Revise

Read through your rough draft five times with *only one thing in mind each time*.

Revise for Ideas:
- For depth and honesty
- To clarify
- To make sure the thesis still fits the paper
- To cut irrelevant sections

Revise for Details:
- Add details for support
- Sharpen vividness and concreteness
- Cut details that do not fit the main idea

Revise for Order:
- Each paragraph should be about one idea
- Paragraphs should divide logically
- Add transition words to move from point to point

Revise for Word Use:
- Conciseness
- Vivid verbs
- Metaphors
- Precise word use
- Variety in vocabulary

Revise for Spelling, Punctuation, and Sentence Structure:
- Search for errors you made in previous papers
- Circle all words, punctuation, or sentences you're not 100 percent sure of and look them up in a spell checker or Chapter 17

Refer to Chapters 7, 8, and 17.

> **Warning:** Writing Is Not This Orderly. The Sentence General has determined that the writing process is sloppy. A write-by-number approach may be dangerous to your best writing. You are normal if you do not follow this process exactly. The process may more accurately be described by the diagram below.

Correction Symbols Your Professor May Write on Your Papers

AB—Abbreviations, See **pages 476–477.**

Agree or Ag—Agreement. Nouns, verbs, or pronouns don't match each other. See **pages 471–472.**

Awk—Awkward. Your professor doesn't have a category for something clumsy.

C—Comma error. See **page 453.**

Cap—Capitalization. See **page 465.**

Format—See **page 477.**

G—Good work here.

Irr. Verb—Irregular verb form. See **pages 473–475.**

MM—(1) Mixed metaphor. See Chapter 8.

OR (2) Misplaced modifier. See **pages 470–471.**

Org—Organization. Two points mixed together or one point split apart. See Chapter 5.

¶—Paragraph needed. See Chapter 4.

?—Confusing section. Look for missing words awkward sentences, illogical idea, or misused words.

Red—Redundant. Needs cutting. See Chapter 8.

R.O. or C.S.—Run-on or comma-spliced sentence. Needs a period or semicolon. See **pages 468–469.**

Ref—Reference. Usually unclear pronoun reference. See **pages 472–473.**

SF—Sentence fragment. See **pages 467–468.**

SS—Sentence structure. May be awkward or nonparallel construction. See Chapter 8.

Tense—Verb tenses don't match. See **page 471.**

Thesis—Thesis needed or unclear. See Chapter 5.

Trans—Transition needs improvement. See Chapter 4.

Vague—Need clarification or more detail. See Chapter 2.

Wordy—Be more concise. See Chapter 8.

WW or Usage—Wrong word used. See Dictionary of Usage, **pages 477–481.**

IDEAS AND DETAILS

Tell as much of the truth as one can bear, and then a little more.

—JAMES BALDWIN

Ideas and Details

A Guide to College Writing

SEVENTH EDITION

M. GARRETT BAUMAN

Monroe Community College Emeritus

WADSWORTH
CENGAGE Learning™

Australia • Brazil • Japan • Korea • Mexico • Singapore • Spain • United Kingdom • United States

WADSWORTH
CENGAGE Learning™

Ideas and Details: A Guide to College Writing, Seventh Edition
M. Garrett Bauman

Senior Publisher: Lyn Uhl

Development Editor: Laurie Runion

Assistant Editor: Amy Haines

Editorial Assistant: Kyley Caldwell

Senior Media Editor: Cara Douglass-Graff

Marketing Manager: Jennifer Zourdos

Marketing Coordinator: Ryan Ahern

Senior Marketing Communications Manager: Stacey Purviance

Content Project Manager: Corinna Dibble

Senior Art Director: Jill Ort

Senior Print Buyer: Betsy Donaghey

Rights Acquisition Account Manager Text: Tim Sisler

Rights Acquisition Account Manager Image: Mandy Groszko

Photo Researcher: Catherine Schnurr

Production Service: Pre-Press PMG

Text Designer: Maxine Ressler

Cover Designer: Maxine Ressler

Cover Image: istockphoto/ Victor Melniciuc

Compositor: Pre-Press PMG

For product information and technology assistance, contact us at **Cengage Learning Academic Resource Center, 1-800-423-0563**

For permission to use material from this text or product, submit all requests online at **www.cengage.com/permissions.** Further permissions questions can be e-mailed to **permissionrequest@cengage.com**

Library of Congress Control Number: 2008942513

ISBN-13: 978-1-4282-6231-7

ISBN-10: 1-4282-6231-8

Wadsworth
20 Channel Center Street
Boston, MA 02210
USA

Cengage Learning products are represented in Canada by Nelson Education, Ltd.

For your course and learning solutions, visit **www.cengage.com**

Purchase any of our products at your local college store or at our preferred online store **www.ichapters.com**

Printed in Canada
1 2 3 4 5 6 7 13 12 11 10 09

For Carol
Who lives as I would write

Contents

3 Getting Ideas
*Brain Teasers to Help You Write
on Almost Any Topic* 47

4 Paragraphs
Ideas and Details in Miniature 89

5 Order from Chaos
Thesis and Outline 99

6 The Draft
That Frenzy Near Madness 117

7 Revising Drafts
Writing is Revising 131

8 Writing with Style 149

9 Putting it All Together
From Topic Choice to Published Essay 169

10 Description
Making Your Audience See 183

11 Narration
Telling your Audience a Story 203

12 Informative Writing
Telling your Audience What it Doesn't Know 229

13 Persuasive Writing
Seeking Agreement from an Audience 261

16 A Collection of Student Writings 391

17 Handbook of English 451

Appendix
The Real Rules for Writing Classes (And Maybe Life) 485

Preface

The thesis of *Ideas and Details* is simple and straightforward: Good writing combines fresh ideas energized by vivid details. Within this principle, nearly endless variation is possible, whether you are persuading parents that smallpox vaccines are dangerous or describing a puddle rippling in the breeze. Chapters 1, 2, 3, and major portions of most chapters, are devoted to providing thinking options for writers trying to create and shape ideas and details. Over 100 brain teasers are the backbone of this book, leading students to draw more and better ideas out of themselves and their reading.

In emphasizing the process of writing, this book takes a no-frills approach to theory by reducing terminology and the number of steps so students are not intimidated and can focus on essentials. Offering options instead of prescriptions empowers writers to try different techniques and liberates teachers in class.

Chapters 4 and 5 discuss options for paragraphing and organization. Chapter 6 discusses options for introductions, drafting, and overcoming writer's blocks. Chapters 7 and 8 deal with revision, including advice for peer review and conferences. Chapter 9, new to this edition, ties Chapters 1 through 8 together by examining the creation of a published essay through all the stages from conception to publication. Chapters 10 to 15 cover the most widely taught types of writing, and Chapter 16 offers additional student writings for analysis and modeling. Chapter 17, the handbook, focuses on the essential rules of grammar and provides comprehensive coverage of usage, punctuation, capitalization, agreement, irregular verbs, and oddities of the language.

Ideas and Details focuses on student writing. Most chapters evaluate a student paper for how well it hits or misses principles just discussed based on the peer review sheet for the chapter. Other student papers allow the class to practice for peer review workshops. Each chapter also contains many short practice writing assignments that require immediate application of concepts. These 5-to 10-minute exercises can be done at home or in short bursts in class and often form sequences that build into essays. Visual rhetoric, in the form of over 40 pictures, teaches students to read visuals as they read writing and demonstrates in a visual way the writing principles of ideas and details, brain teasers, thesis, structure, and styles of thinking.

Here's what's new to the seventh edition of *Ideas and Details*:

- **Stronger emphasis on persuasive and informative writing.** I've added detailed guides to revising informative and persuasive writing as well as more student and professional examples. In Chapters 1, 12, 13 and 15 there is expanded emphasis on analysis and critical thinking in sections on annotated bibliography, summary analysis and paraphrase, and applying critical analysis to student and professional writings. *Ideas and Details* teaches critical thinking and analysis extensively through brain teasers as well.

- **A new chapter, "Putting It All Together," illustrates the entire writing process.** It demonstrates the process explained in Chapters 1 through 8 by taking an inside look at how a hazy topic became a published essay, including false steps, outlines, surprises, and collaboration with editors. The essay, "If God Breake My Bones," is about hardships students face and how teachers deal with them, a topic that should appeal to both instructors and students.

- **Seven professional writings have been added, including five complete essays.** There are pieces on campus violence, myths of student travel abroad, economic arguments for legalizing same-sex marriage, why people procrastinate, and cloning humans. Students are instructed in techniques for analyzing professional writing. New student work includes persuasive essays on immigration laws, the Patriot Act, a chilling narrative about a pre-war military expedition in Afghanistan, and an informative essay on abandoned, disabled children.

- **Much has been added on revision strategies.** Chapter 7 contains "How to be Your Own Editor," and the original and revised openings of "The Declaration of Independence" are given for analysis. New, "quick guides to revision" boxes have been added to Chapters 11, 12, 13, and 15.

- **The research chapter has been updated.** Christopher Otero, who writes this chapter with me, has included calculator sites for research format, updated the APA formats, and listed and explained dozens of new research search engines, web sites and multi-media sites. The chapter now guides students through research by following Professor Otero's creation of a paper on the evolution of Hip Hop Music. He demonstrates each stage of the writing and research process, using Hip Hop for a narrative thread through this complicated subject.

- **InfoTrac® College Edition has been moved from the text itself to the book's Web page.** All the instructions, newly updated suggested readings, practices, questions and assignments are available there. A semester-long subscription to InfoTrac College Edition can be purchased by students if it is not available at their university or college. Please contact a Cengage Wadsworth sales representative for more information.

- *Ideas and Details* **now offers all the essentials found in most standalone handbooks—over 100 pages of instruction.** With its expanded research chapter, the chapter on style and its handbook, *Ideas and Details* now contains virtually all a professor can cover in teaching research, style, grammar, and mechanics in a freshman English course.

COVERAGE OF MLA

The citation examples in the MLA section of this book are based on the Sixth Edition of the *MLA Handbook for Writers of Research Papers*. Although the MLA has recently issued a new version of its *MLA Style Manual and Guide to Scholarly Publishing*, the MLA has urged publishers to use the Sixth Edition of the *MLA Handbook* for undergraduates until the publication of the Seventh Edition of the *MLA Handbook*. Please consult the MLA's website www.mla.org for information on the anticipated publication date of the Seventh Edition. A 2009 MLA Updated Edition of this book will publish in Spring 2009.

ACKNOWLEDGMENTS

I have been blessed by wonderful colleagues, editors, students, and friends during the writing and rewriting of this book. The Monroe Community College Foundation supported an early draft. Great colleagues have provided critiques and resources: Lee Adnepos, Nancy Bailey, Heather Beck, Elizabeth Behr, Gail Bouk, Patrick Callan, Stasia Callan, Toni Caramico-Marotta, Carol Cloos, Donna Cox, James Davis, Cheryl Desmond, Alan Glossner, William Goglia, Judy Hall, Erika Hartmann Hayes, Robert Herzog, Tony Leuzzi, James McCusker, Thom Metzger, Martin Napersteck, Suzanne O'Brien, Christopher Otero, Elaine S. Rich, Mark Spall, Ann

Tippett, Deborah Trout, Holly Wheeler, and Carolyn Wendell. To my students and those of other professors who send me letters responding to the book, I am deeply grateful. My wife, Carol, who devoted weeks to research, also does a wonderful job telling me how a student would feel about the readings and assignments. She wants students to enjoy themselves.

In transforming *Ideas and Details* into this seventh edition, I thank Lyn Uhl, Publisher, and Corinna Dibble, Content Production Manager for their encouragement, suggestions, and clarity of intent. I am always indebted to Development Editor Laurie Runion, who has been with *Ideas and Details* for three editions. Her insights, guidance, practical help, sense of humor, eye for art and ability to adapt to changing situations have been invaluable. I also wish to thank Pre-Press's James Reidel, a scholarly and meticulous copyeditor, for sparing the book many flaws and Philominal Bosco for ably coordinating editing.

I am deeply indebted as well to my colleagues at other colleges who honestly and meticulously reviewed the book and made it better, sometimes by demolishing walls, sometimes by realigning bricks. I thank them all.

Leigh A. Adams, *Missouri State University–West Plains*

Sonja L. Andrus, *Collin County Community College District*

Anjili Babbar, *University of Rochester*

Betty Bamburg, *University of Southern California*

Paula Bennett, *Seattle Central Community College*

Wenty Bowen, *Tufts University*

Therese Brychta, *Truckee Meadows Community College*

Lucy Coombs, *Central Maine Community College*

Eric DeVillez, *Moraine Valley Community College*

David Edwards, *New Hampshire Technical Institute*

Dawn Elmore-McCrary, *San Antonio College*

Christopher Gould, *University of North Carolina*

Jeanne Grinnan, *State University of New York–Brockport*

Paula Guetschow, *University of Alaska*

Lisa Hernandez, *St. Edwards University*

Dan Holt, *Lansing Community College*

Zita Ingham, *Arkansas State University*

Pat Kile, *Richard Bland College of the College of William and Mary*

Lynn McDonie, *Antelope Valley Community College*

Janice McKay, *State University of New York–Brockport*

Tim McLaughlin, *Bunker Hill Community College*

Corrie Martin, *South Puget Sound Community College*

Carolyn Mee, *Beaver College*

Michael Miller, *Longview Community College*

Timothy Parker, *University of Tennessee–Chattanooga*

Amy J. Pawl, *Washington University*

Roxanna Pisiak, *Morrisville State College*

Martine Courant Rife, *Michigan State University and Lansing Community College*

Paula Ross, *Gadsen Community College*

Susan A. Schiller, *Central Michigan University*

Mary Sottman, *South Puget Sound Community College*

Ellen Tiedrich, *Gloucester County College*

Ann Tippett, *Monroe Community College*

Arthur Versluis, *Michigan State University*

Troy T. Wolff, *Shoreline Community College*

Jeb Wyman, *Seattle Central Community College*

Robbin Zeff, *The George Washington University*

—M. Garrett Bauman

The Honest Writer

1

MANY STUDENTS ENROLL IN COLLEGE WRITING COURSES with apprehension. Writing is hard work—and there's lots of it in such a course. You probably will have to expose your feelings. And some students say English teachers want to change their style—but isn't style something that's personal?

Let's look at these three issues a little closer. First, **writing *is* hard work,** even for professional writers. All writers have crumpled papers or made trips to the refrigerator when the words refused to cooperate. Sometimes I seem to change 10 words for every five I write. But writing can be made easier by practicing and by learning shortcuts that this book and your professor will suggest. Compare learning to write to learning to play tennis or the guitar or learning to drive a car. How graceful were you the first time you tried these activities? And when you moved up to the next level of difficulty, didn't it seem almost as hard as starting over? Writing is at least this complicated; there are 750,000 words in the English language—750,000 choices. Your professor hopes to make you practice as hard and often as *both* of you can stand it. **For research shows that the best predictor of success in college is effort. Not IQ, not the college you attend, not your SAT scores, age, sex, or race. Take comfort in that. *You* control your own effort.**

Second, what about the papers in which you might have to **expose your feelings or ideas** that may sound strange to others? If you can open

> From the cowardice that dares not face new truths, from the laziness that is content with half truths, from the arrogance that thinks it knows all truth, Good Lord, deliver me.
>
> —KENYAN PRAYER

1

up, you'll learn one great truth about writing: **Telling the truth as you really see it is the only way a writer ever says something worth reading.** Alice Walker, the author of *The Color Purple,* writes openly about being blind in one eye and about growing up in a poor family. She says she was so embarrassed about her "crooked eye" that for six years she did not raise her head, for fear people might notice the "blob" on it. In life these things are embarrassing, but in writing, they make us feel and understand. A reader *wants* a writer to give of himself or herself—to know the writer's truth. As readers we respect such truth and the person who dares to tell it.

Almost all mediocre writers share two qualities—they're vague and they're half-hearted. This is not intentional, of course. Perhaps they fear making mistakes or saying something unacceptable and so choose a vague, comfortable half-truth. A writer should be sensitive to readers' reactions; however, the writer's first job is to create stimulating ideas for the reader to consider. You cannot do that timidly. Besides, your professor will be grading you on how forcefully your opinions are presented and supported—not on your opinions themselves. Your teacher wants the real you to emerge, and if you want to write moving, interesting papers, the kind you enjoy reading, trust your professor and classmates with your story. Zora Neale Hurston's mother, a poor black woman of the last century, told all her children, "Jump at the sun." Zora, who later became a great writer, commented, "We might not land on the sun, but at least we would get off the ground." Use this course to jump at the sun.

Third, will your professor try to **change your style?** Let's hope so! You had a writing style when you were 14. Would you like that same style to represent you on professional reports, letters, and college papers? Your style has changed as you've matured, for change accompanies all growth. Your professor will encourage further change and maturity by asking you to experiment with a variety of styles and techniques so you can find your best. She also wants you to be able to adapt to the many writing tasks life will throw at you after college.

Your professor wants you to become the writer *you* want to be. **And like all intellectual activity, writing should make a person feel more alive and growing.** Consider that the great novelist Marcel Proust was still revising his work on his deathbed, hopeful, alive for the perfect word that would, as he said, "move the world." Near the end he revised a death scene because, now that he was in the same predicament, he saw more honestly how the character felt. Doing so helped him to continue to grow until his last hour.

Perhaps a writer ought to be an optimist, hoping that in the next words, the next sentence, the next idea, something will make a difference to a reader. If you don't stretch yourself to say something beyond what you already know, the writing will be flat. **College should be one of your life's great stretching experiences.** You really don't know how far you can stretch. Perhaps there is a novel or speech in your future; perhaps a letter to the newspaper that will change someone's life; perhaps a report that will get you promoted; or a letter that will calm a family feud. One thing is sure: Safe, predictable ideas won't change either you or your readers.

Trying different styles also prepares you to write for different audiences. Your tone must differ when writing to an angry customer, to an admissions officer you don't know, or to your favorite cousin. When you choose simpler words to speak to a child, use technical terms to discuss a research project with a professor, or eliminate slang when speaking to your grandparents, you are adapting style to your audience. Which is the real you? *All of them.* In being sensitive to your audience, you stretch yourself into a person encompassing many different people.

As with learning any complicated skill, writing can paralyze you at first. *I can't do all this at once,* you think. You're right. That's why when people learn something new they sometimes seem to get worse for a while. Often this is only an illusion. You may simply be setting higher goals for yourself that you must work up to. If you hit the target every try, it's too close. Some assignments and techniques in this book may seem artificial at first, but with practice they will become part of your unconscious process. If I write for a while without giving an example—as I have been—a little twitch reminds me. At other times a subconscious detector tells me I'm stamping out the same bland verbs over and over. But every writer has to struggle *consciously* to learn these things before they become automatic. This book will focus on the essential concepts you need.

■ **PRACTICE 1-1** Complete this sentence: "One hard aspect about writing that I want to work on this semester is . . ."

■ **PRACTICE 1-2** Complete this sentence: "One topic I'd like to dare to write about is . . ."

A Professional Attitude

The writing you do in this course should be considered professional writing. It is real writing for a real purpose, not practice exercises. I say this because nothing you learn in college will be as important to your professional success as the ability to write well, no matter what career you choose. You may be able to land a first job after college without strong writing ability, but promotions and recognition will get harder at each level. Engineers, businesspeople, nurses, counselors, technicians, and teachers write far more than you might think—and always there is more writing as careers advance. The computer age has made writing more important than ever. Fax, e-mail, and the Internet are replacing the telephone and the personal visit.

Let me use as an example a friend of mine who is not a college graduate. Rick is a carpenter—a physical labor job, right? That was true as long as Rick worked for a boss. But he wanted to be independent, keep more of the profits, and do more creative carpentry. So he established a small, three-person building company—and found himself writing more and more and hammering less and less. He writes letters to inspectors *explaining* variations in housing codes; he writes *persuasive* complaint letters to customers and suppliers when he feels cheated; he writes accurate and vivid *descriptions* of additions or remodeling projects so customers can visualize them; he's become sensitive to audience, tone, and word choice, knowing they sell his houses as much as his reputation for craftsmanship. He's come to realize his business success has a lot to do with his success as a writer.

From a career standpoint, you owe it to yourself to learn to write effectively for these reasons:

- A boss may avoid asking you to do work that would otherwise enhance your career if you cannot write well. Poor writing embarrasses the company.
- Writing well helps you control your destiny; you don't have to depend on an assistant to fix your work.
- A boss or client feels rapport when reading clear, organized writing, but alienated when reading stuffy, disorganized, or vague reports.
- Good writers create new ideas; think of the benefits this brings a career. In Chapters 2 and 3, you will learn to write on almost any topic thrown at you in college or at a job.

Most businesspeople today put writing ability high on the list of what is desired in an employee. Many rank it above even courses in your career field. And poor writing can hurt a career. In 2004 a Philadelphia federal judge reduced a lawyer's fee by $31,500 because of his poorly written briefs. And U.S. Army General John W. Vessey once said, "More has been screwed up on the battlefield and misunderstood in the Pentagon because of a lack of understanding the English language than any other single factor."

Never underestimate the usefulness of good writing. I usually ask my students to do some real professional writing tasks for real audiences, and some have met with the kind of success that makes them realize the power the written word gives them. Mike, who was recently promoted to manage a computer chip lab, wrote a paper for class that became a safety brochure for his company. Rob was upset at the city law forbidding people to keep cars without license plates in their driveways. He'd gotten a ticket. For a class paper, he wrote a proposal to have the law changed so people who couldn't afford big garages could keep a rust-bucket car for the winter and a cleaner car for the summer without paying for two license plates and two insurance policies. The city council agreed and changed the law. Darlene, a single parent returning to college, had a male boss who made sexist remarks and discriminated against her in assigning tasks. She wrote a tactful letter of complaint to him (it's easy to blast someone and get fired). Her letter was so well explained and supported that the man not only treated her better but admitted it opened his eyes to the way other working women were mistreated. These are examples of professional writing in its broadest sense.

Of course, your college writing must show professional polish. This means not just the kind of grammar and spelling you'd want on your résumé, but also a professional attitude toward ideas, details, and honesty. Professionals revise (literally, *re*see). Your professor may challenge you to look again at words, ideas, and details in an effort to help you think more professionally. This is natural; expect it.

Some college writing assignments in courses across the curriculum may seem boring or irrelevant to you. A paper on "Plato's Concept of Justice" in a philosophy course or "Prison Conditions in the Nineteenth Century" in Criminology may not excite you. But a person with a professional outlook will be able to get into almost any topic assigned. If you believe the world is interesting, you will find interesting things to think and say. If you expect boredom, you will probably find it. **Although I cannot promise this will always be true, most topics are made exciting by the concentration and curiosity the writer brings to them.** A professional thinker takes this approach.

Why does college require so much writing? Because you learn more about a subject by writing about it. **Studies have consistently shown that you will retain three-to-five times as much knowledge by writing about a topic than by simply reading or hearing about it.** You make ideas part of you by actively describing them in your own words. If you really want to learn the material in your psychology or biology course, don't just highlight the book. Write out a few paragraphs after finishing your reading.

■ **PRACTICE 1-3** Think of a financial or job situation in your life now in which a strong letter might solve a problem or do you some good. To whom would you write and why?

The Struggle Against Silence

Personal reasons to write well are as important as professional reasons. You can write to touch someone you care about. You can write to discover who you are and what you believe. You can write to preserve important moments in your life or to make your life more your own. As Mexican writer Carlos Fuentes said, "Writing is a struggle against silence." The writer does not just accept life, but works to understand and respond to it.

Chances are, in trying to stretch you, your professor will require both professional and personal writing. But most college writing will require a deeper honesty than you may have been asked for to this point. Not that people try to be dishonest. What I mean is that **in college it may not be enough to just write what you *already know or already feel* about something; instead you must *discover more* about your subjects.** It is dishonest to think that what you already know and believe about a subject is the entire truth. Sometimes you will discover new ideas through research, but many times they can come through looking closer at your own experiences and feelings—probing deeper into what you may have accepted too easily in the past.

I recall an older student who was in a wheelchair. Tom had been shot three times in the lower spine, shattering two vertebrae and leaving him unable to walk. This happened long ago during the Vietnam War. Tom had spent many years in veterans' hospitals. He decided to attend college, even though he had been a high school dropout. He sat in the front corner of the classroom—isolated—wearing purple and silver mirror sunglasses that hid his eyes. The few things he said were sarcastic snaps, and the other students shrank away from him. He was in the class but not part of it. His papers were poor in grammar, but even worse to me, they were bland. "Nothing ever happened to me in my whole life but one thing," he said after I returned a D-minus paper to him. "I don't care about this stuff."

"So write about that one thing that did happen to you," I said.

"No way!" Tom said. "I don't want to. If I do, a lot will come out I don't want out again. It's no good. You don't know what I might do if I get upset." During the semester Tom had trouble with the police regularly. Once he showed me a bruised knee he said the police had given him during a brawl when he refused to leave a buddy's room in the spinal ward of the hospital.

"You're kind of proud of that, aren't you?" I asked.

He admitted he was. "I guess I like fighting cops."

"Do you know why?" I asked.

It was then that Tom reached up and slid off his mirror sunglasses, slowly, reluctantly. I suppose he wanted to see me better, but I saw his eyes for the first time. They were old, exhausted eyes. "Yeah," he answered, "I know why."

After this, Tom began exploring his inner landscape—his own heart. It is the most wonderful and terrifying subject any of us have. Tom wrote several papers that gripped his readers. He read one to the class, and people sat near him to be in his workshop group so they could find out more. **His writing made him real to them,** and they wanted to know what he'd been through. They didn't pity him; they simply hungered for his experience, because real writing makes a reader live more, too. He explored the day he was wounded, what Vietnam meant to him, the father who deserted him, his own son he hadn't seen since becoming disabled, a girl he loved. He made us laugh when he described how scared walking people are of those in wheelchairs, how when he noticed their look of fear he'd pretend he was going to run them over. Tom's life poured on paper, and the class read it and cared. Tom taught them they could write for real, and some people who had previously hidden behind safe topics took a chance, too.

Tom turned his pain into power. He'd feared going over these events because they hurt, but he learned that holding them inside hurt him again and again, while they lost their terror and control over him as he shaped them into words. Tom still had a long way to go at semester's end, but he told me, "At least my mind's started walking again." Tom's is an exceptional story of self-discovery, but most writing teachers can tell stories about how writing has freed writers from self-imposed handicaps.

■ **PRACTICE 1-4** In half a page, tell about a time when your own habits, fear, or laziness held back your growth as a person. Remember Tom.

What Do You Know?

Let me reinforce this point another way. In college most of your papers will be essays. The word *essay* comes from the French *essai*, which means *to try* or *to attempt*. Michel de Montaigne, a French writer who in the sixteenth century invented the term to describe what he wrote, saw the essay as a trial of an idea, an attempt to express something as clearly and honestly as possible. He was reacting to the fake, predictable, and overly idealistic writing of his peers. **For de Montaigne, writing was liberation—a way of freeing himself from what he was supposed to think.** Not only society, but our own habits, fears, and laziness prevent us from seeing and thinking freshly and honestly. For instance, when we become accustomed to seeing work as duty and drudgery, we may block out the pleasures work gives us. We may forget that we work because we love someone or that work makes us stronger, more capable people and makes us proud. Can you think of two other benefits from work besides money?

When de Montaigne tried an idea, he wasn't satisfied until he turned it upside down, cross-examined it mercilessly, wrung every last possible drop of truth from it, and exposed every possible half-truth or lie hidden in it. He even cast a medallion that he wore on a cord around his neck. It read "*Que sais-je?*" or "What do I know?" This curious phrase changes meaning as you emphasize "I," "what," and "know." See if you can discover those different meanings.

De Montaigne's unrelenting honesty comforts me. He makes me believe humans can find truth, can write it, and perhaps can even live by it. **Use this book and your writing course to free yourself of old ways and dead notions and to find ones you can live by today.**

Here are some examples of things we think we know but don't question carefully. Let's start with a cold scientific fact: Water boils at 212 degrees Fahrenheit. It's one of those things you memorize in elementary school. But water does not boil at 212 degrees on a mountain top or below sea level. Nor if it's salt water or carries dissolved minerals. Nor in a vacuum. The truth is more complicated than the simple fact I'd like to believe. Besides, how do *I* know it's 212 degrees? I've never tested it.

Next, consider this story. As a teen, I watched live television pictures of the first man stepping on the moon. I saw Neil Armstrong's boots kick up gray lunar dust as he planted a flag there. I went outside and stared at the pale moon and wondered if I'd ever walk there. The next day I went to my summer job at the warehouse and asked people what they thought about the moon landing.

They laughed. "You really believe a man's on the moon?" one guy said. "It's all made up in Hollywood."

"Sure," another said. "You go to college to believe *that*?" I sputtered and argued feebly for a few minutes, then gave up. Did I *know* men were on the moon? No. And I didn't know enough to prove it to these people, most of whom had not graduated from high school. In fact, how did I know it wasn't a Hollywood trick? I do *believe* men landed there, but I was basically taking the government's and the media's word for it.

My point is that **a lot of what we think of as factual truth is based on blind trust of authority and our own prejudices and**

preconceptions without firsthand observation, hard logic, or research. We hear and we believe—and that makes us vulnerable. College aims to help you think more deeply through **critical thinking** and **analysis**—the intellectual honesty of an educated person who is skeptical and digs beneath the surface of ideas. The critical thinker looks for fudged facts and unintended consequences, considers alternative viewpoints, and actively seeks out his or her own blind spots and prejudices instead of hiding them. In a world where virtually anyone can post exaggerations, distortions, and outright lies in hoax e-mails, blogs, and *Wikipedia,* it is in your best interest to train yourself to separate wishful thinking from fact.

■ **PRACTICE 1-5** What are two ideas or facts you accept only because you have been told to believe them? Try for one from your personal life (something family or friends have told you) and one from political, historical, or scientific areas. Raise questions about them.

■ **PRACTICE 1-6** Think of three good reasons why college tuition ought to be doubled next year. You'll need to step outside of yourself to do this.

Let me end this chapter with a few ideas that are as honest and direct as I can be about writing. First, in your personal and professional life, there will be times when you will be asked to use language to comfort sleeping minds—to reassure and soothe your listeners with predictable statements. This is civilized dishonesty. We all do this. But it is not the best that is in us. Use this course to strive for a deeper honesty, one that does more than avoid the obvious lie—one that tries to touch the heart of a topic. In the long run, these will be the only things you write that will matter to you or anyone else. **The enemy in college (and life) is not other people or our duties, but our own passivity.** To listen without speaking, to follow the feet ahead of us instead of peeking behind the blackberry bushes—that is our enemy. **Each half-truth we accept or repeat without really putting it on trial shrinks our intellect. Intensity expands our intellect—and our well-being.** Psychologists such as M. Scott Peck say that the intense, sometimes painful pursuit of truth leads to happiness and mental health, while unhappiness and mental illness are more likely to come to those who passively accept things as they *seem* to be. This is true for the psychological health and survival of societies as well. Democracy does not prosper unless people question what their officials want them to believe. It was Adolph Hitler who said, "What good fortune for governments that people do not think."

Second, **talent in writing is overrated.** Ninety-nine percent of all writing tasks do not require genius, just a reasonable intelligence and a willingness to work. You *can* do that. *Will* you? Annie Dillard, a Pulitzer Prize winner, goes so far as to say, "There is no such thing as talent. . . . We all start out dull and weary and uninspired. . . . Genius is the product of education." She says people *want* to believe in genius because they can blame their genes instead of working to improve themselves. So don't begin with excuses. Your professor will not ask you to write Pulitzer Prize–winning books. But if you work hard, you will write better than you think you can. **The effort to revise also separates good writers from the pack.** The funny thing is, anybody can revise a paper one grade better with an hour's work. Few do. And revision separates the really honest writer—the one who will put his first thoughts on trial—from the writer who chooses a lesser honesty.

If you ever say to yourself, "My teachers said I had no talent in English," you might keep in mind that Einstein did not speak until he was four years old; Louisa May Alcott, future author of *Little Women,* was told by a publisher, "You can't write"; Beethoven was called "hopeless" as a musician; a newspaper fired Walt Disney for lack of imagination; and Michael Jordan was cut from his high school basketball team. Are you going to let people you've left behind tell you who you are or what you can do?

Third, **write for a real purpose to a real audience.** When your writing course allows, write your papers about topics that matter to you and imagine sending them to a particular person. Write your paper on alcoholism to your friend's alcoholic father; write your paper on energy taxes to your senator or to the owner of a local trucking company or even to the pollution-sensitive owl in your backyard; write your paper on prenatal care to your sister and her new husband. If you cannot think of an audience, imagine that listening carefully as you write is someone who is not judging you but rather who needs help visualizing your ideas, asks questions, and wants to learn something from your paper.

Most students want simple formulas for writing. I'd like to give them to you, but they don't exist. Good writing balances rules and creative freedom. This book will strive for clear guidelines, but remember that rules often rule out great possibilities.

Putting Pictures on Trial

To test these concepts of honesty and critical analysis, let's look at the subject of war in two famous paintings. Both depict the wars of Napoleon of France (1804–15). Theordore Géricault, a Frenchman, painted the picture of the French *Officer of the Hussars.* At the time, he supported Napoleon who was ridding Europe of brutal, corrupt monarchies. (Later Géricault changed his mind.) Francisco Goya, a Spaniard, painted *Execution of the Defenders of Madrid* after Napoleon's army invaded Spain. It shows French soldiers shooting Spanish war prisoners. Both artists were honest in their feelings; yet their paintings present different ideas about what war is and what it means. Examine the pictures carefully.

■ **PRACTICE 1-7** What message about war does each artist express? Try to state it in one sentence each. Now put the paintings on trial; how have both artists loaded the dice to make us accept their messages? Look closely at the details and style. Last, does the passage of 200 years and putting the pictures side by side create a new message? If you were to use *both* pictures as examples in a paper on war, what message would you convey?

Géricault's "Officer of the Hussars"

Officer of the Hussars, 1814 (oil on canvas), Géricault, Theodore (1791-1824)/ Louvre, Paris, France/The Bridgeman Art Library

Goya's "Execution of the Defenders of Madrid"

■ **PRACTICE 1-8** Now, consider these recent photos. What do they convey about war? How do the details help create the point and the way you feel seeing it? How honest is each?

For other perspectives on war, read the student essay "49 Hours in Afghanistan" on p. 406 and the photos on p. 285.

J A Giordano/CORBIS SABA

Reuters/CORBIS

Writing Suggestions and Class Discussions

1. In your opinion, what makes a piece of writing outstanding? List four or five qualities and star the most important. Bring a short, published example to class, noting sections you believe are particularly good.
2. *Try,* in de Montaigne's sense of the word, any current issue (the war in Iraq, using cell phones in cars, or genetic engineering, for examples). Suspend judgment and ask, "What do I know?" Play around, and take all sides.
3. Write several paragraphs describing your relationship with a past teacher of writing. Which guidelines for writing do you remember best? What did you like or not like about that teacher's approach to writing?
4. **Honesty Assignment:** Briefly describe an embarrassing moment and one thing it taught you that you may not have realized at the time.

(One of mine was during my first lecture to a large class. I leaned forward on the lectern—to show how relaxed I was—and the entire table and lectern collapsed with a crash, my notes floating down amid the class's roaring. It knocked some stuffiness out of me and made me realize how tentative my position as professor was.)

5. **Honesty Assignment:** Think about one weird idea you have—something not socially acceptable, something even your friends would think strange. Explain it in one paragraph.

6. Honest writing often balances two realities—our inner, private one and an outer, public one. Write a paragraph about an important moment of your life as honestly as you can. Then write a second paragraph about how someone else might have seen your experience differently. Tell who this person is.

7. How will you use writing in your future career? Whom will you write to and why?

8. Make a list of 10 things you really care about. They may be people, ideas, beliefs, objects, goals, or whatever else matters. Write one or two sentences about each. Your teacher may ask you to share these with the class or a small group and help you develop them into topics for future papers.

9. Label each of your topics from #8 as descriptive, narrative, informative, or persuasive. If one could fit two categories, mark it that way.

10. Think about a person who died or passed permanently out of your life. In freewriting style, not worrying about grammar or sentence structure, record what you remember of that person. Don't stop until you have several insights that you didn't know before you started. Stretch your knowledge and feelings.

11. How will you use writing in college? List five writing tasks you will have to do in your major field and in other courses while in college.

12. Read pages 392–394 on the journal and write a journal entry.

13. Create your personal blog or begin contributing to your class's Web site.

THE BLOG

Accessible to the public, a blog (short for *Web log*) is a Web site that records its creator's ideas—like a journal, it may include personal stories and thoughts, a record of your activities, your opinions on issues, or information you gather from other sources. Recent surveys indicate that nearly 40% of young people regularly read and/or write blogs. Why? Because you can find like-minded people online and expand your audience beyond your family and usual friends.

In blogs you can let yourself loose and experiment with ideas you →

might not try at home. You can discuss Goth clothing, Shakira's music, being a single parent, or why the voting age ought to be raised to 25 or stopped at age 80, and find others who will be interested and respond. Writing counts more when you have an audience, and putting your ideas out in public forces a writer to a greater level of honesty and thought.

Assignment: Write a home page for your blog that tells who you are and what your blog will do and write a sample paragraph to post. You might include a rough drawing or add pasted pictures to create an image of the home page. Blogging "communities" include well-known *My Space* and *Facebook*, but also *Xanga*, *Live Journal*, and the Hispanic *Bitacoras*. *LinkedIn* is a more career-oriented professional blog site.

14. Write an e-mail to your professor introducing yourself. You might list your interests, assess your strengths and weaknesses as a writer and/or perhaps ask about an aspect of writing that puzzles or frustrates you.

15. In peer groups, take one of the following clichés and test it for honesty. First, decide what the quotation means by paraphrasing it in your own words. Next, give an example of how it might be true. Then explain why it might be an incomplete truth. Remember, your job is to discover how much truth is in the saying, not to simply label it true or false.

- "What goes around, comes around."
- "Every cloud has a silver lining."
- "You can't teach an old dog new tricks."
- "You can't judge a book by its cover."

16. Read the following essay that was written by a student in response to Writing Suggestion 3.

STUDENT ESSAY

Chicken at Wegman's
Jennifer M. Horton

She always arrived after the bell rang. Of course we chattered and shuffled our papers and sat on our desks, but when she appeared in the doorway we all settled.

→

"Oh, you are so good to me," she would purr in her Lithuanian accent, for she knew she was the only teacher to whom we granted such respect.

To look at her, one might expect to see her buying grapes or yellow daffodils at a fruit stand. She was a big woman with a round, wise face. Her almond-shaped eyes were sharp, icy blue. They were eyes that had seen much of life—her family had escaped the Soviet Union during World War II, but her father and brother had been killed along with millions of other refugees. She had high cheekbones and straight, short gray hair. When she spoke, her consonants were sharp but not harsh. They gently clicked and ticked across her teeth. Her vowels were slow and smooth, and she rolled her "r's" when she got excited. She had no use for an extravagant wardrobe. Simple skirts and sweaters suited her best, but they were always warm pinks, bright blues, or mustard yellows.

Mrs. Litvinas was our Advanced Placement English teacher during our senior year of high school. Most of us had come to the course on recommendation from previous teachers. Most of us had understood the intricate books we had read. Most of us could write a well-developed essay explaining the political symbolism of Madame DeFarge's crocheting. We joined the A.P. elite, but few of us expected what was to come.

We learned to be alert in her class, never knowing what morsels we might find in her lectures. She challenged us every day to work harder, learn more, and be better than we had been the day before. "Today you will write for me," she would say as she passed out the assignments. "You will tell me how Faulkner uses time as a structuring device in the first half of his book." Some of us cringed silently; others moaned audibly.

"Thank you, Mrs. Litvinas," she prompted us. "Thank you for helping me to become a better person." "Thank you, Mrs. Litvinas," we all mumbled in singsong, then laughed at ourselves.

I can still hear her. Each day she passed out an in-class writing assignment, she would plod up and down the aisles, saying, "If you have not read, you will write on your paper, 'My character needs improvement.' When you finish that, you may sit quietly and contemplate your immortal soul. Do not philosophize! I do not care to read your little philosophies. I want to know if you have read the

→

book. You must read the books in order to pass my class. If you do not read, you will never survive me. I will break you!" Her voice still rings in my mind.

Sometimes she'd mock our papers by reading in a nasal tone, "And so therefore I believe that I think that in conclusion . . ." and pound her fist on the podium. "No! Don't insult me with that garbage. We both know you can do better. All of you."

When our papers were returned, more often than not they were covered with red markings: a "NO!" beside one passage, a triumphant "YES!" beside another, or perhaps an "I know where you stopped reading."

In class she would say, "Be glad there is still room for improvement. Life would be so dull if you were already perfect." When we discussed the "lock theory" in *Darkness at Noon* or Faulkner's southern code of honor or Ionesco's social criticism, she would slice the air and say things like this: "Nothing is a throw-away. Only a small writer would put that sentence there for no reason. You must drink every word in. You must read it over and over until it becomes part of you." And so we drank and drank until we overflowed with Shakespeare and Conrad and Chekhov and Forster. We became, as Mrs. Litvinas would say, "masters of the craft."

Strangers might think Mrs. Litvinas mean, maybe crazy, but those of us who knew her loved her. We waited for her philosophical wanderings. "You must be with people who make you more," she insisted with a broad sweep of arm. "None of this drinking beer at parties. Get a bottle of wine and take your mother on a picnic. You have got to realize, ladies and gentlemen, that there is more to life than chicken at Wegman's [a local supermarket]."

This was her favorite line and we all knew what she meant about what was important in life. Those of us whom she touched with her strength, knowledge, wisdom, and love went out into the world perhaps a little better prepared to face the challenges that life offers.

Discussion/Writing

1. What makes this essay honest and not fake praise of a teacher?
2. How do you react to Mrs. Litvinas's teaching methods? Honestly look for both good and bad aspects.

3. Describe a teacher you had whose strong personality left you with mixed feelings. Balance your honest gut feelings with an honest, objective evaluation.

PROFESSIONAL ESSAY

FUELING A CONTAGION OF CAMPUS VIOLENCE
James Alan Fox

The gun smoke had barely cleared from the lecture hall at Northern Illinois University where last week a former graduate student had executed five students before killing himself when local and national scribes began speculating about a new trend in mass murder American-style. The *Chicago Tribune* Web site, quick with coverage of the tragedy some 75 miles away in DeKalb, noted that the shooting spree was the largest on a college campus since the Virginia Tech massacre. Meanwhile, the Associated Press disseminated a list of more than a dozen campus shootings occurring since 2000.

Are college students indeed the latest mark for heavily armed avengers? The 1980s witnessed a string of shootings by disgruntled postal workers, inspiring the term "going postal." The '90s featured a flurry of multiple murders at middle and high schools nationwide, as "Doing a Columbine" became shorthand for a schoolyard threat. Will this decade be remembered as the time when the ever-popular "College Survival Guides" shifted focus from tips on how to study for a midterm to advice on where safely to sit while taking the midterm?

Epidemic thinking can tragically become a self-fulfilling prophecy by fueling a contagion of bloodshed. The overpublicized acts of two alienated students at Columbine High in part inspired the Virginia Tech shooter to outperform his younger heroes. As the death toll rose that fateful Monday morning last spring in Blacksburg, on-air news anchors tracked the unfolding drama as ignominious records began to tumble. Shortly after announcing that the shooting had become the largest campus massacre ever, eclipsing the 1966 Texas Tower sniping, television commentators declared, with nearly gleeful enthusiasm, that it had surpassed in carnage all

→

other mass shootings in the United States at any venue. For the remainder of the day, viewers were told repeatedly that the Virginia Tech massacre had been the biggest, the bloodiest, the absolute worst, the most devastating, or whatever other superlatives came to mind. Notwithstanding the cruel absurdity of treating human suffering as any sort of achievement worthy of measuring in such terms, little positive can be derived by highlighting such records. But there is one significant negative: Records exist but to be broken.

Unquestionably, the overwhelming majority of Americans who watched the news about Virginia Tech or Northern Illinois would have identified with the pain and suffering of the victims, their families, and the entire campus communities. However, a few would instead have identified with the power of the perpetrators. Imagine, for example, the reaction of some disgruntled student watching one network's newscast last week in which a computer simulation was shown of the gunman at Northern Illinois blasting away at a classroom of students.

The source of contagion extends well beyond the mass media, however, landing right at the steps of college campuses everywhere. In the wake of recent high-profile tragedies, college administrators have made campus safety and security a priority. Not only are colleges feeling compelled to divert scarce resources away from important academic needs over to security technology, but an overemphasis on protecting the campus from active shooters can do more harm than good.

Extended dialogue with students and their parents about safety rather than scholastics as well as efforts to transform open campuses into locked fortresses send two perilous messages. Not only do they advance the overblown image of students as walking targets, thereby reinforcing rather than calming fears, but they may also challenge a few to prove themselves powerful and invincible.

At the same time, efforts to upgrade security beyond what is reasonable based on the limited risk would hardly provide a pleasant campus climate. What student wants to attend classes in an armed camp?

→

It is reasonable, of course, for colleges to develop contingency plans and seek sensible ways to ensure a safe campus. But as with any tragedy like the ones at Virginia Tech and Northern Illinois, our society often embraces—and even demands—extreme responses to extreme and aberrational behavior. Such actions, in hindsight, aren't always prudent.

Consider the measures that many colleges and universities are taking to avoid becoming the next Virginia Tech or Northern Illinois. Though sounding good, they are not necessarily sound.

Safety first: Admissions counselors are quick these days to point out safety features of their campuses. For students and their parents, choosing the right college may depend on balancing security and scholarship. Still, the smart strategy is to focus on the traditional selection criteria—academic quality, range of majors and social life—rather than simply security. For if safety becomes the top priority, then the only choice may be an online degree or no college at all.

Lockdown: This is the new catchphrase on campus security, often raised in parental inquiries about safety procedures. Leaving aside the impossibility of truly locking down a sprawling campus, most college shootings take place in one location. Plus, shooting sprees typically end so quickly that locking down students in dorms and classrooms and turning away off-campus students wouldn't help.

Security guards: Beefing up the campus security force can have a short-term impact by making students feel safer, particularly in the wake of a widely publicized college shooting. But in the longer term, what will universities do to pay for the additional security? Raise tuition? Cut back on faculty? Reduce the number of classes?

Profiling students: In the aftermath of a shooting, we inevitably search for clues that may have alerted the campus to a student who was profoundly suicidal and bent on revenge. Yet, predicting rare events, such as a campus shooting, is virtually impossible. Thousands of college students exhibit warning signs—yellow flags that turn red only after the blood spills. Overaggressiveness in trying to identify and coerce a troubled

→

and belligerent student into treatment can potentially intensify feelings of persecution and precipitate the very violent act that we're attempting to avert. Moreover, as with the shooter at Northern Illinois, the warning signs are not necessarily obvious, if even present.

Right to carry: As many as a dozen states are considering proposals that would permit properly licensed students, faculty members, and administrators to carry concealed firearms on campus. Supporters argue that the death toll at Virginia Tech, for example, might have been lower had students other than the gunman been armed. There is no telling, of course, whether more lives would have been lost in uncontrolled crossfire, or whether more episodes of gun violence would result. Still, at least one Nevada college, a campus where many students own guns for sport, has been considering a plan to train the faculty to shoot. For faculty members, however, marksmanship should be a matter of A's and B's, not guns and ammo.

Of course, if the risk of campus bloodshed were indeed significant, then "playing it safe" would be the wise approach. Notwithstanding recent episodes, for the 18 million college students in America, the odds of being murdered on campus are so low one might need a course in college math to calibrate them.

From 2001 through 2005, 76 homicides were reported at American colleges, based on a database of incidents assembled from the Federal Bureau of Investigation, the Department of Education, and various news sources. Leaving aside cases involving faculty members, staff members, and other nonstudents as victims, the count of undergraduate and graduate students murdered at school numbered 43 – fewer than 10 per year, on average. When compared with virtually any metropolitan area, a student's chance of falling victim actually decreases once he or she steps on campus. Most reported cases of campus homicide, moreover, involved interpersonal disputes among friends and acquaintances or drug deals gone awry, not the unprecipitated act of a vengeful sniper.

Ironically, heightened levels of fear, despite being out of proportion with reality, can sometimes motivate important and long-overdue changes that have wide-ranging impact.

→

The Postal Service, for example, was pressured by its blood-stained image to upgrade its approach to employee relations and grievance handling. The Columbine era forced public schools finally to take seriously the widespread and insidious problem of schoolyard bullying.

The renewed focus surrounding mental health services, student "centeredness," and ensuring that faculty members do not abuse their power over the lives and careers of students (and graduate students in particular) are reasonable and responsible areas for change. Whether these improvements will prevent future episodes of campus bloodshed remains questionable; but they will likely enhance the well-being of millions of college students across America.

Finally, what about the ongoing contagion of campus bloodshed that seems to many Americans to be out of control? Like other so-called epidemics of decades gone by, this latest surge should eventually run its course; that is, unless we nourish it through anxiety, panic, and hyperbole.

James Alan Fox is a professor of criminal justice and of law, policy, and society at Northeastern University in Boston. He is working with Applied Risk Management on an assessment of campus violence prevention strategies for the Massachusetts Board of Higher Education. ■

From James Alan Fox, "Fueling a Contagion of Campus Bloodshed," *Chronicle of Higher Education*, February 29, 2008. Copyright © 2008 by The Chronicle of Higher Education. Reproduced by permission of the author.

Discussion/Writing

1. What is the author's message?
2. Is he right? Put the idea on trial and honestly open yourself to revise whatever preexisting opinions you had on the subject. Ponder how you and other college students react to campus violence and the policies meant to stop it. What is the truth here?
3. What places in the essay seem to break through accepted thinking to a deeper level of honesty? How does he go about doing this?
4. If Fox is right, what are the implications of how we ought to approach violence in our society outside campuses?

The Two-Part
Secret of Good
Writing

Ideas and Details

2

YOU PROBABLY DIDN'T EXPECT THE BEST KEPT SECRET of writing to be given away so soon, but here it is. All successful writers—whether businesspeople or professionals—have this ability, and many writers who have serious flaws in other aspects of their writing can get by with just this one skill: **the ability to combine ideas and details.** Another way of saying this is that the successful writer must continually move between the general and the specific.

Ideas and details are the heart of your writing. They alone cause readers to say, "This is great!" or "Let's take this to the board of directors." No one I know ever received an award, a job offer, a kiss, or a promotion for perfect spelling or punctuation. Readers of magazines, love letters, and business reports care about interesting ideas brought to life with vivid details, and that is what your reader will pay attention to unless distracted by poor spelling and organization.

Let's look at what *ideas* and *details* mean, why they're both necessary, and how you can work with them comfortably.

> Eternity is in love with the productions of time.
>
> —WILLIAM BLAKE

Ideas

An idea summarizes; it concludes, highlights, or generalizes. It's usually abstract. Here's an example to study. It is an old saying that deals with loyalty to country and was popular around the time of the American colonies' revolution against England in the 18th Century:

Where there is bread, there is one's fatherland.

If your first reaction to this sentence was like mine, you found it vague or confusing. Most ideas take time to unravel. I would loosely interpret the sentence to mean that people's patriotism and loyalty are given to those who satisfy their material needs. Let me share other first thoughts. If a government stops supplying our needs, do we become less loyal? Is our love of country really disguised self-interest? I wonder if the loudest patriots are the wealthiest? Would Americans trade their precious freedoms and Bill of Rights for bread if times were tougher? Is company loyalty no more than fear of losing a paycheck? I don't *think* I'd care less for my own family and friends if they didn't do things for me, but would I? Are people that self-centered?

I'm not sure if I agree with the idea expressed in this saying, but notice what happened as I thought about it. *My comments moved from the general to the specific.* The idea stands above specifics. It can apply to many possible situations and leaves room for readers to supply their own examples. But because it is not specific, its meaning is vague. In the time of the American Revolution, this quotation could be tied to specific details: reasons why citizens should have the right to revolt against a king and be free—when the king did not feed, clothe, educate, or protect them—as happened in 1776. How would you apply this saying to your own relationship with your country? Think specifically.

Another name for the main idea in a paper is a thesis. This is the point to be proved or the concept you will illustrate with details.

■ **PRACTICE 2-1** Below are four idea or thesis sentences. Any could be the seed from which an entire essay grows. What *expectations* would a reader have after reading them? What kind of details does the writer need to explain them?
- Chris Rock may be the funniest person alive.
- Technology today is humanity's greatest hope and greatest threat.
- Growing up on a farm prepared me for life.
- The Internet is not just a communication tool; it has changed our families and our values.

■ **PRACTICE 2-2** *Analysis through summary.* To practice pinpointing ideas and restating them concisely, read a newspaper, blog or Web site editorial or viewpoint essay. Underline its thesis and other main idea sentences. Restate the thesis in your own words and summarize the main reasons the author gives to support it. Attach a copy of the printed essay with your summary.

Details

Let's look at *details:*

> A young man strolls a sandy beach at dawn, picking his way along the line of discarded shells, seaweed, and crab legs brought by high tide. He picks up several souvenirs. He plans to display them on his bookshelf when he returns from vacation. A fisherman casts in the surf a few yards off, and nearby is a pool of water left by the retreating tide. The young man notices a fish in the tidal pool.
>
> "It's a bottlenose skate," the fisherman says. "A lot of them get trapped by the tide." The fish is flat like a flounder, white on the bottom, brown on top with a long, whip-like tail. It thrashes the water.
>
> "Skates are garbage fish," the fisherman says. "They compete with the game fish." The young man looks closer.
>
> The pool is sinking into the sand and the skate gasps. It thrashes, searching for deeper water, then settles into a three-inch deep puddle. "A half-dozen get stranded every day," the fisherman says. "People don't eat them. Look—" he gestures to where gulls peck another skate, which is still alive.
>
> The young man bends, touches the skate. It's slimy. He tries to grasp it, but his hand slips off.
>
> "All right," the fisherman says, setting his pole in its holder. "Get the other side." Between them, the men drag the skate down to the surf. The skate jerks free as it hits water. It surges, tail splashing. The young man's souvenirs jangle into the frothy water and are lost.
>
> The skate disappears.

This little story is a collection of sights, sounds, and touches. It is easier to visualize the first time through than the fatherland sentence because it is concrete and specific. We're not talking about dozens of possibilities here, but of one day at one beach with one fish. **Details can be facts, descriptions, stories, examples.** They give us life close up, one piece at a time. Ideas give us life from the mountaintop, in grand scale. Details make a reader visualize, so what you write seems present and real. **An idea does something else for a reader—it gives a sense of purpose and more significance to the details than first meets the eye.** You might consider details and ideas to be sight and insight—the physical presence and the mental meaning. Readers need both to feel satisfied with a piece of writing.

The story about the skate might end as it is, leaving the reader to figure out what insight is behind these details. Fiction usually does not tell, while narrative essays often make the meaning clearer by climaxing the story with a generalization. Let me suggest some ideas for these details. One thing seems clear—the young man understands better the life that inhabits his souvenirs. In a sense both men have been fishing. Has the older man been resensitized to the lives he takes for sport, or is he just being polite? The loss of the shells in the frothy sea and the fact that gulls eat many skates each day suggest it is futile to save one life. Is it?

The story about the skate has an **implied thesis,** which allows readers to create their own concepts to explain the details. Most of your college writing will require a **direct thesis**, usually stated near the beginning of your paper.

Notice that we had to move to details with the fatherland sentence to clarify and develop it. The story about the skate was a collection of details; to clarify and develop it, we must move toward ideas that give meaning and purpose to the details. Alone, neither is enough.

Read the following, and try to figure out what each paragraph needs to satisfy a reader:

1. Is it fair for a woman who gets raped and pregnant to have to deliver her rapist's baby? Then there's the possibility she may be in danger of dying herself. But there are lots of women who use abortion like birth control and don't give a damn that a little life is involved. And I personally know of at least one anti-abortion protester who had an abortion herself! On the other hand, if we say a woman has total rights over her own body, doesn't that also give her the right to use drugs, be a prostitute, or commit suicide?

2. Education today needs to be more personal. Too much that goes on in schools is theoretical and professional; students and teachers both forget they're dealing with people because they focus too much on the job.

The overall effect of paragraph **1** is confusing; it has interesting examples, but it's difficult to figure out what the writer's main point is. The writer needs to help pull details together with *a unifying idea* or *thesis*. Paragraph **2** is just the opposite. It has a clear, forceful idea, but hasn't come to life with details to illustrate what it means. See if you can complete paragraph **2** with vivid details from your experience and provide an idea that would tie paragraph **1** together. As you write, don't hesitate to *add details or change the idea a bit*. That is how writing gets better!

Aside from the specific facts and skills college teaches, it also aims to move you smoothly into a professional mode of thinking. The amateur thinker thinks only when inspired—which makes that person unreliable. Wouldn't you be shocked if a doctor, teacher, or accountant said, "Sorry, I'm uninspired today. Try me tomorrow." We expect professionals to be able to think as part of their jobs.

This is especially true of writing tasks. You may not be able to write a poetic masterpiece every day, but you should be able to put together a clear, interesting piece of writing almost any day you're asked. We'll be discussing other techniques for doing this throughout the book, but the first and most important is learning to **think in both general ideas and specific details in each writing task.** Ideas and details enhance each other. They create inspirations.

The professional thinker (and you should see yourself this way) tests ideas against details and draws ideas from details. If your employer asks, "Do you think we ought to start a day-care center for company employees?" you've been given an idea to work with. Your first step is to test it against some details—how many employees would bring their children to the center, how much will it cost, is there room, and a dozen other specific questions. This should help develop the original idea.

If your boss says, "We get 40% more damaged merchandise returned from our shipments of widgets to New England than anywhere else in the country," you've been given a fact (a detail) in search of an idea to explain it. Could it be transport (bad roads); personnel (a truck driver who throws boxes); manufacturing (widget psychopaths on the assembly line); or something else?

■ **PRACTICE 2-3** For each of the following concrete details, create an idea that draws a conclusion or generalizes:
- In 1971, 62% of new college freshmen said they thought an important part of college was to "develop a philosophy of life." In 2009, 30% agreed.
- There are many more cells in each human body than there are known stars in the universe.
- Only accidents kill more college students than suicides.
- Strangers commit 16% of the murders in New York City.

What Makes a Good Idea

What makes a good idea? The best ideas are original, but since true originality is rare, your teachers will probably be happy if you present an **unusual or fresh idea** and avoid clichés and commonplace ideas. Fine, but how do you get unusual ideas? It's easy to grab the first idea that comes to mind.

The problem is, those ideas come to everybody else's mind first, too. Chances are, if you take the first idea off the top of your head, you'll be saying something trivial. Look at your facts or story more closely—what truth might lurk there that isn't obvious? Here's an example: When asked to tell a story about themselves, many students write about being in car crashes. Ninety percent of the time the professor can predict the theme—bad news for a writer. After the wounded are treated and the tow truck hauls the once-sparkling car to the dump, the writer will say that he or she has learned how serious driving is and will drive more carefully.

That may be true, but the essays you remember say things like this: "Being in an accident made me realize how close I am to death *all* the time and not really aware of it. A loose bolt, a piece of glass, a flying rock, one drink too many, and I'm gone forever." If the writer then goes on to speculate how people block this out of their minds and still drive, a good idea is brewing.

■ **PRACTICE 2-4** Think of an additional, less obvious meaning to be drawn from car accidents.

Being **brutally honest** leads you toward good ideas. Social pressure to say the acceptable thing and fear of embarrassment or of being different hold back fresh ideas more than a lack of brain power. No one deliberately tries to come up with boring ideas, but too often we censor ourselves. There will be more on this in the next chapter, which is devoted to getting ideas. But for now ask if your idea has an unusual twist or slant to it. If not, dig deeper.

A second aspect to a good idea is **complexity,** because the truth is usually complicated. One way to make your ideas deeper is to **develop several competing ideas.** Your writing will seem shallow if you imply there's only one way of seeing the topic. If you believe in simple explanations, I'd like to discuss selling my old car to you. **To develop the habit of deeper honesty, force yourself to look for ideas that compete with your first ones. Put them on trial**. This means you must dig up ideas that potentially contradict your first idea or offer alternatives to it. For example, if I believe young teenagers try drugs because of peer pressure, I should look for competing explanations before I plunge into a blind defense of that idea. Less parental supervision, films emphasizing risk taking and pleasure seeking, and despair about getting a job in an era of business downsizing are ideas that compete with peer pressure to draw teens to drug use. Can you think of one more competing explanation for why teens use drugs?

Why should you challenge your own idea? First, you will impress readers with your openness and insight. Second, you will write a more honest paper. Third, you will anticipate objections readers may consider and you can answer them. You can write, perhaps, that peer pressure is involved in other causes of teen drug use. For example, peers fill the void left by missing parents and by employers who'd rather fire than hire people.

There will also be more on this in the next chapter, but let me take some time here to discuss competing ideas because they're so important. Students frequently tell me they've been working hard on their next paper, pull out a sheaf of scribbled notes, and then say they're frustrated because, since they've been thinking so honestly, they can no longer figure out which side to take in an argument.

One student had decided to write about television advertising. "Everybody hates TV ads," Carrie told me. "They try to get you to buy things you don't need or even things harmful to you. They lie and deceive. But everybody knows that. I can't write a paper telling people what they already know."

"So what do you think ought to be done about commercials?" I asked.

"Well, first I thought we could just not allow them anymore. But who'd pay for the shows on TV? Maybe we could charge people to watch, like with cable TV. Then I thought, well, what about poor people? And legally, don't the advertisers have a right to say what they want?" She sighed. "But what about *my* right not to hear the same dumb ads over and over? I'm so sick of dogs selling beer! Well then, I thought, why not just turn off the TV set? Maybe enough people not watching would make them create better commercials. Suppose a lot of us wrote letters. ..."

"How about that?" I said.

"Oh, no! People are too lazy. I don't know if *I'd* even bother. The other night I caught myself laughing at a new ad. And I hum the jingles sometimes. I don't know what to write. It's just a mess. I need another topic."

"What? And waste all this good thinking?" I told Carrie to be glad, not upset. Her conflicting emotions and ideas had made her better informed, even though the only research she'd done—the most important kind—was in her internal library.

The temptation for a writer in Carrie's position is to glance at her watch and say, "I've got to get this paper done by Friday. I'm just going to pick a side, call it 'Just Say No to Commercials,' and state that the answer to bad advertising is to twist that little dial to the off position." Then the real idea she's come so close to shrivels and dies. But don't kid yourself. A *fake* paper will still be hard to write because it's tough work to tell only half the truth.

The honest response to confusion is to accept it. Don't worry. Most people are confused when they think. Research into creativity shows that you must tolerate chaos for a time until the confusion rearranges itself into a good idea. You have time to sort out the contradictions later in the last three stages of writing: organizing (Chapters 4 and 5), drafting (Chapter 6), and revising (Chapters 7, 8, and 17). In the thinking stage of writing, don't pick *one* side but gladly choose two or three sides before deciding what the truth is. If one fixed idea comes to you at the start of your paper and never changes, red lights and buzzers should warn you that you're not really thinking.

Work patiently through competing ideas, testing each with details to see if it is supportable. If one answer doesn't emerge during the thinking or outlining stage, perhaps it will in drafting or revision. If *the* answer doesn't come by then, the worst you have is a paper that says, "There's no simple answer to television advertising—the sellers, the station owners, and even the viewers are all to blame. No one solution can satisfy the rights of everyone involved." This is essentially what Carrie wrote. **Sometimes, the contradiction is the answer.**

Despite what I've just said, here's a warning: Deliberately trying to be complex *just to be complex* usually leads to confusing writing. Complexity should be the *result* of honestly exploring an idea—of opening yourself to see as many possibilities in it as you can. It's not something you add to a paper like a pinch of salt.

■ **PRACTICE 2-5** Which of the following ideas promises the most originality? Which could you expand into an essay? Do any go too far?
- Suicide is a reasonable response to misery.
- It's tough to be a teenage parent.
- Racial discrimination continues to make this society unfair.
- Discrimination hurts the haters as much as those who are hated.
- We love innocence in others, but not in ourselves.

What Makes a Good Detail

What makes a good detail? **Vividness! Details must be specific, dramatic if possible, and direct, not secondhand.** Suppose you wanted details to bring the following idea to life: "College athletics do more harm to the student than the supposed benefits of character building we hear about so often." Which of the following gives the most vivid details to support the idea?

1. College athletes spend so much time practicing they have very little time left for studies and they're too tired to do a good job anyway. What does playing basketball, tennis, or football teach them about their field of study? Yes, they're taught competition and winning at any cost, but will that get them a good job when they graduate? Most athletes take easy courses and do poor work. They miss the real meaning of college. A lot of them never even graduate, and after the coaches get four years' effort out of them, they couldn't care less what happens to them.

2. Bill Peterson has just limped back to his dorm from football practice, where he has spent two hours slamming his body into a metal sled. The coach has yelled at him, "Hit harder, Peterson! Drive into his guts!" He's limping because the all-star fullback stepped on his ankle. "Pull those legs in when you go down, Peterson," the coach said. "You could trip the runner." Peterson is a starter this year but has no hope whatsoever of playing pro ball or of making the big money. At the dorm, he picks up his history notebook and heads for his night class—scheduled around football practice. He sighs. The professor has been talking about Thomas Jefferson and the American Constitution as the first institutionalized statement on the dignity and nobility of man. "BOR-ing!" Peterson says. "Maybe I'll sit in the back and catch a few 'Z's."

Is there any doubt that paragraph 2 involves readers more, makes us think more? Paragraph 1 is general and paragraph 2 is specific. Paragraph 1 relies on abstract terms like "the real meaning of college"; paragraph 2 makes those ideas concrete by talking about Jefferson's concept of "the dignity and nobility of man." Paragraph 1 is bland (athletes are "too tired" or "have very little time"); paragraph 2 is vivid, *showing* us how tired Bill is, not just *telling* us.

Finding the powerful detail can be just as creative as developing an interesting idea. Our eye, as well as our intellect, must be trained to see better. One of my students who wrote of hugging an old woman said, "Her chest was as hard and flat as a weather beaten plank." The story of years of living was in that comparison. Another student, writing about working in a nursing home, gave intimate, honest details: "I have put diapers on a 100-year-old woman, helped quiet an old man after a bad dream when he called on his long-dead wife, and put countless people on bedpans only to have them miss and urinate on me instead."

Good detail may look a bit different in informative writing, but it follows the same principles. If I announced that you will probably earn more money after finishing your associate or bachelor's degree, you might not even bother to yawn. But if I told you that the U.S. Census Report for 2006 found that the average college graduate earns $23,000 more per year than a high school graduate, I've given you something specific to visualize. (You can visualize $23,000, can't you?)

The chapters on descriptive, narrative, informative, and persuasive writing will suggest specific ways of creating vivid details for specific writing assignments. But for now, remember that details plant the reader's feet on the ground. Support each of your ideas with at least a couple of examples, descriptions, or facts. Only then will the reader be able to see your idea clearly.

■ **PRACTICE 2-6** Rate the vividness and specificity of each of the following details. Then rewrite two of the weaker ones for more specificity:

• Nurse O'Hare is a real witch.
• Many homeless people are mentally disturbed.
• Platform shoes make women resemble flamingos trying to walk during an earthquake.
• In the last decade more women and minorities than ever before attended college.
• Today 27% of men and 24% of women have college degrees. Twenty-six percent of whites, 14% of blacks, and 12% of Hispanics have college degrees.
• The price of computers has dropped a lot in the past five years.

The Difference Between a Topic and an Idea

Students often ask, "What's the difference between a topic and an idea?" and "How can I tell if my details are detailed enough?" Good questions. Let me respond through an example.

Suppose you decide to write a paper for your English class on growing old. Perhaps you've been noticing your grandmother slowing down and remember bicycling and swimming with her. Your topic is "growing old." But it's not an idea yet. **An idea must make a point about the topic.** And there are hundreds of possible points one *could* make about growing old:

• Growing old stinks.
• Growing old is the high point of life.

- Growing old teaches us about the youth we rushed through.
- Society treats growing old as if it were a disease.
- Growing old comes as a surprise to most people.

These are all complete ideas or theses—they generalize and require supporting details. The first two—first off the top of my head—are superficial. They show a simplistic lack of depth because I haven't subjected them to competing ideas. But all have moved beyond the vague topic stage.

If I decide to write on "Growing old comes as a surprise to most people," I might start by scratching down some supporting details:

"Suddenly, you can't do what you always did, and other people just assume they ought to help you." Is this detailed enough? No! It's **fuzzy detail.** It does support my main idea and it sets up the transition to real details, but it's just not vivid. **You will know you're specific enough when your details do some or all of the following:**

- You name names.
- You refer to a *single* instance, not a group.
- You use exact statistics or numbers.
- You quote people directly.

For example, sharper details for my growing-old idea would be: "At 72, Evita Perez's knee began swelling up after grocery shopping, and her daughter began raking leaves and cleaning out gutters when she visited. Evita laughs about shrinking two inches so that she can no longer reach the top shelf in the kitchen. 'I woke up one day, and the floor had dropped!'"

■ **PRACTICE 2-7** Write down a *topic* (like "volunteering" or "hidden courage") that you care about. Then list three preliminary ideas you have about the topic. Now pick one and write three hard details to support it.

■ **PRACTICE 2-8** Honestly question your idea in Practice 2-7 by stating a competing idea and a detail that supports the competing idea.

Should You Start With Ideas or Details?

Should you start with an idea and then add details to liven it up? Or should you start thinking about papers with details and develop the overall idea from them? Both sides have their advocates and **either method will work as long as you move back and forth between ideas and details.** Let's consider the pros and cons of each as a starting point.

In life outside school we usually learn things by starting with details and drawing conclusions. As children, we touch hot stoves or slobber out half words, and later theories about heat and language emerge. The idea of death was not real to me until, at age 13, I saw my Uncle Samuel looking like wax in a casket. Divorce was an empty abstraction until I lived through one. As we experience things one by one, our brains develop ideas to explain our experiences. Most of our self-learned ideas grow this way over years.

On the other hand, most teaching starts with ideas and asks you to apply them to specifics. Moral guidance from religion or family begins with abstract ideas such as "Thou shalt not kill," rather than letting you kill to see how it feels and discover what punishment follows. Biology professors give you the abstract plan behind a frog's internal muscle and digestive systems and then ask you to dissect a specimen, rather than handing you a frog and scalpel to let you figure out the principles by trial and error.

For a writer, sometimes details offer the best place to start—when you're doing personal writing, for instance, where recalling specific places, people, and incidents will lead you to ideas. William Faulkner was fond of saying that he started his great novel *The Sound and the Fury* because he had a picture in his mind of a little girl with dirty underwear. She had climbed a tree to peer into the second-story window of a house. Faulkner claims he wrote the book to figure out how and why that little girl came to be there.

Your professional writing tasks may more often start with an idea given to you. Your employer may ask you to come up with a plan to reduce employee absenteeism or to persuade a client to stay with your firm. Your job is to supply details. This might also be true with informative essays or reports in which the topic is assigned to you.

Details are easier to get than ideas. They tend to come to us whole. Ideas, however, rarely, if ever, emerge complete—like a light bulb flashing on. We need to play around with an idea, rub it up against details before we can say clearly what it is.

Examine the following as potential essay topics. What will be hard or easy in each?

- Democracy
- Your favorite vacation spot
- Airport terminals
- Artificial intelligence

Democracy is the most abstract and general topic. Therefore, an idea will be easy to get and details will be harder because the topic does not help you visualize it. But much has been said about democracy, so even though *an* idea will be easy to get, saying something fresh will be harder. However, that means competing ideas will be readily available. *Your favorite vacation spot* and *airport terminals* are both visual, so you'll have an easy time with details, but a harder time creating an abstraction about them. The vacation is one of the most common topics ever assigned, so a fresh idea will be even harder. Beware the topic that looks familiar or easy at first glance! The airport topic is more unusual, so as long as you stay away from the obvious approaches (hijacking problems and delays), almost anything you say will be fresh. *Artificial intelligence* (or computer intelligence) is less abstract than democracy but not nearly as specific as the other two. Visualizing will be a problem, and details will be hard to get unless you've studied the subject in depth or are willing to do some research.

■ **PRACTICE 2-9** Evaluate the following topics as I've done with the previous four for ideas and details. Which would be the best topic for you? How could you tweak one to work better for you?
- Earrings
- Zoos
- What conservatives stand for
- One of your family legends

The Three-to-One Ratio

One last point: **The classic formula for details and ideas says about 75% of your writing should be details, 25% ideas.** There's nothing sacred about this formula, but it's a handy guideline. Many college students think abstractions sound more intellectual, more important than homely details. Your professor is likely to tell you, however, that most papers suffer from too few details rather than from too few abstractions. Almost every professor wants more and livelier detail.

In this way writing is like life itself. We need principles or ideas to guide us, but we spend most of our time dealing with little details of eating, working, and loving. We could ponder the meaning of love forever, but eating M&M's and holding hands in a park gives substance to our abstract idea of love. Likewise, we don't continually ponder the direction of our career but do concrete tasks in front of us: answer the phone, plan the next meeting, and collect our paycheck. Once in a while, we need to step back, to see if the details of our job or love life match our ideas, make one life. It's the same with writing.

VISUAL RHETORIC

I hope you enjoy the pictures in *Ideas and Details*, but they are not just decorations. **Most are meant to help you understand the concepts of good writing in a visual way. After all, photographers and painters use many of the same techniques writers use.**

First among these is combining ideas and details—which are the fundamental building blocks not only of writing, painting, and photography, but also of music, science, and social systems. The art of composing writing is called *rhetoric*, so when we apply these concepts to pictures, it is called *visual rhetoric*. It's important to learn how pictures speak to us, for modern communication often combines words and pictures. People do this because they want to involve more of their audience's brain, and as a writer in the 21st century, you are likely to need to do it as well in your career presentations.

HOW TO READ A VISUAL COMPOSITION
FOR IDEAS AND DETAILS

How does it make you feel or think? What do you like? Look closely.
Details: Let your eye find its favorite spot. Then figure out *why* you look there. It's often a clue to what's important.
Idea: Tentatively state what the idea/thesis of the picture is. If it seems to lack a message, state how it makes you feel.
Study the details a second time. How do they connect and support the message—or undercut it? Examine all parts of the picture.
Describe the structure of the picture—the arrangement of parts, the lines, the use of light and dark, the connection of foreground to background. Figure out how they work and relate to the main idea. This is the visual equivalent of what a writer does with pieces of an essay.
Audience: Who is the picture aimed at? Artists, like writers, target specific audiences. How might others in your class or family or in different societies react differently?
Context: How might the picture's historical or cultural background relate to its idea?
Style: What is the feel of the picture—precise, murky, impressionistic, new wave, retro, classical, or cartoon-like? Why might the creator have chosen that style?

I'm going to apply this list of concepts to this picture and then ask you to try it with others. **Context:** This is a photo taken near the end of World War II and shows a Frenchwoman whose head has been shaved by her fellow townspeople because she was friendly to the Nazi occupiers. The Nazis ruled France for four years, and scenes like this occurred as towns were liberated and collaborators punished.

ANALYSIS

My **eye** is drawn to the man and woman in the center. The way they stand with his arm around her suggests a couple, but a couple bonded in brutality. I **feel** ugliness, want to turn away. As I look closer, my eye is drawn to the bright shaved head, and the crude swastika painted on her. Or has it been cut into her head? These are vivid details, the kind a writer needs too.

Phillip Looney/Alamy Limited

Nazi Collaborator with Shaved Head

My **tentative idea** is that the photographer wanted to show how people brutalized by Nazi occupation turned their anger on one of their own who betrayed them. But as I look closer, "justified revenge" doesn't explain all the **details.** Many people lean to get their faces on film, to be recorded on the "right" side now that the Nazis are defeated. A man on the left smiles happily, not in grim revenge, and the central man puffs with pride. He's smug and despicable as if he'd actually fought the Nazis instead of ganging up on one person after they were kicked out. The woman holds a rag—to blot her bloody scalp? **Revised Idea:** The woman is the scapegoat, the one they can load their own guilt on. Most of these people probably meekly obeyed Nazi orders. The crowd doesn't seem angry with her personally, but proud and celebrating, except for the woman to the right. I can't read her look. I also have trouble reading the collaborator's squint—is it just from the sun? Or does she sneer in disgust at the crowd's hypocrisy? Is it her inner ugliness or what the crowd has done to her that makes her look so unappealing?

The **background** suggests masses against one person. The building lines in the far background are crooked, the streets funneling the crowd toward the camera. There's a strong sense of pushing the collaborator forward. "See, take her! She's the one. We showed her!"

Key **transitions** are the lapel lines and two men's heads that lead our eyes to the central woman. The white armband echoes Nazi armbands. Have the winners become the new Nazis?

The **audience** for this historical picture was clearly the victorious Americans, French, and British. It might have satisfied them that justice had come to those who helped Hitler; but it makes me think of people in our century who gang up on those who collaborate with the enemy—in Darfur, Iraq, or local street gangs.

Lorne Resnick/Stone/Getty Images

Heinle/Cengage Learning

The **style** is close up and starkly realistic, a snapshot of a moment in action.

Analyze these pictures. Focus especially on how the ideas and details work together, but look at the other elements of visual rhetoric as well.

Writing Suggestions and Class Discussions

1. "If this were my last day alive, I would …" Make a list of 10 specific things you might do. Then pick two or three and list specific details about them in note form. Be vivid, concrete, and honest. Don't write to impress people. Now, create a single unifying idea that best summarizes the philosophy of your last day. Write a short paper based on these notes.

2. What follows are some famous generalizations—ideas that need details. Pick one and use it for your core idea. Illustrate the idea with three or four concrete details and build it into a coherent paragraph. To sharpen your honesty skills, try to find an exception to the idea and work that in as well.

   "Heaven is under our feet as well as over our heads."
   —*Henry David Thoreau*

   "Most folks are about as happy as they make up their minds to be."
   —*Abraham Lincoln*

   "Failure is impossible."
   —*Susan B. Anthony*

   "We see things not as they are; we see them as we are."
   —*Anaïs Nin*

   "The man who sees the world at 50 the same as he did at 20 has wasted 30 years."
   —*Muhammad Ali*

3. The following generalizations are all about love. Pick two to work into a coherent paragraph. You'll need to supply details—examples, facts, stories, or descriptions—to make them more concrete. Some of the quotes go together easily, but you may find it more interesting to put contradictory quotations together. You may agree or disagree with the statements.

   "Love is perhaps the only glimpse we are permitted of eternity."
   —*Helen Hayes*

   "Love is the delusion that one woman differs from another."
   —*H. L. Mencken*

"It is impossible to repent of love. The sin of love does not exist."
—*Muriel Spark*

"A broken heart is wonderful five years later, when you see the guy in an elevator and he is fat and smoking a cigar."
—*Phyllis Battelli*

"Love is an act of endless forgiveness."
—*Peter Ustinov*

"Love is what you've been through with somebody."
—*James Thurber*

"The face of a lover is unknown—because it is invested with so much of oneself."
—*James Baldwin*

4. Quote a favorite line of yours from a song, and then explain what it means to you, giving specific details.

5. What follows are details about AIDS in search of an idea. Create two ideas that the details suggest.

   - AIDS may be transmitted from mother to fetus.
   - AIDS may lie dormant in a person for as long as 10 years while he or she infects other people.
   - Three-quarters of North Americans say they run "no risk" of getting AIDS.
   - Over 4 million people on earth contracted HIV in 2006.
   - 10 million children worldwide have been orphaned when their parents died from AIDS.
   - Most Americans say they have "little or no sympathy" for those who get AIDS from homosexual activity. Twenty-five percent of these say God is punishing them through AIDS.
   - About 250,000 people in the United States with the HIV virus are unaware of their infection.
   - Thirty percent of AIDS cases are now caused by heterosexual intercourse.
   - Many people in developing countries resist using condoms.

6. For one of these topics, generate a list of details that can be used in a paper: quotes, stories, facts, descriptions. But also list ideas as they occur to you. Try for three ideas and list about 10 details on the topic you choose. Mark each item on your list as an I or a D.

   - Teaching morals to today's children
   - Physical education classes

- Halloween
- War movies
- Abuse of the elderly
- Choose a topic yourself

7. Follow the instructions for number six. This time consciously start with ideas first, freely moving to details.
   - An ethnic group to which you do *not* belong
   - Children's toys today
   - The last person you dated or were married to
   - Dentists
   - Thick pan pizza
   - Choose a topic yourself

8. Write down three *competing* ideas to explain one of the following:
   - Why men under 25 cause far more automobile accidents than women under 25
   - Why bad things happen to good people
   - If teenagers today know more about sex than other generations ever did, why there are more teenage pregnancies than ever before
   - Why peace seems impossible between Palestinians and Israelis

9. **Idea to Details Writing:** Express in one sentence one of your guidelines for living: how to be happy, what is important in life, what is right. Now illustrate your sentence with three specific examples. To be more fully honest, also consider a competing idea or objection someone might have to your philosophy.

10. **Details to Idea Writing:** Describe a powerful dream you've had. Start with vivid details: who's in the dream, where it occurs, objects, events, how you feel, odd or unrealistic aspects. Then interpret the dream—look for symbols to explain how the dream relates to your awake life. Suggest *several* possible ideas before concluding.

11. Write a funeral eulogy for someone you know well who has not yet died. What would be your theme and what details would you use to support it? Imagine reading it at the funeral.

12. What is one idea you have mixed feelings about and would like to explore more deeply? Explain why you have mixed feelings and give a few details. (One of mine is how much freedom a teacher ought to allow students in writing assignments. One side of me says students should develop their own topics completely from scratch. It's democratic. The other side of me says students need to be shown they *can* write on anything and that in their careers they will most often be assigned topics. It's less democratic, but more practical.)

13. Evaluate the following list as potential paper topics. How hard would it be to come up with a fresh, complex idea and vivid, specific details for each? Also consider how these topics match your experiences, knowledge, and biases: What are your *personal* strengths and weaknesses in each?

- The national budget
- Concepts of beauty and ugliness
- Stereotypes of grandparents
- Exotic pets like pythons and ferrets
- Lesbian parents
- Your first encounter with violence

14. Write a letter to your boss asking for a promotion or raise. Present several reasons (ideas) why you deserve this reward and support each idea with specific details. For a sample student letter, see page 429.

15. Write a brief summary of a key concept you're learning about in another course. Write out the main idea so it's accurate and clear, and then illustrate the idea with several examples. Imagine your audience is a student in the class who doesn't understand the concept.

16. Write about a children's game—tag, hide-and-seek, musical chairs. Create the feel of the game with vivid, concrete details, but also look for an idea beyond the fun that the game conveys. How is the game symbolic?

17. Write a brief criticism of an afternoon talk show. Make an overall point about what you don't like, and then support it with at least three specific examples.

18. Write captions (or new ones) for two of the pictures in this chapter. Try to give the visual work new meaning through words.

19. Convey a message through visuals. Cut out six to ten pictures for details and paste them into a collage. For example, find four shots of starving children and four of luxurious houses. Then write several paragraphs to convey the point. Let the pictures teach you to write visually.

STUDENT ESSAY

The Unknown Children
Jodie Rosa

Our new admission was a four-year-old boy who had been shaken by his stepmother. The damage was extensive, or he wouldn't have come to us. The only other thing we knew ahead of time about the

→

little guy was that he vomited regularly. We discovered that he had so much pressure in his head from the trauma that surgeons had removed a softball-sized portion of his skull. Every time he cried, his head pulsated. He cried all night long, and being new to us, his medications had not been completely figured out. Eventually, a cocktail of meds would keep him comfortable. The life he had now was the result of a stepmother out of control. He will never recover. Nor does it seem likely the family will recover enough to care for this child at home. He now lives with us: a long-term care facility unit for pediatrics.

Down the hall is another child, little girl Z, who suffered at the hands of her father. She is blind now and cannot eat: a feeding tube nourishes her. She attends a special school for the disabled; it is unlikely she will ever learn anything we consider normal. But education provides some sense of normalcy and keeps her socialized in the hope that something positive will happen someday. She now lives with us.

In the bed next to Z lies a beautiful 10-month-old little girl. Her fate was a natural occurrence, if we can call it that. She suffered a lack of oxygen during her birth, causing significant brain damage. The size of a six-month old, she can't sit up or roll over, may never learn to walk and is just now holding up her head. She suffers seizures and cries often. Her parents cannot care for her—why exactly, we may never know. The only reason we can figure out is that she was not as perfect as they expected. They visit, but rarely take her home for visits. Her new sibling will be born any day now, so the visits are farther between. Doctors said she could eventually go home, but if a perfectly healthy baby arrives at the house, she will probably continue to live with us.

P is about two. She was born perfectly healthy. Mom put her down to nap, and when she returned, something was terribly wrong. We don't know what happened, but P became blind and deaf. She suffers seizures and sensory stimuli dysfunction—when touched, P goes into crying rages as if in excruciating pain. She is sustained with a feeding tube and will probably have very little quality of life. Her parents, who live hours away, rarely visit. Her grandparents visited often in the beginning but seldom now. She is now living with us.

→

This facility is the home for about a dozen children. The stories of how each ended up living here boil down to parents who are not equipped to care for them mentally or physically. Our employee turnover is tremendous. The sadness is too much for most of us. We dress them, feed them, hug them and stay here with them because these kids need love and stability. We do our best to be the family that has left them here.

COMMENTARY

Ideas: This essay exposes a side of life deliberately kept hidden from most people, so it rates high for topic choice. I also like its understatement and restraint. She never calls the parents "awful" or "selfish," but lets us discover the horror through the facts. Her honesty is strong as well—natural causes account for some injuries. She says, "we don't know" several times. It's a mystery why some kids are there or what will happen. They are "unknown" in several senses. The main idea, expressed in the last line, is that the caregivers are handed these unknown children to love and care for—and they do. That kind of love, I think, is a mystery too.

Details: Jodie uses four children as examples, gives the ages, condition and background for each. One especially vivid detail for me was the "softball-sized portion" cut from one boy's skull. There are some fuzzy details, however: little girl Z will probably never learn "anything." A more specific, "never learn to read" or "never learn to tie her shoes" would help readers visualize. Near the end, she says P will "probably have very little quality of life." This is vague, institutional jargon needing detail.

Structure: She starts the essay and each section with parallel details. As we move through the four children, new ideas keep the essay growing toward the thesis at the end.

Style: The repetition of "home" and "lives with us" has a powerful effect. These contrast to the title and use of letters instead of names for the children. The last line turns the institutional facts into something warmer.

Other student writing to study for ideas and details: "Being Ghetto," page 96 or "Quakers: America's First Feminists," page 384.

STUDENT ESSAY

What Disney Movies Really Teach Children
Amy Seager

Snow White lays seemingly dead in a glass coffin with seven dwarfs guarding her body; then Prince Charming enters on his white horse, and with one kiss his true love returns to life. Does this story teach our young girls that true love conquers all—or that without a man they cannot live? Many Disney movies (*Snow White, Cinderella, Sleeping Beauty, Little Mermaid* and others) seem to tell us that if we love truly, anything is possible. That is the moral we *think* we are teaching our children, but underneath that is another message that leads to submission and degradation of women: "Women need men to survive."

Children hope that someday someone will love them the way Prince Phillip loves Princess Aurora in *Sleeping Beauty*. In *Pocahontas*, we learn that no matter what color your skin is, what you think is civilized/savage or what kind of house you live in, you should still love and respect one another and each other's beliefs. In *Beauty and the Beast* we learn that lesson yet again; you should love people for who they are on the inside and not for what they look like. Belle first saw only a beast, but she learned more about the Beast and ended up loving him. Tramp, in *Lady and the Tramp* doesn't have the best reputation, but to find true love Lady puts that aside and gets to know him for who he is and not what others say about him. Love overcame the odds against them. This positive outlook on life is important to reinforce in our children's lives to give them hope in the future. Some children don't have parents who love each other, so it is great they have good models in movies.

However, under these surface morals, Disney movies have darker messages for girls. Where would Cinderella, Snow White, Princess Aurora or Ariel the little mermaid be without their princes? Snow White and Princess Aurora would still be sleeping/dead; Cinderella and Ariel would still be living unhappily ever after with their families. Snow White would be in a death-like sleep until her true love came to break the spell. But since she was pretty enough (with hair black as coal, lips red as blood and skin white as snow) her prince came and saved her. Most of the Disney movies portray women as extremely thin, with ample curves and beautiful long hair that attracts men—which is not the way young girls are. What message does this

→

give the girls? Cinderella would still be cleaning for her step mom and stepsisters if her prince had not rescued her. How did a simple commoner win over the prince? By being uncomplicated, ordinary, and humble. The mermaid Ariel had to change into a human being to win Prince Eric. Also, she had no voice when he fell in love with her. The subliminal message is that if you are pretty enough, humble yourself, and say the right thing (which may be nothing at all because it is better for women to be seen and not heard), maybe your prince will come and save you. Ariel says, "If I become human, I'll never be with my father or sisters again." Ursula replies, "But you'll have your man."

Some Disney movies show strong women (Mulan and Pocahontas, for examples), but there is a catch. Mulan has to first disguise herself as a boy named Ping. In order to fight in the army and have any respect, she must be a man. When she is found out, they kick her out of the army, and she is left to fend for herself. She still wants to protect China and eventually saves the day, but none of it would have been possible without her first pretending to be a man. Pocahontas is a "princess" in her tribe. She is an empowered woman, stands by what she thinks is right, and gains the respect of the settlers, but she does not get the guy. John Smith (or any man) doesn't want someone who will not change for him. Because she stays with her people, John Smith refuses to stay with her. If she will not change, she will not have love.

When you see Ariel changing from a mermaid to a human for Prince Eric, what do you see? More important, what do the female youth of the world see? Maybe they see that one should do anything for love, because love is worth everything. Or do they see the only way to be loved is to change oneself to be what other people want you to be; that no one will love you just for who you are. That is also what sweet Disney movies are telling our young girls.

Discussion/Writing

1. Think of another hidden message about sex roles for either males or females in Disney movies. Support this with three examples.
2. Are there enough supportive details to convince you she's right about the hidden moral of many Disney movies? What other Disney movies either support or dispute Amy's point? Present two specific examples.
3. How do the examples of strong, active Pocahontas and Mulan reinforce her point?

Getting Ideas

3

Brain Teasers to Help You Write on Almost Any Topic

A FORMER EDITOR-IN-CHIEF OF *Ladies' Home Journal* once said that she learned to be an idea person when she first started working as a young assistant editor. Each Monday, she and every other staff member had to bring to a meeting a list of 25 great ideas for articles. This gave her boss hundreds of ideas from which to choose for the dozen needed each month. It also gave the young assistant editor a headache. For the first few weeks she felt as though each idea was an elephant being born.

Then the ideas began to come easier. Some weeks she began having 30 or 40 ideas—better ones her boss could use. The important trick she learned was to let her subconscious mind work on the problem all during the week and not sit down at 3 o'clock on Friday afternoon to create 25 ideas. All week long she'd jot an idea or two down as it came to her—stimulated by all sorts of things—a taxi ride, a meal in a Hungarian restaurant, an unusual garden she saw, a newspaper article. Soon she realized that almost anything could become an idea for a magazine article. "Just knowing I had such an assignment made me remember things I'd otherwise have forgotten," she said. One of the side benefits of becoming an idea-creating person was that she lived more intensely, appreciated life more.

This is *incubation.* You plant a seed of an idea, and your subconscious brain, which has far more brain power than your conscious brain, will work on the problem. The solution that suddenly comes

Writing is thinking.
—ANNE MORROW
LINDBERGH

There are no limits set to thought.
—EDITH HAMILTON

Not all those who wander are lost.
—J. R. R. TOLKIEN

to you does nothing of the sort. It has been planted in the subconscious, which thinks about it while you go about your normal life, unaware of its activity except in flashes. When the idea has ripened, it rises to the conscious level. My point is this: You don't have to wait helplessly for a magic moment to strike in order to write. You can arrange your own inspiration. In fact, working with ideas creates inspirations. Inspiration comes to those who sniff around a lot for hidden bones. It isn't luck when they dig up a great idea.

There are two things to remember about using your subconscious brain power. The first is that **better ideas come if you make a conscious assignment to your subconscious.** If you ignore the task, your subconscious will work instead on your bowling form or try to recall the telephone number of that great-looking person you met last week. The subconscious likes to be tickled once or twice a day with reminders to keep it going.

The second thing to remember about incubation is that **ideas often don't come out fully formed like a newborn baby.** They usually emerge in misshapen bits and pieces—the arm or leg of an idea. I'm using this grotesque image to describe ideas because most people reject such fragments. Have faith. Be prepared to write down idea fragments as they're delivered. You don't need 3 × 5 cards or a computer—although they work for some people. I'm a bit sloppy myself. I use any handy paper, and as I sit to write my first draft, it looks as though I've spread out the trash in front of me. The novelist H. G. Wells had an unusual system to keep new ideas organized as they emerged in bits and pieces. He kept a dozen big barrels around his home, one for each book he planned to write. When fragments of an idea or details came to him, he'd jot them on a slip of paper that he tossed into the appropriate barrel. When a barrel filled, Wells knew he had enough material to write a book.

There's no need to buy barrels. Two pages of notes are plenty to create a two- or three-page paper for a college course.

"Two pages of notes?" I imagine some students protesting. "Why not just write the essay? I thought you were going to save us work in this book?"

This whole chapter will address this question, but a few comments are in order now. First, I want to help you do a *good* job, an honest, deep piece of writing. Writing a draft without notes is easy if you want to do poor work, but it's the most agonizing way I know to create a good final essay because the revisions go on forever, trying to make up for the thinking that should have been done first. **A little sweat in the notes saves bleeding in the revision.** Notes nail down details, connect ideas, and help us concentrate. Researchers into creativity in many fields have shown that this is how the best idea people operate. They've proved it's dependable, saves time, produces more interesting ideas, and helps blocked writers get going again. Why shouldn't it help you? And remember this—all these notes are *easy writing* because you pay no attention to spelling, word choice, or complete sentences.

So when your boss or professor assigns a writing task, start *that day.* Suppose your anthropology professor tells you to write on "Cultural Differences Within the United States." In your next class, listen to the roll call. Do Mozzamil and Mustapha want to be called "Mo" and "Steve"? Does a woman with the French name "Lemieux" pronounce it "Leemo" instead of "Laymeoo"? Does the woman of Indian background touch other women while talking? Perhaps that afternoon you go to the dentist and get a shot of novocaine. As the needle punctures your gum and the pain shoots through your cheek, you recall that the Chinese use acupuncture, which is painless. Perhaps you run into a woman in a bicultural marriage. Ask her a few questions. Talk to the Japanese fellow on your volleyball team. Eat at a Thai or Mexican restaurant. Read the "World News" in the city paper. **And write down anything relevant. These activities will be fuel for your subconscious,** and when you write your paper, deeper, more original ideas are more likely to arise as well. **Inspiration results from many good ideas banging into each other.**

Now, let me tell you how I got the ideas for the previous paragraph, because I wasn't doing it for a college paper. I knew I needed an example to illustrate my idea on incubation so you could visualize it, so I went to a sheet I keep marked "Examples." I made this up when I began the book. It's about 40 to 50 items long most of the time, and I add and subtract from it continually. I picked "Cultural Differences" more or less at random after considering "Grandmothers" (too easy and sentimental) and "Lasers" (too narrow). Nothing much came immediately. The next day when I took attendance in my class, I noticed the names from so many cultures. Later that afternoon I saw my wife talking with an Indian woman in the parking lot—she touched my wife's arm and hair as they spoke, a cultural difference with westerners. That night our daughter Amy brought a friend to dinner, an exchange student from South Africa named Despo. We had a heated discussion about apartheid and American racism with Despo. That never appeared in my paragraph for I couldn't see how to make such an encounter seem like an average occurrence in most people's lives. As I wrote these details into the paragraph, they brought to mind an American woman married to an Arab man and the incident of the novocaine. (I didn't really go to the dentist, but recalled a lecture I'd heard a year earlier about why Americans never invented painless anesthesia while the Chinese never invented chloroform.) From this messy, haphazard material, the paragraph emerged. I rewrote it as a student might see the assignment, but the incubation process was exactly the same for me—and cost me little brain-squeezing pain.

■ **PRACTICE 3-1** Take five minutes to recall some specific cultural differences you've noticed where you live. Write in list form and do not worry about spelling or sentence structure. Tomorrow, add new things that occur to you from school, your job, travel, or television. Add to the list throughout the day until class time.

Improving Your Ideas

It's easy to come up with dull ideas—they're the first ones off the top of our heads. The tops of our heads are notoriously dull—clichés, television jingles, routine responses, and pass-the-salt ideas live there. The Greek playwright Euripides once said, "Among mortals, second thoughts are best." Believe him! **Second, third, and fourth thoughts create the unusual angles and viewpoints that make ideas creative.** Put ideas on trial, as de Montaigne said; call them into question, as Edith Hamilton said. This is what the successful people who compete against you are doing.

So *how* do you draw out your more original ideas? You cannot order yourself to be profound. Richard Wilbur tells the story of a poet who dove under water and held his breath until he thought up a line of poetry and sputtered verse as he gasped to the surface. It kept him in great shape, but really didn't lead to great poetry. Or, **like most professional writers, you can make a habit of creativity through regular note-taking and incubation.** You can get yourself into the groove of having ideas just as ballplayers groove a batting swing. Columnist Ellen Goodman says she goes "through life like a vacuum cleaner, inhaling the interesting tidbits in my path." Other long-term ways of being creative are keeping a journal and reading stimulating books. They will lead to many inspirations in the long run. But these methods won't help you get next Friday's paper done.

For an immediate improvement in your ideas, use brain teasers—systematic ways of stimulating and exploring regions of your mind to find out what ideas lurk there subconsciously. These are the ways people think. (Brain teasers will be indicated throughout the book by the icon you see here in the margin.) At first, these brain teasers may seem artificial and awkward to use, but when you practice them for a semester or two, they will become part of the way you think and help you create ideas with less agony. They will make it possible for you to write on almost any topic. Brain teasers also help you to be more honest, for they draw out complex, conflicting ideas you may be holding back.

Brain teasers go beyond what you tried in the last chapter. There you *randomly* bounced between ideas and details—a kind of free brainstorming. It's a great technique to get started and may be enough to bring short papers to the Order and Draft stages. But there will be times when simple brainstorming doesn't evoke fresh enough ideas, times when you want more focus. Brain teasers will get you going again, and some even organize papers. If you feel blocked or empty, try one or two brain teasers to reenergize yourself.

All the brain teasers follow the same process. First, **make long lists.** Since your brain contains thousands of ideas, you must never settle for the first few that appear. Write down the obvious stuff, but keep going, for the longer the list, the more you'll have to choose among and the more likely that better ideas and details will turn up. Sure, you'll throw away some of these lists, but we're only talking about a rough list. I recommend a half-page minimum for a brain teaser list. One page is better. It takes time to wake our deepest brain. Why a list and not freewriting? Items on a list are easier to organize than a paragraph. Also, freewriting tends to focus you on one idea; a list leads you to many alternatives. **If you really like to freewrite, first do a short brain teaser list, then freewrite on the best idea your list generated.** Second, how many times have you thought, "I know what I want to say, but I can't put it into words"? To eliminate this problem, **make a list of ideas in rough form—not worrying about wording or grammar.** Turning the ideas into words becomes a separate step. A little sloppiness is good compost: Don't rewrite brain teasers for neatness. Ignore your spell checker and grammar checker. In the early stages of writing, concentrate on what you want to say (the ideas and details), not on the structure (which comes next), the words (which come during the draft and revision), or the mechanics (which come last). **Brain teasers are not word association but a list of ideas and details.** One-word items are too vague. Phrases of three to ten words or occasional sentences will tweak your brain more.

Third, **you must not prejudge ideas or details as you compose an idea list.** Write everything down, no matter how dumb sounding. Judge later when you choose which ones will appear in the paper. If you judge at the list-making stage, you may shut off the flow of ideas.

Good ideas have a way of hiding underneath weaker ones. Research into the creativity of scientists, business people, writers, and many others proves that self-criticism kills creativity if done too early. Save criticism until later.

To summarize:

- Make a long list (half to one page).
- Concentrate on ideas/details, not words.
- Move quickly, and do not prejudge items.

Ten Brain Teasers

1. USE YOUR SENSES

 List sense details about your topic—smell, taste, touch, and sound, as well as sight. This will help you get into the topic and supply vivid details for the draft. Our senses connect our mind to the world around us, so by recalling sense impressions you recreate the subject for yourself, engaging brain and feelings, stirring subconscious memories. Drenching yourself in sense impressions is enjoyable once you catch on—one of the secret pleasures of professional writers. Sure, you look like you're lolling in a chair doing nothing, but you're really stretching your arms on a sugar sand beach as the waves hiss over your toes.

Let's try an example. List all the sense details you can about your mother (or another relative). Imagine your mother. Start visually—picture her face, the way she walks, favorite gestures, the way she looks when angry, sad, or laughing. Then become more specific—try her teeth, hair style and color, her favorite clothes. Bring up other things.

Now move to touch sensations—the way she felt your forehead for a fever, a time she struck you in anger, the temperature and texture of her skin, what it feels like to kiss her cheek.

Now sounds—the tone of her voice, the noise of her steps, peculiar expressions she uses when she speaks, unusual sighs or other noises like snores, wheezes, or gurgles. (Yes, mothers do these things. Be honest.)

Now smells—smell her perfume or kitchen or work odors, the unique odor of her room.

You can't just read my words to understand; try it with a pen or keyboard now. Write down as much as you can about your mother, letting your mind go. Probe deeply for the forgotten or unusual detail. Think sensuously. Recall key scenes. For me, my earliest memory is of my mother pushing my baby brother in a carriage across a busy street, me wondering where my father was; another key scene was the first time she learned to drive a car with a stick shift and made the car jerk up and down the street like a bucking bronco; a third was the night in a darkened hallway when she leaned against me and told me my father was dying of cancer.

Not only does a sense brain teaser prepare details and get you into a topic, but it also leads inevitably to ideas. Write any *ideas* that occur to you as well as details. For example, I noticed in my three key incidents that my mother always comes to my mind with my father, and it makes me recall that he so dominated her life that she really had little life of her own at times. This is an abstract idea, not a sense detail, and could become the main idea of an essay. This is exactly how brain teasers move writers from notes to a paper idea.

Using senses doesn't just apply to personal topics such as mothers. Suppose you're writing about public smoking laws. Use your senses to visualize scenes of smoke-filled cafeterias or restaurants. If you're a nonsmoker, write all the smell and breathing sensations you've experienced in a smoke-filled room—your burning eyes, your raw throat, the film on the windows, the stale odor your sweater absorbs. If you *are* a smoker, use your senses to describe the personal agony you suffer wanting a light—your dry throat, your nervous hands, your eyes involuntarily glancing at the door. **The sense brain teaser is an excellent way to start almost any topic. It draws you into your topic and provides sharp details. It will not help you organize papers.**

■ **PRACTICE 3-2** Make a half-page list of sense details about bus or airplane travel. Move quickly; pay no attention to spelling or writing complete sentences. Be as specific as possible. In class your teacher may ask you to read your list and discuss how to develop it into a paper.

■ **PRACTICE 3-3** Write a half-page list of sense details about a topic of your choice. Other brain teasers in this chapter will develop the same topic in different ways, so pick a topic you care about.

2. SEE THE TOPIC FROM ALTERNATIVE VIEWPOINTS

This brain teaser gives you *perspective* by making you see the topic from outside your own narrow viewpoint. **When using alternative viewpoints, you see the topic as someone else would, inhabit another's mind and eyes for a little while. It helps open our own eyes.**

For example, if you want to write on a personal relationship that has soured, first list all the people whose viewpoint might be different from yours:

- Igor (your ex-boyfriend)
- Igor's mother
- Igor's friends
- Your parents
- Your friends
- Igor's new girlfriend, Bertha
- Your new companion, Lars
- Your children (if any)

Now spend time with each viewpoint, trying to see the breakup as each of them would; what would they think in their secret hearts about it; how would they explain its causes or place blame? Remember that each of them will have a different focus. Lars may care less about the past than the future; friends may think Igor was tied down to you; your mother might take your side, but underneath her sympathy perhaps she hopes the experience teaches you a lesson about jumping too quickly into relationships. Ask yourself as you proceed how much truth is in these ideas.

You can also ask the following *character types* for ideas—they always have viewpoints on any topic. This is a kind of cross section of human opinions. How would the following view your topic:

- An accountant
- A socialist
- A lawyer
- Your religious leader
- Your favorite singer
- Someone in the year 2050
- An ecologist
- A psychologist
- A child
- A politician

You may stereotype a bit here, but just imagine what a lawyer might say about the breakup. He or she would consider it a legal/contract problem. What new facets would that bring up? Your religious leader might relate the breakup to your moral and spiritual beliefs. The ecologist or socialist may not be very helpful on this topic. The person from the future may simply say, "It won't matter by then," and suggest not worrying about it. Give each one a few minutes to "tell" you what he or she would say on the topic or problem. If nothing comes, move to another. **We all have little bits of all these perspectives inside us. To cultivate deeper analysis and honest ideas, give each perspective a chance to speak.**

See who speaks loudest and clearest to you and listen for new ideas. Alternative viewpoints help free you from your usual self so you can probe your deeper, more unusual self.

Here are three examples of people thinking from alternate viewpoints. Loren Eiseley, the great nature scholar, said, "In the world of the spider, I do not exist." Can you see the world as a spider does and understand what he means? In her later years, actress Shelley Winters once said, "I think onstage nudity is disgusting, shameful, and damaging to all things American. But if I were 22 with a great body, it would be artistic, tasteful, and patriotic." Last, there's a story anthropologist Bronislaw Malinowski tells. While working with cannibals, he informed an old chief that the millions of dead in European wars were not eaten by the victors, but buried. The old cannibal shook his head. "How barbaric!" he said. All three make us think by shifting our perspective.

The competition among the different viewpoints will lead to more honest and sophisticated ideas you might otherwise never consider. Good ideas toughen up under pressure from other ideas; poor ones crumble. Alternative viewpoints also help you relate better to your audience because you will think of things your reader may want discussed. Can you, for instance, visualize the world your parents saw when they were your age? How did they feel then about music, war, computers, jobs, and college? What hopes and fears filled their thoughts?

Suppose you're writing on a less personal topic for a communication course, such as how television affects our view of marriage. You can start by listing some alternative viewpoints:

- Young children
- Advertisers
- Teenage couples
- Program writers
- Actors/actresses
- Lesbians and gay men
- Marriage counselors
- Religious leaders
- Senior citizens
- People in troubled marriages
- People in wonderful marriages

Go over each one, writing down the viewpoint of each and giving a specific detail. For example, senior citizens might complain that older married couples are often portrayed as grouchy and unloving. Remember, no matter how you feel about this conflict, each person or group will feel it is doing what's right and will justify these feelings. When you finish, sort through the viewpoints to decide which to use. If you decide on your message before honestly exploring all sides, you'll be a little bit like the Queen of Hearts in *Alice in Wonderland* who wants to have the punishment first and then the trial.

Alternate viewpoints can also mean changing your angle of vision. Consider this symbol: **+** . This can mean something positive, but from a math perspective "addition." From a Christian viewpoint, it can also represent the cross and the symbol of salvation through suffering. But suppose we turn the **+** (or ourselves) a quarter turn. Now we have: **✕** . How does that slight shift in viewpoint change the possibilities of meaning in the sign?

Examining alternative viewpoints is best for honesty, for widening your perspectives, and for audience awareness. It may help you organize but may tend to pull a draft in different directions.

■ **PRACTICE 3-4** Your college is suffering budget problems and is considering reducing costs by eliminating the required writing course. List five people or groups who would have different perspectives on this plan. In a half-page list, explain each of their viewpoints, especially the reasons they would give for their position.

■ **PRACTICE 3-5** Imagine the perspectives four or five different people might have on the topic you chose in Practice 3-3. Fill a half-page with their viewpoints.

3. ATTACK STEREOTYPES, UNQUESTIONED IDEAS, AND SLOGANS

Stereotypes, unquestioned ideas, and slogans are enemies of creativity—blocks that prevent honest, imaginative thinking. All three encourage us to think in accepted, common patterns, which as you know is not really thinking.

Stereotypes place people or ideas in closed-minded categories:

- Poor people don't want to work.
- A woman can't build a house.
- They're white; they're probably racists.
- Fat people are so jolly.

Sentences like these portray a writer who does *not* look carefully at life but who sees groups and generalities, not individuals. **Stereotypes are comfortable lies that make the world seem more simple and**

predictable than it really is. That's why they're hard to break. But when you do break them, your writing leaps to life. Do poor people really not want to work? The fact is that 40% of poor people do work, 45% are children, and 12% are disabled.

A creative and critical thinker must peek behind unquestioned ideas once in a while to keep from being closed-minded. Doing this has led to some of humankind's most creative concepts. The Declaration of Independence challenged the divine right of kings—the unquestioned belief that a king received his right to rule from God. Thomas Jefferson questioned this by stating that "all men are created equal" and that a king should rule, not by God's authority, but by "the consent of the governed." What changes so few words have made in the world!

For centuries the dissection of the human body was forbidden. Until this unquestioned idea was challenged and the body dissected, people believed our emotions came from our hearts (not our minds) and even thought a man's erection came from air in his lungs!

Unquestioned ideas are often invisible because so many people take them for granted, like eyesight or the ability to walk. When I mentioned Thomas Jefferson's famous phrases, did you go one step further and ask if "all men are created equal" and "consent of the governed" have also become unquestioned *today?* If challenging these ideas is upsetting, it's because our belief in them is deeply ingrained.

Slogans are stereotyped uses of words. If you find yourself concluding, "Man does not live by bread alone," or "Just say no," watch out! You're not thinking; you're repeating something off the top of your head. While stereotypes are comfortable and unquestioned ideas are invisible, slogans come to us with a sense of discovery: "Ah, I've got it!" But it usually means just as we had the chance to move into new territory, we found our way back to the worn, common road of thought. Students sometimes protest, "But this slogan is true! I've seen it!" Perhaps. But if it's true, at least put it into your own words to make it *your* truth.

I've lumped stereotypes, unquestioned ideas, and slogans together because the same brain teaser applies to each. **To get fresher, more honest ideas, imagine yourself as a puncturer of balloons. Become a cynic who suspects all commonly held ideas and sayings to have little lies in them that need exposing.** Think like the philosopher Nietzsche, who said, "Distrust is a sign of health."

To attack these three idea killers, **first list all the stereotypes, unquestioned ideas, and slogans** you can about your topic, all the "common" truths. These are the things you'd write in your paper if you wanted to create a below-average paper. **Next, find *exceptions* to items in this list.**

Think of people, cases, and incidents that may contradict the common belief. Write as long a list as you can. After you've attacked the stereotypes, unquestioned ideas, and slogans, you can honestly decide what you really think and will have plenty of material for an outline/draft.

For example, let's assume your sociology professor assigns a paper on "Women in the Workplace." Here are some stereotypes, unquestioned ideas, and slogans I've heard about this topic:

- Women can't do the heavy work a man can. (stereotype)
- A woman's place is in the home. (slogan)
- Working mothers hurt kids by not being home. (unquestioned idea)
- Men will not go to a female doctor. (unquestioned idea)
- Keep women barefoot and pregnant. (slogan)
- Equal pay for equal work. (slogan)
- Would you want women shot if they were allowed in combat? (unquestioned idea)
- Women are too emotional to be president. (stereotype)
- Female bosses aren't feminine. (stereotype)

Notice that these stereotypes, unquestioned ideas, and slogans come from *both* sides of this controversial topic. Now, the creative task is to puncture these balloons.

Some, such as "a woman's place is in the home," are easy to attack. Suppose Queen Elizabeth I, Venus and Serena Williams, Catherine the Great, Marie Curie, Jane Goodall, and Oprah Winfrey had stayed home? My list could go on for pages. What a drab world we would have without them. See if you can poke other holes in this slogan. Notice that the "pop" is more powerful when you use specific examples.

Other statements are harder to attack. I do think it's awful to shoot women in battle. I was taught that women should be treated with a gentler touch than men. Maybe, however, I need to get behind these "manners." Is that sexist? Maybe the real issue is that it's awful to shoot men in battle, too.

I found "equal pay for equal work" to be the hardest slogan to criticize. I agree with this slogan. But my job in this brain teaser is to question what I believe on the surface. So here's how I might puncture that slogan: What is equal work? Doctors may earn as much in two hours as a truck driver does in a week. People with seniority often earn far more for doing the same job as newer employees. What about quality of work? Many mediocre workers get the same pay as outstanding workers.

My conclusion: Equal pay for equal work sounds good in theory, but I discovered that variables not related to the worker's gender make such an idea hard to define, to put into effect, or to enforce. I'm not happy with this conclusion because I want to believe in the possibility of gender fairness, but until I think some more about it, I'll be forced to qualify that generalization. Can you find some exceptions to *my* conclusion?

You can do research to attack stereotypes, unquestioned ideas, or slogans, too. It is commonly thought, for instance, that American workers are overpaid, underworked, and inefficient compared to workers in Japan and Germany. But in a few minutes I dug these facts from a brochure of the U.S. Bureau of Labor Statistics: German workers were paid an average of $22 per hour, U.S. workers an average of $15, and Japanese workers an average of $13. American workers labor 100 fewer hours per year than the Japanese, but 400 more than the Germans. And American worker productivity is 22% higher than the Germans and 24% higher than the Japanese. These put a few dents in the stereotypes at least. Most people also commonly think of Africa as the wild continent, the place of jungles and deserts. Yet ecological surveys show Africa to be 28% wilderness and North America to be 38% wilderness, based on uninhabited areas. These facts break the stereotype that the average African lives closer to nature than the average North American. Or do they? Consider how much of northern Canada is subarctic or arctic wilderness.

This brain teaser reveals walls we or our upbringing have built around our inner world. Tearing down these walls, or at least peeking around them, is one way people think. **Attacking stereotypes is good for creativity and challenging established ideas and a great approach to most college papers. It may irritate traditional audiences.**

■ **PRACTICE 3-6**
- List five stereotypes about men and attack two of them with examples, facts, or logic.
- Treat "all men are created equal" as an unquestioned idea and poke two holes in it with specific cases in which this is not or should not be so.
- List five common slogans used to debate public policy (for example, "Guns don't kill people; people kill people") and pop holes in two of them.

■ **PRACTICE 3-7** List three stereotypes, unquestioned ideas, or slogans about the topic you chose in Practice 3-3. Then attack them.

4. CLASSIFY YOUR TOPIC
To classify is another way to think. **Classifying breaks a subject into categories and places individuals in each category.** For example,

biology divides all living creatures into two main classifications: plants and animals. It further classifies types of animals according to whether they are mammals, fish, or insects. You must figure out sensible, inventive categories that show underlying qualities among members of the same group that may not be obvious at first glance. People classified whales as fish, for instance, until realizing that some not-so-obvious qualities, such as lungs and feeding offspring with milk, made whales closer to mammals than to fish.

In a classification brain teaser, **break your subject down into categories several times until you come up with a creative pattern.** For example, suppose your topic is "Dreams." You could break dreams down into daydreams and night dreams. Too general and obvious? Yes. Suppose I classify night dreams as follows:

- Dreams in which you're chased
- Sexual dreams
- Falling dreams
- Replay-of-the-day dreams
- Dreams in which you can't run or speak

To finish a classification brain teaser, list examples and descriptions under each category. Under "chase dreams," for instance, I might list:

- A mad dog foaming, breathing down my neck
- Peasants, with pitchforks and burning torches, chase me into a barn
- Snowmobiles roaring after me through snowy woods

Suppose your topic is "Education." Off the top of my head:

- Elementary school
- High school
- College

Boring! But it is a starting point. How about focusing just on high school:

- Good high schools
- Bad high schools
- Average high schools

Nope. Still flat. The categories are too vague. How about this:

- Preppie high school
- Learn-nothing high school
- Vo-tech high school
- Parochial high school

This is getting better. I can think of people and facts to put under each. I might get even more specific by classifying types of parochial schools.

Let's go back to our main topic, "Education." I could have taken a different route. Instead of schools, I could have classified students, courses, or teachers. Take a minute or two to imagine several classifications for each. If your first classification is boring, you're normal. Pick one aspect and go deeper by classifying only that.

The more specific your subject, the more you can do with it. This seems like a contradiction, since you might think the broader the topic, the easier it is to think up things to write. Not true. **It's easier to think up common thoughts on big topics, but harder to say something fresh.** Suppose you start with "Technology" as a topic. The possibilities are too overwhelming. Narrow it to medical technology and you can classify it more vividly. Narrow medical technology further to "Types of Gynecologists" or "Types of Sports Doctors," for instance, and the paper almost begs to be written.

You might have one objection to classifying—it seems to create stereotypes! It puts individuals in categories. Isn't that what we were fighting in the last brain teaser? Yes, it was. However, our main objective in this chapter is increasing the ways we have of thinking. Attacking classifications that have become stereotypes is one way people think; creating classifications is another. Classification need not be stereotyping—if you keep in mind and remind your reader that individuals do not all fit their categories perfectly. **Classification helps us see patterns; it is only dishonest if it's applied too strictly. Classifying works well for scientific and technical writing and many college assignments. It is a strong organizer.**

■ **PRACTICE 3-8** Classify types of television comedies, love songs, art works, or country music. Have at least five categories. Now pick one and break it down into at least three subcategories. List three specific examples for each subcategory.

■ **PRACTICE 3-9** Classify the topic you chose for Practice 3-3. Break it into at least three categories and list examples for each category.

5. COMPARE AND CONTRAST YOUR TOPIC

You can lure your brain toward more ideas by comparing your topic with something else. This is another basic way people think. We contrast socialism with capitalism, murder with manslaughter, retailing with wholesaling, the Yankees with the Red Sox. **When we stretch one thing to meet another, we create meaning.** If asked to write a paper on John Steinbeck's novel *The Grapes of Wrath,* you might discover ideas by comparing it to another novel. Steinbeck's novel is about poor people struggling to survive tough economic times, so it might compare well with Alice Walker's *The Color Purple*. Start listing differences:

Steinbeck	**Walker**
People are Okies, white Midwesterners.	People are black Southerners.
The antagonist is the capitalist system (banks, sheriffs, the rich).	The antagonist is the heroine's chauvinist husband.
Characters travel across country.	Character makes an inner journey.
Pessimistic ending.	Heroine succeeds in the end.

This list should continue for half a page. What do I do next with this list? Well, I might create my main essay idea by combining a number of these contrasts, or I might go into one difference in depth: say, to figure out why Steinbeck's characters fail and why Walker's heroine succeeds.

Sometimes comparison or contrast is implied in the question given to you— "Contrast the Democratic and Totalitarian View of the Press," or "What Similar Techniques Do the French Painters Monet and Renoir Use?" Other times you may be given a topic and can discover a useful comparison to bring it to life. If you must write a paper on "Modern Nursing Ethics," think of several possible comparisons:

- Two nurses whose ethics are different
- Two situations that require different ethics
- Nursing ethics of a hundred years ago compared with today's ethics
- The contrast in ethics between doctors and nurses
- Similarities between nursing ethics and those of another profession

You would then explore *one* of these in depth, listing as many comparisons and contrasts as possible.

Listing similarities and differences takes the pressure off. But when done, you'll have some ideas and details and the basis for organizing your paper as well. **Comparison or contrast can open up almost any topic. Its drawback may be getting beyond superficial comparisons.**

■ **PRACTICE 3-10** Think of three possible comparison/contrast approaches to one of these topics: men's clothes, e-mail, or Christmas shopping. Pick your best and create a half-page list of specific points to support your idea.

■ **PRACTICE 3-11** Think of a comparison or contrast approach to your topic from Practice 3-3, and list a half-page of specific details to support it.

6. CREATE METAPHORS

A metaphor is a special comparison, not between things in the same category (two novels, for example), **but between things in different categories** (for example, a novel and a beverage):

- Reading her book is like drinking a cool, clear glass of water.
- Her party was like an insane asylum.
- Rap music is a sermon delivered with hammer blows.
- Love must be made fresh every day—like bread.
- Old-age homes are like warehouses.
- The city is wearing a veil of fog this morning.

Why make such comparisons? Because it's fun, and it stirs a reader's imagination and visualization.

Let's return to the topic of "Education" again to show how you could use a metaphor brain teaser to come up with new topics that did not appear in the classification brain teaser. Start by listing all the comparisons you can think of, not worrying if some sound silly.

Let's try narrowing our topic to "College" and see what bubbles up:

College is like: a factory

the army

a farm or garden

a beehive or ant nest

the ocean

a circus

a meal

a tree

No apologies—this is my rough list. Now I glance over the list, adding a few details to each item to see which ones have the most potential. In trying to compare college to a factory, I think of college courses in which the same work is done in mass-production lecture halls, or how class recess resembles a shift change. The *idea* behind this metaphor suggests that college is routine, uncreative, time serving. Someone who felt this way may have the concept for a paper here.

I liked the circus metaphor, especially thinking about the last week of classes when everyone's a bit wild—people dress outrageously and "clowns" try out their routines in class. As an instructor, I feel like a ringmaster try-ing to keep the show going. Some students give beautiful performances, while that tiger in the front row snarls over his last paper. To explore this concept further, I'd want to make a list of all the circus things I can think of and try to find equivalents in college life. See if you can add to the fol-lowing list and if you can find college equivalents for these items:

- Three rings
- Buying a ticket
- High-wire act
- The elephants bellowing
- The sideshow
- Monkeys
- Peanuts, popcorn, and cotton candy
- The bleachers
- The cages
- The freak show
- Cleaning up the elephants' mess
- The whip and chair

The overall mood a piece like this would create is light, a kind of gentle, sarcastic humor that doesn't take college too seriously, but as an entertain-ing game—much different from the grim metaphor of a factory.

Recently I asked a composition class to help a student with her paper on teenage suicide by suggesting metaphors. Let me recreate the discus-sion to show you how ideas emerged.

Me: What can you compare suicide to?
Student A: An ending.
Me: Okay, what kinds of endings are there? Let's think of endings, and then see if we can come back to suicide.
Student B: A rear end.
Student C: A cliff edge.
Student D: A book ending.
Student A: Yeah, like a book with the last pages ripped out—that's suicide.
Student B: How about a dead-end road?
Student A: Or a road that leads nowhere.
Student E: Suicide's more an escape.
Me: From what? Metaphors ought to be visual.
Student F: An escape from prison. Life's like a jail to some people. They want to be free.

Student E: Suicides like to control what happens to them. They feel like victims until they plan to kill themselves. Then they're in charge.
Me: So what's *that* like?
Student G: Like—writing a play. They make everything happen as they want—for once.

A metaphor brain teaser can lead to a main idea and be the backbone of your essay, and it can create sparkling details. It's good for creativity, visual detail, and humor. In college and business writing, you may want to keep metaphors on a short leash.

■ **PRACTICE 3-12** Pick one of the metaphors for college (or invent your own) and make a half-page list of specific equivalents.

■ **PRACTICE 3-13** Create one or more metaphors for your topic from Practice 3-3 and list a half-page of details.

7. LIST EXAMPLES

This brain teaser provides you with *details*. Simply list all the specific examples about the topic you can think of. If you're writing about abortion, list all the cases you've ever known: ones from the news, people you know, stories mentioned by friends or teachers. **An example must be a single concrete instance, never a generality.** This brain teaser tells you quickly which topics you don't know enough about before it's too late. If it's an assigned topic, it'll tell you what research you need to do.

If I were going to write a paper on alcoholism, for instance, these examples occur to me:

- Matt—a gentle young man who was attending AA during a course he took from me. Several times his writing and class comments were incoherent. He was quiet and lonely.
- Rico—an older man who declared he was a recovering alcoholic. He told me about the hell of shakes and fits he used to go through and how desperate he was to make up for the time he was "dead" for his four children.
- Jeanette—the mother of a teenage alcoholic. Her son had ruined her family, bringing her almost to divorce. She threw him out of the house.
- Ed—a 50-year-old man who stole money from his daughter for booze.

Once I started this list, I realized I knew far more alcohol-related stories than I thought—another 10 or so besides these. One example often hooks more. To develop this list into a paper, I might narrow it to teenage alcoholism or the effect of alcohol on families.

Examples are essential to support or visualize most writing. This brain teaser is a good one to use early in writing a paper but will not help you organize.

■ **PRACTICE 3-14** List a half-page of your own examples for a paper on alcoholism or drug abuse. Fill out some of the examples with details. After you finish, state a point the examples seem to suggest.

■ **PRACTICE 3-15** List a half-page of examples for the topic you chose for Practice 3-3.

 8. MAKE A BUG LIST

One way to approach any topic is to criticize or complain about it. You begin this brain teaser by saying, "What really bugs me about _____ is _____." Then you list all the complaints you can think of. A bug list helps you formulate a problem, and solving a problem is a great approach for many college papers and a great way to impress your boss. In both cases, you start with a bug list and move to solutions.

In preparing to write this book, I made a bug list about texts. Some are too filled with terminology, some too complicated, some too theoretical, and some too impersonal. The bug list told me what I wanted to avoid.

One of my recent students worked at a nursing home, and I suggested for one paper that she use a bug list to decide what she could write on. Christine listed dozens of complaints: about the elderly residents themselves, about the way the home was managed, about the families of the residents, and, most creatively, about her own flaws as an employee. She decided there was no easy way to make the home more humane and caring. She wasn't aware of this until she went through an exhaustive list of complaints. Old Mr. Fitzwater was just a miserable grouch, whose bad humor couldn't be blamed on family or staff. And there was that gloppy un-food served each day. And while she understood why an orderly might feel irritated by continual messes, she didn't like employees handling the old people as if they were machines to be oiled. She even found complaints about the building's design that encouraged isolation; it was more tomb than home. Now Christine could not cure all these ills in her paper, but by listing the problems, she saw how some things could be fixed, and she even brought them to her supervisor. And she found a new bug: He was afraid to do anything about her bugs.

Dissatisfaction has solved many problems, so put yourself in a sharp, critical mood for this brain teaser. Mention little things as well as large, abstract things so you have both details and ideas. Be honest.

In reviewing your brain teaser list later, you may decide to tackle a lot, as Christine did, or you may focus on just one interesting or creative criticism and seek a solution for it. **Bug lists are excellent for career problem solving, argumentative papers, and self-therapy. If not used with other brain teasers, however, they can lead to excessively negative writing.** Don't confuse a brain teaser with the final paper.

■ **PRACTICE 3-16** Make a half-page bug list about public transportation, the World Wide Web, or a fast-food restaurant.

■ **PRACTICE 3-17** Write a half-page bug list about the topic you chose for Practice 3-3.

9. USE HUMOR AND FANTASY

Go wacky and wild. Think of all kinds of fantasy situations about your topic or the humorous side to it. **This form of thinking is often downgraded because it sounds unintellectual or silly, but fantasy and humor have solved many personal and world problems.** The German poet Goethe once said, "The intelligent man finds almost everything ridiculous." Dorothy Parker, the great humorist, said, "Wit has truth in it." And psychotherapist Sheldon Kopp said, "Laughter is the sound of freedom." Think how a grin or joke can often end arguments. Think of all the comic movies, plays, and books that have changed people's ways of thinking. One of the greatest antiwar plays ever written was *Lysistrata,* a story about the women of two warring armies who go on a sex strike until their husbands agree to stop fighting. No sex for any man, the women on both sides vow. It's a hilarious fantasy that makes a serious point about the stupidity of war—that killing and lovemaking don't go together—and Aristophanes wrote it 2,400 years ago. By distorting reality, he made it clearer.

Some people will find this brain teaser hard. But anyone can develop this part of his or her thinking repertoire. Being able to let go, without prejudging dumb ideas, is the key.

Here are a few ways to help loosen your imagination:

1. **Reverse the normal rules of reality.** Gary Larson, who created *The Far Side* cartoon, does this with deer who hunt people, salmon who wear tourist caps and ride a boat upstream to the spawning grounds, and ants in lab coats trying to figure out how to get rid of their pests—humans.

2. **Break a social, scientific, or mathematical law** related to your topic and imagine the results. Do you hate local speed limits? Imagine the results of having no speed limit. Do you hate high taxes? Imagine a world without them, or a world of 100% taxation, or a world without money.

3. **Create a new rule or law and imagine its effects.** Suppose libraries could be recorded on microchips implanted in each human brain at the age of 10. What would happen? If you're interested in world peace, you might imagine a world government or the outlawing of foreign travel.

Humor or fantasy can spark personal writing, fiction, and satire, and occasional flashes enliven professional writing. It's creative, but risky. Know your audience first.

■ **PRACTICE 3-18** Think of a fantastic or humorous way of stopping terrorism, preventing divorce, or reducing traffic deaths. Fill out your idea with a half-page list of details.

■ **PRACTICE 3-19** Think of a fantasy or humorous approach to your topic from Practice 3-3. Fill a half-page with details.

10. ANTICIPATE YOUR AUDIENCE

This brain teaser makes you think about how your reader may react to your topic. Answering these questions suggests strategy as well as new ideas and details:

- Who is my audience? Describe its concerns or features.
- What does my audience already know about the topic?
- What does my audience already believe about the topic?
- How might my audience respond to my opinion? Be specific, especially about objections they'd have.
- What does my audience want (need) to learn?
- What might my audience resist hearing? How can I overcome this bias?

For example, suppose I'm considering writing about garbage. Perhaps I spent a summer working at a landfill, took a course in the environment, and think it's an unusual topic. Here's how I might anticipate my audience:

> My audience is my English professor and a peer group in class. I'd bet they don't *know* much about garbage. Most people leave full bags at roadside each week without worrying where the garbage goes.

But one woman in class made a few comments about nuclear waste. My professor's hard to read; she said she enjoys nature but hasn't said anything specific about pollution. I'll assume she's more interested in good writing than in my environmental views. Probably most people in class *believe* we have too much garbage, but they don't know the details. I'd guess most would like to stop unnecessary garbage but won't put much time into it. About half would resist my pet idea of having lots more mandatory recycling, especially the Republican guy in the front who speaks out against government rules. Maybe I could say something about how rules are necessary until people get more responsible. To convince them, I'll have to motivate them. Plain numbers—tons of aluminum thrown away—won't grab them. They may be more impressed by the loss of trees and ugly strip-mining pits. They'll be most influenced by threats to their health by incinerators burning garbage and poisons leaking into our drinking water or even the rising cost of garbage collection. I'd like to get them to change their personal buying habits, but I'll have to do it in a way that doesn't sound as if I'm accusing them.

Doing this audience analysis clarified my topic, created some ideas, and uncovered objections I must answer in the paper. **Because it stresses strategy, anticipating your audience is effective with argumentative writing. The downside: This brain teaser may draw you away from your beliefs and into saying what you think your audience wants to hear.**

■ **PRACTICE 3-20** Suppose you're writing a letter to your classmates about changing a government policy. After stating your point, describe your audience's beliefs, knowledge, and possible reactions to your idea. You may also ask a peer group to give a "live" reaction.

■ **PRACTICE 3-21** Describe a potential audience's reaction to your topic from Practice 3-3. List a variety of possible responses.

If you can only remember one thing from this chapter, remember this: The more brain teasers you devote to a topic, the wiser you'll be writing the paper. Your idea will be tougher, more resistant to attack if you scrutinize it from many perspectives. Another way of saying this is that **you have to kiss a lot of frogs before you find your prince or princess idea.** People's typical response to a problem like writing a paper is to get *rid* of it; brain teasers help you learn to embrace a problem and make something positive out of it.

Brain teasers should be fun—you are playing the mind's video game, punching all the buttons and zinging electricity through the cobwebs of the skull. Enjoy the show. In some ways college is simply play on a higher level. Brain teasers give you control over your thinking. You can passively accept whatever ideas come to you, not knowing if they're the best or most honest you have, or you can reject intellectual helplessness. **Active use of your brain's capabilities leads to self-reliance, confidence, and mental freedom. Brain teasers help you tap more of what is already in you.**

SAMPLE BRAIN TEASERS

BUG LIST—GROCERY STORES

—Long express lines/people with 20 items
—People with checks, coupons, food stamps, and unscannable items in express lanes
—Trashy newspapers: "Aliens in Congress!" "Lawyer Eats Baby!" "Oprah's Face Falls Off"
—Too much plastic packaging
— Plastic bags—tear, groceries in car
—After your hands are full, the cashier tries to hand you the little receipt slip
—Carts in the parking lot. Wind blows them. Dent cars
—People, especially kids with colds, grab bulk cookies with their bare hands
—Big Ruth!
—Not enough cashiers
—Carts with stuck wheels

HUMOR—FUNERALS

—"Doesn't he look good!" He's dead!
—Telling strangers how sorry you are
—Praising the dead one, even when he was a rat and everyone in his family is glad he's dead
—Soft pillows for the dead
—Old men carrying the coffin
—Justin saw a casket dropped and the corpse rolled into the church aisle. Half the crowd screamed. The rest laughed.

ANALYSIS

Format: Both brain teasers are good starts. They're in list form so the ideas can be extracted. Both are specific without being wordy. The length of each item is good, although "Big Ruth" is too vague to mean much to me. The funeral list is too short. There's just not enough there yet.

How the authors might focus their brain teasers for a paper:
The "Funeral Notes" emphasize ironies—contrasts between appearances and reality. This would make a good theme. But it needs more details. The author might try attacking Unquestioned Ideas and Slogans ("he's gone to a better world" or "her suffering's over"), Examples, Alternate Viewpoints, and Anticipating Your Audience to get more ideas. The bug list on "Grocery Stores" is an easier topic and may be too broad, but it has some sparkling details to work with. To be a successful paper, it will have to be narrowed down. Two focuses I see in it deal with customer behavior and improving the environment of the store. She has avoided the obvious path of attacking the checkout people. If the author wants more to think about, she could try Using Senses, Breaking Unquestioned Ideas, and Contrast (between two stores). What else would you suggest?

■ **PRACTICE 3-22** Which brain teasers would you recommend to someone thinking about writing on the following topics? Why? What kind of paper focus do you envision?
- Trailer parks
- Gangsta rap
- The drug Ecstasy
- Hispanic marriage ideals

Roadblocks to Good Ideas and Details

Despite all these brain teasers, there will be times you will find yourself staring at a blank piece of paper at 2 A.M. All writers have these awful moments, so nothing is wrong with you as a writer if you have blue dry spells. Here are two common writer's blocks you can overcome:

FEAR OF RISK
Despite the desire to do well, **many people are just afraid to put anything on paper that is daring or a bit odd.** They're afraid of being judged as weird or of revealing secrets about themselves. When they sit down to write, the flow of ideas is blocked by this internal censor.

Sometimes safe ideas squeeze through and you can manage to write something. Other times, the hold-back message shuts down the flow of all ideas. You want to write, but nothing comes.

 Solution: write the most outrageous things about your topic— the wildest, grossest, most absurd things. You reduce the fear of risk by telling yourself this is a throwaway list that no one else will see.

If I'm writing about pollution control, for instance, and I'm blocked, I can let loose the little demon in me to say irresponsible, risky things:

1. Let's pollute faster so we kill off humanity—the world may be better off without us.
2. There ought to be pollution hit squads. Instead of taking polluters to court, these action groups could break polluters' windows or dump garbage, oil-killed animals, or chemical wastes on the lawns of the company's president. We could picket their houses, churches, and clubs.
3. To cut down on garbage, we could forbid all wrappers on things that don't need to be sanitary, such as clothes.
4. Use big machines to crush garbage into blocks and build houses with them.

Next, I evaluate my absurd, secret list. Item 1 is just nastiness talking; item 2 is illegal and mean, but modified a bit, it might be usable. Perhaps we could pass laws to hold individual employees responsible for company pollution and prosecute, fine, and jail them as individuals. Item 3 may also have merit if I tame it down a bit; item 4 sounds like a technological problem (to make odor-free garbage houses), but turning junk into treasure is a concept I might be able to use with other items—such as automobile tires or bottles.

INSECURITY ABOUT YOUR ABILITY TO THINK

People with this block are amazed that anything at all appears on paper. When *any* idea appears, they are so thrilled they don't dare try another option. They accept any idea as a gift of the gods. **They think writing is a one-time miracle.**

Solution: Writing is a learnable skill to be relied on, and a wealth of ideas exists in everyone's brain. In his book about human intelligence, *The Dragons of Eden,* Carl Sagan calculated that the human eye can absorb 5,000 bits of information per second and that all this data is stored in the brain, which recombines each bit many times with others, forming ideas and adding to them second by second. The average human brain contains an unimaginably large number of pieces of information and ideas—2×10^{13}—which is *far* greater than the total number of all electrons, protons, and neutrons in the universe! Be impressed with your own brain power. Rely on it.

If you're a thank-God-I-have-an-idea person, you're too humble. Use brain teasers regularly for several months until you build up your confidence that you do have many ideas to choose from. **You must demystify creating ideas. Having ideas is human nature; it comes with our genetic code.**

VISUAL RHETORIC

To practice learning to think in different methods, analyze the following pictures for the artist or photographer's way of thinking in creating the picture. Start by looking for how one or more brain teasers shape the picture. Also analyze the other aspects of visual rhetoric that apply to writing:

- Idea (thesis or feeling suggested by a picture)
- Details (How do they support the idea? Look closely!)
- Structure (How are the parts organized?)
- Transitions (How is your eye moved around?)
- Context (significance of historical or cultural setting)
- Style (How does style help or hurt the picture?)

Here's my take on the dandelion puff:

ANALYSIS

Brain teasers: The picture has strong **sense appeal.** I can feel the soft, airy texture and see the delicate fibers so much clearer than in normal life because of the close-up. It stirs memories of picking and blowing dandelions so the

age fotostock/Superstock

Laura Dwight/CORBIS

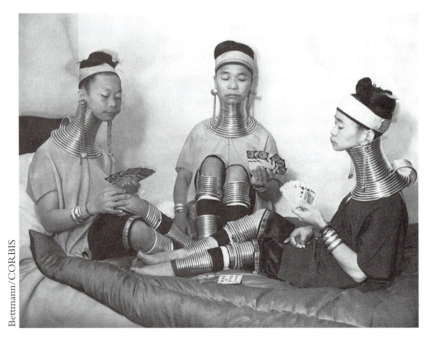

Bettmann/CORBIS

little seeds float like parachutes. Writers often use a close-up approach to put us "inside" a moment. The picture also uses **alternate viewpoints** to alter our normal perspective on the humble weed by isolating it and putting us down in the grass, so it becomes more significant and valuable. The photographer also uses **contrast** between the transparent, delicate puff and the darker splotches below toward which it heads and the sharp lines pointing down from the puff.

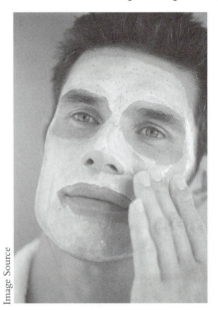

Image Source

Ideas: When I see such pictures, it reminds me that we live in a wonder-filled world and suggests we think things are insignificant only because we don't look closely at them. There is **no direct thesis,** but the picture makes me think about the balance between the beauty and delicacy of new life that is created by the passing of the old in the cycle of death and rebirth. What else do you think about when you look at it?

Details: Other tiny seeds attached to the head are about to let go. Now only one floats freely, but all will follow. Oddly enough—and I don't

Nick Vaccaro/Photonica/Getty Images

know what to make of this—the bright head resembles a dimpled golf ball.

Structure: The intense close-up on a small object gives it significance. An almost empty background makes sense. This is the entire world.

Audience: Someone looking for an artistic experience, not information.

Context: None. The point is to enlarge its importance by isolating it. A writer can do the same thing. Don't describe the entire party—just focus on the eyes of that shy girl.

Style: Soft, slightly blurry for a fantasy effect that heightens the effect of time and life passing.

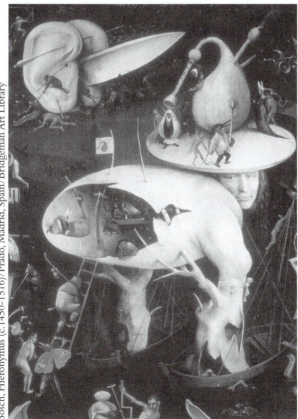

The Garden of Earthly Delights: Hell, right wing of triptych, c.1500 (oil on panel) (detail of 3425), Bosch, Hieronymus (c.1450–1516)/Prado, Madrid, Spain/Bridgeman Art Library

Detail of Hell from "The Garden of Earthly Delights"

Context Note on *The Garden of Earthly Delights.* This strange painting is a detail from a huge, three-part work by Dutch artist Hieronymus Bosch that depicts God's Garden of Eden, Man's Garden of Life Pleasures and Satan's Garden of Hell. Scholars have argued since 1500 about what this disturbing work means. Many think the large face on the central figure is the artist himself.

■ **PRACTICE 3-23** How does one picture I did not analyze display a brain teaser in its way of thinking? Support your response with details and make a tentative statement of the message or thesis the picture conveys.

Writing Suggestions and Class Discussions

· ·

1. **Incubation Exercise:** Your teacher will assign a paper. At each class meeting bring in a half-page list of new ideas and details for that paper.

Note for numbers 2–11: All brain teasers should be in list and note form, not in paragraph style.

2. **Sense Brain teaser:**
   a. List one page of sense details about your first home. Try for all five senses, being as specific as possible. Allow these details to bounce into ideas, but keep returning to the senses.
   b. Same as item a., except list sense details about the first time you ever saw death. Recall hidden details.
   c. Same as item a. on any topic of your choice.

3. **Alternative Viewpoint Brain teaser:**
   a. In a sentence or two, describe one failure you have had. Then list your feelings about its significance, causes, and effects. Now write out how two other people close to you saw your failure differently. Try to think as they would. Now make a fourth and fifth list choosing two of the types of people on page 54 for your alternative viewpoints.
   b. What effects do suicide bombers have on various people involved? Concentrate on honestly seeing the issue as they do. You might think toward a paper evaluating how effective suicide bombing is as a political strategy.
   c. Do an alternative viewpoint list for any topic you choose.

4. **Attack Stereotypes, Unquestioned Ideas, and Slogans Brain teaser:**
   a. Take some unquestioned idea (playing the national anthem at sporting events, for instance) and see if you can expose some unreasonableness about it.
   b. In a few sentences, describe a situation in which someone stereotyped you because of your age, sex, race, physical appearance, or other reason. Then list all the exceptions to this stereotype that you can think of—in yourself or others.
   c. Pick a popular slogan that bothers you and list five to six objections to it.

5. **Classification Brain teaser:**
   a. Classify a type of film into sub-classifications. For example, classify three types of action films or four types of "chick flicks." List several examples for each type and name the key characteristics of each category.

b. Classify reasons why people succeed in their careers; what different qualities does success require? Give details for each.

c. Classify any topic of your choice. Give details for each category.

6. **Comparison/Contrast Brain teaser:**

a. In your Popular Culture class, you are assigned to write on clothing styles of today versus five years ago. List a page of points of comparison, being sure not just to compare details, but also how the clothes' styles reflect changes in attitude or values.

b. Compare or contrast two consumer products of the same type (two models of car or two microwaves, for instance).

c. Write a comparison or contrast brain teaser for any topic of your choice.

7. **Metaphor Brain teaser:**

a. Life is like _____. List six possible metaphors to finish the sentence. Then pick one and fill the rest of the page with details that could develop it. No clichés (no "box of chocolates" or "bowl of cherries").

b. A teen's first sexual encounter is like _____. List six possible metaphors. Then pick one and fill the rest of the page with details that could develop it.

c. Create a metaphor list on any topic of your choice.

8. **List Examples Brain teaser:**

a. You are assigned the topic "Computers and Children" in your introduction to computers course. List at least 10 specific, concrete examples you could use in this paper. Allow your mind to produce ideas as the examples come. Circle any ideas that seem to tie the examples together.

b. List 10 examples of teenage crime. As you review your list, add explanations for its causes or ideas on how to stop it.

c. List 10 examples on any topic that interests you.

9. **Bug List Brain teaser:**

a. Make a 15-item bug list on one of the following topics:
   - Recreational motor homes
   - Evangelists
   - Television advertisements
   - Your job
   - One flaw in your personality

Now circle the two or three items that have the most potential for a paper and try to probe deeper into them by providing details and more explanation.

b. Write a bug list on a topic of your choice.

10. **Humor/Fantasy Brain teaser:**
    a. List all the humorous things you can about one of these topics:
       • Blind dates
       • Family holidays
       • Funerals
       • School cafeterias
    b. List a page of humorous or fantasy ideas about any topic of your choice.

11. **Anticipate Your Audience Brain teaser:**
    a. In one sentence summarize a paper assignment you've been given for a college course. Then list the qualities you believe the professor expects in an A, C, and F paper.
    b. List a page of audience analysis about any topic of your choice.

12. **Peer Review:** Bring to class a brain teaser you're thinking about expanding into a paper. Read it to your group, explaining as you go. Write down the group's suggestions and circle important items. Afterward, write one sentence that explains your paper's tentative thesis.

13. Which two brain teasers do you think would dig up the strongest ideas or details for the following topics? Without actually doing the brain teasers, describe what each will provide for your paper:
    • A report to your boss about which software program the company should purchase
    • A letter to a girlfriend/boyfriend breaking off the relationship
    • A research paper for sociology class on the minimum wage
    • A cover letter for a job application
    • Your own home page or blog

14. Using any *two* brain teasers, develop two pages of ideas/details on one of these topics:
    • Music videos
    • Pornography
    • City life
    • A book you read recently
    • People and their pets
    • A first job

15. You wake up one morning and discover one of three changes in your life:
    • You have aged 25 years. If you're over 50, you lose 25 years!
    • Your gender has changed.
    • Your species has changed.

Thinking from this alternative viewpoint, describe the next 20 minutes of your life accurately.

16. Your peer group's job is to write a bug list of what's wrong with high school, then solve two of the problems.

17. Your peer group's job is to attack television stereotypes of business-people, one ethnic minority, teenagers, or police officers. Choose one, state the stereotypes, and then break them.

STUDENT ESSAY

The following essay began from a sense brain teaser list. Read the essay and then the notes and comments.

Spring Break: Mazatlán, Mexico
Tinamarie Ciccarone

Waiting for the train, I felt like a young child going to the circus. This was my first vacation alone—destination: Mazatlán, Mexico. Like the other hundreds of students, my mind filled with visions: the sun setting into the ocean, the serene beach at night. I was going to have the best time of my life. The Mexican train was scheduled to arrive at 3 o'clock, but that hour came and went. The train station was falling apart: chipped paint, holes in the wall, and the unspeakable rest room. Hyper students and baggage crammed the lobby.

As the hours crept by, I encouraged myself by flipping through the brochures of our hotel. The Riviera was the best beachfront in Mazatlán. I dreamed of crystal water and hours of undisturbed tanning on white sand. My excitement rebubbled, and when the train finally arrived in the darkness like a wobbly earthworm, our eyes widened and faces glowed. We chose seats in the dark and fumbled baggage into the racks above. My aching backside was thankful for a padded seat and we slept.

I opened my eyes at 7 A.M. and scanned the car for the first time in the light. The vinyl orange seats were layered with grime, and my white sweatshirt had become gray overnight. Some seats were loose and shook their occupants. The floor—the original color of which could not be determined—was black, sticky, and wet from spilled beer. Food wrappers, empty beer bottles, and cigarette butts collected under the seats. Someone three seats down dropped a powdered sugar doughnut. An army of ants seized it.

→

Pretty soon a guy with a bunch of keys hanging from his belt came through, yelling, *"Cerveza! Cerveza!"*

I limped stiffly down the aisle. The bathroom knob resisted turning, and the door hesitated before giving in to my push. A wretched smell rushed my unprepared nostrils, and I gagged. I took a deep breath and entered. What else could I do?

The bathroom walls were gray with dirt and slime, the floor wet with either vomit or urine or a putrid combination. The tiny window was closed, trapping the deadly smell. The toilet was black and unusable. The sink was filled with solid human waste. Before I could add to the vile mess on the floor, I jumped out and slammed the door behind me. I stumbled to the booth connecting the cars and sucked in breath after breath of fresh air. Unbelievable! I could not use the bathroom, wash my hands, or change my clothes for another twenty hours.

As I gazed at the countryside, I saw the Mexican people for the first time. We were snaking through a small village. Dozens of identical-looking children, barely clothed, sat in front of houses no bigger than my father's utility shed. Holes in the brick walls served for windows and door. Clotheslines draped across the front yards. The passing train excited them. They shouted, waved, and ran alongside. I waved back and they shrieked joyfully, like puppies behind a fence at my attention. As they vanished in the distance, I walked back to my seat, angry, disgusted, and confused about how I felt. A tear collected—for who?

By the time we arrived, I knew a little bit what life was like for unwealthy, ordinary Mexicans. I had not used a bathroom for 27 unbearable hours. I ate and drank tiny portions, making sure not to run out of food. My body, like everyone else's, smelled like a gym locker. My hair was ragged and tangled and my clothes were now brown. I never thought I'd reach Mazatlán, but of course we did.

Being young, somehow I managed to do some of the wild, fun things I'd planned. I spent hours on the sandy beach, the sun's warmth penetrating and soothing me. The sparkling ocean was filled with sailboats, water skiers, and swimmers. Fancy, modern hotels and sophisticated nightclubs strung along the beach let us in.

But I could see now what else infested Mazatlán. Locals scavenged like rats. Children begged money or food. Sometimes they

→

trailed behind an old, hunched woman, but mostly they hunted alone. By the end of the week I no longer could see the beach's beauty. The hotels were no longer brilliant towers. The ocean lost its gleam, and the sun became plain hot. The happy, carefree college students seemed like mere shadows. What I saw were human beings who did not live like human beings, did not look like human beings. Finally all I could see were the children. Like stray cats, they sniffed through every garbage can in the back alleys, hoping for something, anything. None of them had return tickets in their purses.

SENSE BRAIN TEASER FOR SPRING BREAK: MAZATLÁN, MEXICO

SIGHTS—Train—shabby, dirty, old, worn down, broken windows, opaque with grime and dirt.

Original color gone; the floor was sticky, black, wet in spots.

Food wrappers and garbage under seats.

Spiders, bugs crawled on windows and floor.

The bathroom!!! Filthy, stinky, no toilet seat.

Toilet was black not gray or brown—Black—The sink was gray with a large hunk of human waste.

Flies gathered for a hearty meal.

Mazatlán—the beautiful ocean and beach.

Nice restaurants and nightclubs on one side vs. the poor, hungry, dirty people begging for food and money.

Their broken-down buildings, streets, and sidewalks.

SOUNDS—the train was obnoxious, frightening like it was forcing its motion, like it was going to fall apart.

Constant banging from the connecting doors between cars.

Loud rock-n-roll.

Rowdy laughter, drunken shouts on the train.

The guy who walked up and down the aisles selling beer had a bunch of keys hanging down. You could hear those keys jangle from the other end of the car. He yelled out "Cerveza!" in a scratchy, harsh voice over and over.

SMELLS—the BATHROOM was unbearable! Stench of human waste.

Air stale and uncirculating.

B.O., spilled beer, rotten food.

→

ANALYSIS

Notice that Tinamarie did not use all her brain teaser sense details—some good ones like the flies in the bathroom and the noise of her peers never made the essay. She might have forgotten them or she might simply have found her theme didn't need them. Don't worry about using everything on your brain teaser lists. Notice that other things she barely mentions in her list become much more important in the finished essay—especially the children. A brain-teasing list is valuable not only for what you write down, but for how it helps incubate new ideas when you begin the draft or outline.

Finally, **she mixes sentences, phrases, and sometimes single words,** allowing ideas to flow. Using the five senses as headings kept her on track when one sense ran dry, but you jump around too.

PROFESSIONAL ESSAY

"AMERICAN STUDENTS ABROAD CAN'T BE
'GLOBAL CITIZENS'"
Talya Zemach-Bersin

In September 2005 I boarded a plane to Delhi with 23 other American students for a semester-long Tibetan-studies program in India, Nepal, and Tibet. I set off wide-eyed, hopeful, and full of expectations for what was sure to be a life-changing experience.

The program had promised "exotic" excursions through "traditional and contemporary Tibetan and Himalayan culture," and I was eager to develop a greater awareness of the world beyond American borders. Both my home university and my program provider had informed me that by going abroad and immersing myself in a foreign culture, I would become a "global citizen."

"Total cultural immersion," I was advised, is what makes study abroad such a tremendous opportunity for developing a better understanding of a new culture. I was encouraged to "act like the locals," "be a resident," and "become a member" of my host community. I was expected to assimilate into my new environment by speaking the local language, bargaining for prices, and participating in everyday life as if I myself were Tibetan.

→

But once I arrived overseas, I quickly realized that studying abroad as an American student is far more complicated than simply learning how others speak and eat. International education entails navigating the social, historical, and political realities of what it means to be American in a world of undeniable difference and inequality.

My home-stay parents, Jangchup and Sonam, were Tibetans living in exile in Dharmsala, India—a town flooded with tourists eager to see the Dalai Lama, buy goods made by refugees, snap photographs of themselves with beggars, and trek the foothills of the Himalayas. While Jangchup made peanut butter in the bedroom (the kitchen was too small) and Sonam knitted gloves to sell to tourists in the marketplace, my American classmates and I studied their culture, language, and religion.

Although they called me "daughter," and I called them Amala and Pala, Jangchup and Sonam didn't treat me like family but as a guest of honor. Despite my protests, I always received five times more food than they served themselves, and I was never allowed to make my bed, step into the kitchen, or even turn on the bathroom light myself.

During the last week of my stay, my academic directors handed me a sealed envelope containing a cash payment for Jangchup and Sonam's hospitality, which I was expected to give to them. As a first-world student, I had literally purchased a third-world family for my own self-improvement as a global citizen. While I was more than willing to give Jangchup and Sonam the well-deserved payment, I began to question the relationship of global citizenship to power and privilege.

A few days after we left Dharmsala, my class flew from Katmandu, Nepal, to Lhasa, Tibet, and landed at a brand-new Chinese airport. My classmates and I were aware that our newfound "families," having fled Chinese persecution in Tibet, could not see their beloved home again without risking their lives. As Americans, our national citizenship, passports, skin color, and currency exchange rate all worked in our favor, and—complain as we might have done about having only two shirts to wear, as recommended per our packing lists—there was no pretending that ours was a trip about sacrifice. Unlike

→

our host families, we could go wherever we wanted, from family homes to fancy tourist clubs, from private burial ceremonies and temple ruins to Chinese-owned stores selling imitation North Face jackets. We had bought a product, and we expected to consume our experience.

The cumulative privilege of my race, nationality, education, mobility, and class shone brighter than all of the candles in the Dalai Lama's temple. I was a foreigner in all respects. It was impossible for me to "act like the locals" when everywhere I went I was viewed and treated as exactly what I am: a white, advantaged American. In many places, I could not walk down the street without being asked by locals for money or assistance of some kind. In no way did I feel like a universal or apolitical citizen of the world.

Yet cultural immersion and global citizenship remained curriculum ideals, even when they were far from what my classmates and I were actually experiencing. Caught between a study-abroad education that demanded I "fit in," and an experiential reality that forced me to think critically about what it means to be an American abroad, I found that I had not been prepared with the necessary tools to fully engage with, and learn from, my experiences. Because the curriculum did not include critical discussions about the ways in which my classmates and I were interacting with our surroundings, I had little ability to make sense of the days and months as they flew by.

I came home confused and unable to respond to the flood of questions such as "How was your time abroad?" Or assumptions like "It must have been amazing. I'm sure you have gained and grown so much." Like many other students who study abroad, I found that the program's curriculum focused on cultural and language studies while avoiding the very issues that were in many ways most compelling and relevant to our experiences. Why had we not analyzed race, identity, and privilege when those factors were informing every one of our interactions? Why was there never a discussion about commodification when our relationships with host families were built on a commodified relationship? Wasn't a history of colonialism and contemporary imperialism affecting the majority

→

of our experiences and influencing how host nationals viewed us? Was there nothing to be said about the power dynamics of claiming global citizenship?

My semester abroad taught me that there is a vast discrepancy between the rhetoric of international education and the reality of what many students like myself experience while abroad. Although the world may be increasingly interconnected, global systems of inequality, power, privilege, and difference are always present. That is the reality that many students face during their semesters abroad and continue to think about upon their return.

The U.S. Senate Foreign Relations Committee recently passed a bill that seeks to create an $80-million annual foundation for study abroad, in order to increase almost fivefold the number of American students who study overseas, and to make such study more accessible to lower-income students.

This affirmation of the values of international education is a positive step, but it is important that we examine the quality and content of study-abroad curricula.

American students who travel abroad cannot be expected to transcend historical, political, social, and global systems of power in order to become cross-culturally immersed "global citizens." We can, however, be asked to become internationally conscious and self-aware American citizens who are responsible for thinking about those critical issues.

An international education that focuses on American-based discursive ideals rather than experiential realities can hardly be said to position students in this country for successful lives of global understanding. Rather, such an education may inadvertently be a recipe for the perpetuation of global ignorance, misunderstanding, and prejudice. It is not possible for me to be a citizen of the world, but I am an American citizen. Higher-education institutions would be wise to integrate that same truth about American students who study abroad into the international education they provide. ■

Discussion/Writing

1. What is the author's thesis? State it in one sentence.

2. How do the message, details and attitude of the writer compare/contrast with the student essay, "Spring Break: Mazatlan, Mexico," which also deals with discovering a new culture?

3. This essay thinks through the brain teaser of breaking stereotypes. List three stereotypes she breaks about student study abroad.

4. What other brain teasers might be good to approach a topic like this? Explain why.

5. These student essays illustrate the other eight brain teasers:
   - Alternate Viewpoints: "Bastard," (page 399)
   - Classification: "Marijuana Smokers," (page 417)
   - Comparison/Contrast: "Food for Thought," (page 411)
   - Create Metaphors: "Pa's Secret," (page 395)
   - List Examples: "Being Ghetto," (page 96)
   - Bug List: "Letter to Brad A. Walker," (page 425)
   - Anticipate Your Audience: "Dear Greg," (page 431)

☑ Peer Review Checklist for Brain Teasers

Author: _____

Reviewer: _____

1. Is the brain teaser long enough (at least one-half to a page long)?

2. Are most items phrases (not single words and not paragraphs)?

3. Are most items detailed enough? Circle those that need more specifics.

4. Add two or three new ideas or details of your own to the list.

5. What focus or main idea might tie most of this list together?

6. Suggest another brain teaser that might open the topic further.

Paragraphs

Ideas and Details in Miniature

So far this book has tried to open up your thinking process to create more and better ideas and details through the controlled chaos of brain teasers. In Chapters 4 and 5 we will begin shaping these creative lists into finished writing. Paragraphs are good places to begin thinking about order, for like essays, paragraphs combine ideas and details. **In an essay the key idea is traditionally called a "thesis"; in a paragraph, the key idea is traditionally called a "topic sentence."** In theory, everything in an essay or paragraph must *relate* to the key idea.

In actual writing, of course, paragraphing isn't so neat. What fits together and what doesn't involves interpretation, and it may be tough to realize you are repeating yourself. It's also true that many paragraphs by reputable authors lack topic sentences, contain two ideas, or use repetition for effect. It's simply the nature of writing to break rules. *As long as your reader can follow you,* you'll get away with breaking rules. But it's also fair to say that most good writers *do* follow two guidelines most of the time:

> . . . If design govern in a thing so small.
>
> —ROBERT FROST

- **Each paragraph should combine one idea with as much vivid detail as you can pack into it.**
- **Each paragraph should stick to one idea.**

Three Ways to Build Paragraphs

Here's an example from a student's essay on being a waitress:

> When you wait on tables, remember that people are unpredictable. With this in mind you won't get flustered, annoyed, or irritable when customers ask for margarine instead of butter, whole wheat instead of white, cottage cheese instead of coleslaw, and French fries instead of salad with their linguini alfredo. Nor will you think anything of it when a person orders pumpkin pie topped with chocolate ice cream or scrambled egg beaters (cholesterol-free powdered eggs) with greasy home fries and bacon.
>
> —Lisa M. Agban

This paragraph states its **key idea in the first sentence** and then enlivens it with six compact examples of diners' unpredictability. This common paragraph pattern can be visualized like this:

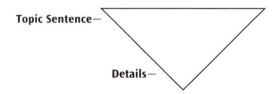

The "broadest" part of this paragraph, its topic sentence, comes first, at the heavy end of the inverted triangle. The "smaller" or narrower details represent the narrow end of the triangle. Since the topic is the job's unpredictability, a sentence about how waitressing hurts your feet or about salary would simply not fit in this paragraph. A sentence about the unpredictability of customer tips *would* fit. The topic sentence-to-details paragraph is common because it's clear from the beginning where you're going. Here's another example of the same pattern from an essay about the destruction of rain forests:

Topic Sentence ⌐ Rain forests contain nearly half of all the plants and animals in the world—many of which have unique medical properties that humans must save from extinction. Some rain forest plants are used to treat

Details = Hodgkin's disease, multiple sclerosis, and Parkinson's disease.

Details —A delicate, tiny blue periwinkle flower found only in Madagascar, for example, is the key element in a drug used to treat leukemia.

Details —Ecologist Norman Myers estimates there are five million rain forest species found nowhere else in the world, and many are becoming extinct before we ever discover what wonder drugs they contain.

—Sally Lujetic

While topic sentence-to-details paragraphs are most common, **good writers occasionally start with details and build to their key idea,** as in this student essay about working in an insurance agency:

Details
> The face of the clock, reflecting the cool, gray wall, reads 8:55. Outside the office, a face presses against the glass door—its nostrils flared, accusing like some grimacing, tribal mask. Do I look intimidating sitting amid disordered files, vagrant pens, computers, and fax machines, and muttering words like "subrogation" or "earned premium"? Inside the bright but still inaccessible office, I almost feel guilt for allowing this person to stand outside while I sit inside. Like a near-realized sneeze, the feeling passes, and I pretend nobody's waiting to get in. When the indifferent clock reads 5:05, similar masks reappear at the door, along with pummeling fists. Sorry! The office is closed. "C-l-o-s-e-d," I mouth to

Topic Sentence
> the irate face outside. The clock's indifference has completely become mine.

—*Irene Kuzel*

This intimate, honest paragraph gains power from the delayed message; the sharp details of the author's thoughts and description of the customer, office, and clock make us *want* a conclusion in the last sentence. If we were to visualize this paragraph, it would look like this:

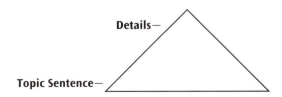

Details—

Topic Sentence—

This paragraph shape works well to build up suspense in narrative paragraphs. Here's another example of the same pattern:

> My first day of school, I wore a frilly pink dress with lacy crinoline puckering out around my bottom. The night before, Mom had to hide it so I wouldn't wear it to bed. I felt so pretty that day, as if I could stand on tippy toes forever like a ballerina. Mom held my hand, smiling. When the school bell rang, I thought everything was going to be okay, but Mom fainted with one of "her things." I tried to catch her, but she slipped through my small, helpless hands to the pavement. A trickle of blood ran down her sleepy face. Epilepsy, we'd been told. I knew she didn't want these things, but why did

she have to have one now? A girl with pretty, carrot-colored hair stared with sympathetic, mocking eyes and asked, "Is that your mommy?" So badly did I want to be accepted by the other children, I lied as I walked away. "Oh, no," I said, "That's not my mommy," words that haunted me for years afterward.

—Christine Bailey

This paragraph starts simply then expands to larger issues. As an introductory paragraph to an essay, it tempts us to read on for more detail.

Informative or persuasive paragraphs can also use the details-to-topic sentence format, as in this one on the issue of gun control:

Narrative detail
Carol Kolen, a Chicago psychologist, was attacked several years ago at the University of Illinois Medical Center by two men, one carrying a gun. She fought off the rape but was severely beaten. Then one Saturday morning last year, she was attacked outside a neighborhood church. She bought a gun, and practices regularly

Fact details
at indoor shooting ranges. Many people install costly security systems in their homes, double-check their locks, won't walk to the store after dark, and panic if they lose sight of their child in a mall.

Descriptive detail
But does it make a difference if your assailant aims a gun into your back, swings a steel bat at your head, or pokes a knife in your chest?

Topic Sentence
No. The threat lies in the assailant—not the weapon. In a society as violent as ours, the law should not take away our right to protect

More specific re-statement of topic Sentence
ourselves from criminals. Recent bills like the Metzenbaum-Stark bill before the Congress jeopardize our safety, security, and freedom as citizens.

—Barbara Collins

This paragraph plants the reader visually with a specific incident and then gives four other examples before widening to the key idea—that a gun control bill before Congress was unsound. The details-first paragraph makes sense because readers are more easily interested by stories and examples than by abstractions.

Later in the same essay Barbara relies on **a third type of paragraph construction—one in which the topic sentence is surrounded by details:**

Opponent's position
Defenders of gun control say there are too many killings not to outlaw guns. But many killers today are on drugs. According to my

Details ⎡ sociology professor, 75 percent of all murders last year were com-
⎢ mitted by people under the influence of drugs. The person high
⎢ on cocaine or in need of a fix won't stop to wonder if his victim will
⎣ fight back or is armed. His lowered inhibitions make for haste—and

Topic Sentence ⎡ you can't scare him away with threats or a stick. You have to shoot
⎢ because, when a drug addict needs drugs, that is the only thing that
⎣ matters. When I worked at a drug rehabilitation center in Scotia, NY

Extended example ⎡ one summer, a polite, sensitive 16-year-old boy sobbed to me his
⎢ story of cocaine addiction. One day his friends bought from a lo-
⎢ cal Brooklyn dealer and after discovering the cocaine was actually
⎢ cleansing detergent, they hunted the dealer down in a park where
⎢ they beat and kicked him. Then one of the boy's friends handed the
⎢ boy a gun and said to shoot the dealer. In his rage and frustration,
⎣ he did.

This paragraph begins with a statistic and hypothetical examples, makes its main point in the middle, and then concludes with a specific example. It could be diagrammed like this:

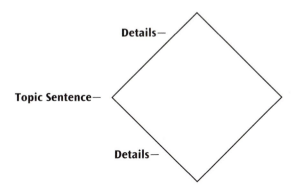

Some paragraphs may not need a definite topic sentence, and **the three patterns only suggest options for arranging details and an idea.** Most writers do not say to themselves, "Aha, now I'm going to write a details-to-topic sentence paragraph." But writers *do* sense the placement of details and idea. **You must always move your reader between the general and the specific.** You want to avoid paragraphs that simply state and restate the main idea and never reach specific details.

Start a new paragraph when you change the subject, change the speaker, change the place, or change the time.

Transitions

Most paragraphs naturally flow smoothly. But if you find the jump between two sentences or paragraphs difficult or awkward, try using transitions to connect them.

Repeat key words. Pick up a key word from the previous sentence. Such a word (in this sentence, it is "word") helps writers sew sentences together. A common way of doing this without being wordy is to use pronouns that recall the previous sentence:

> "*This* is why we must . . ."
> "Because of *this* man . . ."
> "*It* is a problem . . ."

- **Time Transitions:** now, then, meanwhile, before this happened, afterward
- **Space Transitions:** on the other side of the room, farther down the road, nearby
- **Contrast Transitions (to highlight opposition):** however, despite this, although the police say, on the other hand
- **Example Transitions (when giving evidence):** for example, in fact, for instance, one case involves
- **Addition Transitions (amplifying a point):** in addition to, besides, on top of this, also
- **Concluding Transitions (to end a section or essay):** thus, therefore, finally
- **Place Marker Transitions (to move the reader from point to point):** second, next, lastly

These are key trail markers for readers. By numbering your points clearly, you prevent readers from thinking you only have one mixed-up argument; transitions help readers see how things fit with each other. Transitions are invisible—like punctuation. Don't fear boring a reader with them. Many times you will use transitions naturally. However, if people seem confused about how your paragraphs or sentences connect, consciously include more transitional expressions. As an example, read the last three sentences of this paragraph without my two transitions, "however" and "as an example."

VISUAL RHETORIC

Like paragraphs, pictures are collections of details held together by an idea. Write a paragraph in which you explain the message of this picture and support your idea with details. Consider the elements of visual rhetoric (page 36) in developing your analysis.

Superstock

Writing Suggestions and Class Discussions

1. Write a topic sentence-to-details paragraph on one of these topics. Do a half-page brain teaser first and include at least four details in the paragraph. Be creative with the topics:
   • Oil
   • Your favorite television program
   • Men in the kitchen
   • Presidential politics
   • High school dances/proms
2. Write a details-to-topic sentence paragraph on one of these topics. Do a half-page brain teaser first and include at least four details in the paragraph. Be interesting:
   • Bridges
   • Math teachers
   • A scar or flaw in your body
   • One bigot you've met
   • Thanksgiving rituals
3. Write a topic sentence-surrounded-by-details paragraph on one of these. Do a half-page brain teaser first and include at least four details in the paragraph. Be creative:
   • Your favorite sports team or player
   • Litter
   • Laundromats
   • Something in school that's hard to learn
   • The human hand

4. Write a "paragraph anthology" of three paragraphs on unrelated topics. Give each a title. Each paragraph should be about half a page in length. Underline your key idea.

STUDENT PARAGRAPH

Being Ghetto
Shawn'ta Brown

Being ghetto is a funny, creative state of mind, and its language changes like the weather. You don't say "nice," but "fly," "fresh," "butta," or "hott." A loser was first a "nobody," then a "derelict," and now is a "scrub." Who knows what it'll be tomorrow? A girl who sleeps around went from being a "harlot" to being a "ho," a "chicken head," and now a "pigeon." Clothes are "gear." A car is a "whip." When you're rocking in fresh gear, there's nothing better than a hott whip and a girl that lookdid so fly. But being ghetto is hard on English grammar, which is why it doesn't sound butta to management. "Gimme dat thang ova dere" won't get you a job. If the boss asks, "How are you doing today?" don't be creative and say, "Holla at me, baby girl. Ya boy could neva be betta!"

Discussion/Writing

1. Describe the "shape" of this paragraph by locating its idea sentences and detail sentences. What is its plan?
2. This paragraph was written recently, but what details are already "old"? How would you update it?
3. Write a paragraph of your own, making a point about another style of language (computer jargon, professor-speak, or your Italian grandmother's style, for example).

☑ Paragraph Peer Review Checklist

Author: _____

Reviewer: _____

1. Underline what you believe to be the topic sentence. If the rest of the paragraph does not stick to it, suggest changes.

2. What is the most interesting part of the paragraph?

3. Suggest one more detail the author could include.

4. How could one of the details be made more vivid?

5. What is the "shape" of the paragraph?

6. Mark all transitions used. Where might others be used?

Order from Chaos

Thesis and Outline

5

IN THEIR QUOTATIONS, FRANKLIN AND EMERSON summarize the debate about organizing. On one hand, writing needs order. Ideas as they flow from brains—or brain teaser lists—are often chaotic. On the other hand, excessive organization can kill the truth writers hope to convey, for truth has a nasty habit of resisting preplanned schemes. This chapter seeks a reasonable middle ground between these extremes: the minimum organization needed to focus your topic. Why "minimum"? Because except in rare cases, no one ever exclaims, "Your organization really grabbed me." Fresh ideas and vivid detail do that.

That's why brain teasers are crucial. Nothing makes organizing a paper easier than creative, vivid brain teasers; nothing makes organization harder than a vague, skimpy list of preliminary ideas.

Let's start with an attitude. Organization must come from you. Don't cram your ideas into somebody else's box. Nor can you ignore organization, for it rarely occurs magically without conscious effort. The writer who plans how the essay will be structured will discover the holes in ideas, unbalanced emphasis, and redundancy— before the reader does! **In other words, developing a thesis and outlining not only should refine existing ideas, but also should create new ideas and details:** *Structure is a brain teaser, too.*

A place for everything, everything in its place.

—BEN FRANKLIN

A system-grinder hates the truth.

—RALPH WALDO EMERSON

A Working Thesis

. . . .

A thesis is the key point your essay makes—the assertion, message, core idea, or purpose the rest of the essay illustrates or proves. This is where conscious organizing usually begins, because a thesis creates the relationship between a paper's parts, just the way a topic sentence holds a paragraph's details together. Here are sample thesis sentences:

- Many fathers and mothers try to fulfill their lost chances through their children.
- The Social Security system should be privatized.
- The abstract painting exhibit on campus is awful.
- When politics are based on religion, fanaticism and violence soon follow.
- My roommate models her life on a TV soap opera.

Some of these are personal, some informative, some argumentative, but as theses, all display two necessary qualities. **First, they give the essay a flag to rally around.** They lead a reader and writer to anticipate and visualize the essay to come. **Second, they are assertions—complete statements.**

■ **PRACTICE 5-1** What do the five theses promise a reader?

■ **PRACTICE 5-2** Make up two trial thesis sentences on any topic you choose, then say what each promises your reader.

Statements such as "My essay is about welfare" or "Welfare is an important topic of concern today" fail as theses. What *about* it? There's no flag. Is the writer really going to tell us welfare is important? That's obvious. The real message hasn't emerged yet. **A thesis asserts a viewpoint:** "Two solutions look more promising than others to solve our welfare mess: Workfare and Entrepreneurism."

Not all essays need a working thesis. Narratives usually *imply* their messages, and simple reports don't need formal theses. In "How to Repair Your Bike" or "A Summary of the Minutes of the Student Senate Meeting," the main point is obvious. However, **almost all analytical, persuasive, and informative writing requires a thesis.**

Try to develop a working thesis sentence during or after your brain teasers, but before beginning your first draft. You will probably modify it several times during the writing. This is a good sign that your thinking is not too rigid; until final revisions, you should still be learning about the ideas.

A thesis develops in two stages:

1. **Narrow the original topic** until it is vivid and small enough to handle in your allotted space.
2. **Make an assertion or express a viewpoint** about this narrowed topic.

SAMPLE: CREATING A WORKING THESIS

Suppose the professor for your psychology course assigns a paper on love. The topic makes you—and me—panic. Thousands of books, poems, and articles have been written on the subject. How can you say anything significant in four or five pages? Well, you can, and here's how.

First, **narrow the topic before doing brain teasers.** Love? What kind? Sexual? Brotherly? Love of country? Can you list three other kinds? Your brain teaser will be hopelessly vague unless you're more specific than "love." To narrow, think a bit about the *circumstances* of the paper:

- **For whom am I writing?** (audience)
- **Why am I writing this?** (purpose)
- **What obvious topics should I avoid?** (freshness)

These three questions apply to most writing tasks and will save you wasted work on doomed topics. In this case, your psychology professor is the audience. You may grab an uninformed audience with a general topic, but not her. **Your purpose is to show you've learned something; you can't just throw back her lectures.** To be fresh, avoid topics and approaches common to other students. With this in mind, I must avoid the topic of sexual love. Many psychology classes dwell on it, and I'd guess most students will choose it or parent–child love. I would pick the less traveled topic. "Love of Country" cries out. Honestly, I'm skeptical that I can write something decent about this, but let's try.

To narrow it more for vividness, I do some brain teasing by asking questions:

- Is Love of C. different in socialist countries than in democracies?
- Does a divided country like Iraq really have L. of C.?
- What was it like in Hitler's Germany?
- How do governments manipulate patriotic love?
- Should I deal with the people's need to love?
- Should I contrast L. of C. during the Vietnam War with today?
- Should I deal with L. of C. in different races or cultures?
- Would people today really say "I regret I have but one life to give for my country" like Nathan Hale?

This brain teaser helps me understand what's involved in this topic; I'm *learning* more. **At this point I'm going to try an example brain teaser** on Love of Country:

- U.S. purple mountains/fruited plains—L. of C. based on beauty.
- What do the Soviet, French, or Nazi German patriotic anthems say? Research?
- Hitler's ranting speeches—the spell and regimentation. The goose-step parades, the **sieg heil** salutes. Frenzy.
- The shame of Germany after WWI—a broken country.
- The Soviet May Day parades with missiles, tanks, and blocks of soldiers. The gray mass of people—somber—dull.
- U.S. parades on Memorial Day—dancing, fun, music, entertainment. A sprinkling of soldiers. More loose and individualistic. A day off for most people.
- The tomb of the unknown soldier.
- The newspaper editorial critical of the U.S. Iraq policy on July 4th.
- State-controlled press for Nazis and Chinese.
- Japan: highest L. of C. was *kamikaze* pilots.
- U.S.: draft resisters during the Vietnam War said that they loved the U.S.

I learned or reminded myself of much while doing this and think I'll narrow my topic further to "a comparison of the psychology of love of country in Nazi Germany to America today." My brain teasers kept returning to this, and I'm reasonably sure no one else in class will have such a topic. If I'm not sure the professor will accept it, I'll ask her for approval.

Now I'm ready for the second step in creating a thesis: *to make an assertion*. Since I've decided to write a contrast paper, I should do a contrast brain teaser for more detail. Here's a start on it:

Nazi Germany	U.S. Today
Poverty-stricken	Prosperous
Ambition to be on top	Already on top
Chaos, emotional insecurity	Orderly society, more secure
Resents outside intrusion	U.S. intrudes in other lands
Fervent, frenzied L. of C.	Cool, cynical L. of C.
L. of C. meant obedience	L. of C. means . . . who knows?

In psychology class perhaps you've studied Abraham Maslow's hierarchy of needs,[1] and you recognize that some of these contrasts fit his categories. The Germans may have been patriotic because they were broken by World War I and poor; they had strong safety and esteem needs that Hitler appealed to by promising prosperity and a powerful empire. The United States already has considerable material prosperity and national security, so its love of country can afford more open-minded cynicism. So here's my **trial working thesis:** "Nazi German and modern American love of country differ because the needs of the citizens differ."

This section you've just read is pretty much as it came from my head so I could demonstrate how the process works. It *is* sloppy, and I had no idea what thesis was coming. If I'd taken different paths (for instance, developing the contrast in U.S. attitudes during Vietnam and Iraq), the thesis might be radically different. I've tried to reveal the connections between topic choice, brain teasers, and thesis formulations, but I know at each stage there are unseen jumps of thought. You must make these on your own; they are what make ideas truly your own. To develop a good idea, you must play back and forth between thesis and brain teasing.

Here are alternative ways to narrow a topic and conjure up the thesis lurking in your early thoughts. **Write the following sentences, and finish the incomplete idea.**

- "What I really want to say is . . . "
- "Reader, what I really want to tell you is . . . "
- "What interests me most about my topic is . . . "

If you're still stuck, back up. **Make a short list of key words from your brain teaser lists and formulate a thesis sentence from them. Or first create a trial title for your paper—a phrase of three or four words—and build a thesis sentence from it.** Imagine you have 15 seconds to convey your main idea. If you use a computer to create a thesis sentence, I recommend not trying to edit your first attempts. Just press enter and start over. After you write four or five versions, edit the best one.

[1]Maslow believed there is a hierarchy of human needs: moving from the basic biological needs (hunger, thirst, and safety) to the more complex psychological needs (self-fulfillment, appreciation of art).

■ **PRACTICE 5-3** Choose a topic for your next paper and suggest three ways of narrowing it. Then write a possible thesis sentence.

VISUAL RHETORIC

■ **PRACTICE 5-4** To practice thesis writing, create a one-sentence thesis to explain what this picture seems to be saying. What details in the picture support your idea? What details from real life could you refer to for additional support?

Image 100/Alamy Limited

Looping

Some students skip a working thesis, saying, "I'll just write a draft and fix it later." A few people can do this—but if you question them closely, virtually all of them really have done brain teasing and thesis work in their heads beforehand. Most writers who skip thesis preparation start confidently for a sentence or two. Then the next paragraphs fumble into new ideas or repetition. Somewhere halfway through the paper, the writer realizes what the thesis might be, and the paper smoothes out a bit near the end. Revision of this tangled stuff is torture; the ideas smear together and the details are skimpy. It's almost a sure route to a poor grade. In effect, the writer is using the draft to generate ideas, organize them, and find the right words to express them. It's too much to ask of one sitting.

You *can* freewrite to generate ideas and structure, however, by looping. **To loop, write freely for 10 minutes, without censoring ideas, much as you do during a brain teaser, except that instead of listing, write full sentences, letting one flow to the next. Then** *extract* **the key sentence or concept from this freewriting and copy it on another sheet of paper.** Write for another 10 minutes using the extracted sentence as a guide, then extract the best key sentence from *that* freewriting until you formulate a thesis. Looping works well for people who like writing connected sentences rather than the helter-skelter of brain teasers.

Rethink your thesis several times. A perfectly formulated thesis that never changes during draft and revision is a red flag. You may be grinding down the truth for the sake of the system. Slop around in the topic before settling on a working thesis. Find out what's there, pile up some building blocks, and—with a *working* thesis—have a rough plan before constructing the essay. As Shakespeare's King Lear said, "Nothing will come of nothing." All this work on theses has *not* led to just one sentence! It spades up new ideas and makes the glue that will hold everything together.

■ **PRACTICE 5-5** Create a working thesis sentence for one of these topics. First, list three to five potential narrow topics within the general one, and choose one you think will be fresh. Then do a half-page brain teaser. Finally, write a working thesis. Show your work on paper.

Or, try looping; write three free-form paragraphs, extracting a key sentence from the first to start the second, and from the second to start the third. Your thesis must still be narrow and stated as an assertion.

- Freedom of the press
- Tourism
- Underwear ads in newspapers and magazines
- Single fathers or single mothers
- Choose your own topic

Outlines

Like theses, outlines create a Ben Franklin–Ralph Emerson debate. I've heard students say of former high school teachers, "My God! She said we had to have fifty 3 × 5 index cards and a two-page outline. The outline had to have five divisions and each division had to have at least two subheads and *they* had to have two subheads and they . . . " However, I've heard other voices: "My teacher said not to worry about an outline: Just write what we feel and it'll be true. Just be loose. Well I'm really loose—I'm totally disorganized. I need help." I advocate a middle ground. Here's why:

The detailed outline on multiple levels looks like this in the abstract:

I.
II.
    A.
        1.
        2.
    B.
        1.
            a.
            b.
        2.
III.
    A.
    B.
        1.
            a.
            b.
            c.
        2.

Its relentless order seems as inevitable as fate. **But just because you are organized doesn't mean you've said anything worthwhile.**

Second, it may kill spontaneity in the draft. Advocates of this system *want* to eliminate the dangers of spontaneity—disorganization, uncertainty about what to say in the next sentence, redundancy. But they kill spontaneity's virtues, too—coherence of mood, surprise, discovery. Over-outlining often creates dead, lifeless drafts. The writer simply colors inside lines already drawn.

Third, ruthlessly detailed outlines create unnecessary labor because they're seldom used in practice. As philosopher Søren Kierkegaard once commented, "Most systematizers are like a man who builds an enormous castle but lives in a shack nearby." Most advocates of intricate outlines don't use them themselves. They usually write from humbler shack outlines. We get hung up on detailed outlines because humans like abstract order and want to believe that creativity can be planned perfectly. It can't. Actual writing based on a minutely detailed outline usually is dull. Much good writing fails to meet the standards of a multidivision outline.

The other extreme, starting without any outline, may work for some people, but it, too, is flawed. **Without any plan, you *are* going to stumble, wander around, repeat yourself.** If you want to do a good job, you will do heavy rewriting to separate the brilliant tidbits from the garbage and simply to see what you've said. This path, of course, is the one writers must take when composing at the last minute. This approach gives the writer the illusion that a draft is being produced because pages fill up.

The Scratch Outline

The scratch outline is a single-level outline of main headings (only the I, II, and III in the example). For a two- or three-page paper, three or four headings will do. For a four- or five-page paper, five headings will do. An essay entitled "The Dangers of Seatbelts" might be outlined this way:

- Introduction
- Pregnant women
- Fire during an accident
- Drowning during an accident
- Back problems

The writer then assigns details from brain-teaser lists to the appropriate heading and starts drafting. The scratch outline *does* offer direction but *does not* stifle creativity. **Within each section, details are fluid so you have some spontaneous creation and still know where you're going next.** A scratch outline can be seen as a whole; headings can be easily added or rearranged. Most professional writers use this kind of bare-bones outline.

To turn your brain teasers or other notes into a scratch outline, I'm going to suggest **three options professional writers use.** Let's assume that my topic is "Death" and that I've already narrowed it down to "Deathbed Moments."

USE BRAIN TEASERS THAT HELP CREATE OUTLINES

Classification, comparison or contrast, and alternate viewpoints create structure by their nature. For example, if you do a classification brain teaser on "Death," you may classify different ways people behave while dying:

- Calm—death is natural, a part of life
- Begging forgiveness—to make up for wrongs
- Humor—playing a joke
- Philosophical—the "deep thoughts" death
- Religious—death leads to afterlife

This is already an outline. You only need to make a thesis assertion and find examples to illustrate each heading, and you're ready to write. As examples, you might use stories from deaths you've witnessed or from famous people. For humor, I recall that the comedian W. C. Fields—a life-long atheist—was found on his deathbed reading a Bible. "What are you doing?" a friend asked Fields. "Looking for loopholes," Fields answered.

Distribute your examples to the headings. If you have headings with no examples, you drop them. If you have interesting examples with no heading, try to invent a new one. For instance, I just recalled that Revolutionary War hero Ethan Allen was lying on his deathbed when someone whispered to him, "Sir, the angels are waiting for you."

General Allen snarled, "Goddammit, let them wait!" I might add a new category called "Defiance."

Your thesis might assert which approach to death makes the most sense and defend it. ("Of all the ways people die, going with a joke makes the most sense.") Or it might explain the motivation behind each type of death. ("The way you die tells the world how you lived.")

One danger of using brain teasers with built-in outlines is fall-ing into a cookie-cutter approach: stamping out outlines without thinking of your message first. *Never let a pattern interfere with what you think is true.*

■ **PRACTICE 5-6** Make a scratch outline on "Interracial Dating" or "Athletes as Role Models," using contrast, classification or alternative viewpoints to shape it.

■ **PRACTICE 5-7** Make a scratch outline for your topic in Practice 5-3, based on one of the brain teasers. Note: You may have to rewrite your thesis to match.

■ **PRACTICE 5-8** Make a scratch outline for the thesis you created about the picture earlier in this chapter. Your examples should include details in the pic-ture as well as observations from life.

USE BULLETS TO OUTLINE YOUR BRAIN TEASERS OR FREEWRITING

A "bullet" is a little dash, star, or dot like the ones that mark lists in this book. Read through your brain teasers or freewriting, and, on a separate sheet of paper, write the highlights in list form, starting each one with a bullet. **Imagine that your notes are a lecture from which you're trying to pick out the key points for a test.** These should be ideas, not details—for they are your potential outline headings and should sum-marize other items. If you end up with more than four or five headings for a short paper, try combining some. Fewer than three headings means you may need another idea or two. For the topic of deathbed behavior, I might end up with something like this:

- Defiance
- Humor
- Religious
- Philosophical

   To get my bullet outline ready for a draft, I have two options. First, I can use my four headings as labels and **label each item on my original brain teaser list.** I circle labels so they stand out on a messy brain teaser. On a computer, insert the heading in bold before each item. An example brain teaser listing famous deaths might be labeled like this:

(DEFIANCE)

Beethoven shaking his fist at the sky a moment before death.

(RELIGION)

John Donne lying in his coffin to have his picture painted.

(HUMOR)

Dylan Thomas's last words: "I've just drunk 18 straight whiskies—that's a new record."

(PHILOSOPHICAL)

Gertrude Stein's last words: "What's the Question?"

(PHILOSOPHICAL)

Thoreau—when somebody asked if he'd made his peace with God, he answered, "I wasn't aware we'd quarreled."

(HUMOR)

W. C. Fields, looking for loopholes.

(DEFIANCE)

Ethan Allen telling the angels to wait.

(??)

Houdini (escape artist) saying, "I think this thing's got me."

HUMOR–RELIGION

Ramon Narvez (espionage agent) was told by his priest to forgive his enemies. "I have no enemies, Father," he said. "I have shot them all."

When you write your draft, start with a sentence or two describing what you want to say about the defiant death, for example, and then scan your notes for each "defiance" label and add them as details.

A second option to finish a bullet summary outline is to **rewrite the brain teaser details under the headings.** Read through your brain teasers and rewrite each item under one heading. Here's how this method would look in scratch outline form:

Defiance
    Beethoven
    Ethan Allen

Humor
    Dylan Thomas
    W. C. Fields

Religion
    John Donne
    Narváez(??)

Philosophical
    Gertrude Stein
    Thoreau

When you compose your draft, everything is in place, but you'll have to rewrite your notes. With both options, if you find details that don't fit the headings, you must cut them or create a new heading. You can also begin to scratch out the dumb stuff you encouraged during the brain teaser.

USE CLUSTERING, A VISUAL DIAGRAM

For this third method, write your general topic in the center of a clean page and then draw lines out, like radiating spokes from a wheel hub, to related ideas. It stimulates ideas (as a brain teaser does), yet keeps the key topic at the center of focus. **Each item must connect to another by a line— either to the central topic or to any radiating headings.** Go through your brain teaser lists and assign each item a place on the cluster sheet. Try connecting each item to headings first. If it doesn't belong, connect it with a line to the main topic. When done, you'll have a visual representation of your ideas—where you have the most ideas, what fits with what.

An outline for "Deathbed Moments" developed by **clustering** would look like this:

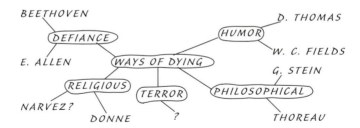

Your last step is to decide what order the outline headings should follow. Rearrange the headings a few times to see how they'll flow when you write the draft. **Most writers save their most creative idea for last**.

■ **PRACTICE 5-9** Suppose your research for the classification of deaths topic uncovered these examples:

- John Greenleaf Whittier's last breath: "My love to the world."
- Mark Twain's last written note: "Death, the only immortal who treats us all alike, whose pity, peace and refuge are for all—the soiled, the pure, the rich and the poor, the loved and the unloved."
- Emily Dickinson's last words were disputed: either she said "Oh, is that all?" or "I must go in; the fog is rising."
- Theodore Dreiser prepared these last words, but did not say them: "Shakespeare, here I come!"
- O. Henry's last words: "Turn up the lights. I don't want to go home in the dark."
- Thomas Jefferson died on July 4, 1826. His last words: "Is it the fourth?"
- J. J. Rodale, organic health food advocate, uttered these words on a national TV interview just before he dropped dead: "I'm so healthy that I expect to live on and on."
- James Thurber's last words: "God bless … God damn!"

Incorporate these examples into one of the scratch outlines or clustering diagram. You may use some categories developed in the chapter, but create at least two new ones.

■ **PRACTICE 5-10** Do a page of brain teasers for your topic from Practice 5-3 and distribute the material to your scratch outline from Practice 5-7.

SAMPLE DRAFT FROM OUTLINE

THE FINE ART OF DYING

How will we spend our last breath when facing the brink of eternity? As the soul shakes free, will we defy death? Or reach into philosophical depths for the meaning of life? Will we pass silently away? Or congratulate death with a sporting handshake and a joke? Or will we go with faith in a new life?

I suspect the few people who think about dying imagine approaching the grave with dignity, summoning up spirited words or actions that will reveal their true hearts. The notorious atheist W. C. Fields was found reading the Bible on his deathbed by a friend who had come to pay his last respects. The religious friend smugly asked what Fields was doing with the Holy Book. "Looking for loopholes," the comedian replied. Death himself must have grinned at such pluck and integrity.

Perhaps the simplest dignified response to death has been defiance. On the brink of reckoning, people dare the cosmos to take them. Beethoven sat bolt upright when he spotted a flash of lightning. Long cursed with deafness by the Powers-that-Be, he shook his fist at the heavens, sank back, and expired. There was music in this gesture, one last measure beating valiantly against the silent tomb. Told to confess his sins, 15th-century Italian painter Perugino refused because he didn't believe in an afterlife. Were demons gleefully stoking a fiery pit for the unrepentant? Good! He would find out, he vowed.

For those of a philosophical mind, Gertrude Stein's death . . .

ANALYSIS

Because you went through the notes and predraft writing with me, you can see them behind this draft. Notice how the introductory paragraph sets up the classifications to come. Instead of simply saying, "I will discuss five types of deaths in this essay: defiant, philosophical, silent, humorous, and religious," the essay poses questions to make readers think about what they might do or say. These questions set up the categories. W. C. Fields is used to visualize a specific example early but also to create the thesis that our death shows how much integrity we have had in the way we have lived. The same point should be made in each of the categories. Notice that each of the next paragraphs focuses on one of the outline headings, and examples illustrate each.

Concluding Comments: Outlines are like bones. Nobody sees them, but a person would sag into a baggy lump without them. You need some skeleton to help your essay stand up. Your thesis is also almost invisible—like a brain—but it makes your essay walk straight instead of reeling and wobbling. **How do you know if you're organizing too much or too little? If you feel lost during drafts, try more organization. If you feel bored and confined, try more brain teasers and maybe looser organization.** The one thing you cannot do is simply write the way you always have if it's not working. The writer who really wants to improve can do so at *every* stage of writing: thinking up fresher ideas and details, making theses and outlines, writing the draft, and revising.

Writing Suggestions and Class Discussions

1. Narrow three of these topics into ones you can handle in two or three pages. Concentrate on freshness—anticipate the obvious things others might say. Some topics may seem "boring"; you must *make* them interesting. Prepare brain teasers for each as you work along. *Or* try looping to narrow two of these topics.
   - Road construction
   - Disaster films
   - Courage that's overlooked
   - A book you've read
   - Prejudice you've suffered
   - High school versus college
   - Open topic
2. Now, create a working thesis for each of your narrowed topics. Be sure it's a complete sentence and makes an assertion the rest of the essay can relate to. If you "looped" in suggestion 1, you're done!
3. For your best thesis sentence in suggestion 2, write a scratch outline. Aim for three or four main headings and assign your best brain-teaser material to them. Use any outlining method discussed, but tell which kind. Bring all work to class.
4. Write a draft for the outline.
5. Evaluate the following as potential theses. What strengths and weaknesses does each have? Imagine what you'd have to do as a writer to fulfill reader expectations for each.

- Pets bring out the worst in their owners.
- Chinese products have been extremely successful worldwide.
- Noise pollution is bad.
- Statistics on teenage pregnancy don't tell how it hurts one young woman at a time.
- Christina Aguilera is a better singer than Shakira.
- I'm going to write about my first love and my latest love.
- The New York Yankees and the Boston Red Sox are rivals.
- San Francisco is the Paris of the United States.
- We ought to have mandatory recycling of tires.

6. Write a brief, *tactful* letter of complaint to a company or organization that has mistreated you. Make a half-page list of ideas and details, formulate a thesis that specifies what you want from the organization, and then outline your letter. Consider your reader's viewpoint.

7. Write a three-year review of your life. Your object is to *evaluate* your last three years, not simply to tell what happened. Although the topic is already narrowed, you need to create a thesis and an outline with details for each heading.

8. Create an outline for your blog. A blog is a personal Web page that often focuses on a specific topic: a hobby, a political agenda, or the author's life. What would your focus be? What headings would your home page contain?

☑ Peer Review Checklist for Thesis/Outlines

Author: _____

Reviewer: _____

1. Is the thesis narrow and clear? If not, suggest other angles.

2. Does the thesis have spark? Freshness? Suggest how to improve it.

3. What promise does the thesis make for the coming essay?

4. Suggest one change in the outline for the author to consider.

5. Ask the author to describe details he or she is considering for several headings.

The Draft

6

That Frenzy Near Madness

"WHY IS IT THAT I CAN NEVER GET A PAPER GOING! I was into the topic—did some brain teasers and made an outline. Yet my fingers freeze when I sit down in front of the computer. Everything I write looks awful—if anything comes at all." I've heard this many times over the years, and I've often felt exactly the same way myself. Most writers sometimes experience choking uncertainty when starting a draft. It may be fear of commitment to one idea or switching from note taking to thinking in sentences. Whatever the reasons, here are a few ideas to make the draft go easier.

> There was a world in my eye.
> —ALICE WALKER

> Planning to write is not writing. Writing is writing.
> —E. L. DOCTOROW

The Concrete Introduction

WARM-UPS ARE FOR LEFTOVERS

The introduction can be particularly hard because most people don't put much prewriting thought into it. A typical outline just says "intro." Yet we instinctively know that our introduction will set the tone for the whole paper, will grab or sedate a reader, and will either point us in the right direction or bog us down in swampy confusion. So, as our first task in the draft, we must write a key paragraph without the prewriting help the rest of the paper has. No wonder writers hesitate at that first sentence. I do. I've already thrown out two introductions to this chapter.

> If my doctor told me I had only six minutes to live, I'd type a little faster.
> —ISAAC ASIMOV

Many introductions are "warm-ups" as the writer gropes for the right tone, the properly phrased thesis, and an interesting lead-in. When I tell students their introductions are too long or vague and that they should get to the point quicker, they sometimes respond that the reader has to "get used" to them. But what's really happening is that the *writer* is getting used to the topic. **Nothing gets a reader used to you faster than a sharp opening; nothing makes a reader feel uneasy sooner than an introduction that mushes around a topic.** How does this one make you feel?

> Homelessness is a very important topic today. The future of our society depends on solving this problem. So many people are suffering, and homelessness is different than it was 10 years ago. It's time we did something to cure this blot on society.

This introduction evaporates if you try to squeeze a specific idea out of it. To avoid introduction paralysis, start your paper not by warming up but by being hot. Warming up is for leftovers; an introduction should set a fresh appetizer before your reader.

 One strategy is not to write the introduction first. Start by drafting the first main heading in your scratch outline, and write the introduction after the rest of the draft is done. As your draft evolves, the introduction you write later will fit the paper better. The weakness of this approach is that you may miss the self-guidance the introduction provides. You can compromise by starting the paper with this simple working sentence: "The purpose of this paper is . . ." Obviously, you'll have to improve this bland opening during revision.

Many professional writers try another method for the first paragraph. Their first few sentences attract and stimulate the reader's *interest*. Once interested, a reader is ready for your thesis, so **a good introduction frequently starts with several concrete, perhaps puzzling, details, then presents the paper's main idea in the last sentence of the opening paragraph.** All six of the introduction types below share this principle.

One specific technique is to start with an **anecdote**—a short story related to your main idea. It can be a personal, researched, or hypothetical story. Here's an example that could substitute for the vague introduction on homelessness.

> Hattie McBride's dress was torn and dirty. She pushed her shopping cart into an alleyway, pulled out the folded cardboard from the lower rack and spread it under a fire escape. She rummaged

among the wadded clothes and utensils on top until she pulled out a bottle of cheap wine. After settling down on the cardboard, she sighed. She was a grandmother and once owned her own home. Now, like thousands of other street people, she's become a social problem. Let's look at one solution for people like Hattie.

These details should make a reader hungry for the idea that would explain them—the thesis sentence, which comes next. In this way the concrete introduction also helps *you* focus your ideas and blast through writer's block.

Another opening starts by asking a good question. That's the trick—a *good* question. Superficial questions or those needing only yes or no responses don't arouse our interest. Examples of bad questions: "Would you like to be a street person?" or "Are most homeless people happy?" There's mild interest in these, but they don't push the reader toward a theme, just a yes or no response. A better question is one with open-ended answers, such as this:

> Every time I walk downtown and see men, women, and children shuffling around in rags and scavenging like stray dogs, I wonder why. Why would a person *choose* to grub in garbage dumpsters, sleep in abandoned cars, and huddle around wine bottles? What can be done to help reclaim these people into society? After talking to some of these people and reading about the topic, I think there are three main reasons why people end up on the street, and that there *is* hope for some of them.

These questions are specific and involve readers by asking them to account for a situation, not simply respond true or false. Whether readers do think of an explanation or are simply puzzled, your audience will be primed to listen to what you have to offer, and that's the introduction's job. Notice also how concrete details attract our eye as these questions develop.

A third technique is to start with a striking fact or facts:

> Nearly two-thirds of all homeless people once held responsible jobs and 25 percent are employed; one-tenth attended college; over half have families, most of whom know about their present condition. Homeless people should bother us not because they've degraded themselves, but because they point out how industry, education, and family have failed.

The same pattern holds here: vivid details followed by the author's thesis. A striking fact must be something unexpected. The following doesn't qualify: "Many automobiles produced in our high-tech society continue to be unsafe." But this does: "Twenty percent of the cars we drive today have life-threatening flaws in their construction." Always remember the power of the specific.

A fourth technique is to start with a quotation that leads to your thesis:

> "For God's sake, get them off the beach!" said one of the contest organizers. "Get the security people—now!" It seems during a publicity session at the Miss America Contest in Atlantic City that several homeless men crawled out from under a lifeboat the gorgeous women were using as a photo prop. The men had slept all night under the boat. Police officers escorted them off so the photos of sea, casinos, and American beauties could continue to maintain the image of America the beautiful, home of the brave and free. Cruel as the organizer's words sound, they may reflect a typical American attitude toward the homeless: We don't want to think about you.

Strong quotations dramatize an idea—interest readers by creating conflict or mystery. You read on to find out why the person said it or what the author of the paper will say about the quotation. That leads to your thesis.

 Fifth, open with a problem or dilemma—viewpoints that contradict each other. Present several sides of a controversial situation before working toward your solution in the thesis:

> Being homeless means being powerless. No money, no stake in your society, no knowledge of how to escape. Most citizens are ashamed of homelessness, especially of homeless children. Yet without an address you can't vote, receive welfare, and, often, attend school—things that give you power. However, there is good reason to require addresses. Society must protect itself from being cheated by fake voters, welfare frauds, and parents sneaking children into better schools outside their towns. In a conference in Washington, D.C., advocates of the homeless think they have found a way around the address dilemma: Social Security numbers assigned on birth certificates.

 Sixth, ask yourself, "What will people first think about this topic?" and speak directly to the reader's concerns. This is how I began this chapter, imagining negative thoughts some students have starting a draft. First, vividly identify with your readers' viewpoint, and then lead them to consider a new idea. Addressing the reader as "you" may help:

> Perhaps you've seen the wino curl on the grate by the post office, the plastic sheet "tents" spread over bushes outside an office building at night for homeless people, the man who emerges from a doorway to ask for a dollar you're too afraid not to give him. There's a pretty good chance he's desperate for drugs. Perhaps in disgust you want to shout,

"You shouldn't live this way! No human being has to accept this!" I felt this way, too, until I met Robert Coles, the philosopher of the homeless.

Three final points. **One, avoid the dictionary definition introduction:** "*Webster's Dictionary* defines homelessness as 'the state or condition of being without a domicile; indigent.'" Dictionary definitions are superficial and corny. They might work if you were really going to pick apart the definition in your paper (Is it really a "condition" or an attitude? What is a "domicile"?), or if the definition had things in it most people wouldn't know. It's far better to create your own definition with ideas that are different from what a reader expects. Writers who start with predictable dictionary definitions usually ignore them and move on. So will the reader.

Two, your introduction hooks the reader, but it also *promises* **the reader what will come.** As in the striking fact example, you may even list the main points to be covered. But be careful not to promise what you can't deliver—the essay will be like a flashy car that gets repossessed during a big date.

Three, be brief. A play reviewer once estimated he spent a year and a half of his life waiting for curtains to rise. Don't do that to a reader.

VISUAL RHETORIC

■ **PRACTICE 6-1** Find a strong picture of a homeless person on a website or in a print publication. Write an introductory paragraph to a paper of your own on homelessness, starting with the picture you found as your concrete detail that leads to your thesis. Attach the photo to your paragraph.

What to Focus on While Writing the Draft

Once you get past the introduction, you may be fortunate enough to experience that frenzy near madness—a compelling rush of energy and concentration that carries writers. You may need only to refer briefly to your notes to start a cascade of sentences. If this happens and the draft still sparkles in the cold light of the next morning, consider yourself lucky.

But the frenzy of inspiration has a finicky way of not showing up or of teasing a writer with a two- or three-sentence burst and then vanishing. The writer who depends on inspiration will have some lucky effortless compositions, but much more despair and frustration. The fact is that most writing—just like most living—is done at an ordinary pitch of mental excitement and must be done in a professional manner. Fine frenzies are memorable and cherished because they are not everyday happenings. All writers must learn to write without them. Ironically, it's when I'm plugging away at an ordinary pitch of concentration that inspiration sneaks into my brain. While I cannot promise that this fickle muse will carry you off, you can improve the odds of an inspiration through concentrated prewriting and focus during the writing of your draft. Here are four suggestions:

1. **Most importantly, concentrate on ideas and details.** Think visually as you bounce between ideas and details. As you give examples, think of the conclusion you can draw to round out the paragraph.

2. **Use your outline intelligently.** Your scratch headings should become topic sentences for paragraphs most of the time, and the listed details will fill out your paragraphs. But don't think of this as a coloring book in which you're simply filling in spaces. Think up new examples and recast ideas as you write. Don't let an outline chain you. But also don't run off in totally new directions for long without referring back to your notes—you could end up confused or with what should be two papers. If you really see a whole new direction for the paper as you draft, take a few minutes to throw together another scratch outline, scrap the old draft, and chase your new thoughts.

3. **Move fairly quickly as you write the draft.** It helps things stick together. If your mood changes between writing parts of the draft, the tone may change. Ideas you mean to bring up later (but that aren't written down) tend to be forgotten during interruptions. Ernest Hemingway believed that the best time to interrupt the draft for the day was at a spot where he knew exactly what the next sentence would say. That way, the following day, it would be easy to recapture the feel of his work and start up. Other writers tend to stop at a tough spot, hoping incubation will solve the problem for them overnight.

Some writers do work slowly. The French writer Gustave Flaubert was known for drafting only one paragraph per day during the composition of *Madame Bovary*. But for most writers I'd recommend a fast pace—a two- to three-page paper should be drafted in one sitting if you've done good prewriting work, and a four- to six-page paper should be no more than a two-sitting effort. It takes a certain sustained effort to engage your mind in the topic. The speed record may be held by Isaac Asimov, who claimed he could draft a nonfiction book in 70 hours. That's hot!

4. **To ease the flow of words, imagine speaking your draft to** **someone** as you compose. If it's a personal essay, imagine the person to be a friend. If it's an argumentative or informative essay, imagine speaking to your intended audience. If you don't remind yourself this way that you're writing for people, you may treat writing as a mechanical process, and the sparkle of a human voice will evaporate from the draft. Visualizing your audience helps you fill in gaps and keep a consistent tone. Some writers speak aloud and then type. Others compose aloud from the outline into a tape recorder and then transcribe to paper, just to get this effect of audience. As I "talk" to my reader, I imagine her saying things like "What's that word mean?". . . "Get to your point!". . . "How does all this relate to me?". . . "Keep my interest—give me a story.". . . "Where did you get that fact?"

WHAT NOT TO FOCUS ON IN THE DRAFT
- Mechanics, spelling, or sentence structure
- Word choices and style

Why not? Because secondary matters bog down a writer during the draft and interrupt the smooth flow of ideas and details. If a great metaphor or vivid verb comes to you, fine. Take it. But don't spend five minutes during the draft searching for one. Save this effort for revision.

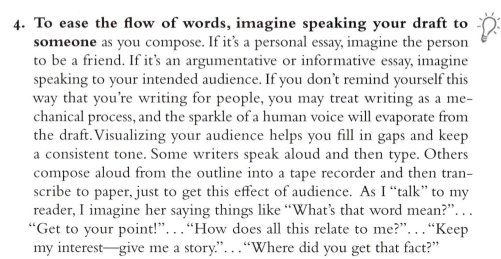

7 TIPS FOR WHEN YOU GET STUCK

Notice, it's not "if" you get stuck. All writers spin their wheels occasionally. You can continue to gun the engine and splatter goo, hoping you will wiggle loose, or you can try alternative strategies to get you to the dry land of the next sentence. Here are some specific tips I use when I get stuck.

1. **Use brain teasers discussed in Chapters 2 and 3.**
   - Move from ideas to details or from details to ideas.
   - Visualize the topic with your senses.
   - Imagine an alternative viewpoint to your last sentence.
   - Classify or compare the last point you made.
   - Think of a metaphor for your last or next point.
   - Attack stereotypes about issues you've just raised.
   - Try a humorous or fantastical touch.
   - Give an example.
   - Think about what bugs you about what you're saying.

Jack Hollingsworth/CORBIS

2. **Study your scratch out-line, then use a transi-tion phrase to start the next point**:
   - "On the other hand . . ."
   - "The next reason to support this proposal is . . ."
   - "Secondly . . ."
   - "However . . ."
   - "Despite this fact . . ."
   - "The next morning . . ."
3. **Reread the last page you wrote.** When you reach the blank space, you may build up enough momentum to leap across it.
4. **Reread your thesis and ask how the next point should relate back to it**.
5. **Ask what your reader would want to know at this point.** Would she have a question? Would he protest a point? Use the responses as a cue.
6. **Skip the tough section and write it later.** You may discover that it's illogical or doesn't belong in the paper.
7. **Write several alternative sentences to see which sounds best**.

Blocks During Drafting

As I mentioned in Chapter 3, fear of risk and insecurity about your ability to think can disable a writer. These can also occur during the draft. You suddenly fear you're going to say something really dumb or embarrassing, and your typing hesitates. You think, what will my professor think if I say I've used co-caine? Is my idea juvenile? Maybe I should just scrap it all and start over.

These are common fears. You must risk sounding silly to get anything drafted. The fact is, **no first draft sounds polished.** And dealing with embarrassing facts forces you to be more honest about the topic. In any case, there's time to reconsider these things in revision. At the draft stage, trust yourself and keep moving.

Inability to start can indicate lack of commitment. If you sigh a lot and say to yourself, "I just don't want to do this," remember the story of Cortez. In the year 1519, the Spanish explorer landed his soldiers in Mexico, and then burned all the ships. He told his men there was no alternative to fighting for their goals, no escape. They fought hard! **You, too, must burn your ships to be really committed to college.** You *are* going to graduate. Not writing this paper is *not* an option. Behind you lies only empty water. Ahead, on the other side of this paper, lies your fortune. Write!

Unfortunately, additional blocks may emerge during drafts.

FEAR OF MESSINESS

We've heard it so often: "Neatness counts." And neatness does count in writing, but *only in the final draft*. Many people want to write drafts logically, grammatically, progressing word by word to a perfect conclusion. They're doomed. Within a few sentences they see the imperfections, the ideas that contradict each other, the detail that doesn't fit exactly, the awkward sentence. "All right," they say to themselves, "I'll write slower, more carefully." Before long they're up to their hips in quicksand and the writing stops. Why? Because they're asking too much of themselves. **Even an average genius cannot think, organize, draft sentences, and consider words and grammar at the same time.** Shakespeare and Mozart *may* have churned out masterpieces with little revision, but the history of literature by writers as great as James Baldwin, E. B. White, and Mark Twain is a history of messy cross-outs, redrafts, thrown-away pieces, and ink spots. Bob Dylan said, "Chaos is a friend of mine"; and Thomas Wolfe claimed he cut 100,000 words from one novel (that's about 150 papers of the length you might write in this course). If ideas, details, honesty, organization, brilliant word choices, and grammar could come at once, we'd all be best selling authors.

Solution: Go play in the mud. Enjoy the surprises and messiness of thinking. Most ideas creep out of dark and sometimes dirty places. If you demand perfection, when misshapen creatures peek out they'll be driven back inside your brain, and new ones will be slow to emerge. Accept the fact that writing emerges incomplete. Write your sentences with inserts written sideways on the page and arrows to the back of the paper, and your brain will send others—ones that may be better or that may transform the frog into a prince.

POOR WORK ENVIRONMENT

Your neighbor's music rattles the floor. Your desk is too low, which makes your back ache. The room is stifling hot. You just ate and feel sleepy. Your paper's going nowhere. **Anything relating to your physical environment can affect your ability to write.** Some people like to be comfortable and cozy. That makes me fall asleep; I like a hard chair in a cool room. Some people must turn on music or the television. Others can't concentrate through such distractions. Some people require absolute silence and privacy. Others like to sense people moving around them because utter silence is intimidating. Some people are morning people, some evening people. And so on.

Solution: Control the things you can control. **Manipulate your environment so it helps instead of hinders you.** Put books under your desk legs (or saw them down an inch) so you're comfortable. Work at the time of day you are at your best. Don't kid yourself—maybe you really *are* watching the television. Try writing in silence. A few years ago one of my students had a mother who interrupted him just as he sat down to write. She'd want to talk or make him do chores or complain about some aspect of his behavior. Mike began to suspect she saved these things until he opened his books. I suggested Mike finish his work at school. He did, and his writing improved one grade almost immediately.

People serious about thinking and writing give their minds the best environment they can, instead of letting a poor environment control them. If you really want to write, you will get it done. When your little brother dumps cola on your keyboard, remember Cesare Cantio—who wrote a novel in prison using a toothpick for a pen and candle soot for ink.

Nail Your Conclusion

Don't dawdle. A murky, wordy ending obscures your message. You want a sharp, crystal sentence or two that highlights your key idea. I'll give you specific suggestions for conclusions to narrative, persuasive, and research papers in later chapters, but **one all-purpose conclusion simply returns to a concrete example, fact, anecdote, question, or dilemma from your introduction.** Our sample essay on the homeless might conclude this way:

> Hattie McBride died of malnutrition on her cardboard mat under the fire escape. If the work-for-shelter program and tenement rehabilitation plan I proposed were enacted, we might not find more Hatties dead in alleys.

STUDENT ESSAY INTRODUCTION

Tougher Punishment for Sex Offenders
Pamela Fleming

Silver, a 30-year-old executive, was raped and beaten in her home by an ex-boyfriend and another friend. During the assault she sustained a black eye, busted lip, and bruises to her arms and thighs. She was choked, leaving welts around her neck. Caramel, a student, was raped by an acquaintance in the front seat of her car after he asked for a ride. During the attack, she sustained bruises on her left breast, along with aches all over her body. Both women were subjected to this ordeal at the hands of men they had once trusted.

Since sex offenders disregard the physical and psychological pain they inflict, here is a way of dealing with them. I propose that sex offenders be punished to fit the crimes they commit. A convicted first offender might be sentenced to ten years in prison without chance of parole and should receive a penile electric shock once daily during that time. Repeat offenders should be incarcerated for twenty years and given two shocks daily.

ANALYSIS

The opening **two examples grab our attention,** and the proposal is equally vivid. It's shocking (pardon the pun) and should be controversial reading. It uses **the classic introductory pattern of details moving to thesis,** but spread over two paragraphs. In a short paper, I'd like the introduction in one paragraph. It promises to convince us to agree with her punishment scheme—a tough sell, perhaps. **Issues she might cover** are the Eighth Amendment to the U.S. Constitution, which prohibits "cruel and inhumane punishment." Another is the possibility that a rapist would be more likely to kill a woman rather than risk her testifying against him under Fleming's plan. She addressed these in her paper. The **length** could be reduced by cutting the last sentence of the first paragraph. It's not really part of her point. **Suggestions for wording:** "Sustained" is used twice and is vague. The beginning of the second paragraph could be cut to start "Here is how I propose dealing with rapists." The first part of that sentence argues the point before saying what it is. Overall this is a powerful introduction.

Writing Suggestions and Class Discussions

···

I. Evaluate the following student introductions. The "Peer Review Checklist" on page 130 will help guide you.

A. "Great, *another* one with gonorrhea, and this one's only 15-years old," the pathologist reading the slide announced. This was the seventh slide today with that diagnosis. It's only 10 A.M. It's not going to be a good day. While I don't like hearing the results of the test, I do enjoy the challenge of the rest of my job in the hospital pathology department.

—Courtney Palte

B. Madonna's "Like a Prayer" echoes through the house, and pants and sweaters fly through the air as we frantically search for the hottest outfits to wear to the club tonight. The world seems right and everything perfect. As I dance to the closet, I smell something foul, like rotted fruit. I open the door, poke my head inside and find approximately 30 plastic grocery bags, all tied in double knots and piled atop each other in rows. Confused, I pick one up before realizing it is bulging with brown vomit. The smell is so strong my eyes water and stomach starts to convulse. The pants, sweaters and make-up do not matter any more. I have to deal with a best friend who is bulimic.

—Erin LaBore

C. The program *20/20* showed a four-year-old boy who'd been abused by his mother's boyfriend. Beatings with a heavy object caused permanent brain damage. His back had inch-and-a-half deep whip marks from a leather belt. And the abuser carved his initials into the boy's backside. This boy will never ride a bike, walk, or even talk. He is fed intravenously and must urinate through a tube in his penis. He received a lifetime of retardation and pain. Yet the abuser received 15 to 20 years in prison, and the mother who let this happen received five years. Another baby burned to death after kerosene had been poured over him. The only two adults in the house were never even put on trial. Beyond how they could do this and what we can do to help, the question we must ask is: What is wrong with our judicial system?

—Tara Geska

D. This is addressed to heterosexuals. Twenty years after lesbians and gay men threw coins, bottles, and parking meters at the cops who attempted to arrest them for being queer, many of you still see no reason to fight for our rights. Most of you are not by our side. Yet homophobia hurts you almost as much as it hurts us.

—*Allan Richards*

2. Bring to class two magazine articles that have strong introductions and explain why they work well.

3. List three environmental conditions that encourage *your* thinking/ writing. List two things that hinder your thinking/writing. Discuss how to change the poor conditions and create or maintain the good ones.

4. For your next paper, bring to class two alternative opening paragraphs, using two of the six methods suggested. Both introductions should be on the same topic but use different approaches.

5. Suppose you had to write a paper on family stress for a sociology class. Write two trial introductions, using a different technique in each. For the last sentence of the paragraph, invent a thesis or main idea that leads from the details to the paper.

6. Write introductions for two of these topics. Try to hook the reader's interest, then lead toward a thesis the paper will develop:
   - Men's or women's hairstyles
   - 2 A.M.
   - Animal experimentation
   - Dates who drink
   - Birthdays
   - Survivor shows on television

☑ Peer Review Checklist for Introductions

Author of Introduction: _____

List three possible titles for your paper:

_____

_____

_____

Reviewer: _____

1. Which title do you find most intriguing and why?

2. Does the introduction grab your attention and set up the paper? Why or why not?

3. What promises or expectations does the thesis give a reader for the essay? Suggest issues or questions the author should cover.

4. Make a suggestion to improve the wording of the introduction. Mark your suggestions on the draft itself.

5. Is it too long or too short? If so, suggest how the author might revise.

Revising Drafts

Writing is Revising

7

MANY PEOPLE ASSUME A WRITER'S JOB IS 95 PERCENT done when the first draft is complete. Now, they think, we'll correct spelling and typos, read it over to see how it flows, and then print a clean copy.

I wish writers could operate that way. But experienced writers—whether they publish essays, write business reports, or compose senior theses—know that "revision" means "reseeing." **A writer is simply not doing the job if reseeing is limited to fussing over spelling and a few surface blemishes.** That's amateurish. You must resee and refeel the entire paper, down to its roots. Ralph Ellison revised *Invisible Man* for 10 years, and Boris Pasternak said his first draft of *Doctor Zhivago* was "disgusting." The person who writes a company's annual report or the committee that writes your college catalogue may revise for months. The inspired genius who whisks out immortal masterpieces on the first draft is 99.99 percent myth.

For virtually all writers, including Nobel Prize winners such as Pasternak, revision means a total, word-by-word reseeing of the draft. Revision means rewriting good parts as well as bad. Only during revision does most writing move from poor to acceptable or from acceptable to good or outstanding. Your professor does not expect from you the fanatical dedication of published writers

The manuscript revealed the usual signs of struggle—bloodstains, teethmarks, gashes, and burns.

—ANNIE DILLARD

My pencils outlast their erasers.

—VLADIMIR NABOKOV

[Writing allows] mediocre people who are patient and industrious to revise their stupidity.

—KURT VONNEGUT

such as Ernest Hemingway, who revised the last paragraph of his great World War I novel, *A Farewell to Arms,* 39 times. But your professor *does* want you to revise more than just the surface. Your writing *will improve* through honest, close revision, and only then will you know how good you are as a writer.

Revision Myths and Realities

Revision draws from a different part of your brain than brain teasing or drafting. **Creating is self-centered, accepting, and sloppy; revising is reader centered, judgmental, and orderly.** Although most people find one easier, we're all capable of both.

The lonely writer tapping away in solitary confinement is also largely myth. Most writers in professional situations depend on advice and criticism from others during revision. They give us perspective; they remind us what we forget to mention or point out what might confuse a reader. Even Shakespeare had help. His acting company commonly deleted scenes and suggested changes during rehearsal for such classics as *Hamlet* and *Romeo and Juliet.* Most bosses ask for drafts of proposals, reports, or significant letters their employees write—and suggest changes. Or they may ask *you* for suggestions on *their* drafts. Grant writers, legislators, and scholars all ask peers for criticism before the public sees the written document. The word "criticize" in this sense does not mean to rip the writing apart, but to highlight weaknesses *and* strengths and to make *positive* suggestions.

Let me illustrate how a writer combines personal revision and outside criticism by using this book as an example. In 16 years of college teaching, I'd written hundreds of assignments, course outlines, and instructions. Some bombed! Each semester I revised flaws and pursued new ideas, finally expanding these into a short "Guide to Writing" used only at my college. Teachers and students told me what worked and what didn't. More revision.

When I mailed sample chapters for an expanded book to publishers, my future publisher sent these to professors at other colleges for their reactions and criticism. The reviews broadened my limited viewpoint. New chapters had to be written; others combined, relocated, or eliminated. One chapter expanded from 10 to 40 pages and helped me discover exactly what process of writing I believed worked best. More reviews (75 pages in all) and voices helped me. For this seventh edition, more new voices and ideas helped me revise. Over 60 professors and editors and hundreds of students have their fingerprints on this book, and they have helped me write better than I can alone.

I was happy to have new things to think about, because with each draft, I exhausted myself. Do you know this feeling of being wrung out, as though you have said everything you possibly can about the topic? **Well, peer criticism jumpstarts a writer's dead battery if it's the right mix of honest encouragement, suggestion, and flaw finding.**

An important part of your college education is to learn how to handle both kinds of revision—on your own and with the help of others. Let me suggest some things to look for and a process to follow when revising first drafts.

HOW TO BE YOUR OWN EDITOR

- Write your draft early so new ideas incubate for revision and there will be time for your draft to sound fresh when you come back to it.
- Start by revising major things first—ideas and details—and then secondary items such as organization and word use. Tinkering distracts writers from more important issues.
- Imagine you are your peers or professor reading. Slip behind their eyes as you read.
- Fix the errors, but also try to improve what's already good.
- Read your draft through for one focused thing at a time. Writers often get "sick" of drafts because they follow it, instead of demanding specific things from it. If you keep rereading for a "bump" to jolt you, you will fall asleep. I recommend reading through and revising the draft once for each of the following aspects:
  — Ideas
  — Details
  — Organization
  — Word Use
  — Mechanics

A two- to three-page paper can be revised for all of these in an hour, and careful revision is almost sure to raise your grade one level.

■ **PRACTICE 7-1** Try the five-step process that follows with the draft of a paper. Stop and do each step separately before reading on.

1. REVISE IDEAS
Honesty, Freshness, Coherence

 Clarify the main idea. First, read through your draft quickly. Now, without referring back to the essay, try to state your main point or purpose. Write it out in one sentence. You may be surprised that you'll be able to say it more sharply after reading the paper. Compare it to the existing thesis sentence and substitute the new one if it's better or revise the old, if necessary. If you had trouble writing a statement of purpose, your paper may ooze in several directions.

 If your paper lacks sharp focus, try this technique: Read through the paper again, copying down sentences that seem to state purpose. Try to combine these sentences into one statement. If this works, great. Replace the existing wobbly thesis. If you can't combine the purpose sentences, you'll have to accept the fact that you mixed two or three paper ideas together. You must then divide the essay into parts, some of which will become your paper and the rest of which will leave the house in a brown bag.

Second, **test your main idea for honesty and freshness.** I read through the paper ruthlessly one time to see if I've slipped into superficial thinking or oversimplification. Qualify or moderate extreme sentences. Be particularly alert for contradictions or potential rebuttals to your arguments. Don't ignore them. Your paper will be stronger and more honest if you confront and respond to them (see "Refutation" in Chapter 13). For example, as I reread this section, I worry that I'm simplifying revision by making it seem too mechanical, too much like a write-by-number activity. No techniques substitute for your intense concentration or involvement in your ideas. A checklist is only a reminder of things to look for.

 Third, **read through the draft as your reader will.** If you have a particular reader in mind, *be* that person. What will confuse him? What points will she deny or contradict? What have you left out that will be important to her? This is a wonderful brainteaser for revision.

■ **PRACTICE 7-2** Reread your last paper and (1) underline key sentences that reveal purpose; (2) combine these into a one-sentence statement of purpose; (3) find two places in which you could have raised an objection or modified an idea for more honesty or freshness. Make the revision.

2. REVISE DETAILS

Visualize and Support

Read the draft again, just for details. Are they vivid and convincing? **Support each major generalization by adding examples, sense details, descriptions, and facts.** Suppose you had written the following in a draft of a paper on Tennessee Williams's play, *The Glass Menagerie:*

> Laura lives in a fantasy world. For instance, there's her glass menagerie, the old phonograph records she plays, and her visits to the greenhouse. She can't even attend business college.

The right information is here, but it's not vivid enough to make us see Laura's fantasy world. Let's expand just *one* of the details:

> Laura lives in a fantasy world. The greenhouse she visits is full of exotic flowers—tropical plants that can't exist in the cold world of St. Louis where she lives. Their fantasy world is protected from reality by artificial heat and fragile glass, just as Laura can go on living only because her mother and brother protect her from the cold reality of the Depression.

In revising for detail, remind yourself that a reader is hungry for facts, quotes, pictures, and examples. Feed him details.

■ **PRACTICE 7-3** Find three places in your last paper that could use more details. Pause a moment to visualize, and then add them.

3. REVISE ORGANIZATION

Make It Easy on the Reader

Check the essay's *overall organization*. While doing this it's better not to read in the normal sense—just skim the main sentences. If it's more than three pages, I usually take notes on a separate page by jotting down a heading for each paragraph or section. Imagine you are creating a **table of contents** for your paper. This helps me see more clearly what my main points are, if I'm repeating myself, if I should combine two sections and if my details match each idea. Now's the time to cut redundant paragraphs or draw arrows to move things around.

Next, **check that each *paragraph* sticks to one idea.** Are the *transitions* smooth between them? (If not smooth, add key markers like "On the other hand, . . ." "Another reason to support this proposal is . . ." or "Once outside, Fergusen saw . . ."). **If you see a lot of skimpy one- and two-sentence paragraphs or one paragraph runs over a page, a red**

signal light should buzz. You may be able to join the bitty paragraphs or insert paragraph breaks into the elephant-sized ones, but it may be a sign that as you motored through the first draft, your thinking became scattered. **Make sure every sentence points at the same target.**

Finally, **flip directly from your introduction to your conclusion. Is your main point consistent?** If not, scream, and then revise.

■ **PRACTICE 7-4** Revise your last paper just for organization. Outline the paper, check paragraph unity, and add transitions where needed.

4. REVISE WORD USE
Waxed Words Sparkle

At this point you know which sentences and paragraphs will be in the final paper. Now focus on polishing words. **Look small.** Tinker. Wax and polish. Do you repeat the same words, or challenge the reader with a few exotic *palabras?* Be ruthless to clichés—they are corpses in your living essay. Did you define key terms? Be more concise. Punch up bland verbs. Substitute slashing, red-eyed adjectives for dull ones. Create a metaphor to make a boring paragraph crack with lightning. Consider sentence variety. Unlike the previous sentence, which was a short, imperative sentence, this complex one delays the main subject and verb with an introductory phrase. Both kinds snap the reader to attention. Chapter 8 is devoted to word polishing.

■ **PRACTICE 7-5** Pick any paragraph from a previous paper and improve three word choices and perk up a vague or dull spot with a metaphor.

5. REVISE MECHANICS

My grandmother told me always to wear clean underwear. She wanted to be sure that if I was hit by a car and taken to the hospital they'd know I was from a decent family. I think of my grandmother when I revise for mechanics. I do it for decency's sake.

Reading through the paper lightly for mechanics will only catch the errors you *don't* normally make. That's fine, **but the deadly errors are the ones you make regularly and don't see. Go through the paper once searching just for the errors teachers repeatedly mark on your papers.** This must be a conscious effort, or you won't improve. If your vices are sentence fragments and apostrophes, go through the draft once, searching only for the little vermin. **Work with the handbook in Chapter 17; don't guess.** If you're a weak speller, check any word you wouldn't risk in a $1,000 bet. After two or three papers, they won't be *your* errors.

■ **PRACTICE 7-6** List your three most common grammar, punctuation, or usage errors. If you don't know what they are, examine your last few papers. Use this as your own individual checklist. Write them in your notebook.

Revising with Others: Peer Editing and Teacher Conferences

By this time, you have exhausted your own resources. Your draft should be scratched up with improvements. Now your professor may ask you to give it to other students to read (peer editing) or talk it over with you (conferencing). These can be your most valuable opportunities to really learn to write. **Peer editing and conferencing do more than help with one paper. They teach skills that will serve you a lifetime:** Giving and receiving positive criticism leads to renewed enthusiasm and ideas in marriage, career, sports, and friendship as well as writing. You'll write for a real reader, not a cardboard one; you'll see how others write; and you'll learn how to revise your own writing better by helping your peers revise their papers. **Research has consistently shown that the person who peer edits gains as much or more improvement in his or her writing as the person who receives the suggestions.**

HOW TO HELP EDIT PEER PAPERS

When called on to critique another student's paper, **your goal should be to help the writer create better ideas, sharper details, smoother organization, and more vivid word choices.** You may also repair punctuation and spelling.

The reviewer/editor must be honest. The person who writes on your paper, "I love it!" or "I wouldn't change a thing!" may flatter you momentarily, but such excessive praise doesn't help you one bit. You may be shy or feel unqualified to criticize, but making an honest effort to help someone else improve a paper will teach you to revise better yourself. You'll learn to see some of the hidden possibilities behind existing words, to see your own drafts more objectively. Teachers who encourage peer editing expect *both* parties to learn.

You must be tactful, of course. The person who scrawls changes all over the paper and says, in effect, "revise everything" is just as dishonest as the person who wants to award the Nobel Prize. Help the writer to his or her destination.

Because most writers need help recognizing what they have written and help understanding how a live audience reacts, **it's probably best to start your comments simply by mirroring back to the writer the message or feeling the essay gave you.** Start by saying, "What I remember best about your essay is . . ." or "The main point I get from this is . . ." **Or you might make a bullet summary of the main points as you read.**

After the author lets you know you're aboard the same spaceship, you can move to suggestions for ideas, details, organization, and wording. Work together. If you were confused at a certain point, for instance, brainstorm with the author for several possible clarifications. Whatever you react to strongly in any way should be discussed with the writer. Try to *enjoy* peer editing; allow yourself the pleasure of inhabiting someone else's mind for a while.

HOW TO RECEIVE PEER CRITICISM

If peer editors feel confused, you may point out things that you think clarify the point, but you can't tell them they're not confused. **What peer editors tell you is something you can never see for yourself: how another person receives your communication.** You can never be your own reader.

Strike a balance between total acceptance and total rejection. If you're too pliable, you may accept changes you shouldn't. It's *your* paper; don't let a strong peer dominate your idea. On the other hand, some closed-minded writers seem to say, "It's written this way because that's the way I wanted it. It's my paper, isn't it?" This person supposes the paper came out exactly as intended. I'm skeptical because that has never happened to me or any other writers I know. More importantly, papers *shouldn't* come out exactly as intended; to me that's a sign that I haven't *learned* as I moved through the stages of writing. **Your paper is not a monument to what you thought at one moment, but an attempt to communicate an idea as freshly and vividly as possible to someone else.** Listen to what your readers say. Before rejecting changes, ask the reviewer, "Why do you say that?" You don't have to follow each suggestion slavishly, but do welcome new possibilities as potential friends.

Bring questions to a peer editing session. Ask about things you've wrestled with or wondered about. For example, "Is this a corny sentence?" or "It seems too long. What should I cut?" or "I'm worried I sound too harsh. What do you think?" Only by showing yourself eager to find weak spots will reviewers really open up to you. It's fairly easy to stifle criticism in workshops—just get defensive. But then you won't get any help either.

A Sample Revision

Here is the opening paragraph from a letter written by Tina C. Maenza. First is the rough draft as brought to a peer review session:

Dean H. Freericks

Assistant Vice President for Facilities Management

John Beane Center

SUNY AB

Buffalo, NY 14261

Dear Mr. Fredericks,

    As you probably are already aware of there is a major problem with student parking at our school. At the end of every class one can be sure to find a line of students in their cars waiting for people to leave so they can park. Not only is this an inconvenience, but it causes arguments among students racing for empty spots, and it makes us late for class. You should consider building parking garages or consider some other possible solutions to this problem.

The reviewer thought the thesis was clear, but suggested that the author "put in a story, more details" to catch the reader's eye. She also pointed out a few flaws in the letter format, the choppiness of the first sentence, and exaggeration in line 2 ("every" and "be sure"). Here is the same text with the author's revisions penned in:

July 14, 2009

Dean H. Fre~~d~~ericks   *de*

Assistant Vice President for Facilities Management

John Beane Center   *Looking at their watches every 30 sec.,*
they wonder just how late they will be to
SUNY (AB)   *class today. Teachers are not sympathetic*
+ some threaten to penalize tardy students
Buffalo, NY 14261   *by reducing their grades.*

←Dear Mr. Fredericks,   *What can we students do?*

exists
←As you probably are already aware of, there ~~is~~ a major problem with

almost   almost
student parking at our school. At the end of every class one can be sure to

find a line of students in their cars waiting for people to leave so they can

park. Not only is this an inconvenience, but it causes arguments among

making
students racing for empty spots (and ~~it makes us~~ late for class). You should

consider building parking garages or consider some other possible solu-

tions to this problem.

Notice that the author revised additional items beyond the ones suggested. Next is the final draft with more improvements. The new visual details certainly help, as do the ironed-out sentences and "little" corrections, including the reader's name!

July 14, 2009

Dean H. Fredericks

Assistant Vice President For Facilities Management

John Beane Center

SUNY At Buffalo

Buffalo, New York 14261

→

Dear Mr. Fredericks:

As you probably already are aware, a major problem exists with student parking at our school. Following most classes, one can almost be sure to find a line of students in cars waiting for people to leave so they can park. Looking at their watches every thirty seconds, they wonder just how late they will be today. Most teachers are not sympathetic, and some threaten to penalize tardy students with reduced grades. What can students do to make class on time when we drive? Besides being an inconvenience and making us late, it causes arguments among students racing for an empty spot. Please consider building parking garages to solve this problem.

TEACHER COMMENTS

Your teacher will probably be the most attentive reader you will ever have. If you write a boring or confusing letter to customers or supervisors, they will stop paying attention. Your professor will persevere and mark the rough, confusing, or vague spots. Since *improvement* is the point of this effort, **the most important marks on your papers are not the grades but the comments.** Each one is a guide for future papers. Study each comment on returned papers carefully. If you don't see where you went wrong or how you could improve a section marked "awkward" or "vague" or why a teacher wrote "good" somewhere, find out. Ask. Be hungry for feedback; that's how you move forward. If you think of comments as simple test scoring, you've thrown away a road map. If you don't understand, look the problem up in this text, talk to your professor, or go to your college's writing center. Take the time to figure out the symbols and abbreviations your teacher uses. Some common ones are listed in a table opposite the title page.

If your teacher has conferences about rough drafts, think of them as opportunities. **Come with prepared questions.** "Why does my opening sound flat?" or "Did I overdo the facts on the dangers of nuclear waste?" **Take notes and mark sections your teacher discusses so you remember.** As with peer editors, be open to suggestions and try to resee your work objectively through your professor's eyes. However, if the professor seems to have the wrong idea about where you want to go with the essay, make clear what you really want to accomplish and ask for suggestions on how to get there.

The Final Draft

Title. The best titles convey information and also a concrete image to hold the eye. Which of the following titles promise boredom and which promise an experience?

- English Paper #2
- Air Pollution
- Whose Poison Gas Is It?
- Death Stalks Your Home

Good titles often come from phrases near the end of your paper, from metaphors you use, or dialogue you quote. Why waste time thinking up a bunch of titles? Well, Margaret Mitchell's first titles for *Gone with the Wind* were duds: *Ba! Ba! Black Sheep* and *Tote the Weary Load.* **The title symbolizes the whole work.** Each semester, students ask, "Does my paper have to have a title?" The answer is "Yes—just as you have to have a name, so you can be picked out in a crowd." So make the title memorable!

Format

- Use black ink.
- Write your name and class in the upper left corner.
- Center the title one-quarter of the way down the page.
- Capitalize all letters in the title. Do not underline or put it in quotation marks.
- Number the pages.
- Double-space and use only one side of the page.
- Leave one-inch margins.
- Staple or paperclip your essay.

Proofread after printing and make corrections—that's what professionals do. If you have more than a few mistakes, print a corrected copy. Here are some basic proofreader's correction marks:

¶	New paragraph
No ¶	No paragraph
⌐	Reverse order of items enclosed
∧	Insert mark (write new items above line)
ℯ	Delete mark
≡	Capitalize letter
ℓ	Lowercase letter
#	Space needed
Stet	Ignore the changes

REVISING ON A COMPUTER

Computers are wonderful for writers, but there are some drawbacks. First, you'll be tempted to focus on small items. You may be deceived by a neat surface appearance into not really studying the logic and sentences. **You've got to dig up a draft, no matter how polished the work appears.** Second, spell-checkers give the illusion that your spelling is fixed. However, if you type "affect" where "effect" belongs or "kiss" instead of "kill," the machine recognizes a legitimate word and won't alert you to your error. **Grammar-check programs can help fix some errors, but they are wrong about half the time.** Use them, but also learn to rely on your own knowledge.

Since you can do so much revision with a computer with such little pain, you should experiment: Combine paragraphs, separate them, move them around, add details, rephrase. You can ask most computers to count the number of times you used "I" or "was" if you're afraid of monotony. But please!—only one font per paper, and avoid script fonts that are hard to read. This is one place I advise you to be bland.

VISUAL RHETORIC

Like writers, artists and photographers do preliminary sketches or drafts before creating their final works. They change angles, add and cut elements and rethink their themes. Many famous pictures are the result of 50 tries to capture the moment. Consider the picture below as a rough draft that you might revise. What idea does it project right now? What are the significant details? What might you revise? Think about additions (props, even new characters), cuts, modifying details, a different angle or setting, changing the style of the shot. How will your changes alter the picture's idea or effect?

Janine Wiedel Photolibrary/Alamy Limited

■ **PRACTICE 7-7** Create your own picture using figurines. Bring it to a workshop to get revision ideas. Then take the final photo and attach a paragraph explaining its meaning and structure.

■ **PRACTICE 7-8** Find an interesting newspaper or online photo and suggest revisions to the picture. Attach a copy of the photo to your paragraph.

Writing Suggestions and Class Discussions

1. Make up three questions about the draft of an essay you're working on. Leave room for responses and attach them to your rough draft for your peer editor or professor. Try for a mix of broad questions on thesis or organization and specific questions about particular words or sentences.

2. To have a sample on which to practice revision, write a half-page paragraph on one of these topics:
   • Adult toys
   • Children and toys
   • Wise elders
   • What I don't like about my present job

- " ___ " is a great song because . . .
- Open topic

3. Revise the paragraph from suggestion two on your own:
   - Rewrite the main idea/topic sentence without looking at the original and compare it to the original. Use the clearest one or make changes.
   - Sharpen the details—make at least two points more specific.
   - Circle all transitions and improve if necessary.
   - Improve three word choices and rewrite any clichés. Then find two or three needless words and cut them.
   - Check all spelling and grammar.

4. Bring your revised, retyped paragraph to class for a peer editing session. Attach two questions about the paragraph for the reviewers. Using peer suggestions, revise and submit a finished paragraph.

5. Write a draft of an idea for your blog and collaborate in revising it.

6. Your peer group will write an ad for a commercial product. Your client wants one picture and about 100 words to appear in the Sunday newspaper and on its Web page. Your group will submit a draft to the client (played by your professor), and then revise.

7. The first draft of the United States' Declaration of Independence written by Thomas Jefferson originally read:

> We hold these truths to be sacred & undeniable; that all men are created equal & independent, that from that equal creation they derive rights inherent & inalienable, among which are the preservation of life, & liberty, & the spirit of happiness; that to secure these ends, governments are instituted among men, deriving their just powers from the consent of the governed.

After peer editing from John Adams and Ben Franklin (a nice group to be in!), the final version approved by the colonies read:

> We hold these truths to be self-evident, that all men are created equal, that they are endowed by their Creator with certain inalienable Rights, that among these are Life, Liberty and the pursuit of Happiness. That to secure these rights, Governments are Instituted among Men, deriving their just powers from the consent of the governed.

Mark each wording change and discuss how three alter the *ideas* in the declaration. Can you think of other word options and how that might affect our interpretation?

8. Read the following student essay. How would you advise the writer to revise it?

STUDENT ESSAY AND ANALYSIS

Bastard
Miguel Martinez

I have always been awed by the strange bonds fathers are supposed to have with their sons. Literature, television, and film have shown these relationships to be complex and intense. Even my friends in school would relate stories of massive power struggles. The part about love they left out but I knew it was there.

I grew up believing my father to be dead. At least that's what my mother told me when I asked her. I know the only reason I did ask was I had just entered kindergarten and my classmates were always talking about this strange being, a sort of god, they called "Daddy." Contrary to popular belief, those of us having only one parent do not feel that anything is missing. At least I didn't until I found out I was an oddity. There is no biological instinct inside us saying that there should be someone else. There was just me and my mother. Period.

Off I went through school. My mother was involved with other men, and we lived with two of them. They were never "Dad," just "Uncle." These relationships didn't work out, and when I was six, my mother gave up on men entirely. We moved to the east side of the city, and she started working. For the next ten years, my mother and I didn't see much of each other. She was a waitress, keeping odd hours, and I was in school or playing. She did make a big point of eating together, even if it was in the greasy spoons she worked in.

When she was able to spend more time with me, I was sixteen, and pretty set in my ways. I suppose I should have let her have her way, but the arrogance of youth took hold again. I left. I didn't have anywhere to go, I just wanted to travel. I spent the next 8 months traveling the country. I did return eventually, only to find my mother filled with a sense of failure. It hurt knowing I had caused someone such hard feelings. She begged me to enter the Navy, and while I wasn't a big fan of the military, I went. The night before I was to leave for boot camp, my mother sat me down and asked if I ever wondered who my father was. I told her, quite honestly, that I didn't, that she had said he was dead. Well, she gave me his name and told me he was living

→

in South Carolina. She told me he didn't care about me, as he had always known who I was, but never made any attempt to contact me.

The news didn't faze me. Friends will ask if I have any urge to find him. I get satisfaction from their expressions when I tell them I have his address and phone number. But just as they can't understand my apathy toward him, I can't understand their reliance on fathers.

Here are comments on the draft by the writer, peer editors, and professor:

THE WRITER'S CONCERNS ABOUT THIS DRAFT

1. *I didn't explore the aspect I wanted to—it seemed too general and jumpy in what I was trying to get at.*
2. *One sentence that drove me crazy was "Off I went through school" (third paragraph). It just didn't flow.*

PEER EDITOR ANALYSIS MADE BY STUDENTS READING THE DRAFT

1. *The only "jumpy" part was the fourth paragraph. Time seemed too compressed. You were six and then entered the Navy.*
2. *You need more detail on growing up without a father. The most vivid detail was your not asking about your father. The least was why your mother wanted you to join the Navy. I'd like to see more about why you didn't miss or need a father.*
3. *Paragraph 3—for ten years you didn't see much of your mom???*
4. *First paragraph needs more detail.*

TEACHER'S ANALYSIS

1. *It's strong in honesty. Daring. Potentially a powerful paper.*
2. *But it doesn't follow its nose to the end of the idea. Your purpose is unclear, as you suspect. Are you dealing with (1) the mother–son relationship; (2) the life of a single mother; (3) the social problems of bastards; (4) your lack of need for a father, or . . . ? All these are here, but you need to decide what main point the others will support. Conclusion is inconclusive.*
3. *Paragraphs 1 and 2 are good——a snappy start.*
4. *#4 needs more detail——it's abrupt, seems to start a new idea.*
5. *#4 Last sentence is awkward.*

You will find a revised, final draft of this essay on page 399. Although the student followed some reader suggestions, notice how he found new areas to explore simply as a result of talking about the essay and hearing what other people saw there.

☑ Peer Review Checklist for Revision

. . . .

Author of Paper: _____

Reviewer: _____

Instructions:
1. Read the paper slowly and carefully.
2. Mark parts that were confusing or problems with a "?".
3. Mark strong sections with a "G" or "★".
4. Write out comments.
5. Return this sheet to the author and discuss your reaction.
6. Do not mark small things like spelling.
7. This sheet should be attached to the final draft.

One question or problem the author wants the reviewer to help with:

One sentence the author is not satisfied with (mark it and explain why it bothers you):

My response to the author's first concern is . . . (discuss and brainstorm with author):

Here's a possible rewriting of the weak sentence:

I feel the purpose (thesis) of your essay is:

One area that could use more detail or support is:

Find a paragraph needing smoother transition and suggest it. (No, it's not perfect!)

Suggest at least three word or sentence structure changes.

Writing with Style | 8

After revising your draft for ideas, details, and organization, comb through your words. Words help ideas croak or sing, convey an authoritative or awkward tone, and arouse or sedate readers. A smooth, clean style proves a writer sweats the words. It isn't luck. It isn't a genetic gift.

The headnote quotation from Nietzsche reminds us, however, that glittering words cannot somehow brush fancy makeup over a bad idea. **Revising words means revising ideas, for words and ideas are inseparable and together create style.** Katharine White reminds us that the struggle to find the right word is normal. And Toni Morrison reminds us we must sweep away the signs of our struggle.

> To improve one's style means to improve one's thoughts.
> —FRIEDRICH NIETZSCHE

> She would write 8–10 words, then draw her gun and shoot them all down.
> —E. B. WHITE ON KATHARINE WHITE'S WRITING

Honesty

. . . .

VOCABULARY

Some writers think big words sound more sophisticated. They use a thesaurus to find fancy synonyms. With happy enthusiasm, they might revise my previous sentence this way: "They inaugurate a scrutinization of a thesaurus in diligent quest for ostentatious synonyms." I hear readers snoozing. An expanded vocabulary does create options, but **the big-word approach usually doesn't work.** First, if the writer doesn't *really* know her words, they tend to be used off-center: sometimes confusing a reader

> The language must be careful and appear effortless. It must not sweat.
> —TONI MORRISON

149

or showing the writer's *un*sophistication. Second, big words rarely impress good readers who want a smooth journey, not a sojourn over gargantuan, albeit splendiferous, boulders. Usually the simplest, most direct word possible is best. The fancy word draws attention to itself—and away from your ideas and details. Use the occasional fancy word or technical term when you need to; don't sprinkle them like salt over the entire paper. **Write within yourself.**

This does not mean you can get away with dull or monotonous words. Your vocabulary should be colorful and vivid, but that rarely requires big words.

■ **PRACTICE 8-1** Revise the following for more direct vocabulary:
- The industrial unit will downsize operations to maximize return on investment.
- My antagonist inaugurated a campaign to terminate my presidency of the Ostentatious Vocabulary Association.

ACCURACY

Honest writing demands accuracy, and this means **revising the sloppy word choices** we *all* make in rapid draft composition. If you don't find three or four inaccurate word choices in each paragraph of a draft, you're either a genius who will soon be famous and rich as if by magic, or you're not searching hard. Ask if each word presents exactly the tone or picture you want. **It's obviously wrong to misstate a fact or statistic, but it's also dishonest to exaggerate or use absolutes:**

- Al *always* arrives late.
- Marcie's *never* had a sick day in her life.
- You'll *love* the new Ford ignition system.
- Drug dealers are murderers, *pure and simple.*

Absolutes are words such as "always," "never," "all," "every," or "none." Leaving no room for exceptions, they sound dramatic and make writers feel forceful, but they are often dishonest. Notice, I did not say "always dishonest." Some absolutes are true: *All* humans die. Ask yourself in revision if an "often" or "usually" might better describe Al's lateness or if a "hardly ever" or "as long as I've known her" might more accurately describe Marcie's health.

To say someone will "love" an ignition system is probably an exaggeration for all but the most fanatical car owner. Why is it exaggeration to say drug dealing is murder, pure and simple? Because it's neither pure nor simple—drug dealing differs from strangling someone, or from selling automobiles that may also end up killing the user—and you must show *how.*

Being tough with words will make your ideas tougher too. Question key words ruthlessly. **Hunt for "weasels":** words that seem to say something but weasel out of it. For example, "Computers *may* help you write two grades better." (Bananas *may* help you write two grades better, too.) Inaccurate language makes you appear to be an unreliable and sloppy thinker.

■ **PRACTICE 8-2** Revise these sentences for accuracy:
- The antiabortionists never consider the lives of pregnant teenagers.
- The United States has been completely humiliated by a bunch of rag-tag terrorists.

EUPHEMISMS AND CRUDE LANGUAGE

Euphemisms are expressions that make things sound nicer or grander than they are. When a used car is called "pre-owned" or "pre-enjoyed," a trucker a "commodity relocation engineer," or a garbage collector a "sanitary engineer," the writer is prettying up the truth. And which is more visual: "trailers" or "mobile homes"; "swamps" or "wetlands"; "addiction" or "substance abuse"; "hospital" or "wellness center"?

Notice that **many euphemisms hide behind crooked use of big words.** In a famous letter leaked to the press during the Vietnam War, orders were given to assassinate a secret agent, but the words "assassinate" and "kill" never appeared. The agent was to be "terminated with extreme prejudice." Euphemisms do have their place in conversation. If your friend Bob is fired, you may choose to say he "lost" his job, "was laid off," or "was furloughed" to spare his feelings. But unless you need to spare your *audience's* feelings, writing demands a stricter standard of honesty. If Bob was fired, say he was fired. Consider whether it's more accurate to describe an agent as "shot," "murdered," "assassinated," "blown away," or "eliminated." How do these each have different implications? At a funeral, the dead person may be euphemistically referred to as "the dearly departed" or "the late Bertha Smith," certainly not as "the stiff" or "the corpse." The dead are "conveyed to their final resting places," not "hauled to the worm farm."

Notice that some alternatives to the euphemisms here are unnecessarily brutal. **Crude expressions,** like euphemisms, give you power or distance over unpleasant facts; euphemisms deny them; crude words exaggerate them they can be laughed at. **In revising for honest words, ask if your choices are *appropriate to the subject*—not sickeningly sweet, not unnecessarily crude.** The honest writer can't be so polite that the message is wimpy or so impolite that the message is forgotten. Obscenities, therefore, should only be used if necessary to duplicate the way a person speaks; the drama they create is usually dishonest—a cheap way to shock the reader. They are inappropriate in professional communication.

■ **PRACTICE 8-3** Revise these sentences for euphemisms or crude language:
- When buying a reconditioned car, delve into the mechanical functioning as well as the amenities or you may own a less than wonderful vehicle.
- The judge thinks a surrogate mother is just a uterus with legs. (Said in a television news broadcast.)
- A senior citizen in faulty prescription eyewear could not locate the lavatory tissue in our retail establishment.

CLICHÉS

Clichés are dead places in your essay. Like all blah word choices, they often creep into rough drafts. **Revision must root them out and plant live words in the empty holes.** Some writers may defend clichés by saying, "Everyone knows what a cliché means." I disagree. For example, is the expression "toe the line" or "tow the line?" Visualize it and you'll see different images for each spelling. A student who described a nasty woman as "an old batilacks" had no idea the original expression referred to a weapon, a "battle axe." Nor do readers pay close attention to clichés. They know there's no new idea, no new, interesting word use that requires attention. Do you really want your readers to drift away? Complete these images:

- Hungry as a _____
- Gentle as a _____
- Quiet as a _____
- Eats like a _____
- Busy as a _____
- Slippery as _____

Most people will complete these images with the same one or two words; the expressions are *that* predictable. Clichés slide easily in *and out* of readers' minds. If you want to show how slippery a political issue is, for instance, don't compare it to a "greased pig" or an "eel." Compare it to a wet gangplank, a slimy creek bed, an icy wheelchair ramp, or a salesman asked for a refund. As Hollywood producer Sam Goldwyn used to say, "We have to get some fresh platitudes." **Start by picturing what you're describing. Feel, see, hear, taste, or smell it as a *thing*, not as a word.**

New clichés are born each year, sounding exciting and creative. A few years ago you may have heard someone say, "Give him props. His music's butters. It's mad phat. And that girl's a dime." Translation: "Give him credit. His music's great. It's very cool. And the girl's outstanding (a 10)." Then they were creative. But these expressions already sound almost as stale and corny as "souped-up car," "pinko," "sexpot," "mod," and "D.A." do today. (Ask your professor what these expressions meant—he or she may have been around then!)

■ **PRACTICE 8-4** Invent two creative alternatives for each of the clichéd expressions in the list you completed above. Be visual and fresh.

■ **PRACTICE 8-5** Revise these clichés to be more fresh and visual:
- Don't put all your eggs in one basket.
- Curiosity killed the cat.
- Fight fire with fire.
- The economy is going down the tubes.

SEXIST LANGUAGE

Aside from the ethical argument that sexist language contributes to bias against women, sexist language can alienate readers (both male and female) who find it offensive. You may also create a picture of yourself as a sloppy thinker who stereotypes and generalizes without much thought. If you always refer to lawyers or scientists as "he," for instance, you should know that nearly 50 percent of all current law students and 40 percent of all advanced degree science students are women. Here are three options for dealing with the "she-he" problem:

- **Use "he or she" or a pronoun without sex reference.** "A student should prepare his schedule . . ." could be "Students should prepare their schedules . . ." or "A student should prepare his or her schedule . . ."
- **Sometimes use "he" and sometimes "she,"** as this book does. Just remember, some nurses are male, some mechanics are women.
- **Use a gender-neutral term instead.** "Salesman" can be "salesperson"; "postman" can be "postal worker" or "mail carrier."

Do these little variations matter? Some people might claim that everybody knows "mankind" includes both males and females, as do jobs that end in "man." But even though we "know" it, hearing "man" used thousands of times in our lives to describe the species, respected positions, and important activities probably has hammered values into all of us. These constant small messages affect our self-image, confidence, and the goals we set for ourselves. Whether you agree with this or not, it's undeniable that most educated people, most businesses, and most public institutions are sensitive to sexist language. The penalties far outweigh the rewards for using such language today.

■ **PRACTICE 8-6** Revise these sentences to make them less sexist.
- An athlete must accept his responsibility to be a role model.
- A chairman must control his audience.

Vividness

Someone might ask, "If I weed out big words, extreme words, clichés, and sexist and crude language, won't my style be dull?" No. You're cleaning away the debris to make room for real style. **Honesty and vividness come from concreteness and from improving key words—especially verbs, modifiers, and metaphors.**

CONCRETENESS
During revision, **replace general or vague words with concrete words that are specific or appeal to the reader's senses.** This is the difference between pretend meaning and real meaning. If you can't pin a sentence down to specifics, cross it off. You haven't lost a sentence but *gained* clarity. Notice how wimpy the following sentences are:

- The Saturn is a *good* car.
- We had an *exciting* time!
- Abused children suffer *mentally* as well as *physically.*

The vague words needing pep are so general that a reader has no specific image from them. In revision, choose words that relate to specific details:

- The Saturn is a sporty, economical, reliable car.
- Our blood pressure blasted off, and we screamed ourselves hoarse.
- We see the scars and burn marks on abused children, but a mother screaming, "I wish you were never born!" scars them, too.

Here's a brief list of common vague words that muffle vividness:

good	bad	great
nice	fantastic	beautiful
ugly	cute	sad
happy	success	awesome
awful	terrible	big/little

If you try to improve these words with a thesaurus, you may substitute "salubrious" or "benevolent" for "good," or substitute "deplorable" or "grievous" for "sad." Though slightly more specific than the originals, these still don't *define* or *visualize*. **In revising for concreteness, resee the thing described; think in pictures, not in words. Replacing vague words with specific ones will do more than any other technique to make your writing more tangible and clear.** Instead of saying, "He's a good man," write, "He'd take in a sick, stray dog," or "He donates five percent of his paycheck to the soup kitchen."

■ **PRACTICE 8-7** Rewrite the following sentences for more concreteness. This requires you to interpret the writer's purpose, because the sentences are vague:

- American foreign policy toward Muslim nations is messed up.
- He is really a great friend.
- Angelina Jolie has an unusual beauty.

■ **PRACTICE 8-8** Using concrete words, describe two of these in a few sentences:

- An ugly aspect of nature.
- The taste of lemon or mustard.
- Your best friend's face.

VERBS

Because they convey actions, verbs should be the strongest words in any sentence. Yet when I ask my students to underline all verbs in their papers, 80 percent turn out to be forms of "to be": was, were, are, is, am. "To be" is the dullest English verb. Other colorless, bland verbs include "go," "have," "get," "do," and "become." Some vivid, action verbs are "hack," "spring," "peel," "plow," "flick," "gobble," or "rip." Study this sample sentence from a student draft:

> **Example:** As the rush of people walk through the downtown area, the clanking and shaking of the old train is heard.

This sentence buries its vivid words "clanking" and "shaking." Make them the main verbs and scratch out the weak "is heard" at the end. Also, "walk" is a weak verb when the writer has the word "rush." Here's how the writer's peers revised it:

> **Example:** As the people rush downtown, the old train clanks and shakes past.

In the next sentence "is" saps potentially stronger verbs:

Example: To many people a college education is a burning desire.

Better: Many people burn for college educations.

■ **PRACTICE 8-9** In the next examples, restructure the sentence around a stronger verb.
- The question often asked by apartment dwellers is, "How am I going to furnish this place?"
- There was a clashing of negative events that helped me find myself.

Some verbs like **"look" or "walk" are so general, I almost always substitute more specific ones.** "She looked at me." Boring. Did she stare, leer, examine, peek, glance, or glare? Notice how the substitutes are more specific and visual than "look." Each adds tone and attitude. Many flat sentences spring off the page with new verbs.

■ **PRACTICE 8-10** List 10 words for "walk" that are more visual and more specific.

ADJECTIVES AND ADVERBS

You may have been told that adjectives and adverbs describe. True. But adverbs (which modify or describe verbs) and adjectives (which modify or describe nouns) are *helpers.* **Rely on better nouns and verbs first.** Which of these pairs is the sharpest:

- Janet walked very, very slowly.
  Janet dawdled.

- The car moved quickly away.
  The car sped away.

- Jack was an extremely big man.
  Jack was a Goliath.

In each case the second is more precise and visual because a weak adjective-noun or adverb-verb gave way to a strong noun or verb.

One particularly flat type of adjective or adverb is the **intensifier,** a word that says, "yeah, well, even more than the next word." These are the most common ones:

very	-est (ending)	excessively
so	extremely	least
too	definitely	most
really		

Here's how they puff air into sentences:

- He was the happiest man alive.
- It was a really easy assignment.
- The oil spill was extremely bad.
- Laws for handicapped rights are so very hard to pass.

Replace intensifiers with more concrete nouns or verbs. For example:

- He was ecstatic.
- The oil spill covered 300 square miles.

■ **PRACTICE 8-11** Revise the other two examples above and these:
- It was very cold that night.
- She was too unprepared for boot camp.

METAPHORS

Vivid writing often relies on metaphors. Albert Einstein used the metaphor of riding a light beam to help explain his theory of relativity, and scientists F. H. Crick and J. D. Watson used the metaphor of two snakes wrapped around each other to describe the structure of the DNA molecule. In Chapter 3 you learned to use metaphor as a thinking strategy. In revision, sharpen metaphors for *compactness, coherence,* and *concreteness.*

Metaphors should be compact. Metaphor power comes partly from suggesting a lot in a small space. Don't explain yourself away like this:

> Cameron was very tall and very thin and has often been compared to Ichabod Crane. His most distinguishing feature would be his long fingers. If you've ever been to a costume shop and put on a pair of phony fingers, you'll know what his look like. Well, maybe not that long, but they are bigger than yours and mine.

This writer had an interesting, vivid comparison, but he diluted it into a thin tea.

> **Revised:** Tall, thin Cameron is an Ichabod Crane. His fingers are like the scrawny, phony fingers in a costume shop.

Elizabeth Taylor—an actress involved in several seamy scandals—captured how she got away with such a life in a concise metaphor: "Success is a great deodorant." You can **suggest metaphors** sometimes with just one word—the ultimate in compactness. Here are winners from student papers:

- Sandy chirped a reply.
- This popcorn kernel of a man was a marine?
- Bill's cabbage brain couldn't understand.

■ **PRACTICE 8-12** Write a one- or two-sentence metaphor and then rewrite it compactly with one star verb or adjective. For example, "Our economics course is like a maze in which you cannot find your way out, like experimental rats in a psychology experiment" could be reduced to "We groped through the maze of economics all semester."

Metaphors should be coherent—everything in the picture should fit together. The following metaphors pull the reader in several directions:

> **Example:** Our household was emotionally *barren*, much like the *deserts* of loneliness people create to save themselves from being *bruised* or *hurt* by someone else. **Analysis:** The writer creates an effective desert image but then stirs in a new metaphor with "bruised." He needed to continue his desert image, perhaps with a reference to being lost, thirsty, or victimized by sun or desert predators.

> **Example:** Even though James Brown possessed extraordinary potential as a musician, his motivation was like an *abrupt red light* that *faded* in and *slithered* out periodically. **Analysis:** The word "slithered" switches images. Red lights can fade but they can't slither. The writer should have stuck with the traffic light imagery.

■ **PRACTICE 8-13** Revise the two examples listed above.

Metaphors must be concrete. They should appeal to our senses with sharp sights, smells, sounds, tastes, or touches. Notice how the following improves with more specific visualizing:

> **Example:** Her dreams were ruined by fear, like the presence of an ugly pollutant in a clean body of water.

> **Revised:** Her dreams were ruined by fear, like chemicals seeping into a pristine pond.

■ **PRACTICE 8-14** Rewrite these sentences for sharper metaphors:
- The city fire chief was a tower of strength.
- We are at a crossroads where we must sink or swim.
- His voice was like a lion's. It made a lot of noise and it felt like it was coming after you down a hallway if you tried to get away.
- Peace comes like rain.

Stylish Sentence Structure

VARIETY

Glance at your sentences. Do they all follow a subject–verb–modifier format? Are most stubby or are they long, twisted snakes? **Readers like variety.** Reading many short, choppy sentences is like picking up a handful of beads; help the reader string them together. A page of continuous long sentences is like a jungle to hack through—you want more air and light. Break up a series of straight statements with an occasional question. Mix simple, compound, and complex sentences. (See Chapter 17 for more details.)

■ **PRACTICE 8-15** Find a place in your last paper in which three sentences in a row are nearly the same length or use almost the same structure. (Hint: Look for ones using a subject–verb–modifier pattern.) Change the length or pattern for variety.

■ **PRACTICE 8-16** Just to see what your sentence lengths are, count the number of words in each sentence of your last paper. What is the shortest? What is the longest? What is the average length? In class, compare with your classmates.

PARALLEL STRUCTURE

Parallel structure means you must match words or groups of words in a series or on each side of a conjunction:

> **Wrong:** The president ordered troops, ships, and bombed the airfield. (The last item is a mismatch.)

> **Correct:** The president ordered troops, ships, and planes overseas. (*Troops, ships,* and *planes* are all nouns and all ordered by the president.)

> **Wrong:** She wanted to stop the civil war, the votes of Americans, and open the harbors for oil tankers. (The second item, a noun, mismatches.)

> **Correct:** She wanted to stop the civil war, unite the American people, and open the harbors for oil tankers. (Three verbs with modifiers and all are things she wants.)

You might consider one other aspect of parallel structure when working on a particularly important sentence: **the items should build to a climax.**

Good: His childhood days were filled with fear, cruelty, and a concealed love. (Because the student contrasted love with negative things, it springs up at the end like a surprise blossom; in the middle of the list, it would lack emphasis.)

Weak: The congressional plan backfired; 3,500 soldiers were killed unnecessarily, Congress was recalled for an extra session, and the plan cost $100,000,000 more than expected. (The deaths are most important and belong last.)

■ **PRACTICE 8-17** Write two sentences that list parallel items in a series. Each item must be a phrase or clause of at least three words.

Conciseness

Essayist and children's book author E. B. White recalled his former writing professor, William Strunk, leaning on the lectern in class, peering over his wire-rimmed spectacles, and barking, "Avoid unnecessary words! Avoid unnecessary words! Avoid unnecessary words!"

I'd like to leave it at that so Strunk's ghost doesn't haunt me, but I need to make a distinction. I receive a number of papers each semester that are *brief,* say, half the length asked for. They're usually not *concise,* however. **Concise writing says as much as possible in as few words as possible.** This means keeping a reader interested, supplying vivid supporting detail, and emphasizing key points. Many brief papers simply state a thesis without bringing it to life, or they simply cover less than a concise longer paper.

Few people could top President Calvin Coolidge for brevity. Once asked by his wife what the Sunday sermon was about, Silent Cal replied, "Sin."

"Well, what did the preacher say about it?" his exasperated wife asked.

"He was against it," Coolidge replied.

This brevity says nothing. However, most great writing is concise. The Lord's Prayer is 56 words; Lincoln's Gettysburg Address is about 200; the Ten Commandments are under 300; and the Declaration of Independence is about 1,500.

Most writers can trim 20 to 30 percent of their draft. Much small-scale wordiness takes up space but contributes nothing:

Wordy	**Better**
"He went on to say …"	"He added …"
"The hat was red in color …"	"The red hat …"

"We proceeded to depart."	"We departed."
"In my opinion it seems to me ..."	"I believe ..."
"Ken was slugged by Joe."	"Joe slugged Ken."
"Due to the fact that ..."	"Because ..."

Here's an introduction that spins nothing into cotton candy:

Example: It is very interesting to compare what different essay writers have to say about writing essays. In our book we have different essays on writing by E. B. White, Alice Walker, and Joan Didion, who are all famous modern authors today.

Notice the repetition and lack of a clear thesis; the writer may think she's started, but the reader knows she's still clearing her throat.

Improved: E. B. White, Alice Walker, and Joan Didion present three different views on writing essays.

Nothing important is lost; the sentence is improved for being direct. **Like watery wine, wordy writing doesn't offer enough pop per ounce.** Readers expect a certain density of information per paragraph. A high-octane effort means not only using high intensity concrete words and vivid verbs, but removing the water.

Redundancy: A hat that is "red in color" says it twice; red cannot be a shape or a smell, only a color. Is the "honest truth" more true than just "the truth"? Chop redundancy to strengthen the following sentences:

- The Constitution was totally demolished.
- He is a completely unique artist.
- The railroad was extended a distance of 60 miles.
- I plan to enter the field of nursing.
- In the fall of the year school once again reopens.
- At that point in time, we faced a serious job crisis.

All writers puff up first drafts; good writers condense final drafts. Concentration and practice, not talent, will make your writing concise.

Connecting words such as "that" or "which," or anything not carrying the main weight of a sentence may be fluff. Cutting two verbs to one strengthens sentences, especially if you exterminate a "to be" verb:

Wordy: The bureaucrats avoided some *of the* work *they were* assigned.

Concise: The bureaucrats avoided some assigned work.

Wordy: The catalytic converter *is used for the purpose of* reducing air pollution.

Concise: The catalytic converter reduces air pollution.

■ **PRACTICE 8-18** Make each of these sentences more concise. Save vivid words, and convert hidden strong verbs into active ones.
- At that point in time, Lee attacked north for the purpose of scaring the Yankees.
- The Capitol was entirely destroyed by fire.
- He had a long gray beard that had not been trimmed very recently.
- Ike brought tears of laughter to a great number of people with his jokes.
- Those who commit murder are not deserving of the state's mercy.

Using a Computer to Revise Words

Computers are great for word revision. A thesaurus feature can find synonyms for poor word choices and a word search will tell if you overused one word. You may be able to instruct your computer to beep at suspect words: absolutes like "always," intensifiers like "very," clichés you want to put a lid on (beep!), vague words like "good," or "to be" verbs like "was." Then you scroll through your draft and consider changing each. You don't have to change all of them, but the computer is ruthlessly honest about telling you exactly what's there—if you want to know.

■ **PRACTICE 8-19** Create a hot list of style words and instruct your computer to alert you when your draft uses absolutes, intensifiers, vague words, and forms of the verb "to be."

Playing with Language

The best way to improve your style is to play with language. Rearrange words the way you rearrange furniture in a room to see how it looks or the way you try a new batting stance. Is change always good? Of course not. But you will never be any better than you are right now unless you try new things. Besides, **as you play with language, you should find that it stimulates new ideas and details like any other brain teaser.** Suppose you were asked to give your opinion on the *Survivor*-type television shows in which people compete to be the last one "alive." You could say:

> The people who are on these shows are freaks and idiots. They give up all their secrets and privacy to be famous for a few weeks. Everybody laughs at them and says what jerks they are.

Analysis: Now, this is direct and bold—but flat. Nothing is supported by concrete detail. All three sentences start with subjects and verbs. Almost all the verbs are bland ("are," "give," "to be," "says," and one action verb "laugh"). It slips into absolutes ("all" and "everybody"), which stereotypes all contestants. It does not use crude language exactly, but "freaks," "idiots," and "jerks" come close, making the writer appear snobbish. Am I condemning the writer's idea? No. In fact, I tend to agree. But the style does not convey it well.

■ **PRACTICE 8-20** Supply concrete details (examples and descriptions) and play with the sentence structure, verbs, absolutes, and labels to improve the paragraph on Survivor-type shows. If you disagree with the writer, rewrite the paragraph to fit your opinion.

VISUAL RHETORIC

To explore the concept of style more deeply, compare these portraits. Consider how the photographer's presentation affects the theme or feel of the picture. Look for focus, contrast, depth, angle and mood.

For additional portraits to examine for style, see Chapter 11.

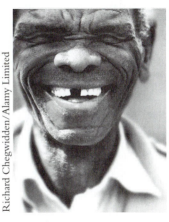

Tom & Dee Ann McCarthy/CORBIS

Richard Chegwidden/Alamy Limited

Writing Suggestions and Class Discussions

Revise the following for honest word use, vividness, parallel structure, and conciseness.

1. It was a blistering June day; the heat could be seen radiating from the pavement.
2. Joaquin is definitely one of a kind.
3. We must grab the bull by the tail and face the situation.
4. The first time I encountered José, it was in a foreign country.
5. The aftermath of Hurricane Katrina was filled with a great many human atrocities.
6. Dr. Baikman is a short, dark man who looks as if he's beginning to get old.
7. She has a way of making people feel very special.
8. Alan's superficialities were especially on my bug list.
9. Queen Morena dumped on the Count. She declined his matrimonial proposal.
10. A garden is in her face where roses and white lilies grow.
11. Americans must give up drugs if they want to escape the prison of this filthy crutch they use to bury their weaknesses.
12. After returning from the little girl's room, I proceeded to expostulate on the numerous beneficial phenomena of mixed-gender lavatories.
13. When I was at the age of 12, my mom started to become a little better, treating us more like human beings, although the discipline was still there.
14. Upon my arrival, I quickly apprehended the culture change and beheld the New Hampshire accent and idioms embellished by the McCormack family.
15. After the whistle, Sam attacks his opponent with a killer instinct, driving him to the mat and gratifying what he sets out to accomplish.
16. There was a fear of anyone approaching him.
17. His right eye was dangling out of its socket, his lower lip was stretched under his chin, his nose was almost completely torn from his face and hanging facial skin.
18. Her medication was putting weight on her that was visibly noticeable within a few days after it was prescribed.
19. Carolyn's life was like water, moving and shifting with no anchor.
20. It's always too late to straighten a kid out after he's been in jail.
21. There are many different variations in color.
22. Halle lacked a confidence factor.

23. Negotiations will either grind to a halt or be hammered out.

24. At 7 A.M. in the morning, the weatherman predicted major thunder-storm activity.

Make a chart listing "male" and "female" at the top and write the qualities brought out with each reference to gender in these 24 sentences (e.g., fear, purposeful). Then evaluate the overall sexist slant to the sentences as a whole.

THREE WAYS TO REVISE STYLE

1. Exchange rough drafts with another student in class. Do all you can to help each other with honest word choices, vividness, sharp sentences, and conciseness.

2. Your professor will mark one paragraph in your paper needing stylistic pruning and pep. Revise it thoroughly.

3. Find an example for 10 of the following in the draft of a paper you're preparing. Then revise. Most people can find at least two of the starred items in drafts:

- Overly fancy vocabulary
- Absolutes
- ★Exaggeration
- Weasels
- Euphemism
- Crude language
- Clichés
- Sexist language
- ★Areas needing more concreteness
- ★Dull verbs
- ★Weak adjectives or adverbs
- ★Intensifiers
- Weak metaphors
- Monotonous sentence structure
- Nonparallel sentence structure
- ★Redundancy
- ★General wordiness

A CYBER GAME FOR STYLE

Create an online personality and introduce yourself to a chat room. You might respond to a posted issue or ask a question. This personality should be *unlike* yourself: a person from a different region, country or different social class and have a different career goal or college major, different sex or age, and/or different philosophy of life from your real one. Your job is to create a believable self by using vocabulary, sentence style, clichés or other aspects of language that your imagined personality would have. If your class has a class Web site, your professor may ask you to submit your personalities there anonymously through a new username. If you have a blog, you might role-play as a viewer responding to your own blog. Please be ethical and make this a harmless game: you should not be abusive, offensive, or mislead readers in any way that might cause harm.

SAMPLE REVISION FOR STYLE

Here is a rough draft of part of a student essay, with suggestions made for style. The author is Mary Updaw, and the comments were made by her and others. Ignore the comments as you read, then go over each of them.

REVISED STUDENT ESSAY AND ANALYSIS

Good Intentions

WORDY and weak verb

I was in urgent need of a tracheotomy operation a year ago.

-VAGUE not concrete

Since then, some difficult situations have occurred. So this is for the strangers whom I meet daily and their good intentions.

unnecessary   *weak verb*

When you get on an elevator with me, do not suggest I go see my doc-
weak verb-ride? enter?
tor if I cough. I do not have enough time between floors to explain to a

perfect stranger my condition. Please do not stare at me with sympathetic

eyes if you notice my trach bib. I am not some poor little lamb you should
Absolute
feel sorry for, and I resent any indication that I am. Please do not ask fool-

ish questions if you see me using my inhaler. I am not a drug addict, and
cut intensifier   *redundant*
wordy   I feel it should be quite obvious I am taking medication for my health. I do
weak verb   *better verb*
not go up to people I see popping aspirin and ask if they have a headache.
stare ?
If your child happens to look in my direction, please do not whisper in
used twice-cut one
his ear and steer him in another direction. I am not some kind of freak he
wordy   *a*
should be afraid of. To the strangers who want to swap medical war sto-

ries, I say forget it. I have not been graced with a Purple Heart for my con-
too crude!
dition; they are only for the men who deserve them, and, frankly, it's none
harsh + unnecessary
of your [#*!%] business. For the well-wishers who secretly are glad it is

me and not you, you are more transparent than you realize, and I don't
redundant-
care to be around you. *this is obvious*

ANALYSIS

Reviewers knew this draft based on a bug list had strong potential. Honest and direct, it hit the reader hard. They also liked the style of the sentences, which are balanced and parallel to make Mary's structure clear. The notes focus on cutting wordiness, replacing vague words, weak verbs, and sharpening the existing sentence structure. The final draft is 20 percent shorter but more lively in style.

FINAL DRAFT

GOOD INTENTIONS

I urgently needed a tracheotomy operation a year ago. But the real shock came later—dealing with strangers and their good intentions.

When you ride an elevator with me, do not suggest I rush to my doctor if I cough. I do not have enough time between floors to explain my condition to a perfect stranger. Please do not stare at me with sympathetic eyes if you notice my trach bib. I am not some poor little lamb you should feel sorry for, and I resent indications that I am. Please do not ask foolish questions if you see me using my inhaler. I am not a drug addict; it should be obvious I am taking medication. I do not ask people popping aspirin if they have a headache.

If your child glances at me, please do not whisper in his ear and steer him in another direction. I am not a freak he should fear. To strangers who want to swap medical war stories, forget it. I have not been graced with a Purple Heart for my condition; they are only for the men who deserve them. For the well-wishers who secretly are glad it is me and not you, you are more transparent than you realize.

☑ Peer Review Checklist for Style

Author: _____

Reviewer: _____

The reviewer should read through the rough draft **only for style.** Make suggested changes on the rough draft itself.

1. Find two weak verbs (is, are, has, or get) and suggest more visual action verbs to replace them.

2. Accuracy/honesty: Find an exaggeration or absolute that ought to be modified. Suggest a revision.

3. Concreteness: Find a cliché that needs a fresher image or an unsupported generalization that needs more detail. Suggest a revision.

4. Find an intensifier and suggest a stronger noun or verb to replace the weak one the intensifier tried to build up.

5. Look for an example of sexist language or stereotyping and suggest a revision.

6. Conciseness: Pick one paragraph of the essay and make at least three suggestions to eliminate redundant or empty words.

Putting it All Together

From Topic Choice to Published Essay

YOU'VE READ ABOUT THE WRITING PROCESS IN Chapters 1 through 8. Now, to demonstrate in detail how a vague, uncertain idea grows into a finished piece of writing, I'm going to reveal all I can about the creation of an essay I published in the *Chronicle of Higher Education* (March 2, 2007).

First, please read the published essay. Then I'll peel it apart so you can see how it evolved through the process of topic selection→brain teasers→thesis→outline→draft→revision. I will include my false steps—the ugly tracks writers cover—and explain how techniques such as brain teasers led me to ideas I didn't know I had. I'll try to be as honest as I can, but as you'll see, some mysteries remain.

> Education: a succession of eye-openers, each involving the repudiation of a previously-held belief.
>
> —GEORGE BERNARD SHAW

> If you do not expect the unexpected, you will not find it.
>
> —HERACLITUS

If God Breake My Bones
M. Garrett Bauman

John Donne, the devout 17th Century cleric who had lived much of his early life as a notorious sinner, once said in a sermon, "If God breake my bones, it is but to set them strayter [straighter] . . . if he draw his knife, it is but to prune his Vine." I think about that when I meet a class for the first time. Which of those September faces have been broken by fate, mistakes, bad luck or cruelty? And what can I do for them?

Zoë, pale, fragile-framed and 18, informed me that she had Crohn's Disease. Ulcers, abscesses, and perforations in her digestive tract caused excruciating pain. Surgeons had removed part of her small intestine and all of her large intestine, but the disease

→

---

still raged. Premature severe osteoporosis from using steroids to combat the condition made her walk stiffly. She grimaced bending for her backpack, like a woman 50 years older. Yet she studied ferociously and attained the class's highest average. When I asked about her goals, she jolted as if pricked by an electric wire: "Once I wanted to be a doctor . . ." Now she hoped only to attend college for as long as possible.

Would John Donne tell Zoë—who had been no hedonist before contracting Crohn's—that fate's knife was charitably pruning her corruption? Where was a divine plan in carving this sensitive, smart woman into pieces? I was amazed that someone in such agony, and who was unlikely to reap the fruits of her education, cared so much about her studies.

Ricardo was a handsome young man with the kind of sweet smile that would make any mother sigh in relief if he dated her daughter. When he was fifteen he was playing baseball in a schoolyard when someone hit a pop fly onto the roof. Ricardo volunteered to retrieve it. He climbed the two-story brick wall at the corner by wedging his sneakers into seams between bricks, then grabbed the gutter and pulled himself onto the roof in triumph. After tossing the ball down, he swung his legs over the gutter to descend. As he probed for a toehold, Ricardo slipped and plummeted to the asphalt.

Four years later he sat in a wheelchair in my class, his rubbery legs strapped down so they wouldn't sway loosely. His hands were bent backwards at the wrists as if trying to touch his elbows.

When I asked students to write something, Ricardo struggled, elbows in the air, to lift his pen. He pincered it between the heels of his hands, then clamped his teeth on it and bent to the wheelchair tray, bobbing his head and sweating. I felt awful watching him, but to excuse him would have been worse than letting him continue. He needed this small, public victory.

Later he told me that he had lain in bed for two years. His legs were "dead," and he lost small motor control of his hands, which warped more each year. Trauma to his head affected his thinking. "I used to be smarter," he said. After he got out of bed, he spent another two years learning to write using his mouth and to operate a wheelchair. Sick of television, isolated, and desperate for activity, he entered college.

"What are your plans?" I asked.

He shook his head. "To learn to drive a van with hand controls." That was all that seemed possible to him.

→

What else should I offer him? Yes, programs could help him through college, but what career could he have? His broken bones were not going to be straightened, and I saw no signs of Donne's promised revelation. Ricardo had made a child's mistake and been punished with a cruel life sentence. He'd been a decent person before the accident—not needing straightening or pruning.

Chip was a veteran of a minor U.S. "intervention" in another country. Although not physically wounded, he had been shell-shocked and now twitched continuously. His head and body went into spasms perhaps 20 times a minute. Chip's doctor verified that the twitching continued during such sleep as he managed. To avoid notice, he sat in the back of the room, but his trembling still rippled through us. When he approached me, his voice was broken by head jerks: "Some men's b-bodies can take battle and-d some men can't-t."

His problems ran deeper than tics. He could not concentrate for more than a minute or two. If he made a point and another student responded, when I asked Chip for a rebuttal, he simply shook his head. His first paper was a series of linguistic twitches as well, disconnected sentences. I didn't know what to do for him and neither did our counselors. Finally, he handed me a withdrawal slip. "I've g-got to get this under cont-trol first," he told me. "I can't think-k." I mustered cheerleader bravado. "Well, when you're ready, sign up for my class again." He looked at me grimly. I patted his shoulder and felt it twitch—a small bump, that's all. Yet within two months, Chip committed suicide.

Heather hid her secret beneath tense silence until one day when I asked her class to write about a moment of revelation in their lives. She wrote about standing outside her apartment the previous summer. She had been wearing a shabby blue bathrobe and had wept as her husband loaded the family car with his clothes, their computer, and whatever else he wanted. He gave no explanation, simply announced that he was leaving. When the car could hold no more, the husband, without a word or glance back, drove away, leaving Heather with their two children, no car, months of unpaid bills and an eviction notice. He had not contacted her since.

"This is me," she wrote. "This is my revelation. I am still standing on the sidewalk in my bathrobe, waiting. For what?"

We live in a bent if not broken world. You can hide from that fact a little longer in gated communities, country clubs and elite universities, but most colleges enroll many people who have been in life's serious accidents. Professors do not expect their career to

→

wring their hearts. I begin each semester intending to teach Flannery O'Connor's short stories or *Twelfth Night.* I like the high-achieving, articulate students who zip along education's straight track toward goals they will reach. Their performance in my classes is reassuring and purposeful. But the broken bones and "pruned" minds of other students make me question that track and where it leads.

King Lear asks, "Is there any cause in Nature that makes these hard hearts?" We would like to answer, yes, there is a cause in our genes or environment, or that terrible suffering is part of a benevolent divine plan withheld from humans; otherwise it makes no sense that such pain exists. There are scientific reasons that our bodies create diseases like Crohn's, but despite traditional rationalizations, no good moral reason. Nor for why a boy's back must be broken for simple childish *hubris*, or a man driven to suicide because he was a pawn in a minor skirmish. These students expose how close to the edge of disaster we *all* are. They tell us how life really is: there is no ivory tower, only a world of casualties or those about to become casualties. We all witness them.

I teach grammar to a young man who will never write a business letter, philosophy to a man who cannot sustain an idea for two minutes, literary analysis to a woman who will soon be incapacitated, and composition to the broken-hearted. Yet these people have faith that college will somehow help them to bear fruit. For them college is a life raft in a sea of desolation and destruction. If we cannot guide them to a career, maybe we can help them to cope and understand. Working hard at study can release a person from the burden of self-absorption. Literature provides tools with which to grapple with existential anguish. There is consolation in having professors as witnesses and cheerleaders, and a kind of redemption in learning for its own sake—not to win jobs, grants or promotions, but simply to know why. These students may be the purest scholars in all of higher education.

I need these students as much as they need college, for they have faced essential issues that we merely study. They teach those still humming along the "strayt" track that we are all condemned, eaten away inside, broken backed, and plagued by twitching, even as we hide behind luxury, power or beauty. All of us in higher education, focused on progress, often forget that education's greatest task may be to begin the work of helping us accept our mortality. I wonder if that is part of my job as a professional purveyor of futures. As John Donne said elsewhere, "Never send to know for whom the bell tolls; it tolls for thee."

Boguslaw Mazur/Shutterstock

■ **PRACTICE 9-1** Reflect on the essay. What parts did you like and not like? How did it make you feel? What was its main point or thesis? What brain teaser lies behind it? How does the style differ from my usual voice in *Ideas and Details*? Now, let's find out how this essay began.

Finding the Topic

I am still awed by students. They make teaching exciting and sometimes deeply touching, and I frequently write about students to grasp the experience better and to learn how to teach better. One term several students suffering hardships—Zoë most of all—made me want to share with others their brave struggles. Many ideas swirled in a confused dust storm in my head. Really—professors feel that way too. I did have a clear image of my **audience** because I planned to write for the *Chronicle*—the professional newspaper for college professors and administrators. I wanted to express for them some despairs and hopes they might have had about students who moved them. I scrawled three tentative topics on scrap paper. I've deleted the doodling and scratch outs and put it in computer script so you can read it:

WHAT STUDENTS TEACH TEACHERS—FUNNY & SERIOUS

   • You can endure disaster—Zoë

   • Cancelled class is joyous

   • Profs need to remember how to daydream—Keenan

   • Students teach us to hope—Renee, Shaquaan

   • We all ought to resist growing up—Malvin, Anna

SECRETS OF THE HEART—SAD, TOUGH STORIES OF ST. LIVES

   • Students opening themselves in class & papers.

   • Confessions of tragedy. A relief to spill their guts.

   • Sometimes causes turmoil. Zoë, Heather, Chip, Keenan

MYTHS AND REALITY—COLLEGE'S OFFICIAL AGENDA VS ITS HIDDEN

AGENDA—

   • Prepare for jobs vs prove you can survive

   • Quote college V.P. vs what Mike _____ says

   • Different view of success—Zoë

■ **PRACTICE 9-2** Which topic do you like best at this stage? Which one seems closest to the finished essay?

Brain Teasers

To explore the topics more deeply, I laid my pen aside and imagined the topic through the focus of various brain teasers. "Myths and Reality" begged for "Breaking Stereotypes" to shatter myths about college: "Most people think college is _____ but it really is _____." I punctured several stereotypes in my head, but in visualizing an audience of professors and deans, I realized my ideas would seem obvious to them. Better to leave that topic for a more general audience.

With "What Students Teach Teachers," I could "Classify" ways students teach professors how to stay young, love life, face hardship, and be happier. My audience might like that and it could be humorous. But it felt wrong to combine Zoë's tragic story with lighter ideas.

"Secrets of the Heart" would focus on hardships. That felt more on target. First, I tried an "Alternative Viewpoints" brain teaser: the different ways professors, administrators, students, and the public feel about students who endure tough lives. It came out bland and boring, and I'm glad I threw it away so I don't have to show it to you. Bad ideas are the norm at first—the trick is to have other options. Classification, contrast, even bug lists had potential, but if this essay was going for the heart, I needed visuals, intimate stories. So I wrote an "Examples" brain teaser to evoke memories and details of students who tugged my feelings.

LIST EXAMPLES BRAIN TEASER

Secrets of the Heart

—Earl—letter to parents apologizing for his drug use and drinking (started at age 9). Won track scholarship to Fla. U. Dropped out. HIV positive

— "Puddles of moonlight" class discussion. Emily tells of first sex experience—infected with S.T.D. Sweet, innocent-looking. Ruined by one mistake.

—B-ball cap guys—Ray, Zack, etc. Seething, holding back—what's their secret rage? "I dare you to teach me" attitude.

—Zoë—Crohn's disease. Operations, agony, "A+" work. Future dreams shot. Loved reading

—Jessica: Ultra-shy, tongue-tied in class. Opened up on class nature walk. Single mom. Wanted to participate, couldn't. Brilliant papers.

—Quote Pierre De Beranger: "My friend the enemy." Trouble makes us stronger.

—Chip: war vet. Stammer and shakes. Shell-shocked PTSS? Drops out. Patting his shoulder. False hope. Suicide. Could I have helped more?

—Roxanna. Gave up her baby to her mom. Deal? College for baby? Why did Rox do it?

—Heather—Husb abandoned her and children. Drove off with all they had. Now she was starting fresh. Scared.

—Rachel: Dated man and slept with him. Next morning, he sent her a package. Not a romantic gift, but a small black coffin. Note inside: "Welcome to the wonderful world of AIDS."

My pen flew—a strong signal that I now had my topic.

Thesis Ideas

At this point I had nine examples of students under great stress. Some, like "Puddles of Moonlight," mean little to you, but it was shorthand for me—a phrase Emily used to describe the romantic scene in the park the night she first had sex—and contracted an STD. The quote, from Pierre-Jean de

Béranger (which is *not* an example), just popped up, drawn by the examples. I wrote it down anyway. (Remember, don't censor brain teasers!) Could that be my thesis? Perhaps the hardships students face (their enemies) help them become stronger, so in a sense the hardships become their friends. Since most of the stories would be sad, I welcomed this positive idea.

But the thesis still seemed thin. So I did a **thesis brain teaser**—listing possible theses to tie together my examples. You can stop yourself at any moment in writing to create your own mini-brain teasers to figure out what to do next: Just ask what you specifically want, and then list options.

Thesis Brain Teaser

• *Professor as the receiver of secrets.*
• *Hardship helps students become stronger.*
• *Some students are comeback kids—the real American Dream.*
• *College classrooms are life labs where students face real tragedies.*

These are uneven: the last two items dug up new ideas, while the first is not a thesis, just a topic. That's all right. **You have to take your ideas as far as you can, keep going, and trust that if you toss your brain enough ideas and details, it will throw you something back.** Especially with theses, it often takes writing and revising a draft for you to fully grasp what you want to say.

Concentrating on the thesis popped another example into my thoughts—Ricardo, in a wheelchair with a broken body because he chased a baseball onto a roof. Hmm. Broken body, broken bones. These were broken people, but some refused to act like they were broken, didn't they? It seemed like a metaphor. And here—I confess I don't know exactly how the connection was made except that it was drawn from my subconscious by brain teasers and by bouncing between ideas and details—I recalled the quotation from John Donne. Donne believed God breaks people to make them straighter, the way a doctor rebreaks a badly set broken bone to fix it, and God prunes people the way a farmer prunes vines to make them bear more fruit. So perhaps the hardships students endured were improving their character and preparing them for some future purpose. Aha! Just as colleges do! This was a stronger rough thesis.

Time to set up a scratch outline. I had too many examples. Chip, Zoë, and Ricardo had to be in it. Earl, however, caused his own disaster. He was not "broken" by outside forces or bad luck like the others and did not fit as well. I also cut Jessica—her painful shyness was not as devastating. I didn't know enough about the baseball cap guys or about the woman who gave up her baby to her mother.

SCRATCH OUTLINE

Secrets of the Heart

Intro: Donne quote: "If God break my bones ..."

Zoë: 18, Crohn's disease, intestine cut away, brilliant, "I wanted to be doctor"
 Pale, fragile, groans when lifting bookbag.

Ricardo: Paralyzed, heels of hands pinch pencil. Writes with mouth, fell from
 roof, 2 years flat on back, brain damage, mother called me to help her
 boy.

Rachel: mid-twenties, victim of predatory boyfriend. "Welcome to the wonderful
 World of AIDS." Fatal mistake. Smart and sassy.

Chip: mid-thirties. War shock. Brain-damaged, stammer. No focus. Suicide.
 "Some men's bbbbodies can take bbbattle, anddd sssome ccant" Tic.

Emily: 20, innocent, shattered. Puddles of moonlight becomes herpes. "I'll never,
 never get another boyfriend."

Conclusion: DeBeranger: "My friend the enemy."

The Draft

With this in front of me, I began keyboarding, using the Donne quotation as my opening hook. I visualized speaking to my audience of U.S. and Canadian professors and administrators—most of whom probably worried about students like mine, too. I wondered what they would like to know and ended the introductory paragraph with the question, "What can I do for them?" because they would want an answer. That unsettled me, because I didn't have an answer. But my feeling of helplessness really was the honest response, and I did not cover it up as I wrote.

I moved from example to example, adding new details to those in the outline to weave a story for each student, so it was not simply a list of items. **When I switched to a new example, I returned to my thesis** to ask how the student's situation related to Donne's statement. Here's how the first draft ended:

THE DRAFT'S CONCLUSION

We might recall de Béranger, who referred to "'My friend, the enemy'" when thinking about how his enemies spurred him on to be better and stronger, while uncritical, supportive friends made him think he was perfect just as he was. Teachers often find that handicapped students, ill students, or hurting students create more work and can distract a class, but just as their sufferings can be their friends to help them grow, so they can help us as teachers to expand our own horizons.

That sounded pretty good. Now, let's see how it all ended up being cut.

Revising on My Own

The draft turned out to be 2,300 words, well over my 1,500 limit at the *Chronicle*. No problem. I always write long so I can toss the junk overboard. It may seem like extra work to write more and then cut, but it means I'm not tempted to keep less than my best work. I scanned the draft looking only for **big issues first**. What was the overall idea and push of the essay? Which major sections fit and which didn't?

The most glaring flaw was that Emily's story duplicated Rachel's—both were betrayed by lovers. Since Rachel's AIDS was potentially fatal, I deleted Emily. The three examples remaining involved a disease, an accident, and war. It had better balance now. Conversations I had with Zoë's doctor and Ricardo's mother were also cut. I could give the facts of Zoë's disease without the doctor; and the focus should be on Ricardo, not his mother's anxiety.

These cuts strengthened the piece by sharpening my focus. *But as I revised, I realized I no longer wholeheartedly agreed with John Donne.* I couldn't justify what my students endured by saying it was part of a divine plan. It sounded consoling at first, but most of these students were unlikely to be healed or become highly productive. Nor were they bad people who needed to be broken or pruned. I could find no good reason for their suffering. In other words, I **questioned my thesis**. In revising I began to argue against Donne. That honesty gave the essay an edge. Finally, I realized that the quotation that originally led to my thesis, "My friend, the enemy," had to go. The essay had outgrown it. Breaking bones and bearing fruit were images of doctors healing and farmers growing. De Béranger's metaphor was about war. And Donne's lines probed more deeply.

Cutting de Béranger left me without an ending. What would I say now? **Conclusions often "close the circle" by returning to the opening**, but I had squeezed the "breake my bones" line enough. How about something else by Donne I could agree with? One time, upon hearing a funeral bell, he wrote that we should never ask for whom the bell tolled because it tolls for everyone. All humans are in the same fix, for disaster and death will come to each of us in time. Other people's misery is our warning. This moved beyond my idea that education can help people cope with suffering. Hurt students were like Donne's tolling bell, teaching the rest of us how to live. Someday we would be in their spot, and their example would teach us courage. *They* teach *us*.

So far, revision focused on thesis, detail and structure. Now I turned to revising smaller aspects, sharpening sentences, cutting wordiness, improving word choices, and fixing grammar lapses. Here's the first draft paragraph from the section on Zoë. The underlined words are ones that bothered me:

One student had Crohn's disease. Eighteen years old, Zoe was pale, fragile and in extreme pain. Her digestive tract had ulcers, abcesses and holes from the disease. Although doctors removed parts of her intestines, that had not helped. She groaned picking up her backpack like an old woman. Yet she studied diligently and ended up with the highest average in class.

Here are the second draft changes and why I made them:

- One student→Zoë (name names!)
- Eighteen years old→move later in sentence (not a primary detail)
- extreme→excruciating pain (turn bland intensifier to a sense word)
- had [ulcers, etc.], that had not helped→disease still raged (stronger verb, more concise)
- abcesses→abscesses (spelling error)
- holes→perforations (medical term seems scarier)
- from the disease→deleted (wordy and obvious)
- doctors→surgeons (more specific and visual)

- parts of her intestines→part of her small intestine and all of her large intestine (more specific and visual)
- groaned→grimaced (more accurate—she did not make noise—she was tough)
- like an old woman→woman 50 years older (more specific, not sexist)
- diligently→ferociously (more visual and honest—she was passionate)
- ended up with→attained (passive to active verb)

Here's the rewritten paragraph from the second draft:

> Zoë, pale, fragile-framed, and 18, informed me that she had Crohn's disease. Ulcers, abscesses, and perforations in her digestive tract caused excruciating pain. Surgeons had removed part of her small intestine and all of her large intestine, but the disease still raged. She would grimace while bending for her backpack, like a woman 50 years older.

Revising with Peers and Editors

During revision, I shared drafts with my wife, Carol, a therapist who offers psychological perspective and common sense, and with my writing buddy, R. H. Herzog, a professor and writer. They helped me toward some of the revisions above.

I cleaned up a "final" draft and e-mailed it to my editors. They liked it and of course had suggestions to improve it. The most significant issue was that one editor at the *Chronicle* had heard a story about an AIDS note in a coffin before! She tracked it down on several Web sites and concluded it was an urban legend. It's possible this had happened to Rachel too, but it was far more likely she had lied. Why, I'll never know.

I did not hesitate to cross it out: this would have been a public embarrassment, and I'm only confessing to you to stress the importance of having outside perspectives on your writing. Be grateful to editors! I replaced that example with Heather's story—so I would still have a relationship "wound."

Like your peer groups, my editors pressed me to think but did not demand changes. They wanted to know which war Chip was in—to add context and a visual. But being truthful was more important. I couldn't remember if it was Somalia or Kosovo, so we referred to it as a "minor intervention." They asked me about the details of Crohn's disease, and I double-checked my notes from speaking with Zoë's doctor by researching the disease on Web sites. That jogged me to remember that she had premature osteoporosis, so I added that. They asked me to verify the exact wording and source of the Donne quotations (commercial publications are not required to use MLA documentation for short excerpts as you are in college papers, in case you're curious, but the *Chronicle's* editors verify every one).

The editors made a dozen small suggestions. For example, they asked how I knew Heather's thoughts when her husband drove away, so I added a phrase about her writing them into a course paper. Simply working over the essay again made me rethink things that had seemed fine. For example, the title that inspired the topic—"Secrets of the Heart"—no longer captured the essay's theme. It's still a good title, but maybe for another essay.

Is the piece perfect now? No! In writing this analysis for you, I've found things I'd like to change. One small example: Chip and I exchange dialogue in the same paragraph; we ought to be in separate ones. One bigger item: I no longer think, "education's greatest task . . . . [is] to help us accept our mortality." Instead, I wish I had said, "Education's greatest virtue is teaching us to face life as it is, not as we wish it were, and that these students show us the courage to do that and keep going."

■ **PRACTICE 9-3** Think of a student you know who must deal with a severe emotional or physical handicap while attending college. Write a brief description of his or her situation. What point would you make about this person? Your professor will be most pleased if this point is different from those expressed in "If God Breake My Bones."

Writing Suggestions
· ·

1. Pick one of these topics or another of your own choice that is not a personal narrative: blue collar workers, bar culture, spiders (or any other animal), advice to high school graduates starting college, or sexual harassment. Narrow the topic into three to four different options. Try for at least one unusual angle.

2. Pen aside, imagine opening up your narrowed topics with different brain teasers from Chapter 3. Pick one topic and write a one-page brain teaser.

3. Do a thesis brain teaser by writing four to five trial thesis sentences to focus and explore your topic more. They should be different theses, not rephrases of the same idea.

4. Write a scratch outline that includes an idea for an opening grabber or hook.

5. Draft the paper, revise it, and have a peer group help you revise it further.

Description

Making Your Audience See

10

Which of these statements are true?

- Description is flowery and poetic.
- Description bogs down writing.
- Description belongs in creative essays, not persuasive or informative writing.

None. They all distort the real nature of description. Fancy, gooey descriptive passages can smother ideas and are unacceptable as professional communication. Such passages give description a bad reputation. **Good description doesn't need to be gooey or fancy.** For example, the following passage describes a seizure a student's infant daughter suffered as a result of a DPT vaccine for pertussis:

> Lying in a puddle of vomit, Katelyn's head tilted to her shoulder, her eyes fixated left, looking like quarter moons. When I picked her up, I realized her head was locked to her shoulder. "Katie!" I yelled. She didn't hear me. Once in her father's arms, her legs locked straight out. Her tiny arms pulled tight against her chest, and her head shot back. My husband held down her tongue just as her jaw locked shut. Her eyes rolled upward, then they were gone.

The question is not what you look at, but what you see. . . . A man has not seen a thing unless he has felt it.

—HENRY DAVID THOREAU

To see takes time—like to have a friend takes time.

—GEORGIA O'KEEFFE

If only we could pull out our brain and use only our eyes!

—PABLO PICASSO

Look! Look!

—COLETTE (HER LAST WORDS)

At the hospital, the child's condition is stabilized, and the author goes on to describe her condition:

> There, lying in a crib resembling a cage, clad only in her diaper, was our baby daughter. Her chest was covered with leads monitoring her heart. Her arms, braced with tongue depressors, were violated with tubes and needles. Inches from her body was a "crash kit" equipped with electric paddles should they be needed.
>
> —*Alana J. Lockwood*

This vivid, factual description draws readers into the author's informative critique of the DPT vaccine, which each year causes seizures in thousands of normal children.

Description breathes life into writing—transforms typed words into pictures, sounds, and ideas. *Good* description makes the writer's idea dance in readers' heads, so they forget they're reading words. *Bad* description, by trying to impress readers with lush words, distracts from the idea. It makes us focus on the writer jumping up and down in a purple wedding dress.

Good description is essential for *all* writing, from business reports to personal letters to poems and persuasive essays. **Description commits writers to honesty by pinning down vague statements with concrete details.** Honest description shows the world as it is with all its pimples and secret beauties. It challenges safe stereotypes and preconceptions by getting down on its knees to examine things and report what's really there. This tough attitude resists gooey description, making writing lean and hard, as in this student example:

> It takes 938 steps to walk from one end of the beat to the other. The air is cold and crisp, the kind that fills my lungs with crystals—like a dagger in my chest. Only an hour and a half left until I'm done. The night is clear, almost too clear. The sound of my boots pounding the frozen turf is the only real thing. Our Air Force bombed Libya two days ago—an act of war. Tonight the lieutenant issued live ammunition. Boring guard duty became relevant.
>
> Step 452, almost to the mid-point, 17 steps away. I can see where I marked the center with a line scratched in the path. The center is an insecure place, where the distance between start and finish is the same. I just hope that the powers that run things have enough sense to go back to the start.
>
> —*Scott Nairy*

This passage makes us *see* as well as understand, which is description's great virtue.

In persuasive or research papers, powerful description can support a thesis in combination with statistics and other facts. In a paper arguing for strong penalties for pregnant women who use drugs, a student's research describes the effects of cocaine on newborns:

> Because cocaine causes fetus malnutrition, when the baby is born, its dry, cracked skin resembles the cover of an old, leather-bound book (Fulroth 70). Cocaine babies are almost always underweight. Their heads are 20 percent smaller than average. Their limbs jerk and jitter constantly, and their hands fly periodically to the sides of their heads, eyes startled wide in terror. Cocaine babies' heartbeats soar, and their lungs pump like hyperactive bellows. They cry inconsolably, a creepy, catlike wail that can last hours and which indicates severe neurological damage (Knight 71).
>
> —*Heidi Daniels*

A Writer's Eye: Six Ways to Visualize Ideas

REEXPERIENCE: DON'T THINK IN WORDS

When I ask students to describe a place, I often receive an essay that begins: "My room is 10 feet 6 inches by 11 feet and painted blue. I have a bed, a dresser, a CD player, a chair . . . ." This dead thing wants to be buried. Some students who realize it's flat "enliven" it with so-called descriptive words: "My room is robin's-egg blue with beige accents. I have an antique maple dresser, an enormous bed, a four-speaker Dolby CD player. . . ." Bury this one in a fancy casket; it's just as dead as the first. Both examples fail because of mistaken goals.

- **Description is *not* a catalog of everything present.**
- **Description is *not* created by thinking up picturesque words.**

Here's an example of a description of a room that does not fall into these traps:

> My room is only a pit stop between the evening and the morning. It has no luxurious, fluffy pillows, no king-sized bed. No extra time is spent in this room. It's get your clothes and out. At sunrise, the light glares off the television in a way that burns your face. In the evening, the coldness sets in, making you pull all the blankets right up to your chin.
>
> —*Scott Smith*

This sample combines a few sharp details with an angle, a theme. *Both* are needed to make writing vivid.

Description *is* created by mentally reliving what you hope to describe. Thoreau and O'Keeffe must have had this in mind when they wrote the sentences heading this chapter. A catalog may help as a brain teaser, but it won't create *quality* description. For that **you must create an *idea* on which the description hangs, and you must concentrate on seeing and feeling your subject, not on choosing descriptive words.** Evoke it inside yourself, and only *then* describe it in words. Reexperiencing often leads to vivid words naturally *and* ties description together.

Suppose I am writing about access for the disabled in public buildings. My first brain teaser list of descriptive details might include the following:

- Wide stalls in restrooms
- Interpreters for the deaf in college
- Low water fountains with large handles
- Wheelchair lifts on buses
- Disabled people I've known

I could use this list to compose a paper, perhaps on "Improvements in Public Access in Recent Years," but these descriptive details aren't sharp enough to write a strong paper. I have not reexperienced them vividly.

Let's take the bathroom stall example. I started to skip this for decency, but I realized that decency allows people to hide many facts about the disabled. Imagine yourself entering that stall in a wheelchair. Experience the bodily movements you need to accomplish this simple act. Go slow: See or feel each moment clearly before going on. Could you do it in 10 minutes between class? I picture myself rolling amid the waists of walking people, bumping open the restroom door and scraping past, rocking and turning several times to shut and lock the stall door, spilling books and papers off my wheelchair tray when I hoist myself by the cold bar, my chair sliding nearly out of reach, contorting to flush the knob behind my back and speeding to class late, bumping cluttered chairs to make a space, and wondering if the professor thinks I'm using my disability to get away with something.

I try to experience Carmen—a wheelchaired student in my literature class one summer. A wonderfully smiling young woman, she loved romantic stories. I experience being her—four feet tall, round-faced, back-bent wrists gripping the chair control knob. I imagine someone dressing me, cramming shoes onto my unresponsive feet, straightening my clothes so they feel right. During those hot classes, did she wish she could shift in her seat like others? Using a pen cost her agony during quizzes. Yet she made no complaints, no special requests, no mention of her disability. She seemed to fly, not to roll.

Thinking of Carmen reminds me of Eva, the old blind woman who lived with my family when I was a boy. Eva never bumped walls or furniture as she walked. From memory, she taught me to read, and she taught herself to read Braille and do leather work for pocket money. She sewed and did all the housework my grandmother did, and when she eventually went to a nursing home, she learned its paths within months. Eva "saw" more than any of the seeing people who lived in our house. Her disability gave her special power and authority.

That makes me recall Tom, a disabled student who scoffed angrily when he was named a hospital's "Patient of the Year" for scoring a 4.0 GPA while working full time. "I'm not a patient," he sputtered. "I'm a man."

I've presented my train of thought roughly as it came out. It's a brain teaser in paragraph form, not finished writing, but it shows more life, more intense description than my first list. Most important, it stimulated my mind. I can advocate disabled rights now with vivid detail. If I advocate a hands-off policy, I have three examples of tough, independent people. If I want to inform people about barriers the disabled face, I have better information.

Although it may seem like I thought in words, I really thought in pictures, touches, and sounds, for that's how we experience things. Experience the subject from *inside,* not from outside. **Allow yourself to become your subject, let it speak through you; don't treat it as an object.** At its extreme, this is the mystical experience of poets and fiction writers, when they swear something "wrote itself." But even a restaurant menu writer must see, taste, and smell dishes to describe them well. Business reports and college papers require it, too. The more you refeel or visualize your topic, the easier vivid description will be.

Some writers can type or write *as* they reexperience, but many writers can't. If words block experiencing, try this: **Sit back, *pen out of reach,* and picture your subject, imagining new details as you expand into it.** Relax. Let the topic talk. Release your subconscious. Censor nothing. Accept everything. Concentrate on seeing even more sharply as you go on. Push your memory, recall facts, try *all* your senses, daydream. Most people stop when the first shadowy pictures appear. You should continue. Go slower, deeper. After a vivid experience gels, record your sensations on paper, still not paying attention to words. Simply record vivid images, allowing new description to flow, too. *Later* you will take control and fine tune the picture. As W. E. B. Du Bois said, "Produce beautiful things, but stress the things rather than the beauty."

■ **PRACTICE 10-1** Experience one of these for five minutes, and only afterward record your descriptions. No catalogs, no fancy words.

• The room you are in right now
• A machine or tool
• Teenage alcoholism
• Senior citizens
• An experience with the police

■ **PRACTICE 10-2** Freewrite a page for a descriptive topic you're considering for a paper.

USE BRAIN TEASERS TO TRAIN YOUR EYE

Experiencing concentrates on unrestricted seeing. **Brain teasers prod your eye in a more organized way.** The two most important descriptive brain teasers are **Senses** and **Listing Examples.** If as you reexperience your topic, you only see obvious things, switch senses. Concentrate on hearing your topic or smelling or touching it. Or consciously list examples for your topic. Then experience it.

Suppose you want to describe to your boss flaws in the design of the store you work in. Be a customer. Walk through the door. Wait! How does the door open? Is it a pull door people always push because it has a horizontal, long handle, not a small grabber? Do you *feel* yourself jolt as the shabby door bounces—loose from the impact of opening and closing so many times? It angers people. How about the entranceway cluttered with gumball machines and a kiddie ride? The *sound* of the whirring, whumpy-whump of the horse ride and kids begging mothers for quarters. Angry mothers, worn-down mothers. Nickel–dime robbery. Now into the store. The first *sight* is the line of people and cash registers, instead of a pretty dress, glittering jewelry, or the *scent* of sweet perfumes. Walk through other stores with your senses. Now you're ready to write.

For fresher description, push past the obvious with a Break Stereotypes brain teaser. Describe the obvious, and then puncture it. Suppose you're describing the wonderful vacation cottage your family rented last year. There's the breathtaking view of lake and mountain, the Fourth of July fireworks display reflected in the water, the fish that beg to be caught, the clean, wholesome country air. Stop! Look closer! Listen harder; didn't you see trash in the stream leading to the lake? Weren't trucks hauling building supplies up that pristine mountain? Didn't motorboats roar past midnight?

Comparisons, alternative viewpoints, and **metaphors** can also stimulate your descriptive eye. If you're describing a local park, for instance, think of alternative viewpoints. Some people might only see broken glass, litter, missing basketball nets, and a rusted fence. Others might never notice the missing net, but just see dunks, layups, spins, passes, the thunk-thunk of dribbling, laughter, and sweaty drama. Yet others might see the park as it was years ago—a bandstand, people in straw hats, and a popcorn wagon. Allowing yourself to experience these other viewpoints makes you see more. We are what we see, so the more you see, the more you become, and the more powerful and alive your description will be.

■ **PRACTICE 10-3** Do a Senses brain teaser and one other brain teaser to gather sharp description for two of the following topics. Experience them for five minutes before you focus on words.
- A childhood place
- An eyesore local authorities should fix or remove
- A commercial product about which you have strong feelings
- Student housing
- The taste of an orange or other fruit

■ **PRACTICE 10-4** Use a Senses brain teaser and one other to dig up more descriptive detail for your topic from Practice 10-2.

USE THE ICEBERG PRINCIPLE

Ernest Hemingway explained his descriptive technique as "the iceberg principle." He said powerful writing only shows the tip of the iceberg, nine-tenths of which rides under water. In essence, he meant that less description is sometimes more because it can suggest more than is visible. When faced with describing a complex or huge topic, *don't feel obligated to cover everything!* You may end up with a shapeless catalog. Instead, **search for a few key details that capture the essence of the larger picture—like a camera close-up.**

The iceberg principle draws readers in close. That perspective creates surprise and drama. It also requires you **to trust your reader. By relying on a small, intimate detail, you hope the reader will infer the larger picture by actively imagining along with you.** If someone writes, "Ralph set fire to the child's kite," there's no need to add, "I think it was cruel."

Describing a red-veined, bulby nose and a sleek, powdered nose suggest quite different things about the noses' owners. Such description can carry the idea of an essay by symbolism or by representation. To describe a group, you don't have to describe every member of the group. Pick *typical* representatives. If I wrote about women in their thirties, forties, and fifties returning to college, here are two examples of "iceberg tips." Bernie, a little volcano of a woman, erupted into life after being bottled up for years. She had raised her children and, at fifty-plus, wanted to go into real estate and politics. College started her lava flowing again. She laughs at her mistakes, loves combat in class discussion, and relishes risks. Then there's Alecia, early thirties, petite, and shy under her long hair. She's afraid she'll fail, but is even more afraid of never trying. She knows something creative lives in her, but the world has squashed her before, and she hesitates to risk herself in front of 30 people. She's taking two courses, just dipping a toe into the water to see if sharks will bite.

These two examples don't capture all the problems and feelings of being an "older" woman in college, but as the tip of the iceberg, they stimulate a reader's imagination and memory. Icebergs strike more ships than watery generalities. Here's another example. While describing her mother's hands in close detail, a student reveals much of her mother's life and their relationship. Think about what the details imply:

> My mother's small, wrinkling hands have nails cut short and tough skin on the tips from playing piano all her life. Vivid blue veins branch out like a leafless winter tree and are raised as if ropes are strung through them. I love watching her little fingers jump on the keyboard. They gently whisper in my ear and scream in agony. Her soul is in her hands. She thinks her hands look old and unattractive, but since I was little, I wanted my hands to look like hers. They may seem worn and tired, but to me they are beautiful.
>
> —*Anya Gilbert*

■ **PRACTICE 10-5** Take an iceberg approach to one of these topics to describe the group to which they belong:
- "Older" men in college
- Suburban houses *or* city apartments
- Local election campaigns
- Health food stores or products
- The youngest or oldest child

■ **PRACTICE 10-6** Take an iceberg approach to your topic from Practice 10-2.

 TRY OTHER EYE-TRAINING TRICKS
- **Describe your topic as if to an audience unfamiliar with it.**
  A colleague of mine often asks his students to describe a ballpoint pen

and its use (or any other object of modern civilization) to a hermit Tibetan monk. If you imagine that your audience knows nothing, you must see freshly.

- **Think of your topic as part of a *process*—**not as a thing. A static thing invites dullness, but few things are truly static. The entire earth rockets through space a million miles per day, rotates at 1,000 miles per hour, and its crust rises and falls two feet under us each day. Everything has an origin and an end and is recycled into new life. Open your mind to see your topic as a process in time and space. A simple description of your room, then, connects to all the people who lived there before, how it came to be, and what will happen to it after you're gone. If you're writing about handling customer complaints at work, make your audience picture the process all parties go through before and after confrontations.

- **Describe what's *not* there.** A person who doesn't smile, cry, or become embarrassed may be interesting for that. The fact that my first word processor could not combine single and double spacing was a major drawback. The lack of dorms shapes atmosphere at many community colleges. Here's a brief description of scars, created through what's missing:

> When you touch your scars, they feel like they are not parts of your body. They are numb, as if that area of your body has fallen asleep. You can tell there are nerves under your scars, but, like vague memories, you can't quite reach them.
>
> —*Katy Lancaster*

■ **PRACTICE 10-7** Look closely at a small natural object, like a moth's antennae, an ant's face, or a few grains of soil. Try two of the "other" techniques to think descriptively. Pull your details together with an idea. Do the same for some *overlooked* part of your anatomy.

■ **PRACTICE 10-8** Use one of the "other" techniques to dig up more description for your topic from Practice 10-2.

Revising for Vivid Description

To this point I've suggested ways to think descriptively. Now, here are a few tips to sharpen description when you revise wording. Be open to change. *All* words describe; we want your description to move from shadowy first-draft description to the kind you can rap your knuckles against. You want your readers to *see* your subject, not just hear *about* it.

THE SENSE TEST

Ask if your descriptive passages pass the sense test—**can you see, smell, taste, touch, or hear something in every passage?**

> **Example:** The accounting procedure is awkward to use.
> **Revised:** The procedure requires flipping back and forth among three pages.

"Awkward" is an abstract word we understand intellectually, but it cannot be experienced by readers' senses. "Flipping back and forth" suggests awkwardness and helps readers experience the procedure more fully, with sound, sight, and touch.

> **Example:** The tenement smelled dirty and rotten.
> **Revised:** The tenement smelled like mildewed shoes.
> *Or*
> The tenement smelled of urine and stale beer.

The revisions create different images, but both are sharp. "Dirty" and "rotten" are not sense oriented.

THE SPECIFICITY TEST

In revising, ask if existing description can be more specific. Test your honesty—**how concrete and exact can you be?** The broader a description is, the vaguer it reads; the narrower it is, the sharper. Try *several* options for unspecific words before deciding.

> **Example:** Heather walked into the room.

Specify the word "room" as "lecture hall," "kitchen," or "men's room" and the sentence focuses instantly. Also specify "walk" as "strutted," "dashed," or "limped" and the sentence leaps at readers.

> **Example:** Ordinary household lawn chemicals cause harmful side effects on a human being's health, including respiratory, skin, and neurological problems. They also can seriously pollute and deteriorate the quality of nearby watersheds.

Here's how a student made this topic more specific and tangible:

> Lawn chemicals cause headaches, runny noses, rashes, and nausea. Other symptoms may include vomiting, heavy sweating, dizziness,

and disorientation. Their nitrogen seeps into groundwater, ending up in streams and ponds. This causes algae buildup, reduction of oxygen, and, eventually, dead water.

—Jeanette Crouse

Specificity names names. Change "car" to "Lexus" or "Mazda" and change "candy" to "M&Ms" or "Peppermint Pattie" to help your writing jump into a reader's eyes.

Specificity enhances your meaning as well as visual appeal. Scan these two phrases:

- A beggar with a cup.
- A beggar with a Burger King cup.

Why describe the cup? It visualizes, but also pinches us with the contrast of "king" and "beggar." Pounce on description that carries meaning as well as visual appeal. Don't describe just for more words.

■ **PRACTICE 10-9** In the following sentences, first mark words that could be more specific or appeal to our senses and then suggest three alternatives for each. Don't limit yourself to one-word replacements.
- Bill ate his lunch noisily.
- The union leadership called for a protest.
- The summer breeze off the water is lovely at night.

■ **PRACTICE 10-10** Revise one of your practice writings on your own topic by applying the sense or specificity test.

THE FRESHNESS TEST

For fresher description:

- **Replace clichés with original expressions.** (See Chapter 8.)

   Cliché: The 100-foot canyon walls stood over us.
   Fresher: The canyon thrust out its 100-foot chest.

- **Create a metaphor to improve dull description.**

   Example: He had scary eyes.
   Revised: He had eyes like half-peeled grapes.

- **Cut flat details.** If you can't improve a dull spot, leave it out—see if anything's really lost. If you wanted to sell a head of lettuce, would you leave on the brown, wilted leaves?

- **Do a mini-brain teaser for weak descriptions.** Freewrite until something vivid emerges. Select the best for the revised description.

■ **PRACTICE 10-11** *Create a fresh metaphor for two of these sentences:*
- The funeral parlor was so quiet.
- She looked angrily into the car at her boyfriend and Marsha.
- The old alcoholic fell down the railroad embankment.

THE THEME TEST

You may not have a clear theme when you begin a descriptive essay, but in revising, be sure you do. Beautiful description without a purpose is like a glittering speedboat without an engine or a whiz-bang laptop without a battery. Themes make description move and live. **Read through your draft one more time to ask if each descriptive detail helps point to one central concept.** If not, consider cutting the irrelevant details and build on those that support your theme.

■ **PRACTICE 10-12** In a short paragraph, describe the food you hate the most. Strive for vividness and creative detail, but also work toward a theme beyond "I hate this stuff." How is the food symbolic of some other issue?

VISUAL RHETORIC

To develop your descriptive eye, study the three pictures that follow. Look for the basic elements of visual rhetoric (ideas/theme, details, structure, transitions and audience), but focus especially on these descriptive techniques: iceberging, what's not described, process, breaking stereotypes, metaphors, contrast, and freshness of viewpoint.

■ **PRACTICE 10-13** Where do you see the iceberg technique, brain teasers, what's *not* there or process used to describe? Finally, evaluate how good the pictures are at creating a *vivid* moment with a strong *feel*. Try to explain why.

Tim Flach/Stone/Getty Images

Peter Hoist/The Image Bank/Getty Images

Heinle/Cengage Learning

Writing Suggestions and Class Discussions

1. Write one long descriptive sentence about the greatest meal you ever ate, your favorite childhood toy, or your favorite piece of clothing. Use as many senses as you can. Pack in details but without making it sound like a list.

2. Write your own abstract, dictionary-like definition of love, hate, or madness. In a separate paragraph, *show* the definition in action. Experience an incident or example. Use picture words, no abstractions.

3. Describe the youngest person you know who is pregnant, homeless, on drugs, in college, dead, or rich.

4. Describe a hospital room. Find four *overlooked* details that, like the tip of an iceberg, represent the hospital experience.

5. Bring a music recording, photograph, or reproduction of an art work to class. Before playing or showing it, read aloud a one-paragraph description you wrote of it.

6. Blind writers like Homer, Jose Luis Borges, John Milton, and Helen Keller rely on other senses. Sit in an unfamiliar setting like a bus stop or mall, close your eyes, and *experience* only through your other senses. Spend 15 to 20 minutes. Then write a vivid description. Show, don't tell.

7. Describe a technical process you know better than most people (enhancing digital photographs or replacing a car's brakes, for example). Describe this process clearly for a reader with average knowledge.

8. Describe a common object like a button, key, scar, or can opener. Discover details others might overlook. Write one paragraph.

9. **Descriptive Challenge:** Describe three of these:
   - The sound of an engine stalling
   - The way your feet feel standing in the surf
   - The sound of a dog shaking water off itself
   - Eating a submarine sandwich
   - The face of a famous person (as if telling a blind person)
   - The smell of turpentine, mushrooms, or rain
   - A soap bubble

10. **I Spy Assignment:** To develop your descriptive eye, *discreetly* observe a stranger for 10 minutes, learning all you can. Study clothes, habits, quirks, speech patterns, as well as physical features. Write several paragraphs. **Warnings:** Don't intrude on the person, and do this in a public place. One student of a colleague of mine got carried away (literally!) when he hotly followed his subject for an hour, and the man turned out to be a detective who arrested him and phoned the professor to verify the "weird alibi."

11. Write a descriptive paper on a place. Vivid detail should support a theme or idea. Write two to three pages. **Visual rhetoric option:** Include a photograph of the place with your paper. Think about how to make the picture's idea, details, structure and style add to your verbal description.

12. Describe a group you belong to—a company, church, club, team, or clique. Describe it vividly and develop a theme.

13. Peer groups will reexperience an area of the college: bookstore, library, or cafeteria, for example. Dig up creative, vivid descriptions, not through fancy words but by discovering sharp details. The groups will spend part of the period observing and writing, then reassemble to share their notes. Strive to find overlooked details. **Visual rhetoric option:** Include a photograph of the location.

14. Describe your worst fear in bone-chilling, graphic detail. Scare yourself!

15. **Visual rhetoric:** Create a poster for your favorite sports team, club, church or other group. Mix visuals with words. Try to create excitement and interest, but do not use a hard sell.

16. Write an entry for your blog about the latest popular clothes style among your age group, or about how collecting unemployment or

welfare affects someone you know. Describe concretely with facts and specific details until the end. Then suggest what message your description implies. Invite readers to react.

STUDENT ESSAY AND ANALYSIS

The Model
Nell Kuitems

As I hurry toward the brick building, I am the only one who isn't carrying a large black portfolio bag. The wind is cold and bitter, stings my skin through layers of sweat pants and coat. I wave hello to a few students struggling against the ripping wind. I will see them in class, but I am not a student, and I am not the teacher. I am the subject studied—their model for figure drawing class, where they study the body in its natural, naked form.

As we enter the room, the lights are off except for two spotlights that shine on a platform in the center. The platform is covered with "paint-spattered" drop cloths, and a humming space heater blows hot air across them. This is my stage. But for now I wait in the corner while the students line up at their easels and pull out large, crisp sheets of white paper, charcoals and pencils. The professor enters, shuts the door and locks it so prying eyes don't wander where they don't belong.

I open my bag and pull out my dark green blanket, then slip off my shoes and socks. When the professor nods, I doff my shirt and bra, then my remaining clothing. My skin leaps into goose bumps, and I wrap myself into the rough blanket. I wander from my corner through the students toward the platform where the professor waits. He offers a gentlemanly hand to help me step up; as I take it, the blanket slips from my shoulder, exposing my right breast. Oh, well. It's too late to think of hiding myself now. Off comes the blanket, and I spread it and sit, fully exposed.

I glance at the professor, and he nods again, so I create a position for my body. I lie on my right side, legs bent back so my feet nearly touch my butt. My head rests on my right arm, which is bent into a pillow. I tuck my chin close to my chest, hiding my face. My left upper arm molds against my body, then bends at elbow to rest under my breasts. I will have to stay in this position for the next hour

→

and then find it again perfectly after I take my stretch break, so I make mental notes of where all my parts are.

Students wander the room studying me from different angles, seeking new curves and shapes. Do they want me from the back, front or side? Top down or bottom up? They study me as they would a ripe bowl of oranges. I have lost all control; I am only an object to be studied. But when they look at me, I wonder if they think about how the glow of my skin changes the closer it is to the heater. My feet and butt must be red with warmth. Do they notice how my breasts are white and taut, my nipples hard when they pass by on the cold side and create a breeze? What do they see when they study me?

Oh, yes. I watch them back. I see their looks of fierce concentration, eyebrows bent together, lips pulled taut, eyes darting to find every one of my hidden details. I would love to be able to transfer my body to canvas, but I can't. Maybe this is why I lend them my body, to let someone with talent do what I cannot. I am not embarrassed any more—not in the usual sense a naked woman would be. They see me every day. Yet little worries nag me. Do they see the mud under my thumbnail? Do they see the bright red, pulsing zit on my back? Out of these imperfections, they must find beauty. This is why I choose to display myself.

I fall asleep, waking at the end of class when someone tickles my feet. I reach out, pull the rough blanket around me, and stretch away the stiffness. I rise, return to my corner, pull on my clothes and become a person again. The professor unlocks the door, and I am through with work. But before everyone packs up, I hurry around the room to take in what they have drawn, proud of the magic created. I devour their work with my eyes, then leave quietly with everyone else.

Outside, the bitter wind nips at my face, but I don't feel it. I am still warm from the space heater and something else. As I wander through the cold, I wonder what form my body will take next time.

ANALYSIS BASED ON PEER REVIEW CHECKLIST

What point does the essay make? It seems to be about exposure and the mystery of how nakedness becomes art. She knows she's "giving" herself to them and the essay ultimately decides such exposure is not a humiliation, but a transformation. Art changes her imperfections into beauty. An intriguing theme on an unusual topic.

Are there any symbolic messages here? Yes. The author uses the iceberg principle in comparing herself to a bowl of oranges, evoking the whole world of art. The interplay between cold and heat, outside and inside suggest the conflict between two ways of seeing yourself—as art and as a person. The locked door suggests the boundary line must be carefully established. Hiding her face in her pose symbolizes hiding as a person while being exposed as an object of art.

Organization? It moves through time, but it's more like a "slice of life" from a typical day on the job than a true narrative. She starts out in the cold, moves behind the locked door to the heat (but still has one cold side to her), then back to the cold. The organization beautifully reinforces the message.

Give the essay the sense test. The best descriptive details are almost exclusively visual and tactile sensations (temperature, body placement, the tickle, the professor's hand, the zit). I wonder if there could have been some sounds—scratching charcoal, rustling paper, people's comments— but I have mixed feelings about whether she ought to have included this. Her essay has a very self-enclosed feel to it, and that may be right for the emotion she wants to convey.

Where can it be more specific? I'd ask the author to consider doing a bit more describing the drawings the students did of her. I wanted to see how they interpreted her (fatter, prettier, shyer than she thinks she is?) and her reaction to the art. That would complete the theme by making her see her "real" self differently through art.

Where can the description be fresher? The zit was a great, tiny detail, especially the use of "pulsing," which conveys several senses in one word. I think she might have described the cold wind sensation better. "Bitter" and "nips" are okay, but not creative. She uses "wander" four times and "taut" twice. Both are strongly visual, but lose punch with repetition. Normally, using a word twice is no problem, but "taut" appears again within three lines to describe something else. This essay nicely combines an idea with details; the language is direct, not strained by false, picturesque words.

SAMPLE STUDENT DESCRIPTIVE ESSAY FOR ANALYSIS

Simple Life
Debbie Geen

It's a cool, brisk day in November when the air bites your skin. The sun is out, but the sky looks gray and confused as if it might rain,

→

but the air smells of snow. The vegetables have been picked, and everything worth harvesting is already canned or stored. Potatoes and apples, packed neatly in their wooden crates, fill the root cellar.

All that is left are the meat chickens—Cornish-Rock Giants—that had been growing fat for the last eight weeks. Now they're a plump cooking weight—four to five pounds. The process starts when we collect eggs from the nests and bring them into the house where we keep the incubator. An insulated electric heating coil runs through the inside of the unit to maintain a 99.5 degree temperature. A small dish of water inside keeps the humidity up. An acorn-shaped 15-watt light bulb gives just enough light to see that the incubator is working. Thirty to forty eggs are placed on a tray with a screen bottom and wooden dowels keep the eggs in rows. We pull the tray out to turn the eggs a minimum of four times a day to ensure that the embryos develop correctly. After all, a mother hen turns her eggs in the nest 90–95 times in one day.

After 21 days of this careful attention, a faint peeping announces that the chicks are pecking themselves free. They wear bright, inno-cent yellow fur that doesn't really resemble feathers yet and are so damp that they stick to your palms.

Once dry and able to stand, they're all put in the chicken house to gain weight. They need to eat constantly to gain weight fast. A timed light in their house turns on every four hours to wake them to eat. Little do they know what part the constant gorging will play in their fate.

A short eight weeks later, it's time. My Dad stokes up a fire to boil water. The fire crackles, the black smoke twisting and rising toward the clouds. It's chilly and feels good to warm your hands by the flames. Dad made his own cooking pot from a 55-gallon metal drum which he places on top of the fire. A spoonful of dish deter-gent added to the water helps penetrate the chickens' natural oils so the hot water can loosen the feathers. This homemade cauldron holds twenty gallons, and once it boils, we head for the chickens.

To capture chickens, we use a four-foot wooden handle with a metal hook on the end. The hook's just big enough to get around the birds' legs and small enough so their feet can't slip out. This is the only way to catch them once the fear sets in—and it always does. The first few are naïve and easy to grab. After the rest smell blood, they squawk and fly wildly, running each other over and scrabbling into walls to escape. Sometimes half their feathers fall off.

→

Not wanting to waste time, my parents catch two chickens at a time and carry them behind the woodshed. There it is, the old, tattered ash stump, about two feet high and nearly as wide. Since ash is hard wood, it lasts many years and shows signs of the work done on it. Old feathers, dried blood and chips of missing wood tell its story. A rusty nail protrudes from one side. Dangling from it are pieces of old baling twine, some shredded from being accidentally chopped during the beheadings. But one intact piece is looped at the exact length so the chicken's neck will be held in the middle of the stump.

Since two chickens are caught, Dad holds one between his knees, seizes the other by its clawed feet, and slips the noose over its head. By pulling on the scaly legs, the neck is stretched out and centered on the stump. Dad swings his trusty hatchet—freshly sharpened—straight down. With a "whack," the blade cuts through and embeds itself in the stump. The lifeless head falls, the beak opening and closing a few times as if trying to get a final gasp of air. The beheaded body is cast aside as Dad positions the next victim on the stump. These headless bodies sometimes run around for two minutes, as if they don't know they're dead and don't know which way to go first. Sometimes headless chickens even lift themselves off the ground as if to fly away before lying down for good. Chickens are the only bird granted this final run. Larger birds like geese are hung from the tree by their webbed feet to bleed out.

The chicken bodies are now dunked in the boiling water for thirty seconds to loosen the feathers. Then we pluck, gut, and carry them into the house for their final preparation. After a thorough cleaning, we seal them in plastic bags and lay them to rest in the freezer. And we're ready for another day of simple farm life.

Discussion/Writing

Write an evaluation of "Simple Life" as if you were reviewing it for class, using the "Peer Review Checklist for Description" as your guide.

☑ Peer Review Checklist for Description

Author: _____

Reviewer: _____

Answer the questions as specifically as possible and discuss the essay with the author.

Ideas: What is the essay's thesis or main point?

What symbolism does the description suggest to you? Explain.

Organization: Describe this essay's organization. Highlight the main pattern, don't evaluate.

Would the essay be improved by rearranging, combining, or cutting some sections? Which? Why? Is anything important missing?

Descriptive Details: Give this essay The Sense Test. Where does it do the best, where poorly?

Which section(s) could be more specific? What are the most specific details?

Find a place where the description could be fresher.

Narration

Telling your Audience a Story

11

THE EARLIEST WRITERS IN EVERY CIVILIZATION HAVE told stories to convey their messages. Homer's tales of Cyclops, the one-eyed monster, and Circe, whose spells transformed humans into animals, not only entertained but informed and persuaded the ancient Greeks about geography, the gods, and humanity's place in the universe. The ancient myth of Sisyphus, for example, tells of a greedy king who is condemned in Hell to roll a huge boulder to the top of a hill. Just before Sisyphus reaches the peak, the gods make the boulder roll back down, and Sisyphus must start all over again. Up and down the hill he chases the rock for all time. Over the centuries the story has been a parable about the empty lives of the greedy and also about the futility of much human effort.

Jesus frequently told stories to convey his message. "The Good Samaritan" and "The Prodigal Son" seem to stick in our minds much better than, say, a typical sermon on charity. When Jesus told a crowd, "Love thy neighbor," a lawyer asked, "Who is my neighbor?" Jesus, realizing the man wanted to put a limit on whom he was required to love, did not answer directly. Instead he told the story of a man beaten and robbed by thieves in his own country. The victim's neighbors, a priest and local official, walked by without helping. Then a Samaritan, a stranger in the victim's country, stopped, washed the man's wounds, took him to an inn, and paid for his lodging. When Jesus finished, the lawyer knew the

God made man because He loves stories.

—ELIE WIESEL

Real suspense comes from moral dilemma and the courage to make and act upon choices.

—JOHN GARDNER

I want a movie that starts with an earthquake and works up to a climax.

—SAMUEL GOLDWYN

meaning of the word "neighbor," not from definition, but from the actions in the story.

Why have these stories lasted so long? Because stories are more visual, more easily remembered than abstractions. When we recall Sisyphus groaning behind his boulder or the "good" men passing the injured man before the Samaritan stops to help, the writer's abstract message flows along with the story.

Successful speakers know that telling a vivid story can be more effective than facts alone. People view a storyteller as creative and smart, as one who commands attention with powerful images.

Conflict

The heart of a good story is conflict: forces in tension with each other. The four common types are person versus person, person versus society, person versus nature, and person versus self. A saleswoman struggling against an employer who cheats clients is person versus person; a social worker battling the city to hire more disabled people is person versus society; a young man struggling to find the ski lodge after a sudden squall separates him from the group is person versus nature; a woman trying to decide whether she should have an abortion is person versus self.

■ **PRACTICE 11-1** Take a moment now to recall examples from your own life to illustrate each of these conflicts. One of them may become your next paper. I will refer to this "practice" during the rest of this chapter. Write a few lines for each.
- You vs. another person
- You vs. society
- You vs. nature
- You vs. yourself

Let's look closer at what makes a good conflict and why it helps your story absorb readers' attention. First, only real sparks make real fires. **Conflicts that don't deeply affect us won't make strong stories.** A story about a mother forbidding her daughter to date a certain boy does not sound very promising, no matter how it upset the writer. However, if the daughter learns that her mother has deeper motives—if, for instance, the boy reminds the mother of a boy who jilted her or of one she always wished she married instead of the daughter's father—then we have more hope for this conflict. Or perhaps we will discover the mother is envious of the daughter's social success. Or perhaps the daughter is dating a wild boy because she doesn't like the relationship her parents have. Here we have something more meaningful. **The best conflicts draw out some deeper significance in the characters or the action.** If a conflict in your life really stirred you, there's probably more to it under the surface. Peek under the rug.

Readers want conflict so they can care about the outcome, so they can cheer and fear and doubt with the narrator. They also want conflicts *difficult* to solve. Wrong versus right or strong versus weak doesn't grip readers as much as conflicts in which wrong and right are murky or in which the forces opposed are equal.

Our lives are full of both inner and outer conflicts. Here are three almost sure ways to find a strong conflict to write about.

Think about the most intense turning points in your life. These have changed not only the *outer* course of your life but the *inner* course as well by developing your philosophy or identity. Readers want a story to matter to the writer, or it won't matter to them. For this reason it is sometimes harder to write about a personal triumph—winning the big race or election—than about a defeat or a tragedy. Winning tends to keep our beliefs intact; often we learn more in losing. However, I can recall an excellent story a student wrote about winning a state wrestling match, because in his moment of triumph he stared into the eyes of the slumped man he'd defeated. Nor do big tragedies necessarily mean a person has grown. As Isaac Bashevis Singer said, "A wise man gets wiser by suffering. A person without wisdom may suffer 100 years and die a fool." **The moments that make us grow, that tear away the predictable boundaries of our lives, are the ones that make good papers**.

One of my students, a woman who worked at a chemical dependency center, wrote about her conflict with her brother, who was a cocaine addict. Despite what she knew from dealing with addicts, she allowed him to "violate" her with a "merry-go-round of anger, shame, guilt, and fear." Her turning point occurred when she realized that she was "addicted to an addict," that she was "a codependent" even though she never used drugs, because she supported and cared for her brother. Her emotional investment was destroying her, and she learned to let go—to stop feeling responsible for where he was at night, whom he was with, what was happening to his body and mind. She still took him for treatment, but she learned she had to break her own emotional addiction.

Are there moments from your life that are too intense to write about? Sure. If you write a paragraph or two and find you really hate dealing with this material, it may be too fresh to see clearly or too raw a wound to reopen. But give it a few paragraphs to see. You may find that something you thought you didn't want to deal with really sets your mind seething with powerful ideas and images. If it wants to pour out of you, keep going.

■ **PRACTICE 11-2** List three turning points that changed your outlook on life.

Look for good conflicts by thinking about an interesting person you've known: the resident rebel in family or town, the eccentric uncle, the homeless woman who hangs around campus, the "respectable" neighbor who abuses his children. You may be personally involved if you take sides with or against the rebel. You may debate whether to notify the authorities to help the homeless woman. Or, as an honest, intense observer, you may simply report the conflict you see. People who climb outside norms have built-in conflict. Your own rebellions may make good stories too.

■ **PRACTICE 11-3** Describe one of the most interesting people you've known and sketch out a conflict that focuses on this person.

Use classic themes of conflict. Certain topics have gripped readers' imaginations for 3,000 years because they touch the heart of our humanity. **Facing death, rebelling against parents or social taboos, discovering your real identity, or initiation into the adult world of religion, sex, or war are irresistible to writers and readers alike.** You can find all these conflicts in ancient Greek literature, in Shakespeare, and in the hottest book or film just out. A more specific focus like forbidden love, as in *Oedipus, Romeo and Juliet, and The Liar's Club,* may draw on all four themes.

How does this help you? Well, suppose you're exploring a conflict about child abuse in your family for a narrative essay. You can deepen the potential of such a story by going beyond the fear and physical danger—connect it to rebellion, taboo, identity, and initiation themes. If little Joel is beaten regularly for spilling his milk, how does that connect to his teenage rebellion (or lack of rebellion), to his willingness to engage in other taboo acts, to his sense of who he is, and to his sense of what being an adult means? If you're just trying to describe what happened exactly as you remember it, you'll be missing the real purpose of writing a narrative essay, which is to learn more now than you knew when you were experiencing or watching the story unfold in real life.

■ **PRACTICE 11-4** Which of your topics from Practice 11-1 could be shaped into a classical conflict? Explain.

Brain teasers can suggest conflicts for narrative essays. A **bug**
list will surely turn up conflict in your life. You can do a general one first and then pursue the one that most intrigues you. Dig out the depth of your dissatisfaction. The **alternate viewpoints** brain teaser can also help you tell an honest story. Look at the story you're considering from the viewpoint of the other people involved to discover your weaknesses and their strengths. This allows you to make *real* opponents in the story, not just cardboard cutouts. Because a major aspect of storytelling is making readers visualize the story, sense brain teasers will stimulate your imagination.

■ **PRACTICE 11-5** Use a bug list, alternate viewpoints, or sense brain teaser to create more notes for one of the stories you sketched in Practice 11-1, 11-2, or 11-3.

Complication

After finding a powerful conflict, you must make it grow more complicated as the story continues. The novelist E. M. Forster said he always imagined one of his readers to be a person who only wanted to be surprised by new twists, new angles, new insights in each paragraph. **If the story stagnates, it's usually because it has ceased to convey new information.** This does not mean you must have continuous earthquakes and car crashes. **Moving forward can be a matter of mental twists**
and insights:

> The new doctor doesn't seem to care about my infected ear. He makes me do all the talking, stares at me when he thinks I'm not looking. Is he nervous? His hand seems to shake a lot. Is that booze I smell on his breath? Or just medicines? He leaves the room and returns after a long time. Maybe I have some horrible sickness and he's afraid to tell me. He even sends the nurse in to tell me I can go.
>
> When I pay the receptionist and get my prescription, I notice a photograph of the doctor and a girl who looks like me—we could be sisters. "His daughter died last month," the receptionist whispers.

What gives this little story some life is not the surprise ending—that's always too late to interest the reader. What gets it going is the initial conflict—the doctor doesn't like the narrator (person versus person)—and what keeps it going are the competing explanations that flash through the narrator's mind; each complicates the story. Without *them,* the ending would have been flat.

 Creating complex conflict often means discovering competing ideas in yourself. At each turn in your essay, ask if you really felt 100 percent as you wrote. The spots where you waver or doubt need to be in the essay to lead the reader through your honest decision making. Making choices creates conflict and reveals your character and theme. Stories in which things happen *to* a passive narrator lack this element. We *are* often victims of fate, accidents, and bad luck, but **the key moments in our** **lives are the ones we can do something about, the ones in which we choose our destiny.** This is what John Gardner meant in the opening quote to this chapter.

I once had a student, Bill, who was in his late forties. He wrote a gruesome narrative about what happened to his wife when they decided to commit her temporarily to a mental hospital. Once Bill's wife was signed in, the authorities could keep her there until *they* thought she was cured. They began chemical and electric shock treatments that hurt and scared Bill's wife. She begged to be released. Bill began to doubt her and believe the medical authorities that she was far gone because each time he visited her she was wilder, more rumpled, more "crazy looking." Some friends and family even told Bill to "detach" himself from his wife. But something deeper in the relationship drew him back. He believed the authorities were more disturbed than his wife, and he eventually fought in court to release her.

This powerful conflict has a number of twists that keep a reader involved. The most interesting is the inner conflict in Bill—whether to believe "sane experts" or the "crazy" wife he loves. The only major flaw in Bill's rough draft was his portrayal of the orderlies and nurses as snarling sadists with dripping fangs. It's easy to see why Bill felt this way, but he portrayed them in descriptions and dialogue that were too exaggerated. *He projected his feelings for them instead of seeing them as they were.* We worked together using alternative viewpoints and discovered the "enemy" was not cruelty, but indifference. Most employees simply wanted to slide through tough workdays a little easier. People like Bill and his poor wife who asked questions were "troublemakers." The workers were not devils, but people who'd grown calluses over their feelings. Bill didn't release them from their responsibility for his wife's pain, but in looking closer at the orderlies and nurses, Bill discovered the real problem in his wife's mental health care. He believed the employees inflicted pain on patients like his wife to make them act more deranged and therefore less human. If they could feel they were dealing with crazy people, it made their disturbing job easier. It's a powerful, honest insight because it's not oversimplified. The lesson: **be skeptical of any angels or devils you create.**

■ **PRACTICE 11-6** Using one of your practice notes in this chapter, list some complications in the conflict.

■ **PRACTICE 11-7** Under each complication in 11-6, list details—events, dialogue, description—you might use to tell that part of the story.

How to Ruin a Story

Teachers and textbooks don't advise students how to mess up; however, if you're interested in ruining a story, here are three ways to do it. First, **give a lot of background in the opening.** If you're going to tell the story of your great fishing adventure, start the story with getting ready the night before, your restless sleep, waking, breakfast, packing the car, driving to the dock, and casting off. This is boring in one sentence. Imagine how boring it can be stretched out to a full page! If you want an exciting start, begin the essay like this: "I was rebaiting my hook when I realized that a squall had just blocked off the sun and was heading straight for our boat." Or start when your buddy spills the lantern fuel into the campfire. If the story is about meeting a wonderful person during a vacation, start with the moment the wonderful person bumps into you with his cotton candy and tangles it in your hair. *Don't* start with packing, travel, unpacking, and setting up on the beach.

The Romans used the expression *in medias res* (in the middle begin) to describe starting where real conflict begins. **Have your characters** **begin in motion, not preparing to move.** Do this and you'll be surprised how busy you'll be telling the real story and how little time you need spend on that story killer—background.

Here are some openings from student papers that hook a reader:

> I was hunched over my crying baby brother when I heard Joe's footsteps behind me. "He fell," I tried to explain, "he was on the bed but he rolled and I . . . I . . . ." Pain shot through my spine like a freight train had burst through the floor straight into my rear end. As he cocked his boot again, my mother dashed into the room and screamed.
>
> —*Raquel E. Torres*

Night falls by the time we reach the inn. The crisp, country air, ten degrees colder than the city, makes us shiver. Moths flutter around the lanterns that light our passage, and the only sound is the crunching of gravel beneath our feet. Sumie hurries ahead, sliding open the heavy wooden door.

—*Bernadette Verrone*

She was gone—again. I watched her red Trans Am disappear up the gradual grade, then turned to see my bus round the corner, creeping toward me like a bug in the cool, moist dawn. The breeze was cold, and faraway thunder drummed summer out of service. The bus groaned to a halt in a diesel haze. The driver opened the door, and I was sucked off the street.

—*James Babcock*

All three start with something happening. The first uses dialogue and action, the second mystery, the third symbolic description.

A second way to ruin a story is to give away the ending. If the following sentence began a story, you wouldn't want to read the rest: "Little did I know the first time Bob approached me after class to borrow a pen that in seven months we'd be married." It's dramatic but kills the rest of the story. Compare that to this opening: "There was absolutely nothing special about Bob that first day he approached me after class to borrow a pen. I would have completely forgotten him except the next day he handed me a dozen pens with a bow around them. Now I've got a nerd after me, I thought." The second version lets us know something is going to happen, but not what.

Giving away the ending applies not only to events, but to the theme. Good readers enjoy figuring out the significance of the events, and an opening sentence like the following can ruin that: "I don't know if I'll ever marry again, but if I do I'll put my wife ahead of my friends." **The writer of narratives must tease readers a bit, give them new events and ideas and also leave them a bit unsatisfied so they'll keep reading.**

Another way to ruin a reader's enjoyment is to summarize events. Don't bother with details—just cover big chunks of the story in a few words. Now it may seem like you can tell a bigger story by summarizing, but what you're really doing is denying readers the pleasure of watching events unfold in front of them—smelling the air, hearing what the people say, and figuring out how events will turn out. When you summarize, it's like someone rushing from the window to tell about the exciting events happening outside instead of letting you look for yourself.

So how do you make a reader feel "there"? Through scenes and moments seen up close. This means you probably shouldn't write about three years of your life, about your entire football season, or about your entire relationship with a friend. Pick one sunset, one encounter on the team bus, one hour in the hospital's cancer ward. That will **give us the rich detail of the moment.** That's how we live—one moment at a time, and nearly all of them lost as they pass. After they're gone, we put a label on them—a summary. *Summary says,* "Working as a painter of dorm rooms made a lousy, sweltering summer." It may be true, but *the real-life moment says,* "The sweat dripped off my nose and into the paint can as I followed Paul Kratzberg's massive, paint-encrusted butt around dorm rooms." *Summary says,* "Grandma shot down my plan." *The real moment says,* "Grandma told me, 'I never figured someone with my DNA could be so stupid.'"

■ **PRACTICE 11-8** Pick two potential places to begin one narrative conflict you developed earlier in this chapter. Which place seems best and why?

Describing People

If conflict is the heart of a narrative, its body is the characters—the physical presence that moves the conflict. This is where your description must be sharpest. We tend to make people in our stories reflect our own ideas, habits, and values instead of presenting them as *they* are. Using an alternate viewpoint brain teaser is the best way to overcome this. **Give each main character—*especially those with whom you disagree*—a few minutes of rough notes. Think as they do. See as they see.** What motivates them? What do they care about? This is essential for *honest, vivid conflict.* If you've been cheated by a salesperson, you must try to convey what she believes, perhaps her anxiousness to succeed, or she will sound fake.

   Besides understanding how your characters think, you must help the reader *see* **them.** These create a picture of a person in words:

- Physical description
- Habits
- The way they talk
- Their possessions
- What others say about them
- Gestures

The man who empties an ashtray three times during an evening communicates character through this **habit.** If he also picks threads from his sleeve and rearranges the couch pillow continually, his character will be dominated by neatness in a reader's eyes. **Gestures**—like poking a listener with a forefinger while speaking, or wrapping a sweaty arm around your shoulder—also create character. In preparing to write about people, **use the preceding list as a brain teaser,** making a list of details for each item.

How do you know which details to actually include in the draft? Let's take **physical description** as an example. Factual description adds detail, but rarely lights up a page: "Gregory Bates has brown hair and brown eyes and is 5′ 10″ tall and weighs 165 pounds." These details do not bring Mr. Bates to life; they should stay on the brain teaser page. A reader *assumes* a person is of average build unless told otherwise. Brown hair and eyes are so common they only narrow Bates down to several billion people. Instead, **search for and choose unique, distinguishing details:** Bates's Mohawk haircut, tongue stud, the wart on his neck, his gangly arms. The reader will automatically fill in the rest as "average."

Here's another trick to describe people: You want not just the unique features of the person but also those details that convey *more* than simple description. **When choosing details from your brain teaser lists, pick ones that suggest deeper aspects of the person, ones that capture personality or beliefs.**

Take eyes as an example. No other part of the human body is described so often. Yet "the windows of the soul" attract more flies than fresh air, more clichés than fresh description. Soft, brown eyes, sky-blue eyes, and sparkling eyes are dead eyes. A writer needs to find a twist: cow-brown eyes or eyes sparkling like rusty razors. Or are those eyes dung brown, chocolate brown, peanut-butter brown, sooty, muddy, or walnut? Make a list of all the kinds of brown you can think of and then choose the best one for your person's eyes. This will give the reader something specific for *better visualization*. It will also *convey more of the person's character*. Muddy eyes, for example, suggest vagueness, confusion, or even dirtiness of the personality. All of these browns are equally suggestive.

■ **PRACTICE 11-9** What do these descriptors say about the person?

- Lizard-green eyes
- Moss-green eyes
- Faded-green eyes
- Cash-green eyes

■ **PRACTICE 11-10** Take a moment to list several vivid substitutes for these bland descriptions:

• Sparkling teeth
• Rosy cheeks
• Dark hair

Possessions reveal character because they represent choices we make. True, most of us own many things unthinkingly—toothbrushes, pens, underwear. But our unique possessions represent conscious choice— the 20 boxes of baseball cards or chest of grandmother's lace doilies, the pink flamingo or religious shrine in our front yard, the Harley or Kia in our driveway. **Gestures, habits, and what others say about some- one also reveal character. A one-page brain teaser listing details should result in plenty to bring a person to life in words.** If you can't fill a page of notes, you don't know enough about the person to write him or her into the story.

■ **PRACTICE 11-11** Write a descriptive brain teaser for one person in the story you've been developing during this chapter.

■ **PRACTICE 11-12** Here's part of a student's narrative essay that describes a person. As you read, mark the six descriptive techniques and look for unique details that also symbolize Lish's personality or beliefs.

STUDENT ESSAY

The Red Heart
Lisa Neal

I first saw Lish the first day of classes my freshman year at Fredonia. Her parents dumped her at the back door of the brick dormitory like a bag of garbage and then roared off in a black Cadillac.

I was shocked that the left side of her head was shaved and dis- played a small tattoo of a black heart. Her hair on the other side was carrot colored and braided like an Indian squaw's. With her head held high, she sauntered in with two leopard skin bags.

Her arrival sent shock waves throughout the dorm. I'm not sure if Lish felt the rocky movement or just ignored it, for minutes after ar- riving she invaded the bathroom with an old green toothbrush with

→

yellowed bristles and a worn box of Arm and Hammer Baking Soda. I was dismayed she was living in the single room across the hall from me. She left her door wide open as she unpacked her sparse belongings, which included posters of puppies and a Paddington Bear with matted fur and a tattered blue coat. Her night table and dresser were left empty except for a glass incense candle and a fluorescent pink tape recorder.

As the days passed, I deliberately ignored Lish, but her presence oozed under my closed door, and I soon watched her with the curiosity of a child at the circus. At first, though, I only noticed her hair changing from carrot to watermelon pink, the way she dragged hard on her Virginia Slims cigarettes, and the addition of an earring in her nose.

Her parents whizzed in once more that semester, this time in a gray Rolls Royce, to bring her winter clothes. For the fifteen minutes they stayed, the entire hall was pierced by yelling. I heard a few snatches of her father's growled words, calling Lish a "humiliation" and a "disgrace to the family." Her mother whined how Lish should be more like her older sister who was going to become a "respectable and wealthy lawyer" instead of a social worker. The barrage of voices ceased with the sound of shattering glass, and her parents burst out of the room like two tourists fleeing a bear's cave. After a few moments, Lish emerged wearing her usual crooked smile. I was amazed! I would have been in tears. The only reminder that her parents had come was the disappearance of the incense candleholder—reduced to glass shards—and the lingering stench of Macy's perfume.

The next night, while I lay on my pink comforter watching *The Cosby Show* re-runs, my phone buzzed. It was my parents giving me the usual razor-sharp threats to do well in my classes. After our yelling match, I slammed the phone down, pounced on my bed, and smothered my face in my pillow.

Immediately there was a timid knock, and I was amazed and a bit frightened to see Lish. She wore Mickey Mouse slippers and a pink flannel nightgown as she shuffled onto my robin-egg blue carpet.

VISUAL RHETORIC

To help you practice describing people, study the portraits that follow and then use them as models the way an artist does. Paint them for us in words, but don't just say what is factually there—try to figure out what their physical detail, possessions, gestures and habits say about the person in a deeper sense. How do they reveal this person's life story and values? If you're feeling creative, write it in narrative form—tell the person's story.

Peter M. Fisher/CORBIS

Bob Mitchell/CORBIS

Radius Images/PhotoLibrary

■ **PRACTICE 11-13** Find an interesting newspaper or magazine photo, and alter its meaning by writing a new caption for it.

Dialogue

Like other aspects of describing people, dialogue must be distinctive—your characters shouldn't sound like *you* but like themselves. If you use real people in your story, listen for their **unique speech patterns and quirks of language.** If you live in the northern states and have a person from the South in your story, he may use the words "polecat" instead of "skunk," "sack" instead of "bag," or "depot" instead of "station." To a southerner, a Bostonian forgets r's, as in "A bahbah cut my heyuh," but adds r's as in "That's a good idear." When I moved to Rochester, New York, I had to learn that a "red hot and a pop" were a "frankfurter and a soft drink." (Or is it a "wiener and a soda"?) Be careful of stereotypes, however. Few Californians really use Valley-talk ("like, gag me with a spoon, dude"); few southerners say, "Y'all come back fo' grits, dahling"; and few people from New Jersey refer to their state as "New Joysee."

More important are individual speech characteristics: the person who says "hey" or "ain't" or "prevarication" or who addresses people as "honey" or "pal" or "sir." **Education levels** show up in dialogue, too. "You ain't puttin' nothin' ovah on me" and "I'm inclined to disbelieve that assertion" come from two different people saying the same thing. **Age, use of slang, environment, and hobbies all influence our choice of words.** People who are into computers, cars, television, or the military use vocabulary that reflects their interest, no matter what they talk about. Take a minute to think of a friend or relative who has a unique vocabulary or style of speaking.

A storyteller must try to **capture the speaker's voice.** As you see, it's legitimate to break spelling and grammar rules in dialogue for realistic effect. A street punk may not say, "We had quite a blast last night" but, "Freakin' blast last night." Describe these speakers based on their style:

- "Isn't that the cat's pajamas, honey? We sat on the same stoop and I didn't recognize him! Mr. Mahoney, the grocer! He could have been the man in the moon!"
- "We can say with firm assurance that no such knowledge of any event could proceed without the bureau chief's tacit or at least implied consent."
- "It's time for lunch, right? So I get him, right? We meet at the mall, right?"
- "Ice it, pops. You beat up your chops too much."

Someone once said, "Dialogue is what people *do* to each other." In stories, you shouldn't pass the time of day in small talk. Skip hello, introductions, goodbyes, and "please-pass-the-butter" talk. Concentrate on the mean-ingful scenes. **Each piece of dialogue must move the story along.** Dialogue can carry scenes in which important revelations are made about a character, the action, or the theme. For example:

> The father rumbled into my office. "Why the hell didn't you put her on the goddamned bus if she ain't sick? I got work."
>
> "Your daughter has several bruises on her lower rib cage," I said, "and I suspect she may also suffer—"
>
> "I feel fine, Daddy," Rachel whispered.
>
> The man stared at her, his thumb working in his belt loop. "Yeah," he said. "You look awright."

How does the dialogue reveal all three characters in a short time? Here's how dialogue and brief description create an intense scene:

> Everyone from the hood had come up to the court to watch the homies play some b-ball. We were soaking up rays when a gold metal-flaked Honda pulled up with Speed and Little Man and a Puerto Rican girl, Blue Eyes. Blue Eyes remained in the car. Speed and Little Man's pants hung off their butts and showed their boxers. Blue bandannas were tied around their heads. Little Man grabbed a 16-year-old boy named Angel.
>
> "Yo, man! Why you be dissing my home boy? What's up with tha? You best chill 'fore I pop a cap in yo ass!"
>
> Angel pulled away and tried to reason with Little Man. "Bro, I don't even know your home boy."
>
> Little Man pulled a small silver handgun from his boot, held his arms out straight, legs spread apart. His arms shook as he pointed it with two hands at Angel's chest. Angel stepped back, hands up, and pleaded, "Yo! Yo, ain't nobody dissing your homie, Bro. It ain't like that."
>
> People ran from the line of fire. Speed yelled, "Do him! Do him!" Little Man stood, arms shaking the gun pointed at Angel's chest. "You ain't got no props if you don't do him!" Speed yelled. The gun jerked. Again! Smoke rolled from the barrel.
>
> Angel's eyes opened wide. "No!" he mouthed. "No." His head bounced as it hit the ground and his blue tee turned deep red.
>
> Speed cried, "Snap! Snap! Let's be chillin' 'fore five-oh gets here."
>
> —*Dawn M. Schranck*

What parts seem most realistic? How does the dialogue advance the action? Are there any word choices you question?

■ **PRACTICE 11-14** Create four or five lines of dialogue for the people in your story. Work on realistic style and reveal character.

Ending a Story

It's tough to wrap up loose ends, make a point and still have a kick ending when the conflict and action of the story are over. But don't make it harder on yourself than it already is. Rather than trying to explain everything, **it's often better to suggest the conclusion.** If you wrote about your bitter confrontations with your sister, you could end with the doorbell ringing and your hope (or would it be fear?) that it is her. Less can sometimes stimulate a reader's imagination more than opening the door.

Symbols suggest conclusions without stating a message openly. If you wrote about running away from home and were taken to a juvenile detention center, you might end by staring out the window at the road winding away toward the city to hint at the future.

A third option is to echo the opening. This rounds off a story, helps the reader recognize it as a whole. If you began with weather, why not end with weather? Rain could give way to sun—or sharper rain. An opening that begins with a letter from your dying grandmother could end when you find the letter you mailed her on the table beside her bed. Your father's hand steadying your bicycle in the opening can be echoed as you notice his hand as he takes your arm down the aisle to be married.

■ **PRACTICE 11-15** You go to the beach and see your lover/spouse with someone else. Write the last line of the story using suggestion or symbolism.

How to Say Something Worth Saying

How can you make a story convey a good theme?

Tell the truth. Now that sounds simple, but the fact is that the most difficult lies to brush away from the truth are the ones we tell ourselves. Does the theme of your story sound like a candy-coated cliché or a safe, predictable message? You must *refeel* the events; ask yourself at every turn if you missed something or closed your eyes to something. Use the brain teasers on unquestioned ideas and clichés and alternative viewpoints to help break into new truths. But don't worry at the outline stage if your theme isn't outstanding. Theme requires drafting and revision to emerge.

Question your own motives along with everyone else's. Be honest about aspects of the story that contradict your main idea. If the ending was basically optimistic, look for darker meanings lurking there. If it was a sad ending, look for positive aspects. Doing this will separate the superficial paper from the one that's probing. The poet Coleridge once said, "No man does anything from a single motive." Look for multiple causes for your actions and the actions of others.

Why have a theme? Why not just tell what happened? **Because how you feel about what you did or what happened to you is as important as the event itself.** A reader may make up his own mind, but he also wants to know how you interpret it. Working on theme also makes us learn something new.

Here's how one student handled theme in a story about a car crash that horribly maims a young man. Steve's girlfriend, Amanda, helps to nurse him despite his disfigurement and brain damage. Months later, the narrator accompanies Amanda to visit Steve at the care facility for the final scene:

> We wheeled Steve out to the sun porch, a place where we often spent our time. Amanda could barely stand to look at him. Steve was paralyzed from the neck down. He had permanent facial scars and was completely deaf, and both his eyes were damaged. His brain was severely injured. Although he could mutter a few sounds, he seemed to comprehend little of what we said. Amanda said, "I don't look forward to this. I'd like to stop visiting him. It hurts me too much."
>
> "How can you abandon him, Amanda?" I said. "I thought you loved him."
>
> "The person I fell in love with is dead, damn it! All that's left is a pile of mush, some *thing* that can't move, hear, see, or talk. Or even understand who I am or was to him! It's not fair!"
>
> Would it have been better if Steve died in the accident? Maybe Amanda was right. As we walked out of the center that afternoon, I noticed Amanda gently embracing her stomach with both her tiny hands. She rubbed her swollen belly delicately and then smiled slightly. She had lost the most important person in her life. But Steve was still a part of her.
>
> —*Christine D. Reber*

ANALYSIS

The author shows life in its honest complexity. Amanda is neither a saint nor an ogre, but an honest woman who gives what she can. It would be nobler if she devoted her life to Steve—or crueler if she ran off thoughtlessly to another man. Do you like the last paragraph and what it implies?

■ **PRACTICE 11-16** Make a rough statement of what you learned from one conflict you've had—perhaps from a previous practice exercise. Now look for a contradictory message you could have drawn from the same experience.

■ **PRACTICE 11-17** Write an alternative ending to a traditional fairy tale. For example, Cinderella decides if the prince only recognizes her through her shoe size, she's better off without the idiot. State how your change affects the theme or moral of the fairy tale. In this case, instead of the theme being "The worthy will be discovered and rewarded someday despite appearances," it would become "If a person is only capable of recognizing you by external appearances, don't marry him no matter how rich he is."

THE REAL STORY IS IN THE SECOND DRAFT

- Take a break after the first draft. One or two days will help you see your story more freshly.
- Close your eyes and imagine your narrative through the eyes of a person in the story who is not you. What would he/she feel? Where would she/he protest unfair portrayals? What would he/she see that your story does not show? Use this alternative viewpoint for cues to sharpen conflict and honesty.
- Read through the narrative imagining you are another person in your class. Where would she/he have questions or be confused? What might he/she skim? What would that person find most interesting? Use these as cues to build up or reduce parts of the story.
- Improve your narrative by:
  - ✓ Expanding the moment when the conflict peaks.
  - ✓ Stating what the main character should have learned from what happened (you may not want to state this directly in the story, but it will help you see your story's theme better).
  - ✓ Making sure the story begins in motion, not with background information.
  - ✓ Turning an important moment from summary to scene (dialogue/description/action) and turning a less important moment from scene to summary.
  - ✓ Creating one more symbolic detail to deepen each major character.
  - ✓ Making two pieces of dialogue more distinctive to the speakers' style.

VISUAL RHETORIC

To help you develop a better sense of narrative, study the pictures on this page for the elements of a good story—types of conflict, complications, theme, vividness, suggestive detail, and symbolism. What is the story? Where are we in the plot? Should this be the opening, middle or climax?

Greg Epperson/PhotoLibrary

Ben Wiedel-Kaufmann/Alamy Limited

Heinle/Cengage Learning

Writing Suggestions and Class Discussions

1. Tell your best story about a relative.

2. Tell a story of a run-in you had with a relative, but tell the story with the relative as the narrator and you as his or her antagonist.

3. Write a narrative essay about an intense event in your life that changed your philosophy or way of seeing the world. Post it on your blog. Be honest, but keep in mind that others will be reading this.

4. **Dialogue Practice:** Write how *you* would ask where the restroom is at a restaurant. Now, ask as an Englishman, a Texan, a New Yorker, an elderly schoolteacher, a street kid, and a construction worker might ask. Choose words and style carefully.

5. **Fun with Dialogue:** Play a DVD of a section of a film you have not seen—with the sound off. Write the dialogue you imagine the actors might be saying until you have a page.

6. You are 85 years old, and your friends are gathered around your hospital bed. Before you die, you want to tell them one story of the many you've experienced, a story that will reveal to them who you really were and what your life meant. Tell that story. (It should be something that has not yet happened to you.)

7. **Description Practice:** Describe the eyes, mouth, and one other feature of someone close to you. Make a list of potential descriptions, then choose the most revealing for character. Turn in one finished paragraph and your brain teaser.

8. You are a drug rehabilitation counselor and have been asked to address a group of high school students on the dangers of drug use. You're afraid they'll be bored if you start out preaching, so you decide to tell a dramatic story to lead in to your point. Write this speech.

9. Tell a story that brings an abstract idea to life. It may be true or fictional. Use one of these topics:
   • Courage
   • Prejudice
   • Failure
   • Cheating

10. **Alternate Viewpoint Practice:** A mother (or father) aged 39, daughter (or son) aged 18, and a grandmother (or grandfather) live together. The grandparent wants to remarry. Break the class into groups of four—one for each part and one to record notes. Present possible ideas each character would have.

11. **People Practice:** Use the list of character features on page 211 to create a page of details to describe either yourself or a close friend. Go

beyond the obvious. **Visual rhetoric option:** Include a photograph of the person that conveys his or her personality, values or life story.

12. Tell your peer group a story you're thinking of writing. Then ask each peer to express the ideas and feelings of one person in the story.

13. Read and discuss the student narrative essays "Pa's Secret," "49 Hours in Afghanistan," and "Bastard" in Chapter 15, and "Spring Break: Mazatlán, Mexico" in Chapter 3.

SAMPLE STUDENT NARRATIVE ESSAY

Live Abortion
Beatriz Valle

Cooky's baby was born fourteen weeks premature. She was on a ventilator and losing ground. The Hospital, Centro Medico de Mayaguez in Isabella, Puerto Rico, was supposed to have an advanced neonatal intensive care unit. That's why Cooky chose it. My sister had had two miscarriages. Her doctor had even performed a cerclage, tying her cervix shut to prevent one miscarriage that happened anyway. This time the baby was alive, but she weighed only one pound, ten ounces. *[opening conflict / flashback adds a new complication]*

Jessie, Cooky's husband, and I left the tattered furniture in the lobby and rode the elevator to the sixth-floor nursery area. Its dreary yellow curtains were closed. I rang a bell, and a long while later a nurse appeared. "May I help you?" she asked. Jessie couldn't utter a word. His face was drained.

"Yes," I said. "We are here to see Rebecca Rivera's baby. This is the father." As I touched Jessie's arm, my voice broke. *[dialogue raises new conflict and complications]*

"It isn't visiting hours yet," the nurse answered, pointing at the sign on the door.

"He's her father! What if she dies before visiting hours?" I snapped back.

"She is considered a live abortion," the nurse replied, but she signaled us to move to the window.

I could never have prepared myself for what I was about to see. Her head was no bigger than a tangerine. Her eyes were horizontal slits. She had no eyebrows, eyelashes, or hair. Her hands were no bigger than the tip of my finger. Hoses and tubes jammed into every orifice of her frail body. If I could pick her up, she would easily fit into the palm of one hand. I hugged Jessie and we cried. *[description draws us in]*

→

more complications and inner conflict

Later we were told if the baby survived 24 hours and then died, the family would have to make the funeral arrangements. If she died prior to then, the hospital would not release the body. Which was better? I wondered.

Cooky was anxiously awaiting us so she could see her baby for the first time. Jessie wrapped his arms around her as we shuffled to the nursery. Cooky pressed her face against the window and waited for the curtain to open. When it did, she whimpered. Jessie embraced her and she sobbed.

new conflict complication

That evening Dr. Gomez said, "Don't expect to take her home. Don't expect her to leave the hospital alive."

Cooky turned on him. "You are not God. I will take her home alive."

complications

Months later, four-pound Rebecca Beatriz Rivera left the hospital. During that time she survived two heart attacks, fought for each ounce she gained, and was scarred all over from the tube insertions. But we were elated.

complication

Chicky, as she's now called, celebrated her sixth birthday last Sunday. Her vision is very poor and only recently did glasses give her a clear picture of the world. She walks on tippy-toes and often stumbles and falls.

The hospital is not being held accountable for what happened. We found out later that, after the birth, Chicky had been placed on a paperlined tray to be disposed of. After several minutes, she cried. A nurse scooped her up and ran her to the neonatal intensive care unit. Only then did she receive adequate care. Because she suffered from lack of oxygen, she now has a mild case of cerebral palsy.

complication

ANALYSIS

Opening: The opening establishes immediate conflict.

Ideas: Complications build quickly. Cooky has already lost two babies. The nurse's coldness, and later the doctor's, add person–versus–person conflict to the baby's battle against nature. When the narrator worries about what's best, we have some inner conflict, too. The conflict is directly related to the theme. Although this child was treated as if she were already dead, life can beat the odds. In the end the author seems to suggest that although the hospital was not held legally accountable, its presumption of death led to Chicky's cerebral palsy. I like the honest inner battle the author wages: part horror, part love, part anger.

Details: The description of Chicky is powerfully honest and vivid. Comparing her to a tangerine and suggesting what's missing ("no eyebrows . . .") show that the baby is not visibly human. Yet the family refuses to accept appearances. Sharp one-word descriptions of the hospital furniture and curtain are enough for background. More could be done with Chicky's description at age six; we need to see her in full humanity now to prove the theme.

Dialogue: The "live abortion" comment and Cooky's defiance of the doctor are strong. I'd like to hear Cooky say something when she first sees her baby. It seems like an important moment. Punctuation and paragraphing are fine.

Ending: The author did not give away the ending, but a new conflict is raised and left dangling. Although I favor short endings, I'd like the author to tell us how she feels about the hospital's responsibility. The essay falls short in theme depth because of this.

STUDENT ESSAY

Holy Hell: Religion Can Be Our Salvation or Our Destruction
Sherri White

My family's Apostolic Pentecostal religion was fanatical, consuming and oppressive. I attended church Wednesday, Friday and twice on Sunday. Saturday was spent cleaning the church, working the bake sales and spreading witness. Services began at 6 P.M. and ended around midnight. And everyone was expected at fellowship after most services. Each member was to give at least 10% of all earnings to the church, even if that meant the family would need to stand in the government's free cheese line.

One particular service stuck out more than others. The evening began with an hour prayer. Then things began to move. The cold, tan, cinder block walls seemed to warm once we sang the sweet, soulful gospel hymns. The organ bellowed, the piano chimed, and tambourines beat the familiar rata-tat-tat as the voices sang one memorized hymn after another to "make a joyful noise unto the Lord." Hands clapped, then feet stomped and bodies swayed. Just as you thought things could not be livelier, one person stepped

→

from his pew and began walking around the church's perimeter. Others joined him until a train of faith marched around the sanctuary. Around and around they went, young and old, men and women, surrounding the evil in their midst. People began to run, then faster. The Bible says, "David danced before the Lord with all his might." So people began rolling on the floor, screaming, dancing, jumping and whirling in circles.

Somehow my pastor halted this frenzy for his sermon. His subject was the Black Walnut Festival that our town was hosting—with its parade, exhibits and carnival. At that moment, the carnival was no more than 200 yards from us, just across a creek. From church, we could hear people's laughing, screams of delight, gasps of fear and the hissing of hydraulics for the rides. Brother Willis shook his head in disgust and pointed a vibrating finger toward the carnival. It was the work of Lucifer himself to interrupt the Lord's service. He was soon enraged and yelling. Finally, he slammed his fist on the pulpit and shouted, "All those people frolicking at carnival will surely perish in the fiery lake of hell!"

Someone in the congregation answered, "Amen!" and someone else exclaimed, "Preach it!"

For two hours, Brother Willis did preach, assuring us that none of the sinners at the carnival would enjoy paradise unless they converted to our religion and a thousand other things. The wooden pew was so hard my back felt like two-week-old bread. Finally, he made the familiar call to sinners and backsliders within our midst to come to the altar. "If you are not ready when our Lord calls us home, you will burn for an eternity." That night he called us by name, many of us children. He pleaded, "Come forward, little ones! Mommy won't be able to help you in hell!"

This fear had been instilled in me since birth. It was so deep that escape was impossible. The lump in my throat swelled, my palms sweat, my knees buckled. I filled with pure terror. Cautiously, I glanced around—my friends shook with fear as well. Then he called my name. My body rose without me telling it to. I reluctantly shuffled the fifteen feet to the altar, each step an excruciating fight to understand what was happening to me. My mind reeled in confusion. I had been primed for this moment every day of my six years of life, but what now? What was I supposed to feel?

Once at the altar, not knowing what else to do, I prayed. In a flash, I was swarmed by my family like mosquitoes attracted to a porch light.

→

I prayed and prayed and prayed some more. Nothing happened. Something should have happened. I didn't know what, but something. That scared me even worse. Was I so bad that even God didn't think I was worth saving, that He wouldn't come to me? I found out later that I prayed up there like that for an hour. I was exhausted, and finally my speech began to slur. I started to mumble.

"Hallelujah!" screamed my aunt.

"Praise the Lord!" my father said. "Praise Him!"

People said I spoke in tongues, that I had the Holy Ghost in me. People shook in their seats. I don't remember much after that. Some hymns of thanksgiving were sung on behalf of those of us who had been saved that night. Prayers were said and we were dismissed. The lost sheep were saved!

Yet it was all false. I did not speak in tongues. I was mumbling, drugged with exhaustion and confusion. I was no different than I was seven hours earlier. Somehow I found the courage to confess this to my father. He said, "Your Aunt is your elder. You cannot question her." For me that was the beginning of the end. I left the church six years later and did not return to any religion until I was married. It took thirteen years to get the bitter, rancid taste out of my mouth. I am now Episcopalian. Like my former religion, there are financial, time and talent obligations, but it's not an environment of fear but of love. One thing I know: I will not raise my children to be respectful drones.

Discussion/Writing

. . . .

1. Evaluate this essay as a narrative, using the Peer Review Checklist for Narration as a guideline.
2. Write about a moment of revelation you had about religion. "Revelation" means *any* sudden insight or understanding.

☑ Peer Review Checklist for Narration

Author: _____

A question the author has for the reviewer:

_____

Reviewer: _____

	Strong	Average	Weak
Opening: Opening Sentence			
Early Conflict			
Ideas: Complications of Conflict			
Honesty/Depth of Theme			
Details: People Are Vividly Described			
Actions Are Vividly Described			
Dialogue: Realistic and Sharp			
Punctuation, Paragraphing			
Ends with a Punch			

The most vivid aspect of this story is:

Use several adjectives to describe the feel of the writing:

Respond to the author's question. Offer several suggestions if possible:

Make another two or three suggestions about the story and discuss them with the author.

Informative Writing

12

Telling your Audience What it Doesn't Know

A COLLEGE STUDENT USING *IDEAS AND DETAILS* wrote me a note asking, "Why does a person who is going to be a television technician need to know how to write informative essays?" He'll find out. Most college graduates are surprised by how much writing is required in their careers. Nurses, social workers, police officers, technicians, and business people discover writing fills far more job time than they ever anticipated. One engineer recently estimated that she spends 50 percent of her office time writing, not calculating or sketching plans. **And of the writing you will do as a college graduate, more will be informative than any other kind:** technical and business reports, memos, brochures, summaries of meetings, letters, speeches, and perhaps research projects or articles for newsletters in your field. The person who can convey instructions, facts, summaries, and analyses *concisely, clearly*, and *vividly* will have an edge in becoming a valued employee or leader.

Nothing can be loved or hated unless it is first known.

—LEONARDO DA VINCI

There's something in life that's a curtain, and I keep trying to raise it.

—MAXINE HONG KINGSTON

Men occasionally stumble over the truth, but most of them pick themselves up and hurry off as if nothing had happened.

—WINSTON CHURCHILL

Audience and Tone

Informative writing strives for *objectivity*. **This means a reader must be moved *by your information, not by your opinions*.** Using facts to support personal opinions on controversial topics or to make new proposals is persuasive writing—discussed in the next chapter. In informative writing your tone should be unbiased; you should not think of yourself as converting your audience but rather as educating it. **On the most basic level, you can simply report**—as in a research report, a summary of an article your professor asked you to read, or a report of what happened at the student senate meeting. But in college most informative essays you'll be asked to write must **analyze a situation—use your reasoning and interpretive skills to explain.** This kind of informative writing is traditionally called *expository writing*—you expose what might not be obvious. At some point, of course, it can cross a murky line into persuasive writing.

For example, your *informative report* may explain how an abortion is done or contrast the prolife and prochoice positions without any personal opinions. An *analytical informative paper* could go further. It might explain the effects abortions have on women or the reasons men tend to lead anti-abortion activities, but you would cross into persuasion if you try to tell the reader to oppose or support abortion laws. In other words **you should restrain your personal opinions in informative writing.** If, in describing the process of an abortion, you write, "the baby is then ripped in agony from his mother's womb," you have loaded the dice with opinion. Likewise, if you write, "the reproductive wastage is cleaned from the uterine wall," you have loaded the dice the other way.

While personal anecdotes and personal knowledge can provide great detail in informative writing as elsewhere, **be sure to keep the focus on the topic and not yourself.** It may be tempting to describe the abortion process by telling the story of a friend who had one, but you will risk falling into storytelling and becoming too opinionated if you rely only on your friend's story. Here's an example of a student explaining Muslim views on sex education and sex:

> Muslim parents feel uncomfortable discussing sex education with their children, just as their own parents never discussed it with them. Muslim countries don't teach sex education in schools either. They have a saying, "Do you teach a baby duck how to swim or just put it in the water and let it swim?" Muslims also say, "Allah is the same today as he was yesterday. His commandments do not change," but in the wash of moral relativism, Muslim parents in Western countries look outdated, provincial and inconsequential to their children. Here, schools work against parental authority and religious values. For Muslims, sex is never discussed for its mere pleasure and is a dirty word unless related to family life. Sex within a marital relationship is worship that is rewarded. Outside marriage, it is a punishable sin. Virginity at marriage is a virtue. Muslims say husbands and wives are

garments for each other, protecting and shielding our modesty like clothes. Sex is a natural gift from God. We do have powerful built-in desires, but sexuality is also a powerful genie that, if not brought into submission to the Will of God, is capable of tremendous destruction.

—*Serap Unlu*

ANALYSIS

This is a very highly charged topic that can generate intense debate. While her sympathies seem on the Muslim side, notice that Serap does not argue that Muslim ways are right and Western ways wrong, she does explain what lies behind Muslim views on sex education, and she does not rely on her own personal story as a Muslim living in North America. Her details are Muslim sayings and facts. Her tone seems fairly objective.

However, this is a good example on which to use your critical thinking skills. How is this writing too idealistic? Peek under the rug:

- Find broad generalizations, exaggerations or absolutes p. 150.
- Think about what has been revealed about abusive and repressive treatment of women in some Muslim countries in recent years. How might that connect to the way they are taught about sex?
- Think of *other* consequences of not teaching sex education aside from purity and modesty.
- Use alternate viewpoints to see through the eyes of young Muslim women and men.
- For example, how might the wedding night look and feel to them? Think of other viewpoints to help you analyze the topic.

Another aspect of objectivity is your obligation to present all major *legitimate* viewpoints where there is difference of opinion. Which are legitimate? They must be either widely accepted or verifiable through science or direct observation. In the abortion debate, many people believe that a newly conceived fetus has a human soul. So, even though we cannot prove it scientifically, you ought to include that viewpoint somewhere in an informative paper contrasting positions on abortion. However, you do not have to include the supermarket tabloid claim that aborted fetuses are being implanted with computers and grown to be robotic servants of the FBI. The source is untrustworthy, and the claim has not been verified by reputable observers. Scientists do disagree, however, about whether a fetus feels pain during an abortion. They debate how developed the nervous system is at various stages, so both theories should be presented.

But don't think of informative writing as dull or boring, a mere reciting of facts. The writer's job—*always*—is to keep the reader awake, no matter what the topic. Unless your audience requires stiff formality—as in a lab or business report, for instance—occasional humor, vivid anecdotes, and lively words are usually welcome.

Writers do adjust their tone in informative writing for the audience. The amount and kind of information you might use writing about an archaeological dig will vary greatly depending on whether you write a paper for your anthropology professor, a letter to your mother, or a section of a job application. The professor will want technical and interpretive information; your mother may find the events of the trip more important; a potential employer may be most interested in the skills you learned and how well you meshed with the rest of the team.

Suppose you are writing an informative paper entitled "The Gift of Life"—donating your organs to sick people when you die. How would your tone and information differ for the following audiences?

- A sociology professor
- Transplant surgeons
- The family of a dying person
- The general public

To illustrate, here are some details about the procedure. **Which of the preceding audiences especially would or would not want to know the following?**

- Organ donation allows part of the dying person to continue living.
- The donor is usually brain dead (a flat EEG line), but the heart still beats and a ventilator keeps the person breathing during the removal of transplant organs (organs deteriorate quickly without blood and oxygen).
- A neurologist is consulted to declare the person brain dead.
- The transplant doctor does *not* decide when to take the organs.
- The hospital *does* notify transplant doctors of likely cases so they can contact the receiving family and wait anxiously with equipment poised for permission to begin removing organs.
- The Uniform Anatomical Gift Act allows your spouse, child over 18, parent, or adult sibling to donate your body even if you have not signed a donor card.
- Doctors refer to these as "organ harvests."
- It is a rapid operation without anesthetics. The body is simply sliced open—"peeled back" as one doctor said in a professional journal—to

save time. The desired organs are quickly removed. Then the breathing machine is turned off and the person dies.

- The body cavity can be packed and stitched up for a funeral.

As you can see from the facts just listed, **an informative writer must be sensitive to the intended audience.** Even in my list there is obvious slanting of the facts presented. I aimed at a general student/teacher audience, easing back on the technical information.

Packing in Details

Here we are again. There's no way to write well without details, and the informative essay should bristle with them. **Stimulate your brain by asking reporters' questions.** You might start with this overall one: "What would *I* want to know about this topic if I could ask any expert?" Suppose your topic is the effects of a nuclear attack.

Ask personal questions: What would happen to *me* if a nuclear bomb struck a half-mile away, a mile away, 5 miles, 50 miles? Ask for graphic details—what would happen to my skin, bones, hair, eyes, sexual function, and digestion? How would it affect me if I survived? How would I eat? Who would live with me? What would be the odds of finding friends or family? What aspects of society would remain? Suppose it was a terrorist's nuclear "dirty bomb?"

Ask less personal questions: How would the living deal with all the dead and dying? Would society revert to a primitive cave culture as some people predict? Would the survivors be inspired to deeper bonds? Would there be just one bomb or a dozen? Would the atmosphere be poisoned for all life on earth as in Nevil Shute's novel *On the Beach?* How likely is the nuclear winter that Carl Sagan and other experts predicted—should the sun be blocked by billions of tons of dust thrown into the atmosphere? How would we respond if it was terrorism and not war? Can you add three or four questions to this list? Try it now for practice.

It's easier to ask questions, of course, than to answer them, but in asking, sometimes answers emerge. In asking, you also mark which territory you will be able to handle best when you focus the topic more. So the first step is to ask the honest questions—the ones you really care about. Tough questions require tough, gutsy details. They'll help point you toward a good paper.

■ **PRACTICE 12-1** Ask four or five tough questions about the topics below. Suspend what you know about them and ask what you really should know:
- Drug use in junior high school
- Television nature programs

- The value of a college education
- A topic of your choice

Surprise Value

Good informative reports or essays should surprise the reader with *new* **information.** If you only tell us what we already know, you're not informing us of anything. For instance, most people know that nuclear bombs generate great heat and do awful things to human flesh. But when you read John Hersey's *Hiroshima,* you learn that some people caught within a quarter mile of the blast of the bomb dropped on August 6, 1945, were vaporized so suddenly that they didn't even have time to scream or turn away. How do we know? Because they stood between concrete walls and the blast, and exact, perfect outlines of their bodies are preserved on the concrete—a painter raising his brush, a mother straightening the blanket on her baby. Their bodies shielded the wall from the intense heat just enough to imprint their silhouette.

That is information. **Give your reader the same kind of essential, inside information.** "General" information and "official" information usually tell readers only what they already know, unless you pick exotic topics—such as spelunking (cave exploring), cooking Indonesian food, or teaching sign language to the deaf.

Do you have to do research to write informative essays? In a sense, yes. However, you don't have to travel to Japan or work 10 years in a lab. **Your eyes, ears, fingers, and brain research the world every day.** If you can imagine a world without electricity, family, schools, police, hospitals, or law enforcement, you may be able to create a plausible essay on the world after nuclear war. If you can imagine what it might be like to see a dying relative put on a respirator and can honestly picture a doctor asking you to sign over the person's organs, you can write about some of the issues in the "gift of life" topic.

Here's an example of meticulously detailed information based on personal observation. It's from a student essay titled, "Dealing with the Dragon":

> When he returned to the car, Mayito pulled out a syringe from its orange and white shrink wrap and a tiny brown cellophane bag with a palm tree stamped on it. His hands shook as he tore the top and poured the brown powder into a tarnished silver spoon. He meticulously drew up 20 cc of water from a puddle he poured in his palm. With the needle, he stirred the water into the powder in the spoon. He then held a lighter to the belly of the spoon until the mixture bubbled. He uncapped the syringe with his teeth, stuck it into a piece of filter from his cigarette, and drew up the amber liquid. He

then jabbed the needle into a bulging vein in his arm with the skill of a sharpshooter. As he pulled back on the plunger, blood mixed with the drug. He told me, "Turn your head!"

But I couldn't turn away. As he depressed the needle, the fluid returned to his vein, and I felt nauseated. I knew this was how it was done, but to see it! I threw open the car door and stood on the pavement, the sun beating on my head. I was sure I would throw up, but I didn't. Mayito stepped out and stared at me. Tears rolled down his cheeks as he buried his face in his hands.

—Janice Mundorff

Many informative papers you do for college *will* require some outside research. Be sure to document these sources (see Chapter 15). Here's an example by a student who was writing on bulimia, or binge eating. To enhance her personal knowledge, she cited two sources with surprise value in details:

Jessica, a 36-year-old financial analyst from California, gorges herself, then takes three hundred laxatives. She has done this each day for sixteen years. A teenager with bulimia starved herself, gorged herself, and made herself throw up. She died while retching over a toilet bowl (Cauwels 2). Suzanne Abraham recorded one patient's "bad binge": she ate a bag of potato chips, a jar of honey, a jar of anchovies on bread, one pound of rolled oats, two pounds of pancakes, one pound of macaroni, two instant puddings, four ounces of nuts, two pounds of sugar, one box of Rice Krispies, a pound of margarine, two quarts of milk, a gallon of ice cream, a pound of sausage, a pound of onions, twelve eggs, a pound of licorice, a dozen candy bars, and ended with a bottle of orange cordial. This totals 1,071 grams of protein, 1,964 grams of fat, and 14,834 grams of carbohydrates (85). These violent abuses of the body profoundly affect bulimics' social life, self-esteem, and psychological functioning. It may cause death from suicide or cardiac arrhythmia.

—Andrea Macaluso

■ **PRACTICE 12-2** Write a sense and example brain teaser about a natural disaster you have experienced firsthand: hurricane, windstorm, earthquake, blizzard, or fire, for example. Be especially alert for details with surprise value—little things that many people might not know.

Poor Informative Topics

Introductory topics, such as "How to Play the Piano," usually lead to disaster. Basic terminology makes it hard to write an interesting paper. You might do better to focus on "How to Handle Your First Piano Recital" or "What Makes Jazz Piano Sound Different." Another problem with introductory topics is that educated people will be familiar with them. Picking topics such as "Techniques of Safe Driving" or "Your First Garden" will bog you down stating the obvious. Pick an *aspect* of the topic that promises more surprise value: "Why Truck Drivers Are the Safest Drivers" or "Garden Health Hazards."

Broad topics such as "What Is a Good Marriage?" can also doom your paper. You'll only be able to say superficial things about this topic because you promised more than you can fulfill in sharp, gutsy detail. Better choices: "How to Handle a Family Argument over Money" or "Six Questions to Ask Your Fiancé Before Walking Down the Aisle." Notice that in these narrower topics, the opportunity exists to define a good marriage.

Good Topics

Lurking inside all poor topics are potential good topics, and keeping two things in mind help you recognize which kind you have. First, has it been **limited to an aspect you can cover *in depth*** in your allotted pages? Can you really tell us something fresh and fill the essay with vivid details? Second, do you have **a specific slant or message** to convey—a thesis? To help you arrive at a thesis, let me explain a half-dozen time-tested ways of structuring informative writing. This illustrates an important point that sometimes gets lost: **The steps in writing an essay are really interdependent—the thesis helps determine structure; the structure helps create ideas.** The four steps of the writing process described in this book—getting ideas, order, draft, and revision—constantly play back and forth to each other.

■ **PRACTICE 12-3** List three or four potential topics for an informative essay. Narrow each so you can cover it in depth in a few pages. You will be building on these topics throughout the chapter.

Organizing Informative Writing

After narrowing your topic somewhat and doing some brain teaser lists, you can invent your own scratch outline for the material. But here are six common structuring and thinking devices people use to convey information:

- The Process or "How-To"
- The Essentials or "What-Is"
- Causes or "Why"

- Effects or "What's Next?"
- Comparison or Contrast
- Classification

If you start with one of these approaches early in your prewriting, focusing and structuring your informative writing will be easier. This is not to say you should always rely on these devices—the most creative topics often break new ground. Let's look at each.

THE PROCESS OR "HOW-TO"

One way of focusing and organizing information is to present it as a *process*. Imagine yourself telling the reader *how to do* something: "How to Skydive," "How to Win at Poker," "How to Teach Children Manners." Process can also be used to focus on issues simply for *understanding:* "How Refugees Become Terrorists," "The Stages of Juvenile Crime," or "How the United States Was Persuaded to Invade Iraq." **Your scratch outline will consist of** *chronological steps.* Try several scratch outlines until you're satisfied. If, for instance, you find yourself with three stages that have very little information and one bloated with examples and ideas, you probably need to divide that step and combine the smaller ones. If I were writing on skydiving, for instance, the following outline would *not* work well:

- Saying goodbye to family
- Arriving at the airport
- Preparing your equipment
- The flight up
- Diving
- Cleaning up

The first, second, and last items don't deserve full steps in the process. They should be brief transitions. Preparing equipment seems reasonable as a main heading, but the dive seems most important and ought to be divided into several stages itself: the (gulp!) leap, the free fall, opening the chute, and the landing. **Organizing chronologically does not imply that you must give equal time to each element. Focus on the key moments.** Slowing time down at key moments heightens the informative effect.

The Georgia Paramedics Against Drunk Driving, for instance, published a brochure that describes the process of an accident at 55 mph. This brochure describes the *one second* after a car smashes into a solid object. In the first tenth of the second, the bumper and grille collapse. In the second tenth, the hood crumples and hits the windshield. The car frame stops, but the rest of the car still travels at 55 mph. The driver braces his legs, but they snap at the knee. In the third tenth of the second, the steering wheel shatters. In the fourth, the front two feet of the car collapse while the rest still moves at 35 mph. The driver is still traveling 55. In the fifth tenth, the driver is impaled on the steering column and blood fills his lungs. In the sixth tenth, the impact can rip his feet out of tightly laced shoes, the brake pedal snaps off, and the driver's head strikes the windshield. In the seventh tenth of the second, hinges pop and seats break free, hitting the driver—who is now dead.

 After deciding on your scratch outline, braintease again and add details and ideas to each heading. This is true for each of the outline patterns that follow.

■ **PRACTICE 12-4** Describe a process in slowed-down fashion, as the Georgia paramedics did. Try a kiss, falling down stairs, or your own topic from Practice 12-3. Find some overlooked details.

■ **PRACTICE 12-5** In small groups, solve the problem of love (well maybe not all of it) by creating a how-to process: What are the best steps a single person should take to meet his or her ideal partner?

■ **PRACTICE 12-6** State one of your topics from Practice 12-3 as a process topic, list the main steps in the process, and add a few concrete details for each.

 ## THE ESSENTIALS OR "WHAT-IS"

This approach informs a reader of *essential* characteristics of your topic. For example:"The Essentials of a Good Photograph,""Problems Children Have When Parents Divorce," "What's Really Bad About Rats," or "What Is Unique About Mary Oliver's Poetry." **Your scratch outline consists of each key element you will explain.** For instance, for children involved in divorces, you might have:

- Loss of a father/mother figure
- Dealing with parental sorrow and grief
- Feelings of guilt about causing the parents' divorce
- Loss of home if property is sold and divided
- New "uncle-daddies"/"aunt-mommies" in the home
- Loss of friends if the family moves

Under each of these you can list the examples, facts, questions, or bug items from your brain teasers. If you find some items have little information, omit them. If one item draws most of your attention, you might focus more exclusively on it. For instance, one common thread I notice in my list of ideas is *loss*. I might decide at this point to focus on "Things Children Lose During Divorce."

■ **PRACTICE 12-7** Make a list of the essentials of a good relationship with a boss or the essentials of a good shopping mall.

■ **PRACTICE 12-8** State one of your topics from Practice 12-3 as an "essentials" topic and make a scratch outline of main headings.

Is there one "right pattern" for your essay? The topic on good photographs and the one on divorce would also be possible as process essays, describing the stages of taking an action photo or the stages children go through during a divorce. The organization of the paper changes, but it might be equally effective. On the other hand, the topic on rats might not work so well as process—unless you wanted to tell the story of one incident ("Our Apartment Building's Battle with Rats" or "Chicago's History of Rat Control"). **What counts is having a** *plan that does not mix approaches.* **That might confuse a reader—and** *you.*

CAUSES OR "WHY"

Organize your paper by informing the reader of the causes of a particular situation. Here are the same topics from cause perspectives:

- What motivates (causes) a person to skydive?
- What were some hidden reasons that the United States and its allies invaded Iraq?
- What causes a rat infestation?
- Why do children feel guilty during a divorce?
- How are juvenile gang members created?

List causes, reasons or motivations for the situation. Each may become an outline heading and eventually a paragraph in the paper. Add details to each cause.

■ **PRACTICE 12-9** Make a list of possible causes for one of the cause topics. Do not settle for only obvious causes.

■ **PRACTICE 12-10** State one of your topics from Practice 12-3 as a "cause" topic, list three or four headings for an outline, and add details to each in note form.

EFFECTS OR "WHAT'S NEXT?"

 Instead of looking backward for the source of the situation, **look forward to the effects or consequences of a situation.** We can reshape some topics like this:

- Long-term effects of skydiving on your body
- How terrorism affects U.S. foreign policy with other countries
- The psychological effects of rat bites
- When children of divorce marry
- The effects gang members have on their peers

To develop one of these, I would list as many effects or consequences as possible. Under each effect, I would list details until I had at least a half-page.

■ **PRACTICE 12-11** Create an effects approach for each of the following topics. Then list four to five possible effects one of them leads to. Do not settle for the obvious effects.

- Drunk driving
- The 12-month school year
- A change in your neighborhood
- Dating through the Internet

■ **PRACTICE 12-12** Create an effects approach for one of your topics from Practice 12-3, draw up a scratch outline of headings, and add details in note form.

Reasonable causes and effects: Suggesting causes and effects for events may be controversial or lead to logical errors. The informative writer must try to avoid arguing and instead suggest all reasonable causes and effects without bias. For instance, the following would be reasonable causes for the computer revolution:

- To improve business efficiency and reduce human errors
- To reduce information storage space
- To speed up communications
- To save money by eliminating jobs

But how about these:

- To bend the minds of children away from religion
- To help government gain secret control of people's finances

The last two require a lot of arguing to prove they're true and are more appropriate for persuasive papers than informative ones. "But," someone might say, "look how children *are* turning away from religion just as computers became widespread! It's a fact!" No, it's an opinion without the widespread acceptance the first four causes would have. Cause and effect errors are explained more fully on p. 276.

Here is an objective example of cause analysis that explains what clues tell fire investigators that a fire was arson. Notice how the student explains the whys behind the causes:

> The color of the flames is a clue that a fire might have been caused by arson. An arson fire burns hotter than a normal fire, creating brighter flames with less smoke. Due to the heat, there is purer combustion and less smoke. Unintentional fires usually start small, so when bright red and yellow flames roll out the windows, firefighters should be suspicious.
>
> When fire spreads, it moves up and away from its origin and leaves a "V" mark on walls. If the floor is burned from one end to the other, this may be a sign that an arsonist spread gasoline or kerosene. If there is a lack of deep char around the point of origin, it indicates a fast-spreading fire that may have been helped by an accelerant.
>
> —*Bruce Teague*

■ **PRACTICE 12-13** Explain the causes of some social problem today, **or** if you could change one decision you made at least one year ago, describe the effects a different decision would have had on your life. Be as honest and objective as possible.

■ **PRACTICE 12-14** Read "Sterilization for Sale" (page 436) and evaluate the reasonableness of the effects that the author suggests.

COMPARISON OR CONTRAST

Let's try our topic list for comparative structure:

- Skydiving is safer than hang gliding
- Afghanistan and Iraq: Two ways of handling the media
- Rats vs. cockroaches: If you had to choose
- Is it worse for a parent to die or to divorce?
- Teaching manners to kids in the United States and in Italy
- Gangs today and five years ago

Next you would list your points of comparison as headings and support each point with details.

■ **PRACTICE 12-15** Develop a brain teaser list of comparisons or contrasts for one of the topics just listed.

■ **PRACTICE 12-16** Create a comparison or contrast approach to one of your topics from Practice 12-3, draw up a scratch outline of headings and add details in note form.

CLASSIFICATION

Here are some of the topics structured by classification (explained on pp. 59–61):

- Three types of terrorist strategies
- Four kinds of excuses to give professors
- Five skydiving styles
- Three common reaction patterns for children of divorce
- Types of female gang members

After deciding on your main points, fill in each category with details describing it. In your draft, each heading will become a paragraph.

■ **PRACTICE 12-17** Create a classification approach to one of your topics from Practice 12-3, draw up a scratch outline of headings, and add details in note form.

■ **PRACTICE 12-18** Pick one of the following subjects and see it in five of the six thinking structures. Create a one-sentence topic statement for each:
- Evolution (or any other scientific concept)
- *Romeo and Juliet* (or any other literary work)
- Schizophrenia (or any other psychological term)

■ **PRACTICE 12-19** Create a brain teaser page exploring the most promising topic you outlined in Practice 12-18.

Drafting Informative Essays

Informative writing does not have to be dry. Yes, you may have a boxcar of information to convey. But you must also draw readers into the subject, make them visualize, and make them grasp why the subject matters. Your introduction especially should strive to be lively and concrete like those described in Chapter 6. Here's an example by Tom Avril from an essay published on a topic most people would find dull and technical—cancer lab research. It's from an article published in the *Philadelphia Inquirer* (April 14, 2008) and is called, "Scientist for a Day":

With a forceps in one hand and a scalpel in the other, Kim Hagerich peeled back the skin of a white laboratory rat. She extracted a glistening section of pink tissue that was perhaps a half-inch long—a mammary gland—and placed it on a small yellow tray. Mammary glands are of greater interest to Hagerich than to most people, as something went wrong with hers two and a half years ago. She is a breast-cancer survivor, one of eleven who donned white lab coats at Fox Chase Cancer Center. They spend the day as scientists: swirling flasks of pink fluid, slicing up bits of animal tissue to examine under a microscope, extracting snippets of genetic information to understand why some cells run amok.

In his report, Avril will provide statistics and theories about the causes of cancer, but by starting with a cancer survivor participating in cancer research, he puts a human face on his topic and makes us care about it. The animal is being sacrificed, not to vague "science," but to a woman who might have died without such experiments. Now she holds the scalpel.

As you draft, try to avoid unbroken strings of fact upon fact— break them up with analysis (causes, consequences, alternatives) and concrete, vivid examples. Emphasize information from your brain teaser lists and research that will be new to your readers and skim obvious things. Above all, help your reader to visualize. For example, if I were writing on the medical harm body piercing causes, I could list problems:

- Cracked teeth from tongue studs
- Allergic reactions to jewelry
- Infections

All true, but this is only the sketch of an idea so far. The reader will skim it unless specific details focus her eye. Tell us about your friend whose tongue stud caused such a bad infection that his tongue swelled so much that the stud had to be removed surgically. Or illustrate with the woman whose repeated ear infections from piercings led to keloids—scar tissue that grew into large red and brown lumps in her cartilage that required plastic surgery.

MAKE YOUR SECOND DRAFT BETTER

- Close your eyes and imagine your professor and two other professors reading your draft. You're going to borrow their brains to improve your paper, and they'll never know! What parts would they find obvious? What would make their eyebrows flash in surprise? Where would they say you need more depth of analysis? Use these as cues for expanding and cutting.

→

- If a lawyer read your draft, where might she object that you are biased or argumentative instead of objective?
- Use critical thinking to deepen the draft's insights:
  - ✓ Ask how your biases might have blinded you to other possibilities.
  - ✓ Explain consequences—even if you are not taking an "effects" approach, an analytical informative paper should go beyond listing points of contrast or steps in a process. Say *why* things matter.
- Improve your draft by:
  - ✓ Adding two new sharp details with surprise value.
  - ✓ Making a postdraft outline or Table of Contents for your essay. Does it really fit the shape you wanted (process, cause, etc.)? Do all the parts belong where you put them?
  - ✓ Do all the details fit each paragraph?
  - ✓ Write (without looking) your paper's thesis in one sentence. Compare it to the one in your draft and revise if needed.
  - ✓ Search for and correct the kind of grammar errors your professor found in your last paper.

VISUAL RHETORIC

Suppose you were writing an informative paper that classified people's attitudes toward their own bodies, perhaps narrowing it even more to their attitude toward their weight. How do these pictures suggest two attitudes?

Mark Anderson/Jupiter Images

Imagebroker/Alamy Limited

List the characteristics of each person that might define a category and explain which details you would draw from the picture to illustrate your point. Next, find two more photos on your own that represent two additional categories and explain what qualities define those approaches to the body.

Writing Suggestions and Class Discussions

1. List five topics on which you think you can write a nonresearched, informative essay. Highlight the ones you think will offer the most surprise value for a general audience.

2. Narrow the best topic from number 1 further and write three scratch outlines (just main headings). Use three different organizing patterns.

3. Using the same topic, decide which organization plan conveys your message best and fill it in with details.

4. **Audience and Tone:** Suppose you were writing an informative letter entitled "My First Semester at College." How would your tone and information included differ depending on to whom you were writing?
   • The college president
   • Your boss (who reimburses your tuition)
   • Your best friend (who is not attending college)
   Make a list of information for each letter.

5. Rewrite these weak topics into sharper, more interesting ones still related to the originals; give two alternatives for each:
   • How to bowl
   • Today's music
   • How to balance a checkbook
   • Traffic violations
   • Smoking is bad for your health

6. Ask five tough questions about each of the following topics, questions that will lead to surprise value information:
   • Teenage marriages
   • The future of gasoline consumption in the United States
   • Community colleges vs. four-year colleges
   • Satellite television or cable television

7. Write a **process or how-to essay,** packing as much information as you can into one or two pages. Concentrate on vivid details and smooth organization. Topics:
   • How to drink with style
   • How to meet men or women at college

- How to deal with a sexist (or a racist or homophobic) boss
- How to give an "A" oral report
- Open topic

8. Explain how a **process** works that you know well, but which most people don't understand—a CD burner, sink trap, spark plug, antibody, therapy for autistic children. No more than 250 words.

9. **Class Exercise in Process Writing:** Create a diagram or doodle of your own of about the same complexity as this one: Write a process description of it so someone else can draw it without seeing the doodle. Proportion is important, but actual size is not. You will have 10 minutes. Members of the class will try to draw it only from the read-aloud instructions—no changes allowed from your written text.

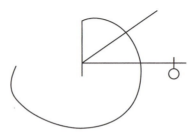

10. Write an **Essentials** essay on one of the following, packing as much information as possible into one or two pages:
    - A good love letter
    - A top action film
    - The most common clichés of television situation comedies
    - Handling being an older adult student in college
    - Open topic

11. Create a brochure for an organization or cause you believe in. Explain its **essential** features in no more than 250 words. **Visual rhetoric option:** Sketch illustrations, use screen captures from Web sites or clip photos from print sources to design a paste-up copy.

12. Create a contest for your blog. Be as straight or wacky as you like, but explain the **essentials** of the rules and prizes clearly. It must somehow relate to the theme of your blog and the people who might read it.

13. Inform a person you're attracted to of your **essential** personality features. This should *not* be a sell, but an *honest* appraisal. Offer at least three key aspects about yourself that a future spouse should be aware of. Pack in vivid, supporting detail.

14. Write an informative essay on the **essentials of a career** you're considering. Interview a person in the field, asking real questions you have. Here are some all-purpose starter questions:
    - What do you like best about your job?
    - What one piece of advice would you give to someone wanting to enter this career?
    - What qualities are most important to be a successful ___?
    - What are you most proud of in your career?
    - What part of your job would you gladly give to someone?
    - What most frustrates or disappoints you about it?

Before calling for an interview, read page 354 for proper etiquette and techniques of interviews.

A sample career research paper is on page 420.

15. Write a **cause** essay on one of these topics. Your job is to consider less obvious reasons as well as ones most people are aware of:
    - Why people get body piercings
    - Why SUVs are so popular
    - Why the drug Ecstasy is popular among younger teens
    - Why divorce is more socially acceptable today
    - Why Physical Education is required in college

    Visual rhetoric option: Illustrate your paper with two visuals.

16. Imagine changing any one historical event and discuss the **effects** that might have. For example, suppose cloning human beings was not made illegal. What difference would it make today?

17. Imagine altering one "law of nature" (such as eliminating winter or not having to kill to eat). Briefly explain why you might change it and then forecast possible **effects.** Look for both positive and negative effects.

18. Write a one- to two-page informative essay **comparing or contrasting** two of your current textbooks. Evaluate them based on the standards established in this chapter for conveying information: adaptation to audience, surprise value, and covering the tough questions. Quote examples to support your views.

19. **Compare or contrast** two competing products, such as the PC versus the Mac or traditional cars versus hybrid cars. Your job is not to judge but to inform us objectively about similarities and differences.

    Visual rhetoric option: Illustrate your paper with two visuals.

20. Write a **classification** essay on one of the following, packing as much information as possible in one or two pages:
    • Male attitudes toward women
    • Female attitudes toward men
    • Levels of racism
    • Student clothing styles
    • Types of video game players
    • Open topic

    Visual rhetoric option: Illustrate your paper with two visuals.

21. The class will be divided into six groups. Each will apply a different one of the six informative organizing patterns to the same topic. Each group should write a focus sentence, an outline, and some details for each heading.

SAMPLE STUDENT INFORMATIVE ESSAY USING A PROCESS PATTERN

Helping the Dead
Elizabeth Biroscak

Lead-in example

You walk into Mr. Allen's room. Around the bed, the curtain is drawn. When you pull it back, the light over his bed makes you squint. Mr. Allen is flat on his back. He wears a faded blue hospital gown. His eyes are partially closed, rolled back and white. His mouth is wide open, dentures half fallen out. His skin has a bluish gray tint to it. He looks like a figure in a wax museum. This is someone who is dead. Many people think that as a nurse's aide you only take care of people who breathe. But too often you will watch your residents take their last breaths. Then it becomes the responsibility of the nurse's aide to give the dead the respect and dignity they deserve.

Thesis

Post-mortem care is a scary, emotional part of my job as a nurse's aide, but a very necessary one. When you perform post-mortem care on one of your residents, done correctly, it can be a great way to say good-bye to someone that you have come to love.

Step 1

Details

When you find someone not breathing, your first response should be to call the nurse in charge to assess the situation. She confirms that the resident no longer has a pulse or heartbeat, calls the doctor and reports the time of death. If the nurse feels the resident

→

has passed from anything other than natural causes (criminal violence, suicide, or an accident such as a fall), she will contact the medical examiner and follow his instruction. If the cause is determined to be natural, the nurse will contact the next of kin and inform them that the resident has passed away. They are invited to come to say good-bye.

When the charge nurse is finished with these things, care is turned over to the nurse's aide. As a nurse's aide, you need to prepare yourself for post-mortem care. For your first time, you may want to ask a co-worker to help. If no one is available, I find that listening to some soft radio music calms my nerves. When a person passes away, sometimes he loses control of bowel and bladder, and sometimes he vomits. When you touch a dead body for the first time, even through your latex gloves, you will be amazed how fast it gets cold and clammy when the heart no longer pumps blood through its veins. It feels like a piece of raw steak just taken from the refrigerator. The skin will be bluish gray—really like zombies in horror movies. You can always tell when someone has been dying a slow death by the color of his or her fingers, arms, toes and legs. As the heart shuts down gradually, it lacks the strength to pump blood to the extremities, so the skin there turns purple from the lack of oxygenated blood. You can actually watch the purple creep up the fingers, hands, toes and legs towards the torso while the person is still alive. It is like nothing else I have ever seen. Most important, you need to make sure that you treat the body with a gentle and kind hand. The dead body you are taking care of is someone's mother, father, brother, sister, son, daughter, uncle, aunt or friend. That person was someone. He should be treated like you would expect your own family to be treated.

Once you are ready to start the actual washing, you need to remove any Foley catheters, IVs or feeding tubes left in the resident's body. If the resident's eyes are open, gently close them without applying any pressure. Start by washing the face, then the rest of the body, working from the top down and leaving the bottom for last. Make sure the side rails on the bed are in the up position. You don't want the body to roll off the bed. Be careful when you roll the body that the head, hand, arm, leg or foot of the resident do not bang against or get wedged between the rails. You will need to clean the resident's mouth with a mouth swab, and if he or she wears dentures,

Step 2

Details

Step 3

Details

→

Step 4
Details

Step 5

Details

Return to
Thesis

make sure they are in and fixed with dental adhesive. No matter how many times you try to close the mouth, it will not stay shut. Also, if he wears glasses, put them on. If the resident has a special nightgown, put it on her. If not, make sure she is in a clean hospital gown or a clean set of clothes.

After finishing the personal care, make sure the resident's bed linens are clean and neat. Place the resident's hands on top of the blanket and put a pillow under his head. Finally, make sure you brush her hair. On your way out of the room, take away any medical equipment (oxygen tanks, nebulizers, IV poles, or suction machines). Now the family can say its good-bye.

You would think that would be the end of the job, but it's not. Sometimes the admissions department will fill the bed with some-one new within an hour of someone passing away. There is no time to waste. The room needs to be ready for the next person. The nurse's aide must clean up whatever the family left behind. You toss pictures, knick-knacks and stuffed animals into garbage bags, and sometimes you can't help but cry when you read a note from a grandchild to a grandparent. It breaks your heart to know that all the things that this person thought enough of to keep, sometimes for years, ends up as garbage. A nurse's aide is expected to just go on with the rest of her day like nothing has happened. She is not allowed to grieve for the dead. Not until the end of the day, that is.

When you have worked in a nursing home as long as I have, you sometimes get callous about your work. As mean as it may sound, you sometimes forget that you are taking care of a human being and not just an inanimate object. Then someone you take care of dies and reminds you that the lives you touch everyday are fragile ones. You never know when they will be gone.

ANALYSIS

Thesis: She is sensitive and caring, but the message is somewhat obvious: the lives we touch are fragile. She needs to incorporate the other side—the brutality and absoluteness of death in her thinking.

Surprise Value: This is a topic many people would avoid—we like to think a dead person magically appears in the casket, if we think about it at all. We especially don't think about what happens to elderly family members in nursing homes. So the topic will have strong, perhaps unsettling, surprise value for most readers. There's a nice combination of tough, honest detail along with recognition of the emotional aspect of helping the dead.

Details: Most are vivid, especially the description of the skin and effects of a slow death on it, dealing with the mouth, turning the body and posing it for family. I found the removal of the dead person's possessions to be a detail with a message: that the staff carefully protected living residents from seeing what would inevitably happen to them.

Organization: Process. It moves in clear stages through time. Some, such as calling the doctor, nurse, and mortician, have weak surprise value, and Elizabeth wisely covers them briefly. Including the preparation of the room for the next resident added zing to the writing, even though it might seem logical to end with the body's removal. It shows how the process of dying continues day after day. A long paragraph in the middle needs to be broken into two, perhaps where she shifts from the feel of the body to its skin color.

Tone: Mostly objective. There are sections where the aide's emotions are discussed, and we know it is the author's own, but she objectifies it by treating it as an issue an aide must face, not to convince us to change the procedures (which would be persuasive writing) or to turn the informative process into the story of her feelings (which would be narrative). She is honest, yet softens the shock in places. References to bodily fluids, for example, are kept general. I think the potential for "Oh, my God!" details was here, but that might unbalance the factual details and human feeling. What do you think? You might compare this treatment with "The Autopsy" in Chapter 16.

Strongest Aspects: I liked how she made me feel like I was preparing to help her by using "you," the combination of compassion with technical details, and the theme that we can help the dead.

Suggestions: Style: Too many sentences follow the subject–verb–modifier format—look at the first half of the first paragraph. While I like her delicacy, I thought there might have been more detail on handling the body's weight and awkwardness and perhaps more about the eyes and mouth. Is that too picky?

SAMPLE STUDENT INFORMATIVE ESSAY USING AN EFFECTS PATTERN

Going to the Chair
Michele Myers

Soft music whispers as you enter the cheerful waiting room. A coffee table holds the latest *Woman's Day* and *Bass Fisherman* magazines. When you check with the receptionist, she greets you with a sweet smile. Soon your name is called by a masked person in scrubs and a lab coat, and you are waved forward. Down the hall you hear the unmistakable whining whistle of machinery over the mellow tune. You sit in a reclining chair that could have come from the set of an old sci-fi show. The assistant clips a pink bib napkin and cool metal chain around your neck. Your eyes focus on sharp instruments on the tray and the water swirling in the tiny bowl. Does this make your pulse increase? You're not alone. But going to the dentist can affect people in many ways.

I have been a dental assistant for five years, and, contrary to popular belief, not everyone is afraid of the dentist. Take Darrell, for example. He falls asleep as we are working on him. It's as if the drill is the soothing sound of the ocean, and after a few minutes, he starts to snore. I can't imagine being that comfortable in The Chair. He told me once that he wants to buy a dental chair for his home to sleep in on Saturday afternoons.

Other patients react to dentists with fearlessness. My mother actually prefers to have treatment done without anaesthetic. She says, "I don't like the aftereffects of the novocaine. It makes me bite my cheek." When I ask her about the pain, she just says, "Yeah, but it's mind over matter. Besides, it's usually over fast." Mind over matter? Is it possible pain is only how we perceive it, that if you tell yourself it won't hurt, it won't?

But I know from experience that fear of The Chair isn't as simple as physical pain. Sometimes pain is just how people express their feeling of lack of control. They fear depending on someone with a sharp, gleaming instrument entering their body. Otherwise I don't know how to explain the effect dental work has on Anna, a mother of five. She works in a factory and has strong, worn, calloused hands; yet whenever she has dental work done, she says, "I'd rather

→

give birth than have a shot in the mouth." She cringes as the doctor tilts her back, and she squeezed her eyes shut as he reaches for the syringe. Like a mother comforting a child, I must hold her powerful, frightened hand until the injection is over.

Roger has a sister who is a hygienist. Therefore, that makes him an expert on dentistry. He questions everything the dentist does because he suspects the dentist is in on some conspiracy. When the dentist leaves the room, Roger asks me, "Should I really have a filling in this tooth?" or "Is it normal to have novocaine for this size filling?" Recently Roger came in with a formula that he thought could re-grow tooth enamel—a mixture of toothpaste and mouth-wash. The fact that enamel is 96 percent inorganic doesn't bother him. He says he's going to have the formula patented.

I will never forget the first time I met David. When I called him from the waiting room, he snapped, "It's about time!" I apologized for being behind, although it was only five minutes. He proceeded to lecture me about how valuable his time was and that I should have told him we were running late. Going to the dentist makes lots of people upset, but when the dentist came in, David turned from the beast Mr. Hyde into Dr. Jekyll. His anger vanished. He smiled and asked nicely about the doctor's family. He released his tension on me, then turned on his charm for the man who was going to drill him.

For pure fear of The Chair, we have John. He spends ten min-utes in our bathroom psyching himself up before he will enter the room. Once there, he paces around the chair until the doctor comes in. Perspiration runs down his face and he hyperventilates. When he finally sits, he gets pale and wilts like a cut flower. His feet shake nervously. Even if it's freezing outside, he will beg us to crack open a window. Then the dentist can examine him. It takes John another 15 minutes of settling in before any real work can be done on him. By the time he leaves, John is physically sick and exhausted.

Sometimes dental professionals glimpse the deeper effects dental visits have on patients. On Steve's first visit, he smelled like cigarettes and stale beer and dressed in Harley biker clothes. He was gruff and scary. He had never liked the dentist, so his teeth and gums were in total breakdown. Now he needed dentures. When told his remaining teeth would be surgically removed, he just shrugged. But at the mention of the impression, he grew agitated

→

and said he had a severe gag reflex. I didn't even get the tray half way to his mouth before he started gagging. In a rush he confessed to me that as a child he had been sexually abused by his father. He told me his father would say to him, "Open up and suck on this." As he spoke, it was as if he suddenly became a little boy again. I felt bad and didn't know what to do. The doctor had to return to take the impression. It was the longest two minutes as Steve coughed and gagged while the material set up.

From my experiences as a dental assistant, I have learned that fear is very real, although it is not always the direct effect of the dentistry. So when David yells at me, I try to remember that he is so nervous, he doesn't know how to deal with it in any other way. And Roger's suspicions are caused by his fear of lack of control. Part of my job as assistant is to recognize patients' nervousness and dis-comfort and do the best I can to eliminate those fears, even if they are caused by hidden factors. That's ok. I don't mind holding a pa-tient's hand, because I hope I'll have someone's hand to hold when I need it.

DISCUSSION

Evaluate this essay using the guidelines from the peer review sheet and the analysis of "Helping the Dead" as a model. Think especially about other possible effects a dental visit has on people.

For samples of student essays using other informative structures, see:

Process: "Simple Life," p. 199; "The Autopsy," (page 414).
Essentials: "Mental Health Counseling," (page 420).
Contrast: "Food for Thought," (page 411).
Effects: "Sterilization for Sale," (page 436).
Classification: "Marijuana Smokers," (page 417).

☑ Peer Review Checklist for Information

. . . .

Author: _____

The organizing pattern I used for this essay is: _____

I'd like help with this paper in this area: _____

Reviewer: _____

	Strong	Average	Weak
Thesis			
Surprise Value			
Details: Vivid			
Enough Detail			
Organization: Clear/Easy to Follow			
Tone: Unbiased, Informative			
Research (if used): Documentation			

Do you agree with the author's assessment of the organizing pattern?

Explain where/how it might be strengthened.

Respond to the author's request for advice:

Evaluate the essay's surprise value. What was new; what wasn't?

What questions about the topic should the essay answer that it doesn't?

What is the strongest part of the essay to you?

Give two additional suggestions for revision:

1.

2.

ANALYZING PROFESSIONAL INFORMATIVE WRITING

SUMMARY ANALYSIS

- State the thesis.
- How does the author shape the essay—by one of the six methods described in this chapter, a combination, or some other? Outline the main sections of the essay.

CRITICAL ANALYSIS

- Evaluate surprise value. What did the essay tell you that you did not know before? Is it mostly ideas or details?
- How thorough was the coverage? Try to find another cause, step in a process, effect, or category or some other place where significant information seemed missing.
- Tone: Is there any editorializing? Explain why it is valid or inappropriate.
- What are the author's sources of information and how convincing are they? What other sources could have been used? Should they have been used?
- Describe whom this writing targets as an audience. Consider age, sex, education, politics, or other issues.
- Where does the author consider alternate viewpoints—more than one way to do something, more than one perspective or explanation. If there are none, suggest several.
- How does the author enliven the facts to draw you in, or where did the author fail?
- Be sure to provide specific quotations or references to the essay to support your ideas.

SAMPLE PROFESSIONAL INFORMATIVE ESSAY

WHY WE PROCRASTINATE
J. Peder Zane

Apr. 15—Purse Punisher. Check Chewer. Money Muncher. April 15 is known by many names. But it is defined by two words: taxes and procrastination.

The painful obligation to send in our returns by midnight tonight brings out the dawdler in many of us. The Internal Revenue Service reports that 35 percent of Americans wait until the bitter end to file. An additional 6 percent of Tar Heel taxpayers are expected to request six-month extensions.

"Every year at this time I am bombarded with people who are in a panic over their taxes," said Geralin Thomas, who owns Metropolitan Organizing in Cary. "Some haven't kept up with their filings, others can't find their receipts, almost all of them feel so overwhelmed by a situation they've been delaying for so long that they just don't know where to begin."

Tax time may be the Super Bowl of procrastination, but it is not just a seasonal problem. Studies show that 95 percent of us procrastinate once in a while and a whopping 20 percent to 25 percent of Americans are considered chronic procrastinators.

For these hard-core lollygaggers, April 15 is just one more day to dillydally. On April 16 they'll continue to defer projects at work, fail to R.S.V.P. for an upcoming party, ignore their plans to see their doctor or take their car to the shop – often at risk to their health and safety.

"Procrastination is their lifestyle, marked by self-deception, bad faith and legions of excuses," said Timothy A. Pychyl, a procrastination expert who teaches at Carleton University in Ottawa. "They're constantly telling themselves 'I have plenty of time,' 'I'll feel more like it tomorrow,' 'I work better under pressure,' anything that will allow them to put off tasks they know they must complete."

Almost everyone puts off boring or difficult tasks – few leap at the chance to do their taxes. Such behavior becomes procrastination, Pychyl said, when people know what they

→

need to do, intend to accomplish it, and then do something, anything, else.

Instead of lazy layabouts, they are usually busy bees, cleaning out their refrigerators, scrubbing their bathroom floors, organizing their files, doing everything except meeting their pressing deadlines.

Technology has been a godsend to these deacons of delay, who use the Web, e-mail and BlackBerrys as cutting-edge tools of distraction. "We found that procrastination accounts for about 50 percent of the time people spend online," Pychyl said. "That's why I call it the procrastination superhighway."

Lots of us do it.

Procrastination is an equal opportunity affliction, according to one of the field's pioneering researchers, Joseph R. Ferrari of DePaul University. Women are just as likely to exhibit the behavior as men; 20-year-olds are as prone to it as 65-year-olds (much older people seem to lose the habit). His studies have also found that white collar employees procrastinate more than blue collar workers, salespeople more than middle managers, business executives more than doctors or lawyers.

More broadly, Ferrari said, there are three basic types of procrastinators:

- Arousal procrastinators are thrill-seekers who tackle projects at the last minute, pulling all-nighters at school and work.
- Avoidance procrastinators habitually put off hard or boring tasks.
- Decisional procrastinators are paralyzed by indecisiveness.

Their behavior has many roots. Ferrari has found, for example, that many chronic procrastinators started early, as a way to rebel against over-demanding fathers. "Finally," he said, "a problem we can't blame on mothers."

But the bottom-line issue, Ferrari said, is self-esteem. Procrastinators care deeply about how others see them; they live in fear of falling short. So they create circumstances that — they believe – will protect their self-image.

→

When they avoid a task, they can't be evaluated on it. When they refuse to make a decision, they can't be blamed if things go wrong. When their rushed work is subpar, they blame it on a lack of time.

They would rather have people think they didn't try than that they can't cut it. They also tend to be charming and personable, Ferrari said, skilled at convincing others to bail them out or let them slide.

It is these psychological benefits that make it so hard to overcome. "To tell the chronic procrastinator 'just do it,' is like telling a depressed person 'just cheer up,'" Ferrari said. "Most of them will need to turn to professional assistance, which most won't seek until they hit rock bottom."

Discussion/Writing

1. Write a summary analysis of the essay.
2. Write a critical analysis of the essay, referring to at least six of the eight items in the critical analysis checklist.
3. Where do you or don't you fit as a procrastinator? Give examples to support your view.
4. Fill in two or three details for each of the three types of procrastinators. Write as if you are the author.

Persuasive Writing

Seeking Agreement from an Audience

13

PERSUASIVE WRITING HAS A BAD REPUTATION. AT ITS worst we picture a slimy hoodlum twisting someone's arm to "persuade" him to tell where the diamonds are. We think of battleships and bombers hovering off the coast of a tiny country to "persuade" its government to change its policies. Cigarette advertisements in magazines "persuade" men that one brand will make them feel as if they're riding a snorting stallion on the range while another brand will make women feel daring and rebellious. How about empty political campaign speeches or a father screaming at his late, tipsy teenager at 2 A.M.? Persuasion is commonly pictured as forcing, tricking, seducing, or lecturing people to buy or do something not really in their best interests. Too often these tactics work. But that's not the kind of persuasion we're interested in here.

Honest, ethical persuasion means bringing readers—through their own reason and emotions—to believe or act as the writer does. In this sense, readers willingly and *consciously* discover that it is in their best interest to agree. This type of persuasion, which will be required of you in many college assignments and in most persuasive writing done in business, professional, and technical careers, is an honest appeal to reason and feeling.

The aim of argument should not be victory but progress.

—JOSEPH JOUBERT

The civilized world represents the victory of persuasion over force.

—PLATO

The most important thing is honesty. If you can fake that, you've got it made.

—GEORGE BURNS

Audience and Tone

Advertising, political speeches, and barroom debates often imply the audience is so dumb or bullheaded that it must be pounded into submission. Reasonable persuasion assumes your audience is uncommitted (unless you know for *sure* you are dealing with supporters or those holding opposite views). It assumes your audience is educated and will weigh your arguments reasonably. This audience wants facts and logic, expects you to be ethical, will be critical of shortcomings in your position, and will not fall for the gimmicks of advertising.

This means that you must achieve a good persuasive tone. You do not have to be somber or dull. In fact, humor not only enlivens persuasion but can demonstrate the writer is broad-minded. Overall, strive for perspective and common sense. Sentences such as "All people who support abortion are murderers!" or (from the opposing side) "Antiabortionists want to enslave women!" share the same hysterical tone. Wild, undisciplined language usually results from wild or undisciplined thinking, and smart, open-minded readers will be skeptical about writers who lose their tempers. **Assume your readers are intelligent, present many facts and reasons for your position, and trust them to see the logic.** If you try to bully readers into agreement with shouting, they won't be convinced—they'll only want to get away from you.

Several years ago I received an anonymous letter from a student. The fact that it was anonymous made me question the writer's integrity from the start. The student was complaining about the revealing clothes a woman in the class wore, arguing that they were out of place in college. I admit the woman's clothes lacked taste, and if I'd received a reasonable letter, I may have gritted my teeth and spoken to her about it—even though I don't think a teacher should be a police officer. But the student's letter used numerous profanities to describe the woman—"slut" being among the nicer. It ended: "I want action! Have *YOU* any sense of decency??!!" Me? Me?! The student steamed and frothed so much that he totally lost perspective. In attacking his reader, he lost whatever chance he had of persuading me to act as he wished. I felt more inclined to counsel *him* than the woman.

Before we agree with an argument, we must trust the arguer. **Give readers reasons to trust you.** Is the persuader ethical? Knowledgeable? Reasonable? Your credibility is damaged by using profanity, bullying, ranting, or threats, by twisting facts or calling rumors "facts," and by relying on slogans, clichés, stereotypes, or other oversimplifications. **The writer who calmly *helps* a reader sort through the complexities of**

a situation, who honestly *shares the difficulties* of right and wrong in the issue, and who *respects the truth* will open doors with a quiet knock. The persuader who approaches with a battering ram or who tries to sneak in a back window is the one against whom readers build barricades.

So before you begin persuading readers, try to put yourself in an honest, helpful frame of mind; open yourself to alternative viewpoints in the early stages especially, so the point you set out to prove is as reasonable and fair as it can be. Keep Joseph Joubert's statement in mind: "The aim of argument should not be victory but progress."

As long as you consider your audience's reactions and are willing to modify your ideas to strengthen them, you will make honest progress. If you seek victory over a reader, ignore or hide facts that threaten your idea, or lose control of your emotions, your case will crumble.

■ **PRACTICE 13-1** Recall two persuasive situations you've been in: one that led to hot tempers and anger and one that led to "progress." Think about the attitude of the people involved in each.

■ **PRACTICE 13-2** Read the student essay "Sterilization for Sale" (page 436), which tries to objectively present both sides of a controversy. Does the author succeed?

To help achieve a good tone, **write to real people for a real reason—** actually send your ideas to someone. My students' persuasive papers have been published in the college newspaper, city newspaper, Humane Society newsletter, Ukrainian Club newsletter, and several magazines. One wrote a proposal to a bank to finance a towing company; another asked a museum curator to reinstate cancelled free art classes for poor children; another used the class paper as an opportunity to answer her supervisor's negative job evaluation of her. One of my students wrote to her town school board to protest a policy against students using calculators during tests. Irene's dyslexic son knew his math, but made simple errors, such as writing 45 instead of 54, without a calculator. Her letter brought a state assistant secretary of education to a board meeting, and the rule was changed. Irene was later asked to address a convention of 500 educators on the topic and help rewrite the state rules. There's no inspiration like writing to real people for real reasons.

You can write to your student loan service center with suggestions, to your boss at the retail store about changing an exchange policy that costs the store thousands of dollars, to a local high school principal to persuade him to make driver's education a required course, to the campus facilities director to add a bus route for the dorm in the woods, to a father to persuade him not to retire from racing, to the Hallmark Company persuading them to sell Christmas jewelry you designed, to Apple Computer proposing a software registration plan that will keep prices low and prevent others from duplicating the software. These are all recent papers my students wrote—and sent. Or, like other students, you can join 35 million bloggers worldwide who post their ideas on their Web sites. Some of these are personal journals, but many develop arguments and debate issues. **Going "live" can give you some of the best education you will have in college.** But do wait for peer and/or your professor's reactions before sending out your ideas.

■ **PRACTICE 13-3** List several persuasive issues you might discuss on your blog. What would be your position, and what would you like your reader to do after reading your posting? Also, name at least one link you could add for readers to get more information (this means finding out what is already on line).

Persuasive Topics

When choosing a topic for persuasion, **you have basically two choices: to take a stand on an existing controversial issue or to make a proposal to solve a problem.** If you choose to take a stand, you will have the advantage of some preexisting arguments but will need to find additional arguments and examples of your own. Often this is called a "**position paper.**" Candidates for political office write dozens of these and post them on Web sites so people can see exactly what their stand and solutions are on subjects of public interest. Committees for nonprofit organizations like the Sierra Club or the National Rifle Association also write many position papers to define the organization's official stance on issues. Freshness of idea will be difficult with some topics such as pornography, nuclear power, and drug laws because most supporting arguments on *both* sides are well known. If you make **a proposal of your own**—a new solution to a problem—you will have to invent all your own arguments. But you will have the advantage of freshness. Proposals sound more stimulating than taking a stand:

- "Students with A grades in a course will receive free tuition; those with D or lower will pay double tuition."
- "No politician should serve more than one term in office."
- "High school students should be required to do two hours community service each week."

But proposals require more careful thinking: Can you think of a serious objection to each of these proposals as well as a positive benefit?

In your career, of course, you will be writing proposals 98 percent of the time. Most employers pay people for new concepts and plans, not rehashing old issues. Persuasion will be needed to convince your supervisor and colleagues, and more persuasion needed to sell clients, government agencies, customers, and other institutions. The higher you rise in your career, the more persuasive proposals you will write, and in fact, writing proposals for new ideas is one way to rise rapidly. Imagine how an employer would react to receiving proposals like these from you under your own initiative:

- We can draw more customers to the store by providing a shuttle bus service from three locations.
- Bookkeeping at the company can be simplified if we adopt the following plan. . . .
- The summer recreation program can be improved if we stagger the children's nap times and alternate quiet tasks with outdoor activities.

■ **PRACTICE 13-4** Write a trial proposal for your employer, college, society, or family. List a few details of the plan.

■ **PRACTICE 13-5** State your position on three controversial issues today.

We'll be developing these throughout the chapter. Try to pick topics about which you have some mixed feelings so you'll have a more honest paper.

Raising Problems That Matter

As in the preceding examples, your thesis should be stated in a single sentence, and in most persuasive writing it appears at the end of the introductory paragraph. This is not unalterable law, but it is a pattern that makes reading easier to follow. It's a mini-map for reader *and* writer. Short persuasive essays may defer the thesis until the conclusion, especially in cases when the writer finds both sides appealing. It is used less often simply because it's trickier to bring off successfully. **What does the rest of the introduction do? It makes the reader care about the problem.** The introduction can also establish your reasonable tone. For example, one might start the essay on "Grades and Tuition" this way:

> Teachers complain that many students are unmotivated. Colleges don't figure transfer grades into one's grade-point average—C is good enough for credit. Many graduates wonder if working hard for a high cumulative GPA is really worth the effort when they might get a job based on their personality. Many good students just slide through with little effort, and the taxpayers foot much of the bill. Perhaps we can motivate students with something closer to home: cash.

At this point the writer has established a problem and has shown she's considered it from several angles (teachers, transfer colleges, several types of students, and taxpayers), and she probably has the reader saying something like this: "Yes, motivation is poor; what should be done about this?" In other words, **by showing us a serious problem, the writer has made the reader hungry for an answer.** Then the thesis is presented as the last sentence of the paragraph followed by the essay that supports it.

The proposal for the shuttle bus might begin this way:

> A customer who wants our product circles the store three times. Our tiny parking lot is full; street parking is full. Will that customer ever return? Unlikely. No one in the area will sell us space for parking, the city has refused to run a bus route nearby, and we have already made our employees park six blocks away. If we can shuttle them, why not our customers?

 One way of starting to think about persuasive writing tasks is to raise all the problems you can about a topic—perhaps by writing a brain teaser bug list. Much of this may turn up in your introduction.

■ **PRACTICE 13-6** Take an issue you find important—perhaps one of your topics from Practice 13-4 or 13-5—and write three or four sentences explaining why it is a tough problem. Be fair to all sides. Then, if you think there is a way to solve this problem, write a trial thesis sentence.

■ **PRACTICE 13-7** Think about a decision you must make, writing three or four sentences explaining why it is a tough problem. At the end write a trial thesis to defend.

■ **PRACTICE 13-8** Pick one of the following questions and list three reasons to support a yes answer and three reasons to support a no. Then take a stand, with whatever modifications to the original you need, and write a one-page essay:

- Should a woman adopt her husband's last name?
- Should government authorities have the right to torture known terrorists to get information to prevent future terrorist acts?
- Should countries that have had long religious or ethnic civil wars (such as Iraq, Darfur, and Israel) be divided into two or three countries?

Supporting Evidence

A reasonable person expects reasonable evidence before believing something. In the previous examples, you'd want to be convinced that cash motivation would work for grades: that it would be fair, that the specific economics of the plan would fly, and that it would be good for students and teachers.

Can you imagine three or four questions you'd want answered before investing in shuttle buses if you were the store's manager? **Always anticipate your audience's barriers to belief.**

When you argue persuasively, pack in as much supporting evidence as possible. **Think of yourself as a lawyer convincing a jury.** There are three types of evidence:

- Facts
- Appeals to values
- Logic

These are new brain teasers for persuasive writing. Make a list of all the facts you know (or need to know so you can research them later), all appeals to value you can use, and all logical arguments you can use.

FACTS

Statistics are one type of fact you can use to support a thesis. A proverb says, "There are two kinds of lies: regular lies and statistics." It means that statistics can be twisted to bolster weak arguments. Maier's law even says, "If the facts do not conform to the theory, they must be disposed of." This attitude may be held by less reputable advertisers or politicians, but **in honest, ethical persuasion, you must be especially careful to handle your statistics fairly and accurately.** If we say, for instance,

"94 percent of people surveyed believe the ban on television advertising for cigarettes is unfair," our reaction to this statistic changes if we learn the survey was conducted by a tobacco company in the town where its factory is located. An ethical arguer must reveal such information or not use the statistic.

The source of your fact strengthens or weakens its impact. **Generally, your facts will be more credible if they are based on recent research conducted by an expert and published in a reputable journal, Web site, or book.** Material from the *National Enquirer,* material assembled by astrologers, or work done 30 years ago in fast-changing fields such as psychology or physics is generally not considered reliable. Even experts are not absolutely trustworthy. Lord Kelvin, Leonardo da Vinci, and Sigmund Freud all made whopping errors in their fields.

Another problem with statistics is simply making the reader *see* them clearly. Today we are bombarded with numbers: billions of dollars, millions of poor people, thousands of recalled products. Despite our modern sophistication, big numbers seem unreal for most people, and **the writer must help the reader see what the number means in a concrete way.** When the United States went past the $1 trillion mark of indebtedness, for instance, most people simply shrugged until one representative of Congress visualized the statistic. He calculated that if we stacked 1 trillion $1 bills on top of each other, the pile would reach the moon! That gave people an image of $1 trillion they could visualize, and it persuaded many people to demand government action, as the representative had hoped. (By the way, 2008 debt was over $9 trillion.)

Here are three facts. Which is the most visual?

- 200 million tons of dirt and rocks were dug to create the Panama Canal.
- A typical hurricane releases 50 times the energy of the first atomic bomb.
- Hoover Dam holds back 10 trillion gallons of water.

I'd pick the second example because we can see 50 atomic bombs (even if we cannot fully comprehend the impact), but without careful calculation I couldn't even tell whether 200 million tons of dirt or 10 trillion gallons of water would be the bigger volume.

■ **PRACTICE 13-9** State two facts or statistics you know about a topic you chose for Practice 13-4 or 13-5. Then help a reader creatively visualize them through a concrete comparison.

Plan on doing occasional research for persuasive writing. The facts I just gave took me five minutes to locate. Statistics give authority to your persuasive voice.

Some statistics can come from your own observations. In a letter to the Vice President for Facilities Management at the State University of New York at Buffalo, a student proposed that the college expand its parking facilities. At one point, she produced her own statistics by driving around campus counting spaces:

> It may also be possible to turn parts of faculty lots into student parking, since faculty lots are seldom full. There are 27,000 students and 4,000 faculty members at UB. All 19,000 commuter students, and, I estimate, one quarter of the 8,000 who live on campus drive to class. There are eight student lots on North Campus, three of which hold approximately 300 cars, five of which hold 200 cars, for a total of 1,900 spaces. Yet there are five faculty lots with a total of 1,000 spaces. On the South Campus, there are four student and two faculty lots, each accommodating 200 cars. I calculate the ratio of faculty to parking spaces is three to one and of students to student parking spaces is eight to one. After viewing the parking lots throughout the semester, I believe you can afford to transfer at least several hundred spaces to students.
>
> —Tina C. Maenza

There's a second kind of fact, one handy for all of us: **examples.** Use examples from (1) what you've seen; (2) what your friends and families have seen; (3) historical or current events; and (4) hypothetical cases.

If you're writing about the law that forbids those under a certain age from drinking alcohol, for instance, you probably know a dozen cases that could support either side—from firsthand experience, from what others have told you, and from the news. Everyone can dig up a couple of examples of drunken teenagers causing fatal accidents—or of drunken middle-aged people killing sober teenagers; of teenagers bribing an adult to buy illegal liquor—or of responsible teenagers arranging a designated driver who will not touch alcohol during the evening.

Historical and news stories carry more weight with a reader—she can think, "Oh yes, I remember that." It is verifiable. **Personal examples** may make the reader wonder if you've colored the facts; however, your own examples give you the chance to write vividly. You can describe the accident scene, quote dialogue from the beer party, build narrative conflict, and write with freshness you can't with historical cases—and you should. **Examples you heard from your friends** are less satisfactory because, as lawyers say, it is "hearsay" testimony. It is one step further removed from the reader and hence less reliable. We all know truth has a way of getting watered down (or spiced up!) as it gets passed along.

Hypothetical examples are necessary to fill in gaps when facts are not available or to project future events for which there are no facts. Hypothetical examples are simply made-up cases of things *likely to happen*. In the abortion debate, for instance, several hypothetical cases are usually raised: "Suppose a woman gets pregnant through rape" or "suppose a pregnant woman discovers the fetus is badly deformed." Both scenarios are likely to happen sometime. We might be able to track down facts about actual women in these cases, but if we can't, a hypothetical example can appeal to the reader's common sense. The reader will test your common sense in explaining the hypothetical case as well. You would be on shaky ground, I think, to portray a woman pregnant through rape as a person who should forget how she became pregnant and within months develop normal maternal tenderness, or look forward to the experience of childbirth the way an intentionally pregnant woman would. There are noble people who can do this—but wouldn't you agree that they are rare? It would be equally rare for normal women, even under such stress as this, to be driven to suicide should they not be allowed to have an abortion.

 Facts and examples are important support for most arguments; pack plenty in your essay, and use them fairly and vividly. Rely most on firsthand experience and reliable sources. Secondhand and hypothetical examples should be used as last resorts.

PRACTICE 13-10 Use a Web site to find two strong facts you could use to support your topic from Practice 13-4 or 13-5. Then add three examples—yours, your friends', historical and/or hypothetical.

APPEALS TO THE READER'S VALUES

People are persuaded not only by facts but by realizing that your proposal supports *values* they believe in. Facts without a context of values seem meaningless much of the time. Amory Lovins, an energy expert, calculated back in 1980 that if the United States were to take all cars off the road with gas mileage of less than 15 miles per gallon and were to replace them with cars with gas mileage of at least 35 miles per gallon, the United States could reduce its gasoline consumption by 15 percent. Ho-hum, right? Well, it becomes more interesting when Lovins reminds us today that if we reduced oil consumption 15 percent, we would have needed to import no oil from the Mideast and may have been less likely to invade Iraq. Do we want to pay for poor gas mileage with thousands of deaths? This puts the fact about gas mileage into a values context.

Some values that writers consider in persuasive writing are *economics, fairness, health, safety, love, environmental impact, freedom, and beauty.* As Abraham Maslow showed in his hierarchy of needs, certain basic needs must be met before people are willing to consider others. We are, therefore, unlikely to consider an appeal to our sense of beauty (put up a gorgeous city sculpture that will delight our minds) if the project will bankrupt us or be dangerous for children to play on. Maslow said we must have safety and basic physical needs met before we strive for "higher" values such as fairness and freedom. After we achieve basic needs, Maslow argued, humans give priority to love, beauty, and spiritual matters. Here is a simplified list of Maslow's values, starting with the most basic:

- **Physiological** (food, shelter, water, health)
- **Safety** (security, order, stability)
- **Belongingness and love** (family, friends, social groups)
- **Esteem** (status, power, recognition, money)
- **Self-actualization** (reaching your *individual* potential; for example, oneness with God, nature, or lover; creativity, justice, beauty, and freedom)

Maslow was being descriptive of how people behaved, not how he thought they *ought* to behave. By contrast, most philosophies and religions insist spiritual values are more important than, say, status, recognition, or even safety. People like Martin Luther King, Jr., or Mahatma Gandhi, as well as thousands of unknown people, have put justice, freedom, creativity, or love above personal health, safety, and status.

You will have to decide for yourself if Maslow is right about what values motivate people the most. Would *you,* for instance, bulldoze a beautiful neighborhood park for an industrial plant if it meant secure jobs for your family? Would most people? Germany, where little wilderness still exists, values nature preserves more than Brazil, which is burning down its vast tropical rain forest for industry in hopes of improving its people's standard of living. **One of the more interesting aspects of persuasive writing is dealing with the changing, conflicting values of people and groups**.

A student of mine served several hitches in the U.S. Navy SEALS. This young man had been in Lebanon when a terrorist drove a truck filled with explosives into a Marine barracks, killing nearly 300 men. He vowed revenge. In one paper he announced he was going into counterterrorist activity so he could torture terrorists and kill them. He described in vivid, gory detail what he would do to his country's enemies and concluded by saying, "I'm doing this so my future children can grow up in a decent, moral world." What hierarchy of values does he hold? Do you agree?

■ **PRACTICE 13-11** Make a list of your most important 8 to 10 values, trying to include several not already listed here. Star the two or three values you think are most important.

In practical terms, the persuasive writer might generate ideas to defend a proposal by going down a checklist of values, asking how each value can suggest new arguments to support his position. Suppose I am proposing that my state outlaw legal gambling and close betting parlors. **The list of values below is written so you can use it as a brain teaser to think up support for many topics.**

- What **economic** benefits will my position have? For whom? How much?
- Will it increase people's **security or satisfy basic needs?**
- Is it **fair** to all parties involved? Think through—one at a time—how various people might see it.
- Will it enhance or limit anyone's **freedom?**
- How will my plan affect **families?**
- Will my plan appeal to the reader's concern for **beauty?**
- Will my plan affect the **environment?**
- Will my plan build **self-esteem or status** for anyone? Who? Why?
- How might this help people **actualize their potential?**
- List **other values of importance to yourself.** How can they be appealed to by your proposal?

■ **PRACTICE 13-12** Go through this list to see what support it triggers to ban legalized betting. Some questions will lead nowhere; just move on.

For example, let me respond to the first question about **economic benefits**. Outlawing gambling may prevent some bettors from losing (or winning) money, but I suspect many would then bet illegally. This would actually increase the gambler's odds of economic success because the government keeps a higher percentage of money bet than bookies do. Outlawing gambling would deprive the state of this money and perhaps cause taxes to rise. If other states don't ban gambling, my state may lose some tourist dollars as well. I realize now I need to research how much is spent in my state on the lottery and horse racing and how much the state keeps.

Here's another example. An 18-year-old student of mine wrote to persuade her parents to rent to her (at less than half price) one of the apartments they owned. Vera admitted to our class that *privacy, freedom, and fun* were the values that interested her most in this proposal. But in her letter, she appealed to her *parents'* needs—how her moving out would benefit *them*. She would no longer mess up their apartment. She wouldn't disturb *them* when she came home late or when her friends phoned at 1 A.M. Moving out would give *them* more room for their younger children; it would teach Vera self-reliance to give *them* more freedom; life for *them* would be more peaceful when clashes with Vera stopped; and finally Vera would do better in school because the children and television would not interrupt her homework. *Thus, she would get her degree sooner, save her parents money, and become a success they'd be proud of.* Let's see—she hit status, economics, environment, freedom, and self-actualization. Vera's parents, as you might guess, saw through the "advantages" to them and said "no" anyway. Why? Because they agreed with Maslow that safety is more important. "You'll shoot your eye out" almost always trumps fun and freedom. And while I admired Vera's cleverness, it was too obvious a ploy.

■ **PRACTICE 13-13** Try the same list (and perhaps your own high-ranked values) with these proposals, looking only for support (we'll do objections in 13-19):

- The United Nations ought to be given command of a permanent, powerful military force.
- Evolution ought to be the only creation theory taught in public schools.
- Churches should pay property taxes.
- The Internet must be censored for pornography and dangerous information such as bomb instructions.

■ **PRACTICE 13-14** Use the value list to create more supporting arguments for your topic from Practice 13-3, 13-4, or 13-5. Write four arguments that appeal to values on the list.

A good persuasive letter targets the needs and values of the **person you address.** It's not enough to show how your idea will benefit you or society. **How will it benefit your reader?** Vera, who wanted her parents to give her an apartment, tried to do this. She looked at the value list through her readers' eyes. But she needed to look at *all* the list. Can you think of a way of allaying her parents' concern over safety? If you want a more relaxed dress code at the upscale men's clothing store where you work, it's not enough to appeal to the employees' comfort. Your boss cares about profits and a classy atmosphere to attract upscale clientele. Can you appeal to that value? This does not mean you have to be dishonest and pander to your reader. It means you have to see how your reader will see your ideas. You might, for instance, suggest that the salespeople could wear the upscale casual wear sold in the store—modeling it as they work.

You might focus on today's more relaxed styles and suggest that old-fashioned white shirts and ties make the store look stodgy. Any other ideas?

LOGIC

Strange as this may sound, logic alone rarely makes readers shout "Amen!" or write checks to support your cause. We tend to agree with ideas partly based on our trust of the writer (how well she connects to us and how fair her tone is), and also partly on our emotional response to the values and feeling behind the proposal. These are seldom totally logical. While good logic may not win agreement, bad logic can kill the deal. Logic draws together facts and appeals to values, and if you do not make a tight connection, the reader will have a good reason to reject your thesis. **In its simplest form logic takes one fact (the minor premise) and one value (the major premise) and shows that if they both are true, a reasonable conclusion drawn from them must also be true.** Let's take an example.

Suppose I want to persuade people that abortion is morally wrong and ought to be illegal. To do this I present a value—killing a human being is morally wrong and illegal. Then I present a fact—that a fetus is a human being. If these two are true, then the conclusion is inevitable: Killing a fetus is wrong and should be illegal. My logic (the connection between the two premises) is valid. Someone who disagreed with me, however, might argue that one or both of these premises are not true. With the abortion issue, people usually question whether a fetus is really a human being. Do you see how the logic of my claim disintegrates if that "fact" is proved false? The opposition might also question my other premise by pointing out that killing humans is morally or legally acceptable in a number of circumstances. Can you name some?

Logic, then, is rarely perfect. One or both of the premises can be questioned. In addition, there are logical fallacies that make any argument that uses them invalid. They are forms of dishonest persuasion. **Here are nine of the most common logical fallacies.**

I. **Endorsement.** A basketball star likes a certain hamburger. The commercial claims you will like it too. A doctor/actor from a TV show recommends a particular kind of coffee. Are you persuaded to buy it? Obviously, we suspect that these people's recommendations are strongly influenced by what they are paid. But the endorsement's fallacy isn't really lying, but logic. There is no necessary connection between the tastes of one person and another. Had a genuine doctor recommended a coffee for its health effects, we might have had a stronger case. An athlete endorsing a hamburger is less logical than an athlete endorsing sneakers. In such cases there should also be an explanation of *why* the product or viewpoint is correct. Does the hamburger use the highest quality meat, cost less, or avoid danger-ous preservatives? These are the real issues. Nor is it enough to say an expert like Abraham Maslow or Rachel Carson believed something. For the reader's understanding you also need to explain how the the-ory works or what the facts are.

2. **Hasty Generalization.** I hate Professor Smith. My friends in the class hate him. Therefore, Professor Smith must be an unpopular teacher. Sorry. You need more evidence. Several students from a class of 25 are too few to support such a claim. Perhaps your group is on Professor Smith's bad side because of poor performance or attitude. How about this: The Democrats always start America's big wars—Democrats were presidents when Vietnam, Korea, and World Wars I and II started. This is also hasty generalization—can you explain why? A hasty generalization means you base a conclusion or claim on too few examples or oversimplified evidence. You can overcome this in your essays by deluging your reader with cases and examples.

3. **Bandwagon.** This is similar to the endorsement, except that instead of picking a prominent person who supports your claim, you say your position must be right because many people support it. There's a quick cure for this fallacy: Just remind yourself how many millions of people thought Hitler and Mussolini were saviors. Closer to home, remind yourself how President Richard Nixon won a landslide election and resigned a year later for illegal activities. Was his presidency justified because many people supported him? No. What makes an argument right is that it *is right*, not that people *believe* it's right. Your job is to show how it's right, not how it's popular. Robert Frost summed this up neatly: "Thinking isn't agreeing or disagreeing—that's voting."

4. **Tradition.** "It's always been done this way" or "My parents taught me to believe. . . ." This avoids thinking. You're hiding behind someone else's thinking instead of walking the reader through the arguments themselves. There's a quick reminder you can use if you're tempted to rely on this fallacy: Suppose the first humans one million years ago had latched onto this principle: "We've always eaten our meat raw and slept in trees. No fire, no caves!" Traditional beliefs prevent people from rushing to each wild, untested idea that floats along, but just because a belief once may have been valid does not mean it still is. Tradition fights good new ideas as well as bad ones.

5. **Unqualified Generalization.** In our enthusiasm we sometimes exaggerate: "Television reality shows are the worst thing for our children's minds today." Really? Worse than pornography? Worse than fighting parents? Worse than an abusive teacher? A statement like the previous one shows the person has simply not thought through the idea. *Qualifying makes it more acceptable.* "Television reality shows are bad for children's minds." It is now no longer at the head of a list of *everything* bad. You could also say, "*Some* TV reality shows *may* harm a child's mind as badly as pornography." The reader cannot toss these away at first reading—he must first see how you support such a view. Avoid words like "all," "always," "never," "nobody in her right mind," or "everyone." Use considered words like "most people," "usually," or "under normal circumstances."

6. **Faulty Cause and Effect.** This means claiming one thing caused another to happen when the only tangible relationship between the two things is that one preceded the other. You may be able to prove the one did indeed cause the other, but a simple time relationship alone does not. "My parents got divorced after I was born. Therefore, I broke up their marriage." Or, "Every time I get a day off, it rains." Or, "The family has deteriorated in the past 20 years—since feminism became strong. That proves how harmful feminism has been to America." None of these are valid logic. In the first case you need to prove that your parents' marriage was solid before you came along and that you were the key problem in arguments your parents might have had. In the second, you'd have to establish that meteorological powers infuse your body on a day off. With the antifeminist statement, think of all the competing explanations for why the family has deteriorated: decline in churchgoing, increased violence, increased sexual activity outside of marriage, increased drug use, increased materialism, worse public morals, a more highly mobile society. All three cases need to show a *connection* between cause and effect.

7. **Sentimentality.** This means pleading a cause based on your feelings (usually misery) rather than on its merits. "You've got to give me a C in this course or I won't graduate"; "You can't withdraw me for absences; I'll lose my state aid." Sorry. The grade in a course says you have performed at a certain level, and your misery at not doing well should not persuade a professor your merit is greater than it is. Your state aid is given assuming you will attend class; you earn it by attending and performing at an acceptable level. "A promotion will make me so happy!" By itself, not good enough. The logical questions are: Did you earn it? Do you show potential?

8. **Attacking Your Opponent.** Instead of attacking a position, value, or fact to advance your case, you attack the person who made the proposal. "Don't support the President's plan to reform government ethics; he's corrupt, too." To a fair-minded reader, this is weak. The plan should be discussed on its own merits. How about these cases; are they valid criticisms?

   • "We shouldn't elect Hilary Clinton president; she stayed married to a cheating husband."
   • "We shouldn't do business with the Captain Computer Company; its head salesman smokes pot."

9. **Either . . . Or.** "Either we enact the governor's plan or the economy will crash." "We should either marry or break up." The "or" part of these statements may happen if we don't do the first part, but there are lots of other possibilities, too. We can compromise on the governor's plan and on dating less seriously. The economy (and our love life) may go downhill for a while, and then recover on its own. There may be several creative alternatives. "Either . . . or" limits the possibilities to only two choices when there are many. People who want you to be either for or against gay marriage, drug legalization, or human cloning, and who refuse to notice gray areas and alternatives, falsify the issue to make it a choice between good and evil. Most of the time, things are just not that way.

■ **PRACTICE 13-15** Think of two arguments that infuriate you: political, parental, peer, or commercial statements. Now, using the fallacies as a guide, expose the logical flaws in these arguments.

■ **PRACTICE 13-16** What is one argument supporting your topic from Practice 13-3, 13-4, or 13-5 that seems to rely on a logical fallacy? It will be easier to find a flawed opposition argument, but be honest enough to look for one on your side—and avoid it!

AN EXAMPLE OF SUPPORT AND LOGIC

In the following selection from a student essay, Candace Northrup proposes that we ought to allow doctors to prescribe marijuana for medical purposes under strict hospital supervision. Here is one of her support paragraphs:

Marijuana has been shown to help people with many illnesses. For glaucoma patients, marijuana reduces fluid pressure in the eye that causes the person to lose vision. AIDS patients use marijuana to increase appetite and decrease nausea. Some multiple sclerosis patients claim marijuana improves their motor functions and reduces muscle spasms and pain (Dickinson 135). Healthy people may not realize the pain these patients endure. My aunt, who has multiple sclerosis, can barely walk because the pain eats away at her. If marijuana was legal, she would suffer less.

Analysis: This scores high for packing specifics into a short paragraph. By listing the benefits of pot for three *types* of sufferers, Candace shows that the issue affects many people. If she had mentioned only one of the diseases, it would lack punch. Pot helps each disease—giving her authority. She appeals to the **values** of health and relief from pain, but also makes an **emotional appeal** to the reader's pity for the sufferers. The concluding example of her aunt personalizes the medical facts.

Candace's essay next raises several **refutations:**

How many people already use marijuana for medical purposes? One researcher says, "Six hundred thousand people now have criminal records because marijuana is not legal for medical use"; as a result, California and Arizona have passed initiatives approving the medical use of marijuana (Ziegler 70). So the government has been forced to look at the issue. Yet General Barry McCaffrey, head of drug policy, was quoted as saying, "Just when the nation is trying its hardest to educate teenagers not to use drugs, now they are being told that marijuana is medicine. There could not be a worse message to young people" (Stiefell 9).

This is one argument against legalizing marijuana—that children will see it as medicine and might think it is all right to smoke for recreation. As a teenager, I don't see that threat. Marijuana was around my small town. Legalizing marijuana for medical purposes is not going to cause much increase in teen usage. I don't see where General McCaffrey gets off saying, "The nation is trying its hardest to educate children on drugs . . ." because I haven't seen much education from the government. Even if we were educated, would it really stop the use of marijuana? Teenagers are curious and oblivious to the world. If teens have their minds set on smoking marijuana, then they are going to smoke it. Even though General McCaffrey opposes medical use of marijuana, the government recently agreed to spend $1 million to look into it (Stiefell 10).

Another question often raised is why legalize marijuana if THC, the main ingredient, is already being prescribed? THC is available as a legal pill (Brookhiser 28). Unfortunately, the pill can take hours to begin working. Smoked marijuana is effective within minutes (Dickinson 135). Second, treating nausea with a pill is not the brightest idea because nauseated patients may not be able to keep the pill in the stomach long enough for it to begin working. One report found that "Oral THC is metabolized through the liver, which neutralizes more than 90 percent of the chemical; smoking delivers the THC—as well as sixty other unsynthesized cannabinoids, many of which are therapeutic too—directly to the bloodstream" (Dickinson 135). Marijuana also seems safer than oral THC. The DEA's own administrative judge, Francis L. Young, declared, "Marijuana is one of the safest therapeutically active substances known to man" (Dickinson 135).

Analysis: The first two paragraphs fairly raise an objection based on the consequences to youth of legalizing pot, but Candace falls into **three fallacies** in responding: unqualified generalization, bandwagon, and attacking one's opponent. The unqualified generalizations occur in her description of teenagers as "oblivious to the world." Qualifiers like "some" or "many" or examples are needed.

■ **PRACTICE 13-17** Find the bandwagon and attacking one's opponent fallacies.

Candace's third paragraph **raises another refutation:** Why not prescribe the chemical in pot without legalizing pot? This is a good objection and one many readers may not have heard. **An unethical arguer might have ignored it.** She does a fine job of responding with facts to refute this objection, providing details of why smoked pot works better for sufferers. At the end of the paragraph—when she quotes a DEA official to contradict the DEA position—**is this an endorsement fallacy or a valid point?**
Now look at Candace's **sources:**

Works Cited

Brookhiser, Richard. "Pot Luck: Any Sick Person Who Wants to Use Marijuana to Help Himself Has to Break the Law." *National Review* 11 Nov. 1996: 27–28.

Dickinson, Ben. "What If Weed Is Exactly What You Need?" *Esquire* Oct. 1997: 134–35. →

> Stiefell, Chana Frieman. "Marijuana on the Ballot: Should a Menacing Drug Treat Some Chronically Ill Patients?" *Science World* 21 Feb. 1997: 8–10.
>
> Ziegler, Jan. "Up in Smoke." *Hospitals and Health Networks* 20 June 1997: 701

The first source is politically conservative, the second liberal, and the last two scientific/medical. Should we care? **Does her list of sources create a stronger image of the writer?**

Structuring the Persuasive Essay

If you have the time and creativity to invent your own persuasive structure, do it. But over 2,000 years from Roman orators to today's editorialists, one model structure stands out. Not only does this model help you organize your ideas, but also it generates new ideas and helps you cover key aspects of any persuasive presentation. The four-part structure is Introduction, Main Supporting Ideas, Refutation, and Conclusion.

 The introduction should begin by intriguing us with a concrete problem that is difficult to solve and end with your solution to this problem, your thesis. You establish an ethical, knowledgeable tone here by showing the reader your familiarity with the issues by mentioning several options people suggested for solving the problem.

The introduction then outlines in detail exactly what you are proposing. *Explain* **how your plan will work, and define key terms:** who will do what, how it will be funded, what the timetable or stages are. Before you defend it, show the reader exactly what you propose. A complex plan may require several paragraphs to explain. Don't skimp here!

The main supporting evidence should be arranged tightly, one paragraph or perhaps two for each main supporting idea, and the paragraphs filled out with examples, facts, appeals to value, and logic that support the idea. Study how Candace's paper does this. In papers of three to five typed pages, you should have room to develop three to four supporting ideas. In papers of one to two pages, two supporting ideas may be all you can back up in depth.

To outline, list the main arguments and fill in support from brain teasers under each. Try several scratch outlines until your main headings are crisp and distinct. The Roman orators believed support should start strong and end strong and that the less strong arguments should be in the middle. Their rule of thumb: Second strongest argument comes first, strongest comes last, and the others in the middle. If you have a flimsy argument, put that in your wastebasket.

■ **PRACTICE 13-18** Drawing on your notes from other practices, make a scratch outline of your main supporting ideas for your topic in Practice 13-3, 13-4, or 13-5.

The **refutation** comes next in the paper. After raising your main sup- porting ideas, take time to **consider one or two major objections someone might have against your views or proposal.** Some people may ask, "Why should I attack my own case?" Why indeed? Well, in a written persuasive paper, as contrasted with a debate, you have total control over the presentation of ideas; no one can question your ideas—*except the reader!* And believe me, when someone is trying to persuade a person, he will raise objections. Most people love to find reasons why things cannot be done. Hiding weaknesses in your position won't work with a good reader. So be honest. Also, by considering objections, you can modify and improve your ideas to be more convincing. It's not only honest but in your best interest as an arguer and will help you improve your ideas. As John Locke once observed, "To judge other men's notions before we have looked into them is not to show their darkness, but to put out our own eyes."

In the refutation section, **one strategy is to show how the objection is flawed. But first you must state opposition ideas with full** **honesty**—so it would satisfy the opposition. Present these as valid questions, not as pesky troublemakers. Then pinpoint *fallacies* in the objection, correct "*facts*" the objection may have mistaken, or question the *values* in the objection. In other words, the same brain teasers used to create support can also create refutations to an objection.

Suppose you have written an essay defending television, saying it contributes much to American culture and is a great educational tool. In your refutation section, you must consider objections people might have to your view. One objection would be that television watching has caused a decline in children's ability to read. This contradicts your claim of television's educational value. To be an honest arguer, you might point out that children do seem to watch television more than they read books; perhaps you might acknowledge that reading scores on standard tests have declined steadily during the past 25 years. How do you refute this now? **Begin by seeing if the objection falls into a logical fallacy.** Faulty cause and effect, for instance, seems to apply. Just because a decline in reading scores followed an increase in television watching does not prove one caused another. We have had Republican presidents most of the past 50 years; can we claim *they* caused a decline in reading scores? Of course not. In refuting, you should also suggest possible causes of the decline *other* than television. Perhaps the schools aren't teaching reading the best way; perhaps school discipline problems disrupt the teaching of reading; perhaps the lack of family togetherness (reading aloud after supper, discussing the newspaper) has contributed.

Question the facts. Are the reading tests outdated? Do the lowest test scorers watch the most television, or do the best readers also watch television? You can get examples from your classmates or perhaps do some quick research. You can also **question the values** behind the objection. You might argue it's too easy to blame a machine for our problems as a society when we ought to blame ourselves for not working hard enough to learn, support, and teach reading.

A second way of handling a refutation is to concede some truth to the objection. "Television has probably contributed somewhat to a decline in reading ability. However, . . . " *Then* writers usually say despite this drawback, there are too many good reasons to let this one objection stand in the way. This is often the only solution where there is no compromise possible, usually because of moral issues. If you were in favor of allowing abortions, for instance, you may have to concede that aborting a fetus really is the taking of a human or potentially human life. You might even acknowledge this would be wrong in a perfect world, but that the misery an unwanted or deformed child endures is worse yet.

Another type of concession offers compromises. People who are against abortions, for instance, might reluctantly agree that a woman in danger of dying in childbirth may be granted an abortion. But they should probably add that the principle of the sanctity of human life is still not compromised—that the taking of a life is to save a life.

The refutation section of a persuasive essay is perhaps the most important; it establishes your integrity as a writer, it forces you to consider your thesis more deeply, and it gives you the chance to make your argument even stronger. Refutation may be placed in a separate section of the essay, or you may handle it as objections might be raised against your supporting points.

■ **PRACTICE 13-19** Raise an objection to two of these proposals (used in Practice 13-13) and then see if you can refute the objections through logical fallacies, facts, or values:

- The United Nations ought to command a permanent, powerful military force.
- Evolution should be the only creation theory taught in public schools.
- Churches should pay property taxes.
- The Internet must be censored for pornography and dangerous information.

■ **PRACTICE 13-20** What two major objections might someone raise to your position in Practice 13-3, 13-4, or 13-5? Refute them with logic, values, or facts; concede; or compromise.

■ **PRACTICE 13-21** Find someone else's blog or a chat room that discusses a controversial issue. Pick a piece of writing you disagree with and write and post a response explaining why.

The **conclusion** in persuasive writing can be a simple reaffirmation of your thesis, but it's usually better to look forward. You might paint a picture of the world in which your plan is enacted, or you might paint a picture of how less effective plans than yours would affect people's lives. Or you might end with a dramatic statistic or example.

QUICK GUIDE TO CREATING PERSUASIVE WRITING

Identify a problem you'd like solved (try a bug list brain teaser)
List three to four possible solutions for the problem:

1.
2.
3.
4.

Choose one (your trial thesis).
List three reasons to agree with your proposal:

1.
2.
3.

List two possible objections to your proposal that someone might raise:

1.
2.

How might you answer these objections or modify your proposal to satisfy them? Why is one other possible solution inferior to the one you chose?

REHEARSING YOUR PAPER'S APPEARANCE IN COURT

- Picture a "jury" consisting of a professor, a classmate, a parent, a businessperson, a scientist, a friend, an elderly neighbor and a judge. Imagine sitting with them while a clerk reads your paper aloud.
  - ✓ Where might they feel as if they're being "sold" something?
  - ✓ Where will each one care most about your topic and where will some yawn?
  - ✓ Who will want more facts and where?
  - ✓ What values that you did not use might persuade some to your side? Where?
  - ✓ Which spots might the scientist, businessperson or judge find illogical?
  - ✓ What refutations would each person raise? Should you consider doing so?
  - ✓ What unintended and perhaps negative consequences of your proposal might occur to some of these people? If enacted, how might it influence other things?
- Now a lawyer from the other side approaches the jury. What evidence might he bring against your paper? How would he cross-examine your refutations?
- Revise the worrisome spots.
- Search for and correct the kinds of grammar and mechanical errors you have made on past papers.

VISUAL RHETORIC

To help you study the art of ethical persuasion, let's look at some pictures that convey arguments. Just as with written argument, you'll be able to evaluate these for persuasive ideas and supporting details, as well as tone, appeals to value, and sensitivity to audience. On the next page are two photographs that at first glance may seem to be simple records of events—just factual moments caught on film. But are they really neutral? **Context:** Both are pictures of Iraqi children wounded during the U.S./British attack and occupation. We do not know how they were hurt. But in such a context, these photos make persuasive statements and ones like them have been used to persuade people to accept political positions.

■ **PRACTICE 13-22** What message does each picture convey to you? How might different audiences react differently? What appeals to value does each make? Could you raise a refutation for each picture? Style: What effects do the two perspectives—distant shot and extreme close-up—have on the message? How would the wording of a caption make a difference?

Warren Zinn/Army Times Publishing Company/CORBIS

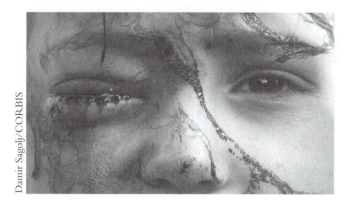

Damir Sagolj/CORBIS

The next two pictures are engravings by 18th Century artist William Hogarth. They are intricate, complex scenes, but ingeniously connected with contrasting details. **Historical Context:** Hogarth created these works to persuade people to support a law to restrict the sale of gin (which passed in 1751). While 18th century water was so contaminated people were forced to drink alcoholic beverages like beer to avoid disease, Hogarth believed the surge in drinking hard liquor, especially gin, was destroying society.

■ **PRACTICE 13-23** What details attract your eyes most in the first picture? What details attract your eyes most in the second picture? What is the artist's overall message, considering both works? List his main supporting arguments and back them up with details from both pictures. Describe his style—is his tone reasonable for persuasion? Ethical? The original audience was England in 1750. How effective is his argument today? Could we make the same argument about Cocaine Lane and Pot Street?

Gin Lane, 1751 (engraving) (b/w photo), Hogarth, William (1697-1764)/Bibliotheque Nationale, Paris, France, Lauros / Giraudon/ Bridgeman Art Library

"Gin Lane"

Beer Street, 1751 (engraving), Hogarth, William (1697-1764)/Guildhall Library, City of London/Bridgeman Art Library

"Beer Street"

Analyzing Professional Persuasive Writing

Analyzing professional persuasive writing draws on the same skills as peer reviews, but most professional writing has already been carefully edited, and a writer who exposes work to thousands or hundreds of thousands of readers pushes hard to have even stronger ideas and logic. So critically analyzing published work will challenge you, but it also creates the chance to sharpen your skills as a writer. After you read a published essay, start by writing a **summary analysis** to absorb and learn about the work.

SUMMARY ANALYSIS

- Mark the proposal or thesis and state it in your own words.
- List the main points used to support the thesis—list ideas, not details.
- List refutations the author raises and the answers to them.

Now, **think critically** to evaluate the essay's arguments and effectiveness. You're doing this not to rip apart the work, but to unpack its meaning.

CRITICAL ANALYSIS

For Facts
- ✓ What details back it up? What other support is needed?
- ✓ Where is it specific and where vague or hypothetical?
- ✓ Evaluate the sources of the facts—why are they reputable or suspect?

For Values
- ✓ What values does the argument appeal to?
- ✓ What other values might oppose the authors point? How?

For Logic
- ✓ Look for places where the author falls into logical fallacies.

Refutation:
- ✓ Be skeptical and think of other refutations. How might the author answer them?
- ✓ What implications or consequences does the author *not* raise?

Tone
- ✓ Look for specific examples of wording that create a positive or negative image of the persuader.

SAMPLE ANALYSIS: THE PROS AND CONS OF CLONING HUMANS

Let's look at a short published excerpt before turning you loose on a full essay. Scientists have worked to clone living creatures for decades. A clone is an exact genetic duplicate of one parent made from his or her cells without any genetic material from a second parent. Frogs and sheep, among other creatures, have been successfully cloned, and since 2003 several organizations have claimed they cloned human beings. While none of the human clone claims have been verified, most experts believe it is feasible, and some governments have enacted laws to prevent it.

Here is a small section from an essay *opposed* to human cloning that appeared in the *Spectator* the day after the first human cloning was claimed. No author was cited. The essay previously criticized cloning because there had been many defects in cloned animals. This would surely mean many defective human clones would suffer miserable lives before the process could be perfected. But the editorial asserted that the following was a much "deeper" reason to forbid cloning people:

> To begin with, there can be no valid reason for anyone to want to clone a human being. A desire is not its own justification; not every human desire is worthy of fulfillment, and life should not be lived as if it were an existential supermarket in which products such as human clones were to be picked off the shelf at the drop of a whim. No one has the right to a child, much less the child of his choice, and any society that forgets that human life is a gift held in trust, not an object for the self-gratification of individuals, is one which is in very deep trouble; for egotism could go no further. In such a society, everyone believes himself to be the Louis XIV of his own life, the absolute sovereign of his own existence, unwilling to accept any limitations to the expression of his own desires, and hence unable to live in true harmony with other, equally absolute monarchs. Either his wishes are met or he rages against the world. . . . Like a spoilt child, he will appreciate nothing; when he encounters the inevitable limitations of human existence, he will react with a querulous and destructive fury. He will hate the world and all it contains with vengefulness.

Summary Analysis: The publication opposes human cloning in this section because it is selfish and encourages social egotism. There is no refutation.

Critical Analysis: Before I start, let me confess I think it is creepy to create another little me, and it does seem egotistical and unnatural. I'm starting out prejudiced in the essay's favor. But I must get past my gut reactions and look more objectively at what is here.

Supporting Facts: Because this is an ethical topic, I should not demand piles of statistics or facts. Even so, I'm surprised to find out, when I examine the piece closer, how thin the evidence is. The author uses the metaphor of a supermarket for a nice visual, but it's not a fact. The only concrete example is of Louis XIV—hardly a reasonable example. The author makes many sweeping generalizations that, while elegantly stated and forceful, lack specific support.

Supporting Values: The author's appeals seem based on these values:

- Accepting nature's rules
- A belief that limits help us live more socially and more happily
- A belief that life is not our possession but a gift (from God? He does not say)

Values that would oppose the essay might include intellectual/scientific freedom (self-actualization in Maslow's hierarchy) and the right (is it a right?) for a person who is sterile to have DNA passed to children (belongingness or esteem needs). Can you think of another?

Logic: I see unqualified generalizations ("no valid reason for anyone," "no one has the right," and more—find them) and the either/or fallacy (see if you can pick it out and explain why it is illogical). These flaws, I think, result from not grounding each idea with details. It leads to simplification. This is ironic for me since I agree with the author that our society confuses personal "desire" with "justification," meaning we think because we want something, it is just or fair for us to have it. There is plenty of evidence that could have been used; advertising slogans such as "Have it your way" (fast food) and "You deserve it" (high-speed Internet), for example. See if you can add three or four examples of self-indulgent attitudes in modern life that could illustrate the author's concept. The author sees modern society as self-centered and thinks cloning oneself is the logical result of that attitude. He believes this urge destroys community and family. It's a creative idea and the editorial writer may be right, but he certainly has not proved it. There's just too little evidence. If I imagine implications or consequences of this essay's attitude, would we also shut down self-indulgent blogs, stop creating hybrid crops that feed the world, or tell Starbucks they can no longer offer 32 customized varieties of coffee?

Tone: It's smooth and forceful, but too absolutist and oversimplifies human motives. I feel as though I'm being addressed from a throne.

■ **PRACTICE 13-24:** Make a list of three reasons to support cloning humans and give examples and details to support each. Think of a strong refutation for one of your reasons and give support for that. If you consult with sources for ideas, be sure to credit them.

Writing Suggestions and Class Discussions

1. Read the letters-to-the-editor section of a newspaper and pick an example of a letter with an appealing tone and a letter whose tone

put you off. Explain why one works and why the other doesn't. Bring the letters to class. **Or** do the same thing with two letters in a chat room or blog.

2. Write a tell-off letter to someone who holds an idea you don't accept. Attack! Be sarcastic, abusive, snotty, and personal. Let it rip! *Then,* rewrite the letter as good argument, as though ten calm, unbiased, decent people have come to listen respectfully to you.

3. Write an introductory paragraph for a paper on teenage sex. Your job is to show the reader how difficult the problem is to solve and also how important it is to solve. Establish a tentative thesis by the end of the paragraph.

4. List a page of statistics, examples, and hypothetical examples that could be used to support one of these theses:
   - Baseball is boring.
   - Most white people have little idea what subtle discrimination most minorities suffer in an average day.
   - The rules of normal life are suspended once you enlist in the armed services.
   - Children are not as cute as many people believe.
   - High school is a time of continual humiliation for many students.
   - Old age can be the best time of a person's life.

5. Use the value list on p. 272 to support *or* refute the following proposals:
   - "The CIA should assassinate known terrorist leaders."
   - "Gay or lesbian teachers should not be hired in elementary schools."
   - "Public television stations ought to be supported by a special tax of $50 on all television sets sold."

6. Write examples to illustrate five fallacies. Label each example with the fallacy it demonstrates.

7. Pick out a web page or print ad, and write a paragraph explaining a fallacy in logic in the ad.

8. **Visual Rhetoric:** Create a serious ad for a product you like or create a spoof ad to attack a product you don't like. Use words *and* visuals to convince us.

9. Analyze a photo essay for its persuasiveness by going to http://www.time.com/time/photoessays.

10. If you could change one historical event, what would it be? For examples, have Jesus not be crucified or warn New York City, London, or Madrid before the terrorist attacks on those cities. Speculate on the hypothetical effects this change would have; then defend your change by appeals to value.

11. Write a response to an editorial in any newspaper or blog. Respectfully disagree with the author. In your introductory paragraph, accurately and fairly present the author's views; then work on refuting logic, facts, and/or values. Send it to the newspaper or post it online.

12. Write a one-paragraph letter/email to persuade your mother you really are working hard at college. Help her visualize the amount of work you're doing by making the statistics (number of pages read, papers done, hours studying, and so on) more visual.

13. Write a personal letter to a family member or friend to persuade that person to change his or her mind about a personal issue. See the sample student letter on page 431.

14. Write a one-page letter to yourself, persuading yourself to reform some habit or trait you know is wrong. Be sure to consider a refutation.

15. Write a one-page persuasive essay on some subject of college policy. Post it on your blog or send it to the college newspaper.

16. Write a letter persuading a company to change its television advertisement that you find offensive. Address it to the Public Relations Department and provide a stamped envelope so your professor can mail it.

17. Write a letter to any bureaucratic official, persuading him or her to change some policy or activity you don't like.

18. Write a proposal to your employer to solve a company problem. After revision, send it to your supervisor.

19. Read and discuss the sample student persuasive writings in Chapter 16.

20. Write a job application letter for yourself. Apply for an actual job you want now or imagine one you will want after graduation. Honestly sell yourself by referring to your main accomplishments, skills, experience, and personal qualities. If there is an obvious refutation (your lack of experience, for instance), answer it.

21. **Group Activity:** *Open Hearing:* The class will be divided into four groups. Each will develop its own proposal to solve a local or college problem, doing research and brain teasing for supporting facts, values, and logical arguments. Each group will present its plan to the rest of the class in an open hearing for feedback: refutations, suggestions for additional research, new ideas. Then each student will write a persuasive paper on the topic.

22. **Group Activity:** Bring to your peer group a thesis and two or three main supporting ideas for a persuasive paper. Each member of your group will role-play a person or group who is likely to have a strong

view about your proposal and express how that person or group might argue for or against your thesis.

23. **Group Activity:** Predict the arguments the following groups would make about this proposal: "The Internet must not be censored in any way."

- A parent of school-age children
- A Chinese pro-democracy leader
- A member of a white supremacist militia
- An FBI official
- A wheelchair-confined person

SAMPLE STUDENT PERSUASIVE ESSAY

Helping Immigrants Is Our Right and Duty
Sandra Marcucci

A small boy huddles in terror as his home is invaded by gun-wielding intruders who drag his father into the midnight darkness. An emaciated girl rummages through a rat-infested dump in search of a meal to bring home to her starving siblings. A mother in Ghana weeps as she sells her child to a fisherman, believing her son is better off as a slave than dying of hunger. Imagine a world in which needy people are not assisted by those able to assist. Imagine a place where starvation, murder, abuse, rape, and other atrocities prevail. These places exist, and many immigrants throughout history have journeyed to the United States to escape such conditions for a better life. The Statue of Liberty regally stands at New York Harbor to welcome all those in need. As members of the human race, we have a duty to help these immigrants.

Between 1892 and the early 1950s, nearly fifteen million immigrants entered the United States through Ellis Island (Brownstone n. pag.). In 2006 more than one million legal immigrants and one and a half million illegal immigrants entered the country. Without a doubt, the vast majority of the population of the United States traces its heritage to ancestors looking for better opportunities. The Statue of Liberty offers safe harbor for all, proudly saying, "Give me your tired, your poor, your huddled masses . . . " Nowhere do the lines on Liberty state that we should do this until it becomes inconvenient.

→

The United States is a free society with an abundance of food, shelter and opportunity for a safe existence. Members of this society have a moral obligation to share our wealth and food with those in need. Thomas Jefferson established this country's basic principles by writing: "That all men are created equal; that they are endowed by their Creator with certain unalienable rights; that among these are life, liberty and the pursuit of happiness." He concludes with the judgment, "And for the support of this declaration, with a firm reliance on the protection of Divine Providence, we mutually pledge to each other our lives, our fortunes, and our sacred honor" (Jefferson n. pag.). Are citizens of the United States more entitled to freedom and dignity than immigrants from foreign lands for the sole reason that they were fortunate enough to be born here? They are not.

An article in *The New York Times* reports that Jorge A. Bustamante, a United Nations human rights expert, said that the United States is not doing enough to protect immigrants' rights and that he had "serious concerns" about immigrants' conditions here. He adds, "The overuse of immigration detention in the United States violates the spirit of international laws and conventions and, in many cases, also violates the actual letter of those instruments." His report said an increasing number of raids by Immigration and Customs Enforcement officers on houses and workplaces had "terrorized immigrant communities" ("Immigration" A11).

Immigrants have fled their homelands to escape evils such as the Nazi invasions and extermination of millions of Jewish people or the ongoing "ethnic cleansing" in Rwanda. Even today epidemics, famine and natural disasters force families to leave in search of food, shelter and safe living conditions. The United States is their hope for a new start. St. Paul writes, "There is neither Jew nor Greek, there is neither slave nor free man, there is neither male nor female, for you are all one in Christ Jesus" (Gal. 3:28). All people have the capacity to love, learn and contribute to the world we live in, and no one should be overlooked or mistreated, regardless of race or other differences, especially in a country founded on equality for all. We have a responsibility to help immigrants achieve equality.

Hundreds of Mexican immigrants live in fear of deportation, which would separate them from their U.S.-born children, as in the

→

case of 28-year-old Liliana Sanctuario. Liliana and her two-month-old son, Pablo, currently live in a space provided by St. Luke's Episcopal Church in Long Beach, California to avoid deportation, which would separate them from her husband and three children who are U.S. citizens and legal residents. Elvira Arellano, threatened with the possibility of being separated from her seven-year-old son, is taking refuge in a Methodist church in Chicago while facing deportation. Churches of all denominations around the country feel the need to provide temporary lodging and assistance to immigrants facing current policies, believing it is their moral duty to help ("Dilemma on Sheltering Immigrants" n. pag.).

Peggy Delarose-Delgado, a naturalized citizen born in the Dominican Republic has had her home invaded twice. She describes the shock of having a dozen Immigration Agents invade her home, terrifying her children (Preston n. pag.). Many immigrants, legal and illegal, have their rights violated and privacy invaded by federal institutions conducting these terrorizing raids. Any parent would be outraged and helpless finding herself in a similar situation in which she could not protect her children. As American citizens we often take our rights for granted. Consider the case reported by *The New York Times* about a Chinese woman who miscarried twins after being taken by authorities to New York to be deported. Immigration officials deny Zhenxing Jiang's claim that she was physically and mentally abused, and denied food and medical care when taken into custody. Ms. Jiang and her husband entered the country illegally in the mid-90s and applied for political asylum, contending that under China's one-child policy, she could face forced abortion or sterilization if she were made to return with two American-born children (Bernstein A14).

How would you feel if your mother or daughter was "forgotten" and left in a jail cell for four days with no food or water as was Adriana Torres-Flores, 38, an illegal immigrant from Mexico awaiting transfer to the county jail after being arrested on charges related to the sale of pirated DVDs and CDs (Nossiter A12)? Stories like this are repeated throughout the country on a daily basis and must be prevented. If a child is starving or shivering in the cold wearing only the tattered remains of a dress, or sick and needing medical attention, regardless of whether she is an immigrant, legal or illegal,

→

it is our moral obligation to do what can be done to change the situation.

Why is it so difficult for citizens to become involved with the issue of immigration? Excuses include that they're too busy, don't understand it or don't think it affects them, so why should they care? But what would have happened if Thomas Jefferson or George Washington did not fight for freedom and human rights? Denial has not solved any of the immigration issues, but only increased them. Immigrants who create successful lives here will not only add to our culture, but will no longer drain the government. In addition, immigrants who have been through similar situations would be able to assist new immigrants. Monies wasted on useless raids that only produce fear and anger could be used to provide assistance to immigrants building new lives. Helping immigrants find a future honors our ancestors who entered the United States in years past for the very same reason immigrants come today: in search of freedom and stability.

Many people claim that because these immigrants entered the country illegally, violating laws, they should be held responsible and sent back. But aren't there more basic moral values than obeying laws? Shouldn't compassion and respect for human rights be regarded as higher standards? Don't we expect the same in our everyday lives? Don't we have an obligation to protect these values, not just for ourselves but for those less fortunate as well?

The golden rule says, "Do unto others as you would have them do unto you." If each citizen made the effort to take one positive action—whether sheltering the needy, feeding the hungry, donating to an organization providing legal aid or financial aid for immigrant children to attend school, or voting to support more humanitarian laws—much could be accomplished. This unfortunate situation must be dealt with, as it goes against the principles that make this country proud, prosperous and free. The United States was founded on moral values and human rights, and all citizens should insure that immigrants can find them here.

Works Cited

Bernstein, Nina. "Asylum for Woman Who Miscarried During Effort to Deport Her." *New York Times* 8 Sept. 2007: A14. *InfoTrac*. Monroe County Lib. System, Rochester, NY. 22 April 2008 <www.infotrac-college.com>.

Brownstone, David M., Irene Franck and Douglas Brownstone. *Island of Tears*. New York: Barnes and Noble, 2000.

"Dilemma on Sheltering Immigrants." *Christian Century* 10 July 2007. *InfoTrac*. Monroe County Lib. System, Rochester, NY. 22 April 2008 <www.infotrac-college.com>.

"Immigration Policy in U.S. Criticized by U.N. Aide." *New York Times* 8 March 2008: A11.

Jefferson, Thomas. "Declaration of Independence." *The Avalon Project at Yale Law School*. n.d. 1–7. 12 April 2008 <www.yale.edu/lawweb/avalon.htm>.

Nossiter, Adam. "Arkansas Woman, Left in Cell, Goes 4 Days with no Food or Water." *New York Times* 12 March 2008: A12.

Preston, Julia. "No Need for a Warrant, You're an Immigrant." *New York Times* 14 Oct. 2007. *InfoTrac*. 21 April 2008 <www.infotrac-college.com>.

Discussion/Writing

1. Which values does the author appeal to most strongly? Which values might a person opposed to a more open immigration policy use in response?

2. What type of supporting evidence is stressed in this paper? How much is facts, statistics and examples, how much value and how much logic? How effective is the balance in persuading you to agree?

3. Analyze the logic in her analysis in the last two paragraphs. Be specific.

4. Evaluate this essay as persuasion, using the Peer Review Checklist as your guide. Other student persuasive writings can be found on pages 423–50.

SAMPLE PERSUASIVE PARAGRAPH

Battling Obesity with Cocaine
Christopher J. Nesbitt

With obesity sweeping across America with the fury of a forest fire in dry season, everyone is looking for the miracle cure. According to the American Obesity Association, 64.5 percent of adult Americans are overweight. Phen Phen, Trim Spa and the Hollywood Diet are just a few of the fads Americans have gobbled up to combat obesity. What if they took crack cocaine or shot up heroin to lose weight instead? Really, when was the last time you saw a morbidly obese crackhead? Poor diets and sedentary lifestyles are major contributors to the overweight epidemic. Narcotic users generally eat very little and are in a constant state of motion chasing their next high. Sure, it's a radical proposal, but Americans love a quick fix. To lose weight today, people have three quarters of their stomach removed, have fat literally vacuumed out of them and even inject horse urine into themselves. Smoking crack is easier; all the user has to do is place a little glass pipe to her eager lips, light up, sit back and watch the pounds melt away. It sounds safer than what people do now. Realistically, what's a bigger drain on our health care system, morbid obesity or some innocent narcotic usage?

Discussion/Writing

1. What values are stressed in this proposal? Which values would best refute his proposal?
2. This paragraph suggests an unstated criticism of American attitudes. What is it? Explain.
3. Analyze his use of the words "gobbled," "fix," "drain," and "realistically."
4. This is a thought–provoking paragraph rather than a fully developed essay. How serious is he? How do you know?
5. Write a similar satire for another cultural issue, such as hair loss or erectile dysfunction.

☑ Peer Review Checklist for Persuasion

Author: _____

Author's intended audience (explain background if necessary):

One concern or problem the author has with the paper is: _____

Reviewer: _____

	Strong	Average	Weak
Introduction: Grabs my attention			
Plan is detailed			
Thesis/proposal is clear			
Tone: Respectful, open-minded			
Ideas: Freshness			
Arguments			
Details: Supporting facts			
Appeal to values			
Logic			
Refutation:			
Documentation (if used)			

Respond to the author's concern:

The strongest part of this paper is:

Here are two things you might work on in revision:

1.

2.

Here's another reason or example to support your idea:

Here's a possible objection someone might raise to your idea:

SAMPLE PROFESSIONAL ESSAY

LEGALIZING SAME-SEX MARRIAGE IS SENSIBLE
Jay Hancock

Feb. 20--Societies that are tolerant, free and diverse tend to be richer and happier than societies that aren't. Maryland has shown this for decades.

Now is the time to extend the legacy by legalizing same-sex marriage. The move would beam welcome signals not just to gays and lesbians but to all members of the young "creative class" who represent the economic and social future. Not co-incidentally, it's the right thing to do.

More and more research shows how inextricably linked tolerance and prosperity really are. No religion, race or sexual orientation has a monopoly on talent. States wanting to stay ahead must show that their doors are open to everybody.

Statistically, a large gay population is one of the best predictors of a strong economy, economic theorist Richard Florida noted in *The Rise of the Creative Class.*

"To some extent, homosexuality represents the last frontier of diversity in our society, and thus a place that welcomes the gay community welcomes all kinds of people," he wrote. "Openness to the gay community is a good indicator of the low entry barriers to human capital that are so important to spurring creativity and generating high-tech growth."

Of course you can carry Florida's observations too far. Trying to start a "gay business district," as Spokane, Wash., did after he spoke there a few years ago, won't bring high-tech nirvana without arts, music, diversity and other attributes the creative class craves.

Some attempts to put gay marriage and the Chamber of Commerce on the same bandwagon are just silly.

Last year, the UCLA School of Law's Williams Institute found that increased wedding-hall rentals from same-sex nuptials would help generate a net gain for Maryland's budget of $3.2 million a year. Folks on both sides of the debate can tell you the stakes are a lot higher than a couple of coins in the state till.

→

But as part of a larger policy of openness and benevolence, legalizing gay marriage makes sense for Maryland. We already boast the culture, tolerance, diversity and educational resources the creative class seeks. Allowing unions for two people who love each other – no matter what their gender — will cement the franchise.

And don't be surprised if they bring economic dividends.

Tolerance toward gays is crucial to Baltimore's future as a high-tech hub, a study by the University of Baltimore's Merrick School of Business found a couple of years ago. Metro Baltimore's "Gay Index," as measured by a professor at Carnegie Mellon University, outranked those of Chicago, Philadelphia, Cleveland and St. Louis.

Such a drawing card can help make Baltimore the first Rust Belt city to successfully transform into "an inclusive, diverse and creative economy," wrote Zoltan Acs, the University of Baltimore study's author.

It's not that gays and lesbians are more likely to seek high-tech, high-paying jobs than heterosexuals. Rather, intelligent, creative people of any sexual orientation are more likely to feel comfortable in places that foster tolerance. Companies wanting to hire them must find them on their own turf.

It boils down to attracting youth, who of course are tomorrow's work force. With a median age of 37, Maryland's population is older than that of 30 other states, including Virginia, California, Georgia, Utah and Texas. Young people are more likely to pick up stakes for attractive areas. They're also more likely to support gay rights and gay marriage.

History has demonstrated the wages of inclusiveness and its opposite. Spain's expulsion of Muslims and Jews in the 1400s prompted a long decline. Welcoming Jews, Huguenots, artists and scholars helped make the Dutch Republic powerful and rich in the 1600s despite an almost complete lack of natural resources.

Nobody chooses to be gay. But by approving gay marriage, Maryland can choose to improve its record of equal opportunity for everybody, which is the only way to run an economy.

→

DISCUSSION/WRITING

1. Write a summary analysis and critical analysis of this essay based on the checklists on p. 288.

2. Hancock only makes a passing reference to legalizing gay marriage as "the right thing to do." Should he have spent more time on the moral issue? Defend your stance.

The Literary Essay and Review

14

DURING COLLEGE YOU WILL PROBABLY BE ASKED TO write papers about poems, plays, fiction, or essays. Why? Partly to sharpen your critical thinking and writing. But also because literature's great works often better express our own unborn or rejected ideas. Writing about literature not only teaches us how the best writers write; it also helps develop thoughts we have not been able to ripen alone. Literature's compact intensity often reveals patterns, emotions, and ideas more clearly than in real life— which is watered down with trivia. In a real sense we become what we read.

Exactly what is a literary essay? What does it do? First, it is *persuasive,* for you must convince a reader with evidence that your analysis is valid. It's *informative* as well, because most literary essays strive for an objective tone and reveal something about the work, not just your feelings. Some require *research*.

At heart, the literary essay *explains* or *analyzes* a literary work. It is *not a summary.* Analysis seeks the *why* under the surface of a literary work. It discovers not-so-obvious patterns, style, or ideas. Analysis creates a *thesis* to be proved about the work:

> "*Moby Dick* is not really about hunting whales but about hunting for the God who runs this world."

In every work of genius we recognize our own rejected thoughts.

—RALPH WALDO EMERSON

Men take possession of art as a means of covering their nakedness a little.

—PABLO PICASSO

> "In Frost's poem 'Stopping by Woods on a Snowy Evening,' the horse represents civilization and order."

> "*The Glass Menagerie* uses music and lighting to create a mood of fantasy."

Notice that each thesis requires supporting evidence from the literary work, and each says something *about* the work that the work's author does not state; it does not simply retell the story.

Here are the same three theses stated as vague summaries—theses that will lead you to D papers or worse:

> "*Moby Dick* is about a man obsessed with killing a white whale."

> "'Stopping by Woods on a Snowy Evening' tells how a man is tempted to enter a beautiful woods instead of going home."

> "*The Glass Menagerie*'s main character is a frustrated young man who lives with a bossy mother and a fragile sister."

A good thesis may also compare or classify several works:

> "Modern detective stories still use Poe's tricks."

> "Marlowe's *Dr. Faustus* and Goethe's *Faust* portray two very different men who sell their souls to the devil."

> "We can see Sylvia Plath's changing view of death if we compare one early and one late poem."

■ **PRACTICE 14-1** Explain what a writer would have to do to prove each of the six good theses listed.

How Much Can You See?

Read the literary work *slowly* (fast reading is for newspapers). Allow the story or poem to lead you into its world. **Suspend judgment at first.** Say to yourself, "Maybe what's going on here is . . . " rather than committing yourself to one idea. **Read it again, marking passages that strike you as important or meaningful.** These may not always be something you understand; in fact, sections that seem irrelevant or puzzling may be the most fruitful because you hope to explain the not-so-obvious.

Your job as a serious reader of literature—and as someone who wants to enjoy it—is to see how much you can see. There's no one right answer the author has hidden behind door number one, two, or three. You will succeed if you patiently explore the literary work by crawling around inside it without preconceptions and without labeling, noticing as much as you can the odd words and unexpected twists, the smells, and images the work creates in your own head. Billy Collins, a Poet Laureate of the United States, says a reader should "drop a mouse into a poem/and watch him poke his way out." Think of that mouse as your own feelings and thoughts. Experience the poem or story with your imagination, emotion, and physical senses. **Leave the abstracting until a little later. First,** **sniff the story, nibble it, check out the interesting debris in the corners and the little holes in the wall.** How does it make you feel? What pictures does it bring to your mind?

■ **PRACTICE 14-2** Read one of the poems starting on p. 321 and mark lines that grab your attention, then finish these sentences:

"When reading this, pictures of . . . came into my mind."

"When I was reading, I experienced feelings of . . ."

"Maybe what's going on here is . . ."

At this point, an *idea* for a thesis may occur to you. The marked passages will be handy *details* for evidence. But if no thesis pops up automatically, several ways of thinking about literature can be applied as brain teasers. I'm going to suggest **four major approaches to get ideas about literature:**

- Use your own gut reactions.
- Try to discover the author's intention.
- Use a critical perspective.
- Explicate or analyze the words in the work.

Brain Teasers for Literature

1. **Use your own gut reactions.** Reading requires *collaboration* between writer and reader. Writers are helpless without readers' imaginations. They rely on readers to catch suggestions, to feel sad or afraid. Your response is part of the literature. You're not simply a visitor looking at an object, but a vital part of an experience, and your presence alters its meaning. In fact, **your gut feelings help create all literary works, for they are incomplete without a reader's interaction. This is the philosophy of reader–response interpretation.**

Start by listing your thoughts on a literary work. **Freewrite your impressions and observations.** Begin by describing the emotions the literature made you feel, what you thought about after reading it, or how you might behave if you had been in the same situation as the main character. Reread the work's significant passages to restart the flow when you stall. If an idea sizzles, continue in paragraph form until the spell cools; then start new ideas.

The drawback to gut feelings is that they may not be in the work. If you enjoyed pet garter snakes as a child, for instance, you may allow this personal experience to misread a poem like Emily Dickinson's "A Narrow Fellow in the Grass." Dickinson's comment that snakes make her feel "zero at the bone" does not allow a cuddly snake interpretation. *You* may write such a poem, but Dickinson didn't. As I will point out in the fourth brain teaser, you must be able to *support* your gut reactions with evidence from the work.

2. **Explain the author's intentions.** One person who should know what a literary work means is its creator. So to understand the work, we might try to discover the author's intentions in creating it. **This involves researching what authors have said about their work or biographical events that relate to the work**. Poet T. S. Eliot attached more than 50 notes to "The Wasteland"—most readers need these comments and explanations to understand the poem. Another example is poet and novelist Thomas Hardy, who often wrote about chance and fate. Two biographical incidents may explain why. Doctors pronounced Hardy stillborn at birth, but he was revived by a skeptical nurse. Weeks later, he was found with a poisonous snake sleeping beside him. These stories, told to young Hardy, shaped his personal mythology and may have influenced the accidents and twists of fate that afflict his characters.

There are dangers in biographical analysis. A book does not necessarily reflect an author's life. Writers often disguise their personal lives, create purely from fantasy, or build a mythical public image of themselves. Robert Frost cultivated the kindly, simple New England farmer image, but his poetry was cynical and elegant. Ernest Hemingway's books are tough and antireligious, yet we know he was a soft touch for friends in need and often slipped into churches to pray. Robert Browning raised another problem. A popular English poet, Browning was asked late in life to interpret one of his first poems, "Sordello," because no one understood it. "When I wrote 'Sordello,'" Browning sighed, "only God and I knew what it meant. Now only God knows." He could no longer explain his own poem! The point is that authors are not omniscient about their writing. Their intentions—if we can really discover them—may strike readers quite differently. **It's perfectly reasonable to disagree with an author's interpretation of her own work—*if* you can prove the words support your view.** If you do find an author's life or philosophy relevant to the work, you must also show evidence from the work to support such an interpretation. Most professors will be uneasy with a totally biographical interpretation of a literary work, but some connections may help develop your ideas.

3. **Consider critical perspectives on literature.** Like biographical interpretations, these ways of thinking step outside the strict boundaries of the text. They relate the literary work to ideology or social issues and give you new ways to think about the writing. Here are some common ones:

    • **Political perspective.** You can interpret literary works as expres- sions of common social problems. John Steinbeck's *The Grapes of Wrath* or *In Dubious Battle,* for instance, can be interpreted as attacks on capitalism during the Depression and as portraits of the struggle to establish labor unions. Your paper could discuss the accuracy of Steinbeck's portrayals of history or the new ideas he created for social justice. Edward Abbey's novel *The Monkey-Wrench Gang,* which advocates sabotaging bulldozers, driving spikes into trees (to ruin saw blades), and blowing up dams, inspired the "Earth First!" group that actually does some of these things. A historical approach could compare Abbey's ideas with Earth First's or debate the ethics of his philosophy as expressed in the book.

    • **Feminist perspective.** You can evaluate literary works' portrayal of women and of gender roles of both sexes. Shakespeare often gets credit for creating smart, witty, independent, strong women like Portia, but is criticized for paper dolls like Ophelia or for shrews like Kate, who is "tamed" into meek obedience by her loudmouthed oaf husband. Or, as some critics suggest, has Kate learned to play along with male egos in public so she can be free in private? Your paper can evaluate or define how women and gender roles are handled in the work.

    • **Ethnic perspective.** Mark Twain's *Huckleberry Finn* has been at- tacked for its portrayal of African Americans. After an explosion, someone asks if anyone was killed. A boy replies, "No . . . only a nigger." Was Twain a racist or using irony to attack racism? Twain's life, we are fairly sure, showed respect, even love, for African Americans, and most critics believe he wanted to make white readers feel the ugly horror of racism. But the book has some nasty dialogue. To write a paper on this topic, you would have to dig up ethnic references from the book and use them to support a thesis. Shakespeare's portrayal of the Jew Shylock in *The Merchant of Venice* has been considered anti-Semitic. Your paper could gather references in the play, research the way Jews were seen and treated in Shakespeare's day, and draw comparisons to current literature.

- **Other perspectives.** Any belief system can be a brain teaser, a window through which you see the text. And each perspective alters what ideas will be let loose in your head. **You can analyze any literary work from a Christian, Hebrew, Hindu, or Muslim perspective. Or from a psychological, mythological, or sociological perspective.** For example, John Barzelay's student paper on page 446 looks at the ancient Greek epic, the *Odyssey,* through the perspective of the psychology of Attention Deficit Disorder.

The danger of critical perspectives is that you may distort the literary work to make it fit your idea. Is Freud's Oedipal theory applied to Hamlet—a latent sexual attraction toward his mother—a brilliant idea or an exaggeration? As with biographical interpretations, you must return to the words in the text for supporting evidence.

4. **Focus on the words.** Many literary critics today say an author's atheism or the work's connection to politics is secondary. They say that since words create meaning, the analysis should focus on them. Virtually all literary critics agree that *any* **analysis should include some explication of the text.** This means a close reading of the text in detail. Your entire paper may be a line-by-line interpretation of a poem or a selection from a short story or, more often, may explicate several short sections to show how the literary work supports your thesis. At the brain teaser stage, work through key passages, explaining lines and tying ideas together. Here's a passage from Thoreau's *Walden:*

> Time is but the stream I go a-fishing in. I drink at it; but while I drink I see the sandy bottom and detect how shallow it is. Its thin current slides away, but eternity remains. I would drink deeper; fish in the sky, whose bottom is pebbly with stars.

Brain teaser: Time is like a stream. Okay. What are the fish? Are they ideas? People? He also drinks from time—we all do. Time nourishes us—like food and water. But Thoreau sees through time and realizes it is "shallow" and "sandy." These aren't really negative words, but they do show how small and impermanent time is—which is ironic because time seems immense to most people. Time flows away and is thin because the present moment is all we can ever grasp and that's gone as soon as it comes. He compares time with eternity. He wants to be nourished by something deeper than time. The sky is like a giant stream, or ocean and stars like pebbles. Magnificent—the cosmic beach. This contrasts with the shallow, sandy stream of time. The sky at night does resemble a giant ocean, but he's talking about it on a deeper level, about the soul or heavens perhaps, finding nourishment from things that do not change and slide away but which are permanent. How do we grasp that, find it? Thoreau's two years at Walden, then, may have been a kind of fishing in time. Self and even nature are incredibly tiny fish.

A few observations on this process: My rough brain teaser opens up potential ideas but must be focused when I develop a trial thesis. It wanders around because I am *exploring* an idea, not writing a paper. Second, notice how long the explication is compared to the original. That's normal—works of genius compress much into a small space. Third, notice that a rough explication moves backward and outward for connections; you cannot simply plod through line by line. Tie ideas together.

■ **PRACTICE 14-3** Quote a few favorite lines from a song or poem you like. Explain the meaning based on your gut feelings, then explain them again using one of the other literary brain teasers to see if you can either add to what you've said or see the lines freshly enough to get a new perspective or possibility.

Brain Teasers for Explication

I. **Theme.** Look for the message in the text, but don't settle for the first idea you see. **Make a list of possible themes.** Very few literary works have one underlined purpose. And often the first ideas that occur to you, as with any brain teaser list, will be superficial. You should be especially suspicious if your theme sounds like a cliché; "What goes around, comes around" or "You can't judge a book by its cover" are probably too obvious for a serious literary work. Also, don't think of theme as the ultimate point of a literary work. Literature is not a sermon in rhyme or dialogue, but an experience of life. There's more to it than a moral.

In its proper form a theme must be:

- **A complete statement, not just a single word**
- **Stated in terms outside the literary work—stated in universal terms**

> **Example:** The theme of *Romeo and Juliet* is that romantic love cannot exist in this corrupt world.
> **Weak:** The theme of *Romeo and Juliet* is love. (What *about* love?)
> **Weak:** The theme is that Romeo loves Juliet too much when their families are fighting. (This is not universal.)

How do you figure out what a theme is? There's no formula, but you might start by putting into words what the main character learns or why the work ends as it does. **Start with a topic word like "jealousy" or "freedom" and try to say what the story or poem *demonstrates* about the topic.**

WHY DON'T AUTHORS JUST SAY WHAT THEIR THEME IS?

- Because authors seldom write poems or stories just to prove a point. Other aspects are equally important to them. You wouldn't want an author to announce as he introduces a character, "Psst! This woman is the villain—watch out for her!" or "Hey, here comes a rhyme!"
- Because authors usually develop several themes simultaneously.
- Because it's more intellectual fun to explore and debate a story when it's not neatly labeled and wrapped.
- Because reading literature is like reading a more intense version of life—if we were told the point, we might pay less attention to living it.

2. **Conflict.** List the forces in tension in the work. In the quote from Thoreau, time versus eternity is most obvious, but you could also list earth versus heaven or permanence versus impermanence. In a short story or play, conflict occurs between characters, in a character's mind, or between a character and society or nature. **List all the conflicts and fill them out with examples or evidence from the story. Then draw a conclusion about the conflict, and you have your thesis:**
   - In *Walden,* Thoreau struggles toward heaven but refuses to let go of earth.
   - In *The Sun Also Rises,* the conflict between the matador and bull reflects the conflicts among Jake, Brett, and Robert Cohn.

   Your paper must then illustrate and prove its thesis with detailed evidence.

3. **Character.** Drama, fiction, and some essays and poems can be approached by thinking about character. Start with gut reactions, but also apply these questions:
   - What consistent qualities does a character have?
   - What motivates the character?
   - What complexities does the character show?
   - Does the character change, and how?

To discover ideas, comment on each question and note details from the work for support. In *The Great Gatsby,* for example, Jay Gatsby is *consistently* polite, gentle, a big spender, mysterious, and oddly detached from real life. He's *motivated* most obviously by wealth and the desire for Daisy, the rich girl he loves but who married someone else. Underneath, there's also his motive of wanting to live in the past. He's *complex* because he has contradictions and inner conflicts: He has gangster pals and a poverty-stricken past and yet can be naive and gallant and really doesn't care about money except to attract Daisy. Does he *change?* Scholars have debated this point since the book was published. This brain teaser can supply ideas and details for any paper on fiction or drama.

4. **Images.** Most literature can be analyzed through its images and symbols—pictures and other sense details. **Scan the work, listing images, searching for patterns and repetitions.** In *Romeo and Juliet,* for instance, Shakespeare uses religious images (saints, prayer books, a shrine) to refer to Juliet. This suggests both love's holiness and Romeo's melodramatic excess in Act I. In *The Great Gatsby,* the author repeatedly mentions the green light on Daisy's dock across the bay. Perhaps Gatsby wants a green "go" light from Daisy to pursue his romance, but this hazy, uncertain light may represent Daisy, who likes the youth and fun Gatsby brings her settled life but who is too selfish to risk herself. Like the light, she is a tease. There's usually something significant behind a repeated image. **Write down page references and your first interpretations. Look for a pattern.**

5. **Form/Style.** Each genre or type of literature has its own principles of style and form. *Poetry* can be analyzed by looking at the rhyme, rhythm, sound devices, and format (sonnet, ballad, and so on). **But you can't just *describe* rhyme pattern, for instance. Show how it relates to the overall meaning of the poem by having a *thesis* about the rhyme:**

> **Sample Thesis:** e. e. cummings uses rhyme that doesn't quite match (off rhyme) in "when serpents bargain for the right to squirm" to show that humans are not in harmony with nature.

Fiction can be analyzed through narrative point of view (who the speaker is and how much he or she knows of characters' thoughts) or by explaining how the time sequence is constructed. **As with poetry, show how the form or style contributes to the story's overall effect:**

> **Sample Thesis:** Nick narrates *The Great Gatsby* because Gatsby is too ignorant of himself and too blind to Daisy to tell the story honestly.

Drama's unique element is staging—the props, actors' gestures, lighting, the set, and visual effects. Show how these elements contribute to the overall themes/conflicts:

Sample Thesis: The main sets in *Romeo and Juliet*—the street, bedroom, and tomb—set up the three main conflicts in the play.

All literature can be analyzed for word choice and "tone" or "mood"—what we might call the writer's *attitude* toward the subject:

Sample Thesis: When e. e. cummings distorts ordinary, simple English words, he is showing his real theme: That people should pay such close attention to the simple, basic things in life that they become strange and new to us again.

■ **PRACTICE 14-4** To illustrate how these concepts work together, read this poem by Robert Browning:

Meeting at Night
The grey sea and the long black land;
And the yellow half-moon large and low;
And the startled little waves that leap
In fiery ringlets from their sleep,
As I gain the cove with pushing prow,
And quench its speed i' the slushy sand.

Then a mile of warm sea-scented beach;
Three fields to cross till a farm appears;
A tap at the pane, the quick sharp scratch
And blue spurt of a lighted match,
And a voice less loud, through its joys and fears,
Than the two hearts beating each to each!

First reading: What's going on? Is a character or the author telling the poem? Any vocabulary you need to look up? First reactions?

Brain teasers: List the conflicts. Who is meeting and why is it so secret? List the images—what pattern emerges? Is there meaning in this? Regarding form, how do the two stanzas mirror each other? Listen to the sounds by reading the poem aloud, especially the end of stanza one and the middle of two. Does this poem have a theme?

After answering some of these, formulate a thesis you can defend in discussion with supporting evidence from the poem. Is it possible our close reading and interpretation will create ideas an author did not intend?

Of course—although we are far more likely to underestimate a professional's rich use of words. **The point of literary interpretation is not to hit exactly what an author meant to say, but to exercise and develop our minds to see and think more deeply and to help a reader see new possibilities of meaning in the literary work. Your interpretations will be legitimate as long as you can support your ideas with details from the literature.**

Next, let's look at one of Elizabeth Barrett Browning's love poems. Please read it twice before going on:

How Do I Love Thee?

How do I love thee? Let me count the ways.
I love thee to the depth and breadth and height
My soul can reach, when feeling out of sight
For the ends of Being and ideal Grace.
I love thee to the level of everyday's
Most quiet need, by sun and candlelight.
I love thee freely, as men strive for Right;
I love thee purely, as they turn from Praise.
I love thee with the passion put to use
In my old griefs, and with my childhood's faith.
I love thee with a love I seemed to lose
With my lost saints—I love thee with the breath,
Smiles, tears, of all my life!—and, if God choose,
I shall but love thee better after death.

What is your **gut reaction** to this poem? Freewrite your first impressions. Now try to state its **theme** (Psst—go beyond "Love is intense." What is the love *based* on?) Next, list the **imagery** the poet stresses.

Now let's play around with other possibilities that emerge when we put this poem beside "Meeting at Night." After all, we're reading two love poems written by a husband and wife around the time they met. Let's start with biographical background to see what that might reveal. Robert's poem was written in 1845 when he was 33 years old. He was still living with his parents because he had not, despite many years of effort, established himself as a poet. Elizabeth's poem was written soon after her marriage to Robert in 1846. Six years older than Robert, she had published her first of many books at age 13, and this poem became perhaps the most well-known poem in England during the entire 19th century! She was so famous, in fact, that for years Robert was called "Mrs. Browning's husband."

But it was not a one-sided relationship. When he met her, Elizabeth lived under her tyrannical father's rule. He forbade all his children to marry. She was 39, unable to walk after a riding accident years earlier and sickly. Robert loved her poetry first, then her, and believed he rescued her from "a dragon" when he secretly eloped with her, and the couple escaped to Italy. Within a year, at the time she wrote this poem, Elizabeth recovered her health and the ability to walk, and at age 40 she delivered their son (named "Pen"!). Was her disability psychosomatic and cured by escaping her harsh father, was it a natural rehabilitation of a physical injury, or was it an example of the curative power of love? No one knows. By all reports, they had 15 very happy years together—in Italy to evade her furious father—until her death.

Elizabeth Barrett Browning

Robert Browning

Stock Montage/Superstock

Portrait of Robert Browning (1812-89) 1859 (litho) (b/w photo), Talfourd, Field (1815-74)/© Dickens House Museum, London, UK/Bridgeman Art Library

■ **PRACTICE 14-5** To decide what meaning lies in these poems and to focus on an interpretation, consider these questions:

- Which biographical details add possibilities of meaning to the poems? How? What specific lines in the poems back up your ideas? Does it matter that Elizabeth lived with her father in a house far from the sea?
- Do the poems say something to *you* aside from the authors' life stories? What?
- How do the two poets' attitudes and messages about love differ (or agree)?
- What would a feminist critic say about the difference between male and female ideas about love in the two poems?
- What would a psychological critic make of the poems and the real life story?

Organizing Literary Essays

After you turn the story or poem over a few times and examine different parts, you're ready to focus on an aspect of the work—to create a *thesis* like those shown already. In developing a thesis, examine your notes for an idea *worth* proving—one with some complexity. In literature this often means recognizing *multiple truths*. Good vs. evil rarely occurs cleanly in life or good literature. More often we face a choice between two partial goods or two partial evils. Gatsby, Hamlet, Ahab, and Hester Prynne interest people because good and evil mix in them. **An honest thesis embraces ambiguity.** A categorical thesis suggests that either the poem or the interpretation is superficial.

> **Weak:** Daisy in *The Great Gatsby* is an evil woman who doesn't care what harm she causes.
> **Better:** Daisy causes much evil from weakness, fear, naïveté, and selfishness (specific, and outlines the four points that will organize the essay).
> **Weak:** Ahab in *Moby Dick* is a lunatic, pure and simple.
> **Better:** Ahab may be crazy, but it's a magnificent, sane madness.

After focusing your thesis, assemble evidence from the literary work—quotes, incidents, details of character—whatever interesting, relevant bits you have combed from reading, brain teasers, or research. Place like material together until you have solid outline headings.

Drafting Literary Essays

A good way to start a literary essay is to explain why your topic is important or puzzling. Why does it matter to you? How does what you're about to prove add to a reader's understanding of the entire work? Your introduction should also let the reader know which three or four main issues will be covered to prove your overall thesis.

As you draft, assume your audience has read the story, play, or poem carefully. **There's no need to retell the plot or identify the characters. You should focus entirely on proving your thesis.** Look for all the evidence in the work that bears on your point, and don't get drawn into other issues. You will need to constantly clarify and support your ideas by quoting relevant passages. Think of yourself as a lawyer building an argument in court. So look deeply into each quotation you present, picking apart the words.

As a general rule of thumb, **your explanation of a quotation should be twice as long as the original.** Why? Because you must point out *how* it proves your thesis.

The following is a nice example of a student assembling evidence to build a point. "Revelation," a story by Flannery O'Connor, is about an older woman, Mrs. Turpin, who feels morally superior to other people. While in a doctor's office, a young woman, Mary Grace, grows upset with Mrs. Turpin and finally throws a book at her and calls her "an ugly old wart hog from hell." The girl has a seizure, so Mrs. Turpin rationalizes by telling herself that the girl was crazy and the ugly one. But Mrs. Turpin's superiority is shaken as the story ends when she has a vision of being one of the last people summoned to heaven. The student's introduction asserts that Mary Grace is not a lunatic as Mrs. Turpin believes but "a manifestation of a supernatural being representing goodness or oppressed suffering," and that Mrs. Turpin, although she represents herself as a charitable, God-fearing woman, may be evil itself. In this section, the student supports her idea of Mary Grace as a supernatural force:

> The most obvious clue that something supernatural is going on is the end when Mrs. Turpin watches the parade of souls going to heaven. However, the whole work is peppered with symbols representing supernatural things, beginning with the title, "Revelation." The "Grace" in the girl's name could be religious imagery suggesting goodness. Then there's this description of Mary Grace: "She was looking at [Mrs. Turpin] as she had known and disliked her all of her life—all of Mrs. Turpin's life, it seemed too, not just the girl's life" (121). The idea that the girl's hate goes back before her mortal life began hints that Mary Grace is not simply a mortal, sensitive teenager. An examination of the waiting room scene shows that Mary Grace flares up angrily when Mrs. Turpin merely thinks evil thoughts. An example is when Mrs. Turpin is thinking about how white trash are beyond help:

> > All at once the ugly girl turned her lips inside out once again, her eyes fixed like two drills on Mrs. Turpin. This time there was no mistaking that there was something urgent behind them. (123)

> If Mary Grace were mortal, her flare-ups, dirty looks, and scowls would be limited to those times that Mrs. Turpin glares at someone or says something nasty. But if she represents the spirit of God's intention that we live in harmony, her anger would rise against the oppression and ridicule in Mrs. Turpin's mind.

—Marjorie Pixley-Ketzak

Copy quotations accurately. If three lines or less, incorporate them into your paragraphs. Should you quote poetry this way, you must use a slash to indicate the actual line ending, as in this example from Marvell's "To His Coy Mistress": "Had we but world enough, and time, /This coyness, lady, were no crime." If a quotation is more than three lines, set it off like this selection from Tennyson's "Ulysses":

> The lights begin to twinkle from the rocks;
> The long day wanes; the slow moon climbs; the deep
> Moans round with many voices. Come my friends,
> 'Tis not too late to seek a newer world.

The lines are indented 10 spaces for both poetry and prose, and no quotation marks are used. Most people double-space all indented quotes, and others stick to the older practice of single spacing. See Chapter 17 for punctuation of tag lines for quotations. Try not to pour on quote after quote. **Quote the best, paraphrase the rest.** (For documentation of quotations, see Chapter 15.)

Revising Literary Essays

Review "Steps in Writing a Paper" inside the front cover of this book. Does your **thesis** still fit what you wrote? Some parts may have to go, or the thesis may need to be rewritten. Have you distorted the literary work's main idea to make your point? Cut where you dwell on the obvious. Beef up your most creative ideas.

Revise details. Too little support? Too many quotes? Sharpen explications?

Revise mechanics and style. Literary essays use the present tense to describe the work (after all, literature is immortal), so you would say, "Flannery O'Connor says . . ." even though she is dead and "said" it years ago.

The Review

Related to the literary essay is the review—of books, restaurants, plays, concerts, art shows, speeches, films, or any other event or work that can be judged by *standards of performance.* **Like literary essays, reviews persuade readers through supporting details**. If it was a bad dinner followed by a worse speech, describe the limp green beans and mushy potatoes as well as the speaker's bad jokes. Like a literary essay, a review can interpret the themes of its subject.

Reviews differ from literary essays, however, in several regards. First, **descriptive summary** *is expected.* Up to half of a newspaper or music review may inform readers accurately about the topic. You can assume readers of literary essays are already familiar with the work being discussed, but a review must help readers sample the work. Teach us! Second, the **review emphasizes** *evaluation.* Your purpose is to make a judgment of value and then support that judgment with evidence. If your professor wants a **critical review,** go heavier on evaluation and lighter on summary. As with any persuasion, **make your standards of judgment clear.** Specify what you mean by "good service" at a restaurant. Some people like a server to check on their needs every few minutes; others consider that pesky. In an art review, does "old-fashioned" art mean the red barn school of painting or anything that does not use lasers or computers?

Chances are good you will write reviews in your career and in college. In your career, you may be asked to review a new product your boss is considering buying or to review another employee's job performance. You will need to set up standards of performance and interpret how well they have been reached, supported by specific, descriptive details. For a product, some standards might be:

- Efficiency
- Ease of use
- Price
- How necessary it is
- Safety

You might outline your review by using these headings, then comment on each with details. Under safety, for instance, you might point out that the new computer tends to give employees eyestrain after a week's use. For a job evaluation, common standards of performance are:

- Amount of work done
- Quality of work
- Reliability
- Ability to work with others
- Initiative

What else would you add?

You will likely review books or theories for college courses. Your psychology professor may ask you to contrast how behaviorist and humanist psychologists would deal with a teenage alcoholic and then evaluate which method will succeed best. What should be the standards of success?

Although people don't usually write reviews of dates or parenting style, in your private life you can use the techniques of a review to help decide what car you want to buy or which career is for you. Prioritizing standards and a sharp eye for supporting detail helps you evaluate with more depth and clarity.

■ **PRACTICE 14-6** Make a list of *your* top five standards of performance for one of the following: art, restaurant, book, film, or theatrical event. Now apply these standards to one specific painting, concert, work, or performance.

■ **PRACTICE 14-7** Write a brief review of yourself as a college student. List four to five standards by which you think college students ought to be judged; then evaluate your performance for each standard. Conclude by stating how you could most improve your overall rating.

VISUAL RHETORIC

To practice writing evaluations based on standards of judgment, study these paintings of Mary and the baby Jesus. This is a classical Christian scene, yet how different the effects! **Context:** The *Virgin and Child* is a work of the early sixteenth century, while *Madonna and Child* is from the seventeenth century. What difference does that make? Well, during this

Virgin and Child (oil on panel), Greek School, (16th century)/ Church of San Martino, Venice, Italy, Cameraphoto Arte Venezia/Bridgeman Art Library

Madonna and Child (oil on metal), Badalocchio, Sisto (1581/5–1647/Private Collection, © Agnew's, London, UK/Bridgeman Art Library

"Virgin and Child," *Greek School*

"Madonna and Child," *Sisto Badolocchio*

passage of time attitudes toward man and God changed and the qualities that were valued in art changed as well. In other words, **the differences between the two paintings are in large part based on different standards of judgment.**

■ **PRACTICE 14-8** Study the two paintings' details for points of contrast, and look at their rhetoric—the structures, backgrounds, transitions and styles. Then formulate an idea that explains the different view of religion or art in the pictures. Support your idea by referring to details from the works. Then, evaluate the two paintings yourself, based on your standards for art or for religion. If you are not Christian, you can still evaluate the paintings based on your standards.

For example, in the earlier painting, Mary and Jesus are slender with washed-out faces. In the later work, mother and child are robust, the flesh plump and glowing. What difference does that make? The later work shows stronger emphasis on God taking on human flesh, on being human. God became a real person with a real body. In the early painting, spirit dominates flesh. It is as though the more flesh, the less divine they would be. To someone who emphasizes life after death in a spiritual kingdom, the earlier painting might have more appeal. The fleshy Madonna and Jesus, they might say, makes human flesh too pretty; after all, our earthly lives are illusions. But if I find the interconnectedness of spiritual and physical worlds appealing and believe God loves the beautiful decaying things of this world, I'd prefer the work by Badalocchio. If I were nonreligious, I might criticize the earlier painting for scorning the body, which is the only life a person has. Look for other points of comparison and the ideas they suggest.

Writing Suggestions and Class Discussions

1. Write a review of a restaurant, film, art show, or other subject with performance standards. Make your standards clear, and support your opinion with specific details.
2. Write a review of your essays written so far for this course. Establish standards of performance and evaluate your work's strengths and weaknesses, quoting from past papers to support your points.
3. Write a job evaluation review of someone who works with you. Fairly and specifically evaluate his or her work, with supporting details. Conclude with a recommendation.

4. Read the sample student review on p. 332.

5. A peer group will research and analyze a literary work. One person each will (a) research the author's life and connect it to the work; (b) apply critical perspectives to the work, doing necessary research; (c) explicate theme; (d) explicate conflict or character; (e) explicate images and symbols; and (f) explicate style. The group will discuss its ideas and report to the class.

6. Choose a literary work. Do preliminary brain teasers and turn in three possible thesis statements you might defend.

7. Compare and contrast works by two authors on the same topic (Gaines and Walker on racism, Millay and cummings on love, for examples).

8. Study how one poet or fiction writer deals with a narrow topic (Yeats on escape, Lawrence on love, Hopkins on nature). Support your thesis with explication of several works and any other evidence you can find.

9. *Explication:* Quote a short passage (5 to 10 lines) from a piece of creative writing you have read recently. Explicate its meaning using any of the tools offered in this chapter. Write at least a page of analysis.

10. Five poems follow. Although from different historical ages and using different forms, *all deal with the idea of time.* Here are several ways you can use these poems to improve your ability to analyze literature.
   • Formulate a tentative thesis about one poem.
   • Look for similarities and differences among the poems. Consider theme, imagery used, and form. Have specific evidence from each poem to support your ideas.
   • Research the author's life for one poem and see if you can draw some connections to the poem. Does the poem alone support your biographical interpretation?

POEMS FOR EXPLICATION AND DISCUSSION

Sonnet 73
That time of year thou mayst in me behold
When yellow leaves, or none, or few, do hang
Upon those boughs which shake against the cold,
Bare ruined choirs, where late the sweet birds sang.
In me thou see'st the twilight of such day
As after sunset fadeth in the west;
Which by and by black night doth take away,

Death's second self, that seals up all in rest.
In me thou see'st the glowing of such fire,
That on the ashes of his youth doth lie,
As on the death-bed whereon it must expire,
Consumed with that which it was nourished by.
This thou perceiv'st, which makes thy love more strong,
To love that well which thou must leave ere long.

—*William Shakespeare*

Vocabulary: *thou:* you; *mayst:* may; *boughs:* branches; *fadeth:* fades; *doth:* does; *perceiv'st:* understand; *ere:* before.

To the Virgins, to Make Much of Time

Gather ye rosebuds while ye may,
Old time is still a-flying;
And this same flower that smiles today
Tomorrow will be dying.

The glorious lamp of heaven, the sun,
The higher he's a-getting,
The sooner will his race be won,
And nearer he's to setting.

That age is best which is the first,
When youth and blood are warmer;
But being spent, the worse, and worst
Times still succeed the former.

Then be not coy, but use your time,
And, while ye may, go marry;
For, having once but lost your prime,
You may forever tarry.

—*Robert Herrick*

Vocabulary: *ye:* your; *succeed:* follow; *coy:* shy or flirtatious; *tarry:* linger behind.

Ozymandias

I met a traveller from an antique land
Who said: "Two vast and trunkless legs of stone
Stand in the desert . . . Near them, on the sand,
Half sunk, a shattered visage lies, whose frown,
And wrinkled lip, and sneer of cold command,
Tell that its sculptor well those passions read

Which yet survive, stamped on these lifeless things,
The hand that mocked them, and the heart that fed:
And on the pedestal these words appear:
"My name is Ozymandias, king of kings:
Look on my works, ye Mighty, and despair!"
Nothing beside remains. Round the decay
Of that colossal wreck, boundless and bare
The lone and level sands stretch far away.

—*Percy Bysshe Shelley*

Vocabulary: *antique:* ancient; *visage:* face.

A Noiseless Patient Spider

A noiseless patient spider,
I marked where on a little promontory it stood isolated,
Marked how to explore the vacant vast surrounding,
It launched forth filament, filament, filament, out of itself,
Ever unreeling them, ever tirelessly speeding them.
And you O my soul where you stand,
Surrounded, detached, in measureless oceans of space,
Ceaselessly musing, venturing, throwing, seeking the spheres to
connect them,
Till the bridge you will need be formed, till the ductile anchor hold,
Till the gossamer thread you fling catch somewhere, O my soul.

—*Walt Whitman*

Vocabulary: *promontory:* a peak of high land overlooking the sea; *spheres:* planets or stars; *ductile:* plastic or stretchable.

Childhood Is the Kingdom Where Nobody Dies

Childhood is not from birth to a certain age and at a certain age
The child is grown, and puts away childish things.
Childhood is the kingdom where nobody dies.
Nobody that matters, that is. Distant relatives of course
Die, whom one never has seen or has seen for an hour,
And they gave one candy in a pink-and-green striped bag, or a
    jack-knife,
And went away, and cannot really be said to have lived at all.

And cats die. They lie on the floor and lash their tails,
And their reticent fur is suddenly all in motion
With fleas that one never knew were there,
Polished and brown, knowing all there is to know,

Trekking off into the living world.

You fetch a shoe-box, but it's much too small, because she won't curl
up now:

So you find a bigger box, and bury her in the yard, and weep.

But you do not wake up a month from then, two months,

A year from then, two years, in the middle of the night

And weep, with your knuckles in your mouth, and say Oh, God! Oh,
God!

Childhood is the kingdom where nobody dies that matters,—mothers
and fathers don't die.

And if you have said, "For heaven's sake, must you always be kissing
a person?"

Or, "I do wish to gracious you'd stop tapping on the window with
your thimble!"

Tomorrow, or even the day after tomorrow if you're busy having fun,

Is plenty of time to say, "I'm sorry, mother."

To be grown up is to sit at the table with people who have died, who

neither listen nor speak; Who do not drink their tea, though they
always said

Tea was such a comfort.

Run down into the cellar and bring up the last jar of raspberries;
they are not tempted.

Flatter them, ask them what was it they said exactly

That time, to the bishop, or to the overseer, or to Mrs. Mason;

They are not taken in.

Shout at them, get red in the face, rise,

Drag them up out of their chairs by their stiff shoulders and shake
them and yell at them;

They are not startled, they are not even embarrassed; they slide
back into their chairs.

Your tea is cold now.

You drink it standing up,

And leave the house.

—Edna St. Vincent Millay

SAMPLE STUDENT LITERARY ESSAY

Structure and Feeling in "Childhood Is the Kingdom Where Nobody Dies"
Carrie Gaynor

"Childhood is the Kingdom Where Nobody Dies" by Edna St. Vincent Millay captivated me with its vivid images and emotional confessions. It defines what it means to grow up. Childhood is a vast place, a kingdom wrapped in the innocence that allows us to act as though time were on our side. But that all changes when the people who matter most to us are snatched away, along with the deception of security. When you grow up, you realize how exposed and vulnerable life is. In order to convey these feelings, Millay blends images with various structures.

Why she chose topic

Thesis

The poem is presented in two parts. The first deals with what it means to live in the kingdom of childhood. Millay then creates visual images that intensify to an emotional climax. To support this progression, she starts with distant relatives, then comes closer to home with the family cat. In describing the distant relatives, Millay speaks in third person in a long, rambling structure. This makes it go fast and seem insignificant:

Outline overall approach in paper

Distant relatives of course
Die, whom one never has seen or has seen for an hour,
And they gave one candy in a pink-and-green striped bag, or a
    jack-knife,
And went away, and cannot really be said to have lived at all. (286)

Supporting quote

Page reference

Notice the matter-of-factness of the words and the lack of emotion. A family gathers and one's great uncle brings a piece of candy. He has nothing to do with your life, and his death is no event.

Explication

In the next stanza, Millay begins to draw the reader into a comparison of sorts. You are home, and your cat, full of life and fleas, lies on the floor, dead. And you place the cat, now in rigor mortis, into a box and bury it under a tree. You weep. Millay creates a personal sense of loss by switching from third-person to second-person narrative, directing the image at the reader:

Style analyzed by comparison

You fetch a shoe-box, but it's much too small, because she won't
    curl up now:

→

So you find a bigger box, and bury her in the yard, and weep.
(286)

Explication of quote

The use of the box symbolizes the child's need to expand her view of the world to match her experience.

The next stanza continues to make you feel words in your belly. The rambling sentence plays with your adrenaline. There is no ambiguity about what now defines childhood:

Quote needs explication

But you do not wake up a month from then, two months,
A year from then, two years in the middle of the night
And weep, with your knuckles in your mouth, and say Oh, God!
Oh, God!
Childhood is the kingdom where nobody dies that matters,—
mothers and fathers don't die. (287)

Transition to last section

At this point, the poem switches to dialogue, signaling the turning point. The reader gets a last glimpse of the child's sense of timelessness while at the same time touched by an awareness that tomorrow may never come.

The final section deals with images and emotions of grieving. This process starts with numb unwillingness to accept loss:

To be grown up is to sit at the table with people who have died,
who neither listen nor speak;
Who do not drink their tea, though they always said
Tea was such a comfort. (287)

Explication

This passage brings to mind a child conducting a tea party for her make-believe friends: the dead. The child continues, despite the dead people's ("they") lack of response. All adults are haunted by the dead, and the desperate child tries to trick her "guests" into participating, returning:

Run down into the cellar and bring up that last jar of raspberries;
they are not tempted.
Flatter them, ask them what it was they said exactly . . .
They are not taken in. (288)

These passive, rational attempts abruptly change to aggression:

Shout at them, get red in the face, rise,
Drag them up out of their chairs by their stiff shoulders and shake
them and yell at them;
They are not startled, they are not even embarrassed. (288)

Quote needs explication

Conclusion

The final act of growing up is learning to accept what is. The last stanza reflects the change from the absence of any control to very

→

careful control. Millay switches back to a matter-of-fact tone as she ends the tea party. Time has passed, the tea grown cold. The child stands. She is no longer part of the delusion and leaves the house. Leaving the house suggests what being grown is: when one is completely exposed, deprived of all security.

The last words are small, the last lines short, and they make the reader feel that way—exposed at the end of the page.

Work Cited

Millay, Edna St. Vincent. *Collected Poems.* New York: Harper & Row, 1956.

ANALYSIS BASED ON PEER REVIEW CHECKLIST

Ideas: Insight. This essay has some wonderful depth of interpretation. Her last paragraph asserts potent truths about childhood.

Sticks to thesis: The opening prepares us for analysis of theme, but the second paragraph announces she will use a section-by-section analysis that combines structure and imagery. She could add a sentence telling us that the structure and imagery support the theme she's discussing.

Details/Amount of support: Plenty. Every section is supported with several direct quotes and other references.

In-depth interpretation of quotes: At times the quotes fly too thick without explication. Just before the concluding paragraph there are eight lines of poem with only one line of explanation. In those quotes I'd like to know more about the "cellar" and "raspberries." A cellar is like a grave, and raspberries, once juicy live fruits, are now preserved there. Since she's been discussing living, dead, or dead-while-alive relatives, this must mean something. Generally, her paper has fine depth. For instance, she perceptively lays out the switch from the impersonal "one" to "you" and ties it to her thesis.

Organization: It's smooth with nice transitional markers ("In the next stanza," "At this point," and "The final section . . . ") to help the reader.

Format: A fine model for handling quotes/citations.

Most creative interpretation: Demonstrating how the relaxed, rambling sentences give way to abrupt, hysterical ones, reflecting the change in the child from calm to shock.

What else ought the writer explain? She ignores the scene in which the dead people sit at the table with the child. It's the boldest, most puzzling part of the poem to me. Are they memories? Ghosts? Living people who act dead? Wishful thinking?

POEM AND SAMPLE STUDENT LITERARY ESSAY

Batter My Heart, Three-Personed God

Batter my heart, three-personed God; for You
As yet but knock, breathe, shine, and seek to mend;
That I may rise and stand, o'erthrow me, and bend
Your force to break, blow, burn, and make me new.
I, like a usurped town, to another due,
Labor to admit You, but O! to no end;
Reason, Your viceroy in me, me should defend,
But is captived, and proves weak or untrue.
Yet dearly I love You, and would be loved fain,
But am betrothed unto Your enemy.
Divorce me, untie, or break that knot again;
Take me to You, imprison me, for I,
Except You enthrall me, never shall be free,
Nor ever chaste, except You ravish me.

—John Donne

Vocabulary: *o'erthrow:* overthrow; *usurped:* taken by force or trickery; *fain:* gladly; *betrothed:* engaged; *enthrall:* enslave.

Three-Personed God
Nancy L. Galleher

In "Batter My Heart, Three-Personed God," the narrator addresses the three facets of God's Trinity: Father, Son, and Holy Ghost. The poem uses images relating to battle and capture to describe man's heart. For the narrator—like all men—has been captured by God's enemy, Satan. The line, "I, like a usurped town to another due" (5), describes this surrender. The word "usurped" means seized or taken possession of by force, wrongfully.

The poem separates the Trinity or "Three-personed God" (1) into three intertwined entities that struggle to redeem man's heart. Whenever God is mentioned in the poem, the words "You" or

→

"Your" are capitalized. The line, "for You/As yet but knock, breathe, shine, and seek to mend" (1–2) describes the Son sent by God the Father to redeem man with tenderness and love. The words all suggest a gentleness embodied by the lamb of God. The word "knock" reminds me of a mural behind the altar in the church I attended as a child. It is a picture of Christ gently knocking on a gate to a lovely garden—which symbolizes the door to man's heart. "Breathe" and "shine" are words of life. "Seek to mend" suggests the care and concern God the father has for man, which is why he sent his son. Man instinctively recognizes and loves his heavenly father in whose image he was created: "Yet dearly I love You" (9) and is desperate that God love him: "and would be loved fain" (9). He works hard to give God access to his heart: "I . . . Labor to admit You" (6), but he fails:

> . . . but O! to no end;
> Reason, Your viceroy in me, me should defend,
> But is captived, and proves weak or untrue. (6–8)

Man's heart is a prisoner of war, "captived" by the enemy. "Proves weak or untrue" suggests betrayal under the pressure of captivity. Man has been given reason by his creator to govern his actions, just as a viceroy who represents a king is expected to rule and carry out his king's wishes. God expects man's reason to defend him better.

In scripture, Jesus is compared to a bridegroom at a wedding feast. He lived among men, died, and was resurrected by God to prepare the wedding feast at God's table in heaven. Man's heart is often referred to as Jesus' beloved or bride. With this in mind, the poet effectively uses the image of marriage in these lines:

> But am betrothed unto Your enemy.
> Divorce me, untie or break that knot again; (10–11)

"Betrothed unto Your enemy" means promised in marriage to Satan, which occurred when man first sinned in the Garden of Eden. Man knows the only way this unholy relationship can be severed is by divorce, which will "untie" or "break the knot." Marriage is symbolized by the knot, an intertwining of two souls. The word "again" refers to the time when man's heart belonged to God alone, before it was captured by Satan.

Man has been given the Holy Spirit to empower him to wage war against Satan. The lines:

> That I may rise and stand, o'erthrow me, and bend
> Your force to break, blow, burn, and make me new. (3–4)

→

describe the bestowing of this gift. When Jesus ascended to heaven, he promised his disciples a power to enable them to carry on his battle against evil. At the Feast of Pentecost, the force of the Holy Spirit sounded like a strong wind blowing ("blow"); tongues of fire appeared and touched every person there ("burn") and filled them with the Holy Spirit ("make me new"). This empowers man to do God's work and resist evil. Man's will must be broken and the wall surrounding his heart penetrated. This is suggested in the plea: "Batter my heart, three-personed God" (1). "Batter" suggests ramming down barriers by repeated attacks that overwhelm and subdue. When God "batter[s] my heart," He breaks those walls that have kept Him out. The force increases in intensity from lines two to four: "Knock" becomes "break," "breathe" becomes "blow," "shine" becomes "burn," and "mend" becomes "make me new." The narrator wants to be recreated, not just repaired.

Man must be a servant—but to which master, God or Satan? He pleads:

Take me to You, imprison me, for I

Except You enthrall me, never shall be free,

Nor ever chaste, except You ravish me. (12–14)

He recognizes that even though he knows which master he wants to serve, the only way he can be certain to serve God is to have his free will taken away and his soul captured. "Enthrall" means to hold or reduce to slavery, as well as to spellbind. However, man has been given free will and is continually asked to make choices about which master he will serve. The last line, "Nor ever chaste, except You ravish me" (14) creates two contrasting images. "Chaste" means pure, holy, and without sin. A person who is chaste is in control of his impulses and actions. The word "ravish," in contrast, implies being overcome by force or rape. How can a person become pure by such an act? The poet seems to suggest that the only way a man's heart can become pure is if his will becomes subdued. Then, and only then, will he be truly free of Satan's grip on his soul.

DISCUSSION

Using the Peer Review Checklist for ideas, comment on the strengths and weaknesses of Nancy's analysis. What else did you see in the poem that she does not mention? What words or phrases might be taken in a different sense?

☑ Peer Review Checklist for Literary Essays

Author: _____

I would especially like the reviewer to comment on: _____

_____

Reviewer: _____

State the author's thesis as you see it. Author and reviewer should discuss the accuracy of this statement. _____

_____

	Strong	Average	Weak
Ideas: Insight			
Sticks to thesis			
Details: Supporting evidence			
Analysis of quotes			
Organization: Smooth and logical			
Format: Page citations			
Punctuation of quotations			

What was the most creative interpretation the paper made?

Respond to the author's request:

What else about the literary work ought the writer explain to prove the thesis or to dig out its complexity?

What questions do you have that are still unanswered after reading the paper?

What lines or events in the literary work might tend to *disprove* the author's thesis? Discuss.

SAMPLE STUDENT CRITICAL REVIEW USING SOURCES

The Texas Chainsaw Massacre
Devra Whitaker

Imagine going on a road trip with four of your best friends. You have already spent a weekend in Mexico and are returning with a piñata full of marijuana to sell once you get home. Things are going swell until you drive past a dirty, bloody, disoriented young woman walking barefoot down a deserted road. Your friends want to leave her, but being the considerate person you are, you pick her up. You and your friends ask her questions, but she does not respond. You continue to drive, and she suddenly starts thrashing and begging you to turn around. Your friends try to calm her, but she pulls out a gun from her underwear, and blows her brains out. As if this wasn't horrible enough, you must drive around with her corpse and try to convince a creepy old woman at the nearest gas station, a disabled old man, and a crooked sheriff that you need help. While doing so, your friends begin to disappear. What's your fate? To go one-on-one with a homicidal maniac who just happens to be wearing your boyfriend's skinned-off face. Sound interesting? If so, the movie *The Texas Chainsaw Massacre* directed by Marcus Nispel (2003) is perfect for you. In researching the movie, I learned it was the true story of Ed Gein who murdered and dismembered several middle-aged women in the late 1950s. Thomas Hewitt, also known as Leatherface, is the psychopathic killer in this thriller, which was previously directed by Kim Henkel in 1974 (Phillips 1). I feel that this movie was excellent because it is based on a true story, it reaches out to put me there, and it provokes strong emotion.

I must admit that I was a little upset that this movie was based on the Ed Gein case, but that made it all the more interesting. Ed claimed that he wanted to know how the human body worked, so he studied books on human anatomy. He also read books dealing with Nazi concentration camp medical experiments. When the police came to search his home on November 16, 1957, they found human bodies hanging from hooks set in the basement walls, a human heart in a pan on the stove, the crown of a skull used as a bowl, and a "woman suit" made from a skinned woman complete with face mask and breasts. There are many similarities between

→

Psycho and *The Texas Chainsaw Massacre*, but I never would have guessed that *Psycho* was the origin. I don't think anyone else would have either.

It may sound strange that a bloody horror flick such as this would actually "reach out" to someone, but it reaches out to me. The fact that parts of this movie took place in 1954 is what really draws my attention to the screen. Some critics describe this as a "lame re-do that lacks thrills and chills" (Vice n. pag.), but how can one see this film as just a re-make? When movies are done over and over about the Titanic or the Holocaust, does one just say, "It wasn't as good as the first one"? This may not have been about a war, major social movement, or leader, but it is about everyday people like us who were minding their own business doing everyday things. They were sentenced to unspeakable deaths just because they were in the wrong place at the wrong time. I can imagine myself there with the fear, anger and shock that they must have felt. To be honest, I probably would not have survived, but if I were in the position of a survivor, the trauma from that event would have ruined the rest of my life. If the thought of experiencing this tragic and disturbing incident isn't enough to scare someone, then I don't know what is. It reminds us that we live in a dangerous world and that too many of us take our lives for granted. Who is to say that we are guaranteed that trip home from our next vacation, school, work or the grocery store?

The general idea of *The Texas Chainsaw Massacre*, of course, was to be frightened, but as I thought about it more, I realized there was more to it than that. Scott Phillips of the *Weekly Alibi* says, "I'm glad the flick is finally rearing its blood-spattered head, 'cause it's entertaining" (n. pag.). Entertaining, indeed, but were directors Henkel and Nispel sending a deeper message to their audience? I sat in the theater with my jaw dropped through the entire ninety-eight minutes and found myself on the verge of tears when Erin (Jessica Biel) is begged by her friend, Andy (Mike Vogel), to use a knife to finish him off. The psychopathic killer had previously beaten him, hung him on a hook plunged in his back as if he were in a slaughter house, and sawed his left leg off. Imagine having to carry out that responsibility on someone you love dearly. Anger filled me when I finally realized that the "incest family" had stolen a baby girl from the previous family that "stopped in." At the end, I sighed in relief when Erin captured

→

the baby and escaped with two lives. But Thomas Hewitt was never captured. So every now and again, caution, suspicion, and "ready to attack" feelings come over me, especially when I am alone.

Over all, I rate this movie an A plus. One critic believes that this was "A frightfully effective remake of the seminal horror classic" (Rechtshaffen n. pag.), but did he realize that this was actually a twisted re-make of *Psycho,* and that Norman Bates was created from Ed Gein? I sure didn't. There were surprises all over, and it should make people more cautious about their surroundings. For those who are into true horror, I challenge them to check out *The Texas Chainsaw Massacre.* I guarantee that if you view this film with these things in mind, you too, will be a little more cautious of your neighbors, co-workers, family, and friends. Have a safe trip to Blockbuster.

Works Cited

Phillips, Scott. "Texas Chainsaw Massacre: The Next Generation." *The Weekly Alibi.* 9 March 1998. 19 Nov. 2003 <http://www. filmvault.com>.

Rechtshaffen, Michael. "Texas Chainsaw Massacre." *The Hollywood Reporter.* n.d. 19 Nov. 2003 <http://www.hollywoodreporter.com>.

"The Truth about The Texas Chainsaw Massacre." *The Texas Chainsaw Massacre: The True Story.* n.d. 8 Dec. 2003 <http://www.geocities.com>.

Vice, Jeff. "The Texas Chainsaw Massacre (2003)." *Rotten Tomatoes.* n.d. 19 Nov. 2003 <http://www.rottentomatoes.com>.

Discussion/Writing

1. What are the standards of judgment in this review? What other standards would you apply to a horror movie?
2. What three main standards of judgment would you apply to any movie?
3. Write a brief review of a movie based on your standards of judgment.

☑ **Peer Review Checklist for Reviews**

· ·

Author: _____

Question or problem for reviewer: _____

_____

Reviewer: _____

	Strong	**Average**	**Weak**
Ideas: Standards of performance are clear			
Depth/creativity of analysis			
Details: Support for evaluation			
Visualization (vivid description)			
Organization: Clear and logical			
Tone: Reasonable			

Respond to the author's question:

What do you think is the best part of the paper?

What standards does the author seem to value most? What others might be used?

Is there anything the author ought to cover in more depth or to cut? Explain:

Offer two other suggestions for the paper:

Research

Written with Christopher Otero

15

IT'S 2 A.M. THE CURSOR BLINKS ON A BLANK document. Your notes are spread everywhere. You've been waiting for someone to return your most important source to the library, and you're still shuffling through articles you e-mailed to yourself. Sites you've bookmarked no longer exist. You believe you'll have to slip a late paper under your professor's door. Even worse, you're thinking about buying a paper online to save your GPA.

OR

It's 2 A.M. The day your research paper was assigned, you created this schedule:

Week One: Do general reading
Narrow topic
Week Two: Assemble books and Web sites
Join an online newsgroup
Week Three: Read sources and take notes
Conduct personal interview
Record bibliographic information
Week Four: Weigh evidence and decide on thesis
Create outline
Write rough draft and bring to peer group
Week Five: Revise paper
Type Works Cited list
Print extra copy for security
Send thank-you note for personal interview

When I slept, armies of footnotes marched across my dreams.

—TED MORGAN

Research is the art of seeing what everyone else sees, and doing what no one else has done.

—ANONYMOUS

Beside each item, as relentless as marching soldiers, checks appeared. *You* snagged the library books first and had time to contact a Web site to get a missing URL. Notes neatly stacked, you're about to proof the paper. The only thing wrong, really, nagging the back of your mind, is that your paper seems bland, lifeless.

The first scenario is chaotic, and the second is idealized, but mechanical. Let's try to balance these two extremes so you can be both on track and creative.

Why Should I Write a Research Paper?

 For your career. If you become a financial advisor, you'll need to know how to research investment trends for clients. As a civil engineer designing a courtyard, you'll need to research water drainage systems. As a nurse, you might have to study new laws about bar coding medications, so patients are administered the correct drugs. Research papers teach you how to discover information you don't know and report it clearly to others.

 For your academic studies. Use your research paper to learn more about a topic your professors *didn't* cover, and you may stun them! Researching areas not covered in class is what leads to awards and doctoral theses.

 For your personal life. A friend of mine suffered labored breathing, sharp eye pains, and kidney stones. After five referrals, she was finally diagnosed with sarcoidosis, a disease with no real cure except for time—up to 20 years, the doctors told her. Lillian searched the Web to learn more about what she could do to ease her symptoms and even provided her doctors with new information about the disease.

Great Research Topics for College

 Choose a topic you care about. Professors assign research papers to encourage creativity—so seek it. Find an exciting angle within the broad, bland topic. Remember: In most cases, readers care about your topic only half as much as you do. So you must be enthusiastic to keep them reading.

Connect your personal interests to class requirements. If your assigned topic for a history course is World War II and you're interested in automobiles, research transportation technology during that period. If you love sports, study the Nazi Olympics or games soldiers played. If you are a computer science major in a literature class, research technology themes in the poems you're reading. If you worry that you're straying from your professor's guidelines, simply ask.

Tap into current events. Check out the headlines of Internet news sites or your local paper to pick up on an interesting new development.

Examine the images around you. *MSNBC, Time,* and the *New York Times* allow you to click on their multimedia or photos links to pull up this week's pictures.

Identify a real audience. If you decide to write about child abuse, would you target teens, parents, victims, victimizers, counselors, or teachers? A specific audience helps you visualize and shape your thesis and details.

Allow your topic to evolve. Narrowing your topic and creating a thesis is not a one-step process. Keep separate notepaper to record new ideas.

■ **PRACTICE 15-1** Let's begin your paper now. Yep. Right now. Narrow two subjects below to find a research topic that interests you:

- Gangs
- Chemical warfare
- Music
- Diseases
- Your own subject

Create Your Key Research Questions

Before you begin to research, ask questions you want answered. These will focus you on the important issues and forecast you how much effort and interest you will need to complete the assignment. I can find interesting aspects in all of the subjects in Practice 15-1. I'm concerned about gangs that use violent crimes as initiation rituals. I'm worried about inexpensively manufactured chemical bombs. Because I'm 40 (and "old school"), I need to learn more about my students' hip-hop scene. I'm also anxious about the potential global outbreak of the bird flu, which in its worst case scenario would kill 142 million humans. To begin, I will ask some hard questions about what I know and what I'll need to learn about both.

Gangs

- How have gangs changed since the Bloods and Crips first appeared in Los Angeles?
- In what ways are gangs substitute families for youth whose families are broken?
- Are there international gangs impacting North America?

Chemical Warfare

- What are the latest chemical weapons most people don't know about?
- What counter-measures can be used if a chemical weapon is deployed?
- What locations are most vulnerable to a chemical weapon attack?

Hip-hop

- How has hip-hop changed since its origins in the mid 1970s?
- What dance styles were born of the hip-hop culture and why?
- Does hip-hop really contribute to violence against women?

Bird Flu

- How does the bird flu mutate to infect humans?
- What would happen to our government, economy, and food supplies should it hit?
- How did countries survive pandemic flues and plagues of the past?

 Raise new questions and scrap ones that grow stale or seem obvious. Early research helps modify your questions. I skimmed a few articles on gangs and wondered how gangs communicate. What graffiti symbols do gangs use to demarcate territories? Which subtle hand gestures cause brawls? As I read about chemical weaponry, I wanted to learn more about terrorist organizations that might use chemicals bombs. Who supplies terrorists with banned toxic agents? For hip-hop, I found an image of 50 Cent, a rapper known for hard core lyrics. This picture of him, on the next page, with a human silhouette target made me think about whether he was reporting or celebrating urban violence. I also viewed another image with Nas tattooed with "GOD's SON." New questions arose: Do hip-hop artists simply exploit violence to enrich themselves, or do they ever contribute to improving their communities? About the bird flu topic, I wonder how much has been spent developing new vaccines, and should the flu infect North America, who would be the first to be vaccinated? Could those without health coverage afford vaccinations?

VISUAL RHETORIC

■ **PRACTICE 15-2** Compare and contrast the images of 50 Cent and Nas. What rap stereotypes do they reinforce or break? How does the style of the artists and the photographers help shape the images?

 Use Brain teasers to bring out what you already know. On the hip-hop topic, a *sense details* Brain teaser could record your impression

Reuters/CORBIS

50 Cent at MTV Music Awards

Jesse Frohman/CORBIS

Rapper Nas

of the music. Play some hip-hop music from the 1980s, like Public Enemy, and *contrast* with Nas's "Be a Nigga Too." Listen for political or social themes. *Classify* hip-hop: east coast, west cost, gangsta, lyrical. *Break stereotypes* about who listens to hip-hop. Use the *bug-list* to identify vulgar, violent, and sexist lyrics; that might ruin songs even though they imbed positive messages. For the bird flu, *sense details* could describe symptoms. You could *compare* and *contrast* the potential outbreak to the 1918 Spanish flu that killed 50 million people worldwide. You could also *classify* Types A, B, and C of flu viruses. You could also *anticipate your audience*: most people are so mired in their own lives, they don't consider large catastrophes, or they believe that infection would never happen to them.

Think actively toward a thesis. Keep asking "why" and "how," especially during your early stages of research. As I searched the Internet about hip-hop, I thought about its role in video games such as *True Crime: New York City* and *Grand Theft Auto*. I thought about adolescents who pretend to be thugs beating prostitutes and shooting cops with hip-hop music in the background. Regarding the bird flu, I wondered how many people in the United States would die should a strain mutate. And then I thought about remote parts of Africa or South America where there might be no impact. Philosophically, would the bird flu be Nature's own way of dealing with overpopulation? Questions like these might uncover more than my original questions—or change my research focus. Right now, I'm going with hip-hop. That I, as a teen, lived it helps my credibility as a writer, but now that I'm older, needing to learn about today's youth gives me a real cause for writing the essay. My early research into the bird flu was bogged down by technical information and contradictory outcomes. Considering my audience—you—I believe that you will find more interest in the hip-hop topic than the unclear, hypothetical future of bird flu.

Choose the topic that works for you and the assignment's requirements. As a college student, you must find a balance between what you *wish* to write about and what you're *required* to write about. Ideally, your essay will address an audience beyond your college classroom, but remember that the required subject, tone, purpose, source types, and word-length are detailed by your professor. If you are unsure of your topic, meet with your professor for direction.

■ **PRACTICE 15-3** For your best topic in Practice 15-1, ask four key research questions, and do a half-page Brain teaser to clarify what you already know.

Library Resources

LIBRARIANS

When you begin to research answers to your questions, librarians can guide you through pamphlet files, computer indexes, and the Web. To keep these wonderful people on your side, come prepared with your key questions as well as your professor's assignment, and read basic references first, so they'll be happier to work with you. If you only bring a general topic such as "chemical warfare" or "disease," librarians might think that you expect them to do your work. Besides, the more specific you are, the better information you'll get.

THE REFERENCE SECTION

Visit your library's reference section or go online to access reference works. **The reference section includes encyclopedias and other books that provide raw facts and statistics.** Because I needed to learn the history of hip-hop, I read an encyclopedia entry about how hip-hop's early originators included DJ Kool Herc, born in Jamaica, whose rhythms set the stage for 1980s lyrics that critiqued urban environments. About the bird flu, I learned that during the second half of January 2008, almost 2.5 million birds were killed in India to prevent the spread of the virus. Curiosity and a few minutes can dig up strong facts on almost any topic. **Try these sources:**

- *Information Please Almanac* (United States, world facts; www.infoplease.com)
- The *Statistical Abstract of the United States* (www.census.gov/compendia/statab)
- *FedStats* (statistics from over 100 federal agencies; www.fedstats.gov)
- *Occupational Outlook Handbook* (careers; www.bls.gov/oco/home.htm)
- *The World Fact Book* (international demographic, governmental, and economic information; (www.cia.gov/library/publications/the-world-factbook/index.html)

■ **PRACTICE 15-4** Use one of the reference works listed above to find an interesting fact/statistic related to your practice topic from 15-3. Bring a copy of the article to class, along with two ideas about its significance for your topic.

BOOKS

Electronic card catalogs locate books at your library and other libraries. The following is a typical online card catalog entry found under the subject of hip-hop:

Author	McQuillar, Tayannah Lee, 1977.
Title	When rap music had a conscience: the artists, organizations and historic events that inspired and influenced the "Golden Age" of hip-hop from 1987 to 1996.
Publisher	New York: Thunder's Mouth Press, c2007
Paging	xvii, 184 p.; 18 cm.
Notes	Includes bibliographical references (p.[165]), discography. (p.[167]–178), filmography (p.[168]–184). Includes bibliographical references (pp. 60–61) and index.
Review	Available (click here).
Subjects	Rap (Music) History and criticism. Rap (Music) Social aspects.
Format	Book.
Call Number	782.4216 M173w

Use the catalog entry to determine whether a book is worth your time. Evaluating a book's reliability helps you think more deeply about your topic and spares you from reading weak sources. Here are some tips:

- **How closely does the title relate to your topic?** This title looks great for my hip-hop topic; however, it only spans nine years and doesn't include information about hip-hop's early birth in the 1970s.

- **Compare the book's length with the size of its topic.** This book is 184 pages long, and the last 20 pages are dedicated to a bibliography, discography, and filmography. With only 165 pages for the span of nine years, it's bound to be superficial—strike one against it.

- **Consider the author's credibility.** Is this author an expert? I searched Amazon.com and read a book review that gave it four stars (of five), but it stated that the work included very few lyrics and that it didn't "present a solid case." I also searched OCLC, an online reference of books in print, and found only one other book by McQuillar—on using "folk magick" to gain money and love. Finally, McQuillar was born in 1977, and she's critiquing rap she first heard at 10 years old. I wonder if her age may skew her perception of hip-hop history. Although the book might be good, McQuillar's publishing credibility is not strong—strike two.

- **Check the date.** Scientific and technological topics often must be published within the last five years to be up to date. Psychology rarely accepts research more than 10 years old. With books about historical events or music, "recent" can mean something published 25 years ago. McQuillar's book, published in 2007, is great for my topic.

- **Evaluate the book's paging and format.** This book's size is 18 cm, which is about 7 inches—pretty small. Amazon.com's "Search Inside" feature let me view the actual text. The large font and the book's small size verified the work would be brief and general.

- **Check for an index.** An index helps you quickly identify information you need. Unfortunately, this book does not have one.

- **Use the book to help you find more sources.** This book includes a bibliography (a list of works the author used to write the book), a discography (a list of songs and musicians), and a filmography (a list of relevant movies). These are plusses.

- **Read the subject line.** This might suggest new phrases to search. Now I know I might find more books under "rap music history and criticism," as well as "rap music social aspects."

Bottom Line: Should I use this book? *Only to lead me to better ones.*

For books worth reviewing, write down the title and call numbers. If you're working online, print the bibliographic information—and use the back of the sheet for note taking.

When you find good books in the library stacks, scan adjacent books. Related books are shelved together.

To locate books not in your library, check *Books in Print* (www. booksinprint.com/bip), which lists all books currently being sold. Search the Online Computer Library Center (OCLC), a worldwide card catalog that connects over 60,000 libraries with access to over 98 million records, or visit Amazon.com and Barnesandnoble.com. **Or ask your college library for an interlibrary loan—it's free!** Bring the bibliographic information to your library's reference desk. It should arrive in a week.

■ **PRACTICE 15-5** Find a book title for your topic from your library's electronic card catalog and another from Books in Print, the OCLC, or an online bookstore. Record complete bibliographic information and evaluate their likely reliability for your topic as I did with the hip-hop topic.

ARTICLES

Why would you want articles if you have a book? Because most new books are already one to five years old the minute they reach the bookstore, due to the lag time in editing and publishing. Magazines also cover topics too small for books. For my hip-hop paper, I might find many articles on artist Jay-Z but no book. Also, you can read many writers' ideas in articles in the time it takes to read one book.

COMPUTER INDEXES AND DATABASES FOR ARTICLES

Don't be tempted to rely on the Web for *all* your research. Your library's computer indexes and databases are better organized and more reliable than most Web sources (*indexes* provide *only* bibliographic information; *databases* usually provide the articles themselves). At the end of this section, you'll find a list of indexes, but for now, I will use *General OneFile,* which provides access to 9,000 journals, as an example of how my research on hip-hop continued.

Using an index is very much like using *Yahoo!* or *Google,* inputting search words and key phrases. Below is the opening screen of the database. Most indexes, like this one, include a subject search and ways to limit the results. I have typed "hip-hop" into the "Find" box, selected only items with full-text, and requested articles between 2004 and 2008.

General OneFile Subject Guide Search

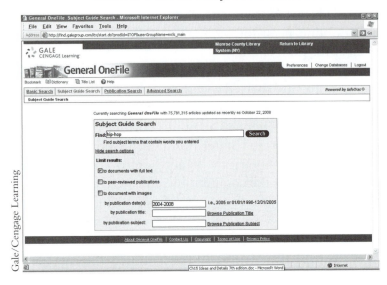

129 items were listed. To narrow my search, I combined "hip-hop" with the words "politics," "culture" and "violence." **These hits helped shift my focus to "hip-hop as a means for social activism."** Great—I had moved closer to a working thesis! So I started a new search on "history of rap." During these two searches, I marked five interesting titles and viewed them. Below is a *General OneFile* screen with my marked references.

Selected Sources from Search Results

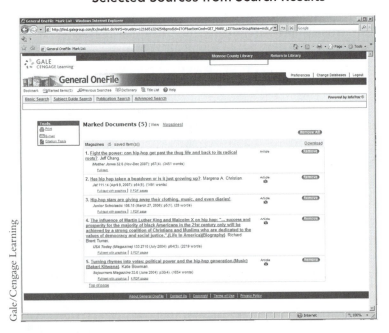

■ **PRACTICE 15-6** Pick two article titles from my list. What do you believe they will cover? How credible is each source based upon the information provided?

I clicked on the first article, "Fight the Power: Can Hip-hop Get Past the Thug Life and Back to its Radical Roots?" partly because of the interesting title, but also because its 3,451 word length would likely provide detailed information. Below is part of the article I e-mailed to myself.

Instant Evaluation of Source: This author is reliable; his well-written content includes information about hip-hop's history and the music industry's financial support of thug lyrics, rather than political themes. My focus began to change to the positive aspects of hip-hop—how it *can* encourage social activism—which is more original than the usual anti-hip-hop rhetoric.

Here are other computer databases your library may offer:

- *ArticleFirst!* (articles from popular sources)
- *Expanded Academic Index* (articles from magazines and Internet sources)
- *FirstSearch!* (humanities, business, and science indexes)
- *JSTOR Electronic Journals* (older articles in business, humanities, social sciences, and science journals).
- *Wilsonselect* (indexes other indexes; full-text articles)

TIPS FOR USING COMPUTER INDEXES AND DATABASES

- **Be patient.** You may find the perfect resource in minutes, but expect to try several times. Each database is like a door in a house. You need to look in all the rooms to find the best information.
- **Start specific, then broaden searches.** Type your most specific topic first ("hip-hop"). If your results are poor, try broader categories ("rap music" or "popular music"), then scroll the list to discover better subheadings.
- **Limit searches by more recent dates.** When I narrowed my search for articles since 2007, I found 10.
- **Change your search options.** Most indexes allow you to search by subject or keywords. A subject search gave me 1,231 hits, but a keyword search turned up 23 that were more on target.
- **Narrow your search by subdivisions.** When I searched "hip-hop culture," *General OneFile* provided me with 43 subdivisions. The "criticism and interpretation" category listed 12 academic journal articles on social and demographic perspectives of hip-hop.

Portion of a Full-text Article

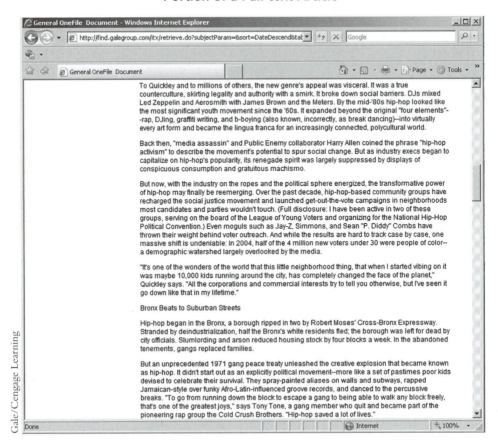

General OneFile Document - Windows Internet Explorer

http://find.galegroup.com/itx/retrieve.do?subjectParam=&sort=DateDescend&tab

Google

General OneFile Document

Page ▾ Tools ▾

To Quickley and to millions of others, the new genre's appeal was visceral. It was a true counterculture, skirting legality and authority with a smirk. It broke down social barriers. DJs mixed Led Zeppelin and Aerosmith with James Brown and the Meters. By the mid-'80s hip-hop looked like the most significant youth movement since the '60s. It expanded beyond the original "four elements"--rap, DJing, graffiti writing, and b-boying (also known, incorrectly, as break dancing)--into virtually every art form and became the lingua franca for an increasingly connected, polycultural world.

Back then, "media assassin" and Public Enemy collaborator Harry Allen coined the phrase "hip-hop activism" to describe the movement's potential to spur social change. But as industry execs began to capitalize on hip-hop's popularity, its renegade spirit was largely suppressed by displays of conspicuous consumption and gratuitous machismo.

But now, with the industry on the ropes and the political sphere energized, the transformative power of hip-hop may finally be reemerging. Over the past decade, hip-hop-based community groups have recharged the social justice movement and launched get-out-the-vote campaigns in neighborhoods most candidates and parties wouldn't touch. (Full disclosure: I have been active in two of these groups, serving on the board of the League of Young Voters and organizing for the National Hip-Hop Political Convention.) Even moguls such as Jay-Z, Simmons, and Sean "P. Diddy" Combs have thrown their weight behind voter outreach. And while the results are hard to track case by case, one massive shift is undeniable: In 2004, half of the 4 million new voters under 30 were people of color--a demographic watershed largely overlooked by the media.

"It's one of the wonders of the world that this little neighborhood thing, that when I started vibing on it was maybe 10,000 kids running around the city, has completely changed the face of the planet," Quickley says. "All the corporations and commercial interests try to tell you otherwise, but I've seen it go down like that in my lifetime."

Bronx Beats to Suburban Streets

Hip-hop began in the Bronx, a borough ripped in two by Robert Moses' Cross-Bronx Expressway. Stranded by deindustrialization, half the Bronx's white residents fled; the borough was left for dead by city officials. Slumlording and arson reduced housing stock by four blocks a week. In the abandoned tenements, gangs replaced families.

But an unprecedented 1971 gang peace treaty unleashed the creative explosion that became known as hip-hop. It didn't start out as an explicitly political movement--more like a set of pastimes poor kids devised to celebrate their survival. They spray-painted aliases on walls and subways, rapped Jamaican-style over funky Afro-Latin-influenced groove records, and danced to the percussive breaks. "To go from running down the block to escape a gang to being able to walk any block freely, that's one of the greatest joys," says Tony Tone, a gang member who quit and became part of the pioneering rap group the Cold Crush Brothers. "Hip-hop saved a lot of lives."

Done   Internet   100%

Gale/Cengage Learning

■ **PRACTICE 15-7** Research your own topic using one of your library's computer indexes. Find at least two articles that seem worth reading.

World Wide Web

. . . .

RELIABLE AND UNRELIABLE WEB SITES

- **The Internet is unregulated.** No official verifies articles' validity. Although published authors make mistakes and distort facts at times, editors try to correct them. Readers cancel unreliable publications. Your odds of reading trustworthy information in a college library or college databases are a lot better than when you log onto Smokin' Billy's Web site.
- **Knowing the type of Web site you're viewing helps you evaluate it.** For example, the National Rifle Association (www.nra.org) and Green Peace (www.greenpeace.org) are nonprofit organizations, yet their commitment to causes means they often provide biased information.

Government (.gov) sites provide excellent data, but watch out for political spins. Commercial sites (.com) often slant information to sell a product, but some offer valid resource links. For example, a company that sells child car seats might provide articles on car safety. Educational institutions (.edu) usually are the most objective. Sites in the United Kingdom (.uk) might indicate alternative world views than those coming from the United States or Canada.

- **Avoid Web sites with advertising banners and pop-up windows.**
- **Numerous grammar and mechanical errors suggest the ideas may be careless too.**
- **If the site hasn't been updated for six months, forget it.** The page's creator is too lazy or uninterested to be reliable.
- **Web sites with their own search engines tend to be the best organized and most reliable.**
- **Sites with "feedback" links indicate that owners care about their relationship with visitors.** And they might give you research leads.

■ **PRACTICE 15-8** Find one reliable and one unreliable Web site for your topic from Practice 15-3. Explain why you rate them this way.

SEARCHING THE WEB

Start with institutions related to your topic, not general search engines. Include "department," "institute," "association," or "organization" with your searches to locate reliable sites. Using these words in my search, I learned that MIT's Women's Studies program hosted a 2005 hip-hop conference entitled, "Hip-hop, Gender, and Culture: A Workshop for Faculty Development and Feminist Debate." The description provided me ideas for addressing misogyny in hip–hop lyrics.

- For social or economic topics, try the U.S. Department of Justice (www.usdoj.gov/02organizations/index.html).
- For historical topics, try the Smithsonian Institute (www.si.edu).
- For health and human services topics, try the Food and Drug Administration (www.fda.org).
- For vital statistics and population growth, try the U.S. Census Bureau (www.census.gov).

Search major news sites.

- *CNN News* (www.cnn.com)
- *National Public Radio Online* (www.npr.org)
- *New York Times* (www.nytimes.com)

Search magazine sites related to your topic.

- For nature and ecology, *National Geographic* (www.nationalgeographic.com)
- For music, *Rolling Stone* (www.rollingstone.com)
- For athletics, *Sports Illustrated* (sportsillustrated.cnn.com)

Use search engines. Search engines attempt to categorize Web sites worldwide. Unfortunately, new sites emerge each minute, and their creators report their presence to only *some* search engines. So which is the best to use?

Your engine should provide alternate search terms. A site like *Yahoo!* provides alternate searches at the bottom of the screen. For example, when I typed, "hip-hop," the site suggested "theological implications of hip-hop"—a topic I thought never existed! *Ask.com* provides easy-to-use links, and an automated drop-down list of re-phrased questions help refine your search.

Your engine should retrieve image and audio files. *Google,* like many engines, lets you limit searches by photographs, streaming videos, and sound files. This was useful for my topic when I wanted to know what Missy Elliott's music sounded like.

Your engine should search other engines. Metasearch engines report only the top hits of other engines, saving you effort. *Dogpile* lives up to its slogan: "All the Best Search Engines Piled into One." It fetches top hits from *Google, Live Search, Yahoo!* and *Ask.com*. Another favorite is *Metacrawler:* It "crawls" through other engines.

Here are addresses for the search engines mentioned:

- *Ask.com* (www.ask.com)
- *Dogpile* (www.dogpile.com)
- *Google* (www.google.com)
- *Metacrawler* (www.metacrawler.com)
- *Live Search* (www.live.com)
- *Yahoo!* (www.yahoo.com)

■ **PRACTICE 15-9** Search two engines listed above using the same word or phrase for your topic from Practice 15-3. Which engine gave better results? Explain.

E-mails to Experts, Newsgroups, and Blogs

EXPERTS

E-mail interviews allow you to reach busy experts or those who live far away. Your interviewee can reply more thoughtfully than in face-to-face interviews. During my literature class, one presentation group stunned us with a letter from Ron Carlson, a short-story author. They located him at a Midwest university and e-mailed questions about his story. Within a day, they received a two-page response!

Visit college Web sites to find e-mail addresses of professors who might share their expertise. Let the person know in advance what your assignment entails, where you are located, and what class you're taking. This openness will increase your odds of getting an online interview.

Post a question at an "Ask an Expert" Web site. Usually within three days, you receive an e-mail response with links to more information. Wanting to compare hip-hop of the 1970s to today's music, I went to *Allexperts.com* (www.allexperts.com) and posted a question to Antoine King, publisher of Bronx's *SPATE Magazine*: "Would you mind sharing some info on underground artists who don't get much radio play?" King provided me links to the *MySpace* pages of Mysonne and Sha Stimuli, who according to King "have positive messages without glorifying being a gangster." These sites included music samples and political lyrics.

■ **PRACTICE 15-10** Post a question related to your topic at *Allexperts.com*, and bring the response to class.

NEWSGROUPS

Register your e-mail address with an online newsgroup dedicated to specific topics. Whenever articles or responses are posted, they are automatically e-mailed to you. *InterBulletin* (news.interbulletin.com) lets you search through 30,000 newsgroups. I found several groups related to hip-hop; however, some seemed defunct. To find a newsgroup related to your topic through a search engine, combine your subject (in my case "hip-hop") with the term "newsgroup." You might also join newsgroups through newspaper Web sites. *Warning:* Some newsgroups are not professionally moderated, and despite their codes of ethics, you may encounter rude participants.

BLOGS

Blogs also vary in reliability because many are personal Web sites. Credible blog sites list their sources of information and links to other resources. Search the Internet using the word "blog" along with your topic. My own search led me to *Hiphopmusic.com*, which provided insightful critiques of today's music and political industry—using text and video. Of course, *MySpace.com* and *Facebook.com* provide blogs by politicians, authors, musicians, artists, and researchers. Both sites require you to apply for a free account.

■ **PRACTICE 15-11** Go to *InterBulletin*, *MySpace.com*, or *Facebook.com*—or search the Web. Find a newsgroup or a blog related to your paper topic.

TIPS FOR ELECTRONIC COMMUNICATION

- E-mails are professional correspondences; use correct mechanics.
- Start with an appropriate greeting, including any titles ("Dear Dr. Martino").
- State your purpose in the first paragraph. Mention you're a student, the class you're taking, and how you found the contact.
- Ask no more than five questions, or your potential source might ignore you. One should ask for leads to other sources.
- Don't wait until the last day.
- Thank the person in advance. You're requesting expertise for free!
- Close your e-mail with "Sincerely" or "Respectfully." Include your full name, college, city, and state.
- When you get a response, send a "thank you" along with a copy of your essay.

Multimedia on the Web

Researchers also use online videos, podcasts, and mp3 files as sources.

Streaming Video. Major online news sites like *MSNBC.com*, *CNN.com*, and *Reuters* (www.reuters.com), provide links to their streaming media content. Visit *YouTube* (www.youtube.com), *blinkx* (www.blinkx.com), or *AOL Video* (video.aol.com) to retrieve media that might not be covered by national and local news organizations. You may have to sift through unprofessional content but the sites provide decent sources within news, politics, science, and technology categories. Using *YouTube*, I found a three-minute interview between PBS talk show host Tavis Smiley and Barack Obama about the role hip-hop might have in the White House!

Audio Files. iPods and MP3 players make access to audio content easy if you subscribe to their company's download sites. If you've already registered for *iTunes* or *Rhapsody*, use them to listen to interviews, speeches, and seminars. Even without these pricey gadgets, the Web provides access to other historical references:

- American Rhetoric (famous US speeches; www.americanrhetoric.com)
- Digital History (speeches and lectures; www.digitalhistory.uh.edu)

- British Broadcast Radio (hourly news and archives; http://www.bbc
.co.uk/radio)
- National Public Radio (hourly news and archives; www.npr.org)

I went to National Public Radio and listened to an *All Things Considered* report on Jay Z's $150 million contract negotiation with concert promoter Live Nation. In the report, Jay Z was likened to Madonna, which tells me that hip-hop is fast becoming as mainstream as pop music, reaching broader audiences than I first imagined.

Overlooked Sources

YOUR COMMUNITY

Use the *Yellow Pages* to contact local organizations or businesses related to your topic. One student researching funeral rituals interviewed several undertakers and was given a *very* detailed tour of one facility. She learned far more than books would have taught her. For gang activity, mentioned earlier in the chapter, I could contact local police precincts or neighborhood associations. For the bird flu, the local Disease Control Center might offer me leads. For the chemical warfare topic, I could contact the local Homeland Security branch. For my hip-hop topic, I could contact local radio stations, visit a recording studio, or attend a concert. Most experts will give information over the phone to courteous callers.

SMART FRIENDS

Ask friends, family, bosses, and professors for leads. For my topic, I called two colleagues who recently lectured on hip-hop's social impact. I also spoke to some of my students who provided me with recordings from underground artists.

Collect your own data firsthand. Student Jennifer Wheeler gathered her own research simply by counting. This paragraph comes from a letter she sent to her employer's clothing store. She wanted the store to eliminate plastic wrapping to "do its part in saving our planet":

> During a typical week in the Ladies Sportswear Department at my store, we receive approximately fifteen rolling racks of hung clothing and between five and ten racks of boxed clothing. Each individual piece of merchandise is needlessly prepackaged in plastic that is thrown away. Weekly, we throw away approximately 3,000 plastic bags and 2,250 plastic hangers. This is only Ladies Sportswear.

My manager informed me that monthly our store discards one ton of plastic. Many of these bags can be reused, and all the hangers can be used in the store instead of switching the clothes to our store hangers. This would save salesclerks six hours of work in our department each week.

TIPS FOR PERSONAL INTERVIEWS

- *Ask* for the person's time a week ahead, and explain exactly why you want it. Suggest a few sample questions and how much time you'll need. (I recommend 30 minutes.)
- Do your preliminary reading first. Your knowledge will encourage your source to provide sharper information.
- Prepare questions, but be open to new ideas during the interview.
- Come with paper and pen. If you want to record the interview, ask permission.
- Dress professionally—you will be taken more seriously.
- Start with an easy question to loosen things up, but move to key research questions before you run out of time.
- *Immediately* after an interview, fill out your notes and record your reactions before they go cold. Be sure to indicate which are quotes, paraphrases, and personal reactions.
- Send a typed thank-you note, along with a copy of your paper.

■ **PRACTICE 15-12** Make a list of three people or organizations that can give you information for your topic from Practice 15-3. List five questions you'd ask.

Note-Taking Strategies

There is no one "right" way to take notes, but here are some suggestions:

- **Skim your sources before reading.** Scan the headings, index, or table of contents to find the best information quickly.
- **Before taking notes on good sources, record the complete bibliographic information:** author, title, volume number, pages, date, and publication information. For Internet sources, include the URL address, date posted to the Internet, and date you read it. These will be required for your works cited.

- **Use Post-It notes as tabs in the margins of books.** Write questions and reactions on them.
- **3 × 5 note cards have two advantages.** They're neater than a mess of papers and can be easily rearranged when you organize the paper—provided you limit yourself to one fact or idea per note card.
- **A large paper pad provides space to write, but will tempt you to put too many ideas on one page.**
- **Paraphrase instead of copying long quotations.** Condense the original, and quote only key sentences or phrases. Avoid referring to the original as you paraphrase so you don't risk plagiarism. This will help *your* voice control the draft. Ask yourself, "What is the one key point I need from this source?" Then write. Of course, if you unearth a sparkling paragraph, copy it. *Quote accurately, use quotation marks, and record page numbers.*
- **Analyze source material.** Be an active, critical thinker, not just a copier, when you take notes. Raise an objection to the author, add a personal anecdote, or connect sources. Be sure to label "My Ideas" or "My Comment" at the top of your notes so you never confuse your ideas with those from sources. Clip comment cards to their source cards. In the following example on hip-hop music, the first card contains source material, quotation, and paraphrase; the second is my commentary on the source.

Bibliography Information →

Chang, Jeff. "Fight the Power: Can Hip-hop Get Past the Thug Life and Back to its RadicalRoots?" *Mother Jones* 32.6 (Nov.–Dec. 2007): 67(4). *General OneFile*. Gale. Monroe County Library System (NY). 27 Mar. 2008 <http://find.galegroup.com/itx/start.do?prodId=ITOF>.

→ Paraphrase and Direct Quotation

Chang states that a treaty between gangs in 1971 gave birth to hip-hop, but it wasn't a political movement, only what youth did to celebrate survival in poverty. He says, "They spray-painted aliases on walls and subways, rapped Jamaican-style over funky Afro-Latin-influenced groove records, and danced to the percussive breaks." He also cites former gang member turned rap artist Tony Tone: "To go from running down the block to escape a gang to being able to walk any block freely, that's one of the greatest joys . . . Hip-hop saved a lot of lives" (n. pag.).

Commentary ←

MY IDEAS:

The early hip-hop scene helped poor kids share their experiences with others, instead of physically feuding over them. But notice how tagging walls and subways cars with spray paint was also an act of freedom. Did this defacement of public property encourage early anti-hip-hop sentiments in society at-large?

The next example combines source and commentary on one card:

Bibliography Information ←

Chang, Jeff. "Fight the Power: Can Hip-hop Get Past the Thug Life and Back to its Radical Roots?" *Mother Jones* 32.6 (Nov.–Dec. 2007): 67(4). *General OneFile*. Gale. Monroe County Library System (NY). 27 Mar. 2008 http://find.galegroup.com/itx/start.do?prodId=ITOF.

Paraphrase and Direct Quotation ←

Chang claims that hip-hop artists encourage followers to vote, particularly during the 2006 elections when 4 million new voters under 30 participated—and that "more than half of them were people of color." Additionally, local hip-hop organizations "have stopped construction of juvenile detention facilities in California and New York City, helped can environmental deregulation legislation in New Mexico, passed a college debt-forgiveness initiative in Maine, created networks for Katrina survivors across the South. . ." (n. pag.).

Commentary ←

MINE: If hip-hop is helping local communities and political activism, why isn't it getting national attention? Chang, earlier in the article, partly blames large record companies for cutting deals with the "thug" rappers, instead of the newer, underground artists, because the image of toughness—along with its misogynistic, "gangsta" ideals—sells easier than political activity. Did these artists sell out their local communities?

■ **PRACTICE 15-13** Fill a note card or sheet of paper on your topic from Practice 15-3 based on a source. Paraphrase most of your source but include a short quotation. Then comment on the material.

Annotated Bibliographies

· ·

Another way to help hone your research material is to write an annotated bibliography. Often, professors require this as a formal stage in writing a research paper.

An annotated bibliography lists your sources and then summarizes their main ideas and how they may relate to your research topic. For my hip-hop topic, here are two sources in proper MLA bibliographic citation with my annotations.

Chang, Jeff. "Fight the Power: Can Hip-hop Get Past the Thug Life and Back to its Radical Roots?" *Mother Jones* 32.6 (Nov.–Dec. 2007): 67(4). *General OneFile*. Gale. Monroe County Library System (NY). 27 Mar. 2008 http://find.galegroup.com/itx/start .do?prodId=ITOF.

The author examines the birth of hip-hop in the 1970s, identifying its role in bringing hope to New York City, as a means to express discontent of urban living. The work details hip-hop's role in preventing violence by artists who used lyrics instead of weapons and dance instead of fights to resolve conflicts. The article also critiques the music industry for offering deals to thug artists. Finally, political activities supported by hip-hop artists are explored.

Christian, Margena A. "Has Hip-hop Taken a Beatdown or is It Just Growing Up?" *Jet* 11.14 (9 Apr. 2007): 54–59. *General OneFile*. Gale. Monroe County Library System (NY). 27 Mar. 2008 <http://find.galegroup.com/itx/start.do?prodId=ITOF>.

Christian interviews popular hip-hop artists and producers in light of Nas's 2006 album *Hip-hop is Dead*. Interviewees include hip-hop stars Nas, Chamillionaire, Russel Simmons, and Chuck D. Some see hope in hip-hop's potential, and others see its decaying evolution as irreversible. The article discusses hip-hop's lack of female artists and says that 58 percent of hip-hop's daily listeners disapprove of its messages. It also examines hip-hop's impact in Brazil, Israel, and Japan.

Organizing Research Papers

· ·

When most of your research reading seems done, reflect upon and refine the focus of your thesis by asking following questions:

- What is the main thing I've learned?
- What idea grabs me the most?
- What angle will impress my audience?

Identify key subject headings. Place note cards into related piles or spread loose papers on a table. Read through your notes, then on a *separate sheet*, list the main points you want to cover. Next, go back to your notes and rewrite or cut and paste the paraphrases or quotations under the headings. For hip-hop, here are my tentative heading notes:

TENTATIVE HIP-HOP HEADINGS:

- Origins of Hip-hop
- Hip-hop Stereotypes of Violence and Anti-Female Content
- Thug Hip-hop Artists
- Socially Responsible Hip-hop Artists
- Hip-hop of Today

Formulate a working thesis statement *before* **creating a detailed outline.** A working thesis helps to structure your piles of notes. Study your list of main points, and then write several trial thesis sentences that tie some of them together. Remember: Your thesis is a *one-sentence statement*, not a question. Here are three possible thesis statements for my hip-hop topic:

POTENTIAL THESIS STATEMENTS:

- Despite negative stereotypes of hip-hop, some are trying to do the right thing.
- Hip-hop is just as crude as other pop music but gets overly criticized because it intimidates white people.
- Hip-hop is rescuing itself from degeneration and now is returning to its roots by helping revive impoverished communities.

INSTANT SELF-ANALYSIS:

My first one seems obvious, and "do the right thing" is vague. I would have to narrow my focus to just a few artists. The second one isn't really true. Hip-hop has more crude language and violent content than most genres, and I doubt I could prove the racist point. I prefer the third. It's honestly complex—and it allows me to investigate hip-hop's origin, its selling out, and its reemergence into hope for poor folks—maybe even in rural areas since it has reached "crossover" popularity.

ROUGH OUTLINE

Stage 1: Origins of Hip-hop's Social Commitment
Stage 2: Early Political and Social Lyrics of Hip-hop
Stage 3: Why Hip-hop Sold Out to the Thug Image
Stage 4: Reemergence of Social Commitment
Stage 5: Hip-hop Dies if New Voices Don't Emerge—Rural

Assign important research and your own ideas to each heading. Clip note cards or papers together to your headings—or cut and paste information—to help keep your details organized.

Work in bold stray facts or quotations. If a good statistic or quotation doesn't fit into your headings, you might use it in your introduction or conclusion. Margena A. Christian's article, from my annotated bibliography, states, "Music sales dropped overall last year by 5 percent, but rap album sales plunged 20 percent" which might be caused by hip-hop's deteriorating appeal. This statistic might be a great way to begin my conclusion.

Write an abstract. Many professors require students to submit research papers in stages for approval. Try not to think of this as an extra chore, but as an aid in writing: Your teacher wants you to think, incubate, and organize early to provide feedback before a grade is at stake. Get used to preliminary reports. Most business and professional research requires an "abstract"—a thesis and one paragraph summary. This is usually submitted for approval and may accompany the final draft. Notice that it briefly identifies why the topic is important, tells what subjects it will cover, highlights supporting evidence, and draws a conclusion. Here is the abstract for my essay.

HIP-HOP ESSAY ABSTRACT

It is easy to dismiss hip-hop as a force for positive social change, especially with lyrics that degrade women, overuse the "n" word, and celebrate gangster violence; however, hip-hop is naturally rescuing itself from degeneration and now is returning to its roots by helping to revive impoverished communities. This essay will examine the early birth of hip-hop in the Bronx as a means to *prevent* gang violence, and then it will examine its political influence in the 1980s and early 1990s, reviewing lyrics from Run DMC, Public Enemy, and →

Kurtis Blow. It will explain why hip-hop disintegrated into the "thug life" due to its easy marketability to the masses. Finally, it will rebut Nas's lyrics that "hip-hop is dead" to show that hip-hop is entering a new era where listeners desire fewer self-loathing victims and more calls to social action. This can be done by studying emerging artists, like Mysonne and Sha Stimuli, who are returning hip-hop to its original state.

■ **PRACTICE 15-14** Formulate a thesis statement and headings for your topic from Practice 15-3. Also create an abstract that briefly summarizes your paper.

Writing Research Papers

Your **introduction** should catch the reader's attention with key research questions, an anecdote, or a strong fact, something to smoothly lead to your thesis statement. Research paper introductions usually preview what you will cover and perhaps why—drawing from your abstract. In my hip-hop topic, I will avoid the typical rant against hip-hop, since it's overdone. Critics make some valid points that I'll address, but I'll focus on the honest, hopeful aspects of the culture. **Work quickly on the first draft,** so you aren't sidetracked by little issues. **Your main goals are to clarify your sketchy ideas and support them with sharp details.** Here is a draft of my essay's introduction.

SAMPLE INTRODUCTION

"HIP-HOP: THE LYRICAL PHOENIX"
Renowned rapper Nas created a firestorm among hip-hop's listeners and producers with his 2006 release of "Hip-hop is Dead." Its opening verse attacks "rich ass niggaz" who guzzle expensive cognac, toke "ganja," flaunt bullet-spitting "llamas," and fornicate with Brazilian "dimes." He cautions wanna-be thugs, that if he "rolls up, it's all sown up," that their excessiveness, which discredits hip-hop culture, will die upon on his arrival. The song also threatens DJs who promote gangster image. To understand Nas's wrathful and apocalyptic tone, however, we need to examine how hip-hop has evolved during the last 30 years, and where it might be heading. It just might be that, like the Phoenix that reemerges from its own ashes, hip-hop is naturally

→

rescuing itself from degeneration and now is returning to its roots of helping revive impoverished communities.

Instant Self-Analysis: It feels good to finally put together sentences after all the disorder of research. Although it's not perfect, I like its edge. I wonder, though, how my audience will accept the vulgarity of Nas's words this early in the essay, or whether it will understand "llamas" (guns), "ganja" (marijuana), and "dimes" (women who score a perfect 10). Although I like the allusion to the Phoenix, I wonder if I'll be able to extend it throughout the essay or if it's too poetic. But this a good start, and I won't let insecurities stifle my progress.

RESEARCH ETHICS

As a college student, you belong to a community of thinkers with a special code of ethics. We are allowed to borrow ideas from each other—but only under certain terms. Fair Use practices require that we **include the sources for information that we've borrowed.** Those who violate these practices are plagiarists and can be severely penalized. Ideas *and* words are "intellectual property" and, therefore, are copyrighted (protected by law). Documentation also shows that our material comes from reputable sources.

It's possible to forget these ethics when you're worn out by the semester's workload and rushing to beat an approaching deadline. It's also tempting to ignore ethics if you see others buying papers from an Internet site. But be warned: Today's professors have easy access to smart search engines and detection software to catch plagiarism. And they do! It's sad to see capable students resort to cheating and fail courses due to plagiarism. At many colleges, students who plagiarize are expelled. It can ruin a student's credibility for years to come. Check out your college and professor's academic honesty policy. The risk is not worth your college degree!

■ **PRACTICE 15-15** Search the Internet for the following phrase in quotation marks: "fired for plagiarism." Print an interesting article, and bring it to class.

■ **PRACTICE 15-16** In a paragraph, describe two tricks students use to plagiarize and figure out how a teacher could catch such tricks.

AVOIDING PLAGIARISM

According to the *MLA Handbook for Writers of Research Papers,* Sixth Edition, "**Plagiarism involves two kinds of wrongs.** Using another person's ideas, information, or expressions without acknowledging that person's work constitutes intellectual theft. Passing off another person's ideas, information, or expressions as your own to get a better grade or gain some other advantage constitutes fraud" (Gibaldi 66).

Rephrasing does not make an idea yours; it only makes the words yours. A citation credits the *idea* to someone else. Quotation marks credit the *exact wording* to someone else.

Introductory taglines, like "According to Dr. Santana . . . " announce where source material begins, and **citation parentheses**, such as (Santana 33), mark the end of source material. Anything else, you are claiming as your idea.

The following must have citations:

- Word-for-word passages by others
- Paraphrases or summaries of other people's ideas in your own words
- Statistics and facts

Common knowledge does not need citation. The core of knowledge possessed by most educated people is called "common knowledge" and is considered the common property of society. Common knowledge includes **famous quotations** like these:

- "I have a dream."—Martin Luther King, Jr.
- "Oh that this too, too solid flesh would melt."—Shakespeare

Common knowledge also includes ideas:

- The First Amendment to the U.S. Constitution protects the right of free speech.
- Most religions say death is a release from the pain of life, not a dreaded event.

Common knowledge can be facts and statistics as well:

- Shakespeare lived in England 400 years ago and wrote the plays *Hamlet* and *The Tempest*.
- The synthetic pesticide DDT, now almost banned world wide, causes the death of birds and fish.

Expert knowledge requires citation. Higher degrees of specific knowledge cease to be common knowledge. If, for instance, you quoted the rest of Hamlet's speech, or discussed the debate over the approval of the First Amendment that took place in 1790, or described the specific chemical reaction DDT causes in bald eagle eggs, it would cease to be common knowledge. Among *experts,* this information may still be considered common knowledge, but until you establish yourself as an expert, you must document.

■ **PRACTICE 15-17** Which of the following is common knowledge? Which is expert knowledge?

- Tupac Amaru Shakur, a famous rap artist, was murdered in Las Vegas, Nevada.
- Shakur's parents were Black Panthers; his mother was pregnant with Shakur while imprisoned in New York.
- "Tupac Amaru" means *Shining Serpent*, after an Incan Indian revolutionary. "Shakur" means *Thankful to God* in Arabic.

Citing Sources: MLA Style

Since different disciplines require different formats, ask your professor which documentation style to use. The two most common are the Modern Language Association (MLA) and American Psychological Association (APA). MLA is used for the humanities: English, philosophy, art, and music. APA is used for the social sciences. **Both formats require four parts:**

- tagline
- paraphrase or quotation of the source
- commentary
- parenthetical citation

TAGLINES

Taglines, or introductory phrases, make quotations, paraphrases, and facts flow with your paper. Taglines introduce the source before you present the quotation or paraphrase: "As one social researcher says . . ." or "After 30 years as a judge, Kristin Landon believes . . ." Taglines transition readers to a new voice and can reveal what authority your source has.

PARAPHRASE OR QUOTATION OF SOURCES

Paraphrase all but the most important sentences. You cover ground faster with paraphrases. Long quotations frustrate readers, who assume correctly that the real message is in your voice. If two or three writers agree on a point, choose only the best one; don't drag readers through redundant quotations. Here's an example of a good MLA paraphrase mixed with bits of quotation from a description of an animal test by student Mindy Reynolds:

Tagline   The Draize Test involves testing cosmetics for eye damage that might occur to humans. Reports describe how researchers smear mascara,

Para-phrase and Quotation for example, over the eyeballs of rabbits. Unlike humans, rabbits have no tear glands to wash it off. The animals are "immobilized" in a stockade device. In some cases, their eyes are held open with clips. As a result, they cannot blink to get even a moment's relief and

Citation ultimately suffer "eye ulcers, bleeding, and blindness" (O'Connor 94).
Author And for what purpose? The tests do not even resemble how humans
commentary use the product.

Use a block-format for any quotations that are more than four lines. Indent all lines of the passage. No quotation marks are needed. Here's an MLA sample block format from an article written by Margena A. Christian in the 9 April 2007 issue of *Jet* entitled "Has Hip-hop Taken a Beatdown or is It Just Growing Up?":

> The industry is the bastardization of the culture that we've seen over the last 15 years or so where there's been an excessive pro-motion of Black self-hatred, sexism, misogyny, extreme materialism, anti-intellectualism and a lack of diversity in the representation of Black people in the music and culture. That's what's dead to me. (Powell qtd. in Christian n. pag.)

■ **PRACTICE 15-18** Below is a paraphrase of Christian's article. Which parts need quotation marks or more rewriting? What additional citation information should be included?

> Given that hip-hop's record sales have decreased since 2006, it's not that hip-hop culture is dead, but rather that the hip-hop industry is dead, according to Margena A. Christian. In her article, she quoted Kevin Powell, and he said that the music industry has bastardized the hip-hop culture over the last 15 years. Powell says that the industry confuses its listeners with representations of Black self-hatred, sexist lyrics, materialism, and anti-intellectualism among Blacks who, like any other humans, are diverse in nature. That's why Powell says that the hip-hop industry, not culture, is dead.

COMMENTARY/CRITICAL ANALYSIS

Agree, disagree, expand, or clarify your source material. If you don't comment, readers might misinterpret your information or not understand how it supports your thesis. Here's an MLA example from an essay against the banning of handguns. It's from the student's refutation section, where Barbara Collins considers arguments opposing her thesis. Notice how she leads us back to her thesis:

Tagline and Paraphrase ⌈According to a *U.S. News and World Report* study, police argue that a gun is six times more likely to be shot at a family member or a friend than at an intruder (Baer, Gest, and Anderson 35). This, however, does⌋

Commentary ⌈not justify banning guns. Let's take the husband who goes mad and wants to kill his family. He goes to the gun case and notices his gun is missing. Does he change his mind and decide to let them live? No. People in a rage use knives, clubs, or their bare hands. The weapon isn't the gun; it's hatred and insanity.⌋

Here is a sample paragraph with sources that might appear in my hip-hop essay:

Tagline Imagine a song that opened with "If I ruled the world, was king

Direct Quotation ⌈on the throne, I'd make peace in every culture, build the homeless a home." The message seems hopelessly idealistic, like something⌋

Commentary ⌈performed for flower children at a hippy concert. It surprises young audiences that these were the first lines of "If I Ruled the World," the 1985 crossover hit by Kurtis Blow who began his career as a break dancer and DJ in Harlem and the Bronx ("Kurtis Blow Biography on Yahoo! Music" n. pag.). Blow's timely 1985 message was delivered when 135,154 violent crimes were committed in New York City—over 15 an hour ("Uniform Crime Reports . . . 1985 to 2005" n. pag.). The same NYPD report indicates that violent⌋

Paraphrase ⌈crimes rose to 20 per hour in 1990. Blow wanted to curb violence through music, but east-coast hip-hop lyrics might have hardened amidst increased crime rates. Interestingly, in 2005, violent crimes dropped to 6 per hour ("Uniform Crime Reports . . . " n. pag.).⌋

Commentary ⌈When will hip-hop lyrics reflect this reduction in crime, and realign themselves with Blow's peaceful vision?⌋

HANDLING AND INTERPRETING STATISTICS

You must also critically interpret statistics. Imagine reading a political science essay on voting. In it, you run into this table from The US Census Bureau's Web site.

Table 404: Voting-Age Population, Percent Reporting Registered, and Voted: 2006

Characteristic	Population	Percent Voting
Total	220.6 million	43.6
18–24 years old	27.8 million	39.0
25–44 years old	80.0 million	68.4
45–64 years old	71.0 million	54.3
65–74 years old	18.4 million	60.5

(continues)

Characteristic	Population	Percent Voting
White	179.9 million	45.8
Hispanic	29.0 million	28.0
Black	25.7 million	38.6
Asian	9.9 million	21.8
Educational Attainment		
Less than 9th grade	12.1 million	17.1
9–12, no diploma	20.2 million	22.8
High School Graduate	70.0 million	37.6
Some College	60.2 million	47.3
Bachelors	58.25 million	59.5

If you're like me, you skimmed this table. It's too much to absorb. In the middle of a research paper, it has the same zero effect. To make it count, you must **analyze and draw conclusions about the statistics.** Here's my point as it might appear in a draft (without the table):

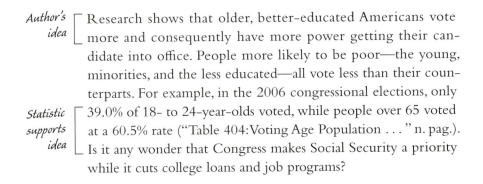

Author's idea — Research shows that older, better-educated Americans vote more and consequently have more power getting their candidate into office. People more likely to be poor—the young, minorities, and the less educated—all vote less than their counterparts. For example, in the 2006 congressional elections, only *Statistic supports idea* — 39.0% of 18- to 24-year-olds voted, while people over 65 voted at a 60.5% rate ("Table 404: Voting Age Population ..." n. pag.). Is it any wonder that Congress makes Social Security a priority while it cuts college loans and job programs?

Another way to incorporate statistics is to use charts in your essay. You still will need to decipher and comment on illustrations. Suppose I continued my analysis of voter participation with charts and text:

Examine Figure A. While 45.8% of whites and 38.6% of blacks voted, only 21.8% of Asians, and 28.0% of Hispanics voted ("Table 404: Voting Age Population ..." n. pag.). Of course, language and cultural barriers may keep many Asians and Hispanics home, but which came first? Do they not vote because the politicians ignore them, or do politicians ignore them because they don't vote? Figure B shows a similar trend in education: College graduates were three times as likely to vote as those with less than a ninth grade education ("Table 404: Voting Age Population ..." n. pag.).

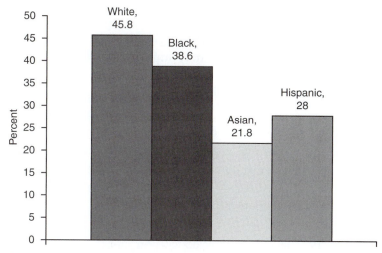

Figure A: Percent Voted by Race in 2006

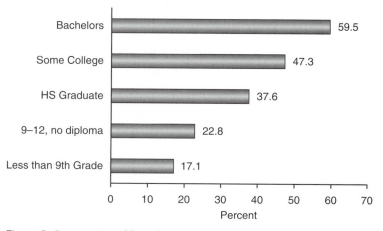

Figure B: Percent Voted by Educational Attainment in 2006

The young, minorities, and less educated should want their voices heard. Yet the "haves" vote most often. Perhaps because they are "haves," they believe in the system. Those who are alienated may feel the system will not listen to them anyway and don't vote because it best expresses how they feel.

Critical analysis of statistics. Notice how my analysis alternates with hard statistics—ideas alternating with details. But as an honest researcher, I must deal with three flaws in my paragraph. First, I did not mention that the voting age population includes non-citizens. This affects my interpretation, since large numbers of Mexican and Cuban immigrants and perhaps Asians in the United States cannot vote. If only citizens were included, the statistics might show they vote at higher rates. I need to find out! The second flaw is an unstated assumption that groups vote as a block in their own self-interest. But a grandmother may want students to have loans, and a young person may support social security. Finally, the data reflects congressional votes, known for less voter participation rates. My conclusion might be different if statistics were based on a presidential race.

Using charts. I chose a bar chart because it dramatized the numbers. Some software allows you to alter the length and sizes of bars, but don't manipulate them to over accentuate differences. Let the program automatically create real proportions. Also, make sure shades are sharply different. Label all axes and data, title your chart, and cite your source.

■ **PRACTICE 15-19** Think of another conclusion that the statistics suggest.

PARENTHETICAL CITATIONS: MLA STYLE

Always use citations in the body of your essay to document sources. A citation is the material in parentheses that follows ideas taken from a source.

- **Basic citation format:** After a paraphrase or quotation, write the author's last name and page number where the material was found, like this: (Toutelli 52). There are no commas or "p" used. The reader can locate the source at the end of your essay in the Works Cited list—arranged alphabetically by the authors' last names.
- **Author's name used in tagline:** If you use the author's name in the tagline, as in "Professor Toutelli declares . . ." then the parentheses would only include a page number, like this: (52).
- **Source with no author named:** Use the *title of the work* in the citation: ("Internet Excess" 31).
- **Source with no page number:** When a source such as an Internet article doesn't use page numbers, use "n. pag.": (O'Shea n. pag.). If, however, the source provides paragraph numbers, then use "para.": (O'Shea para. 3).
- **Two sources by one author:** If you use two or more sources by the same author, indicate which one the material came from by including the title: (Toutelli, *Demon* Data 52). Use ellipsis points to shorten long titles (Toutelli, "Finding. . ." 12). The first citation

is a book, so it's italicized. The second is an article, so it uses quotation marks.

- **A source within a source:** Suppose you're using Richland's idea that was quoted in Toutelli's work. Include both names like this: (Richland qtd. in Toutelli 30).

■ **PRACTICE 15-20** Using your notes from Practice 15-13, write a brief paragraph that smoothly introduces the source and uses a proper MLA citation.

A Quick Guide to MLA Works Cited

. . . .

MLA WORKS CITED FORMATS

- A Works Cited list begins on a separate sheet of paper at the end of your essay.
- A Works Cited list only includes the works used within your research paper—not everything you read for the paper.
- The entire list is alphabetized by the author's last name, so citations are easy to locate.
- If no author is named, start with the first main word of the title, and then alphabetize it among the other works.
- Indent second and third lines to keep the author's name visible.
- Double-space everything, just like the rest of your essay.
- Dates are written like this: 15 Aug. 2009. Abbreviate months except for May, June, and July.
- Include exact URLs (web addresses) followed by the date you accessed the source. If a Web site provides a search option, use the URL of the search page instead.
- Follow punctuation and order of items exactly.
- Title the list "Works Cited" on a separate page at the end of the paper—*without* bolds, italics, underlines, or quotation marks.
- Works Cited lists are tedious, and popular sites such as *EasyBib.com*, *Son of Citation Machine*, and *NoodleTools.com* allow you to input bibliographic information into text boxes to automatically

→

create Works Cited lists. But be wary! They don't always properly format works, and sometimes they do not provide all formulas.

- Consult the current *MLA Handbook for Writers of Research Papers* for more formulas.

QUICK GUIDE TO MLA WORKS CITED

SAMPLE MLA WORKS CITED LIST

Works Cited

Weekly maga-zine →

Padgett, Tim. "Cuba's Chance." *Time* 3 Mar. 2008: 34–37.

Patrick, Brian Anse. "Vikings and Rappers: The Icelandic Sagas Hip-Hop across *8 Mile.*" *Journal of Popular Culture* 41.2 (Apr. 2008): 281–305. ← *Monthly publi-cation with volume*

Previ-ously unpub-lished Web ar-ticle (no author) →

"Pursuit of Happyness and Shared Parenting." *Fathers and Families: Advocacy for the Father Child Bond.* 16 Mar. 2007. 20 Apr. 2008 <http://www.fathersandfamilies.org/site/news.php?id=188>.

Roberts, Cokie. *Ladies of Liberty: The Women Who Shaped Our Nation.* New York: William Morrow, 2007. → *Basic book*

"Senator Barack Obama & Hip-hop 2008 President Super Tuesday." *YouTube.* 3 Feb. 2008. 15 Mar. 2008 <http://www.youtube.com/watch?v=pFSVG7jRp_g>. → *Online video*

Previ-ously pub-lished Web article →

Underwood, Anna. "A Dream Before Dying." *Newsweek* 25 July 2005: 50–51. *Newsweek Society.* 20 Apr. 2008 <http://www.newsweek.com/id/50633>.

MISSING WORKS CITED INFORMATION

Some sources, especially online, do not provide all the information you need. Provide as much information when you can, including volume numbers and issues; if they are missing move on to the next item. But do substitute these abbreviations for the following missing information:

- n.d. (no date of publication)
- n.p. (no place of publication or no publisher)
- n. pag. (no page numbers used)

ADDITIONAL MLA WORKS CITED FORMATS

Book with editor(s), but no author—editor name(s), title, place of publication, publisher, and date published.

> Babic, Gregory Victor Babic, ed. Words to Inspire Writers. Sidney: F. C. Sach & Sons, Publishers, 2008.

Work with two or three authors—second and third authors' names are in normal order.

> Johnston, David, and Scott Gibson. *Green from the Ground Up: Sustainable, Healthy, and Energy-Efficient Home Construction.* Newtown: Taunton, 2008.

Work with more than three authors—"et al." means "and others."

> Fishman, Alfred P, et al. *Fishman's Pulmonary Diseases and Disorders.* New York: McGraw-Hill Professional, 2008.

Book not in first edition—after title, insert edition.

> Turvey, Brent E. *Criminal Profiling: An Introduction to Behavioral Evidence Analysis.* 3rd ed. San Diego: Elsevier-Academic Press, 2008.

Book in more than one volume—insert volume before place of publication.

> Kleinman, Daniel Lee, et. al. *Controversies in Science & Technology: From Climate to Chromosomes.* Vol. 2. New York: Mary Ann Liebert, Inc., 2008.

Work within an anthology—list the author of the work you cited, the title of that work, then information on the book. Page numbers are needed.

> Lahiri, Jhumpa. "This Blessed House." *American Short Stories.* 8th ed. Ed. Bert Hitchcock and Virginia M. Kouidis. New York: Pearson-Longman, 2008. 742–754.

Common reference books—complete publishing information not needed. Edition date only. List the entry under the heading where your information was found.

> "Fauvism." *Encyclopædia Britannica.* 2008 ed.

Lecture—speaker, title of lecture, sponsoring group, location, and specific date.

> Momaday, N. Scott. "The Crisis of Identity Facing Native Americans and Indigenous People." Monroe Community College, Rochester, NY. 8 Apr. 2008.

Quarterly magazine—volume number and issue after magazine title, then the year in parentheses, and page number. If pages are numbered continuously throughout the year, do not include the season in parentheses.

> Nouvian, Claire. "4,000 Meters Below: New Research Reveals the Wonders of the Deep Sea." *American Educator* (Winter 2007–2008): 8.

Newspaper with city in title—include section with page number. If the section here had been a number instead of a letter, you would write "sec. 5:1."

> Thomas, Katie. "Issue for Athletes: Protest on Darfur at Olympics." *New York Times* 1 Apr. 2008: A1.

Newspaper without city in title—include city after title in brackets.

> Leubsdorf, Carl P. "Iraq is a Minefield for Candidates." *Democrat and Chronicle* [Rochester, NY] 23 Mar. 2008: A22.

No author listed—start with the next item needed, alphabetized by its first letter. The following newspaper example would be alphabetized among the Bs in the Works Cited list.

> "Bat Die-offs Baffle Experts in New York and Vermont." *New York Outdoor News* [Elizabethtown, NY] 22 Feb. 2008: 14.

Interview—use book or magazine format if you read the interview, but use the following if you conducted the interview yourself.

> Foster, Carol. Personal interview. 30 Aug. 2008.

Corporate or group author—specific unit listed as author and larger company or group listed after title. "n.p." here means "no publisher listed."

> *Subscriber Agreement: General Terms & Conditions of Service.* Sprint Nextel. Reston, VA: n.p., 2007.

Pamphlet—author, title, place of publication, publisher, and date, if available. In the following entry, no author was named.

> *Renovate Right: Important Lead Hazard Information for Families, Child Care Providers, and Schools.* Washington, DC: U.S. Environmental Protection Agency, 2008.

Television program—episode title, program title, series title (if any), director (Dir.) or producer (Prod) or narrator ("Narr.") or writers ("By"), network name, call letters and city of station (if any), broadcast date.

> "Level One." *Rise of the Video Game*. Prod. Tracy Rudolf. Discovery Channel. 14 Apr. 2008.

Film, Videocassette, or DVD—episode (if any) title, producer ("Prod.") or director ("Dir.") or narrator (Narr.) or by ("By"), distributor, date and format.

> *Sand and Sorrow*. Narr. George Clooney. Home Box Office, 2008. DVD.

Music recording—performing artist, title of song, "By" followed by songwriter (if different than performing artist), recording date (if different than when compilation was produced), title of compilation, production company, year, format (audiocassette, CD, etc.).

> Johnson, Jack. "Hope." *Sleep Through The Static*. Brushfire Records, 2008. CD.

Sound recording—composer or author, title, volume (if any), producing company, identifying number (if any), date, and format (e.g., CD, LP).

> Tertzakian, Peter. *A Thousand Barrels a Second: The Coming Oil Break Point and the Challenges Facing an Energy Dependent World*. Burlington, NC: American Media International, 2008. CD.

ELECTRONIC SOURCES
Previously Unpublished Electronic Sources
"Previously unpublished" means that the material has NOT been printed in a newspaper or magazine before appearing electronically. Although some of the information below may not be provided on the Internet, give whatever is listed. Use < > to enclose Web addresses, also known as URLs (Uniform Resource Locators). Note: If the web address is long, only include the link to the site's search page.

    Article that is only available on the Web—author, title of article, name of website, date placed on Internet, date of your access, complete URL. (Note: The link below goes to the site's search page. Also, since it is a newswire, there is no period after *ABC News*. Had it been a professional or personal website, it would have a period.)

> Leamy, Elisabeth. "Creative Consumer: In Debt? Consider Counseling." *ABC News* 14 Apr. 2008. 15 Apr. 2008 <http://abcnews .go.com/>.

Professional or personal Web site—author, title of Internet article, name of Web site, date published on the web, date of your access, complete URL.

> Ashliman, D. L. "Folklore and Mythology Electronic Texts." *Folk-texts: A Library of Folktales, Folklore, Fairy Tales, and Mythology.* 6 Apr. 2008. 14 Apr. 2008 <http://www.pitt.edu~dash/folktexts.html>.

Newsgroup or bulletin board posting—author, title taken from subject line in quotation marks, Online posting, date posted, name of forum, date of your access, URL of newsgroup or bulletin board.

> Brown, Day. "Female Morals." Online posting. 11 Apr. 2008. *Alt. Sci.Sociology.* 14 Apr. 2008 <http://news.interbulletin.com/cgi-bin/ibwrn/artl=37820/alt.sci.sociology>.

Sound recording or clip—author, title, compilation title, producing company (if any), Web site, date submitted to Internet, date of your access, complete URL.

> Banks, Lloyd. "Southside Story." *The Hunger for More.* Universal Music Group. *RealPlayer 10 Music Store.* 2004. 2 Mar. 2008 <http://musicstore.real.com>.

Video clip—author (if any), title, Web site, date submitted to Internet, date of your access, complete URL address.

> "Senator Barack Obama & Hip-hop 2008 President Super Tuesday." *YouTube.* 3 Feb. 2008. 15 Mar. 2008 <http://www.youtube.com/watch?v= pFSVG7jRp_g>.

E-mail communication—author, title (taken from subject line), recipient of e-mail, date received.

> Stevens, Sean. "Being Al Krux." E-mail to Justin Tucker. 14 July 2008.

PREVIOUSLY PUBLISHED ELECTRONIC SOURCES

"Previously published" means the source was originally printed on paper, then later printed electronically.

 Start with the traditional MLA print format, and then tack on the following electronic information (skip missing items and go to the next item):

- Name of computerized index italicized (*General OneFile, ProQuest, ERIC, NY Times Online,* etc.)
- Name of computer service or producer (Nexis, BRS, Prodigy, AOL, etc.)
- Name of Web site if applicable
- Date you looked it up if online or date of electronic publication to CD-ROM if applicable

- Complete URL or file transfer address if applicable
- Publication medium (when source is from a CD-ROM or diskette) if applicable

Article from a computerized index—MLA citation first (in this case, a monthly journal), name of computerized index, library and library location if available, date you viewed it, and complete URL.

> Austin, Sally. "Seven Legal Tips for Safe Nursing Practice." *Nursing* 38.3 (March 2008): 35(6). *Expanded Academic ASAP*. Gale. Monroe County Library System, Rochester, NY. 14 Apr. 2008 <http://find .galegroup.com/itx/start.do?prodId=EAIM>.

Book on the Internet that was previously published—MLA citation for book, name of computer service or producer, date you viewed it, complete URL.

> Mandela, Nelson. *Long Walk to Freedom: The Autobiography of Nelson Mandela*. New York: Little, Brown, 1995. *Open Book Systems*. 5 Apr. 2008 <http://www.obsus.com/obs/english/books/Mandela/ Mandela.html>.

Article from a CD-ROM—author, title, place, publisher, date when CD-ROM was produced, publication medium.

> "Why Birds Migrate." *The North American Bird Reference Guide*. Seattle: Lanius Software, 2004. CD-ROM.

■ **PRACTICE 15-21** Arrange the following bibliographic information into proper MLA works cited format

- Date accessed online: 13 April 2008
- Newspaper title: *Milwaukee Journal Sentinel*
- City of publication: Milwaukee, WI
- Author: Susanne Rust
- Article title: "Bird Flu Fears Wane"
- Original publication date: 7 April 2008
- Page: not provided
- Computerized index used: *General OneFile* by Gale Cengage Learning
- URL: http://find.galegroup.com/itx/start.do?prodId=ITOF
- Library Used: Monroe County Library System (Rochester, NY)

■ **PRACTICE 15-22** Bring to class a book, a magazine or newspaper, and an Internet article. Be prepared to use them to create a Works Cited.

Citing Sources: APA Style

Use American Psychological Association (APA) documentation style for social, behavioral, and some natural sciences papers.

PARENTHETICAL CITATIONS: APA STYLE

Always use citations in the body of your essay to document sources. Otherwise, you run the risk of plagiarism. Below is a common way to cite sources within your essay using APA style. Notice the use of a lead-in phrase, author, year, and page information.

Publication year after author's name ←——

"According to *Chronicle of Higher Education* columnist Dan Carnevale (2005), The same high-school students who think nothing of going to J. Crew's Web site to order the right pair of jeans—sifting through the plethora of styles that seem to change by the week—are turning out to be equally sophisticated online consumers of college information" (A25).

——→ *Quotation with author's name in tagline*

- **Basic citation format:** Include the author's name, year of publication, and page numbers. Place the publication year immediately after the author's name.
- **When to use page numbers:** Use "p." for single pages and "pp." for multiple pages: (Toutelli, 2008, p. 226). The APA requires a page reference *only* if you give a direct quotation or statistic; general summary needs only a name and date, like this: (Toutelli, 2008).
- **Source with no page number:** When a source such as an Internet article doesn't provide a page number, use the paragraph number instead. For paragraph three, write "para. 3".
- **When to use quotation marks or italics:** No quotation marks are used around article titles, but book, journal, magazine, and newspaper titles are italicized.
- Within the body of your essay, capitalize all major words in titles. (In Reference Lists, only the first word is capitalized.)
- **Author's name used in tagline:** When the author's name is in the tagline of your quotation or paraphrase, include the publication year in parentheses immediately following. For example, "Professor Toutelli (2008) declares . . ." After the quotation or paraphrase, include the page number in parentheses.
- **Multiple Authors:** When two or more names are listed, use "&" instead of "and" between their names. For more than six authors, use the first author's name, followed by "et al." (Espinoza, et al., 2008, p. 49).

→

- **Source with unnamed author:** Use the title of the work in the citation, along with the year ("Excess," 2008).
- **Two sources by one author:** If you use two or more sources by the same author, you must indicate in the parentheses which one the material came from, like this: (Toutelli, 2008, *Demons*, p. 52). Use ellipsis points to shorten long titles (Toutelli, 2008, Finding. . .. , p. 12). The first citation is a book, so it's italicized. The second is an article from a magazine or newspaper, so the title needs no quotation marks.
- **A source within a source:** If Richland's idea was quoted in Toutelli's work, include both names like this: (Richland, as cited in Toutelli, 2008, p. 30).

■ **PRACTICE 15-23** For your note card or sheet from Practice 15-13, write a brief paragraph that smoothly introduces the source and uses a proper APA citation.

A Quick Guide to the APA Reference List

APA REFERENCE LIST FORMAT

- Only include works used within your research paper.
- The entire list is alphabetized by the author's last name, so citations are easy to locate. Initials are used for first and middle names of authors.
- If no author is named, start with the first main word of the title, in alphabetical order among the other works.
- Date (in parentheses) immediately follows author's name. If there's no author, the date follows the title.
- The year always goes before the month and day. Don't abbreviate months: (Example: 2008, July 9.)
- For book and article titles, capitalize only the first word and proper nouns.
- For magazine, newspaper, and journal titles, capitalize all major words.
- Quotation marks are not used around titles.
- Indent second and third lines.
- Double-space everything.

→

- "p." or "pp." is used before all page numbers; "p." is for single pages, "pp." for consecutive multiple pages.
- Abbreviate all states with two capital letters.
- There are no periods after URLs.
- For more formulas, review the latest APA publication manual.

QUICK GUIDE TO APA REFERENCE LIST FORMAT

REFERENCES

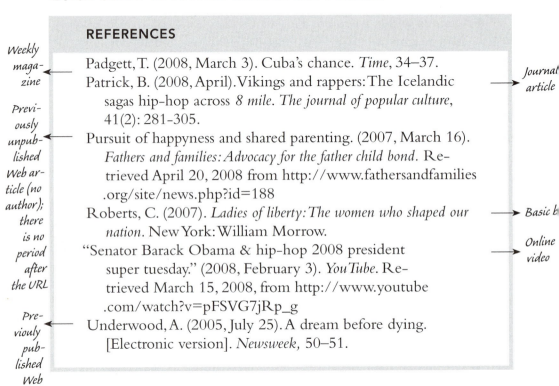

Weekly magazine →

Padgett, T. (2008, March 3). Cuba's chance. *Time*, 34–37.

Patrick, B. (2008, April). Vikings and rappers: The Icelandic sagas hip-hop across *8 mile*. *The journal of popular culture*, 41(2): 281-305.

← *Journal article*

Previously unpublished Web article (no author); there is no period after the URL →

Pursuit of happyness and shared parenting. (2007, March 16). *Fathers and families: Advocacy for the father child bond*. Retrieved April 20, 2008 from http://www.fathersandfamilies .org/site/news.php?id=188

Roberts, C. (2007). *Ladies of liberty: The women who shaped our nation*. New York: William Morrow.

← *Basic b*

"Senator Barack Obama & hip-hop 2008 president super tuesday." (2008, February 3). *YouTube*. Retrieved March 15, 2008, from http://www.youtube .com/watch?v=pFSVG7jRp_g

← *Online video*

Previouly published Web article →

Underwood, A. (2005, July 25). A dream before dying. [Electronic version]. *Newsweek*, 50–51.

MISSING REFERENCE LIST INFORMATION

Substitute these abbreviations for missing information in your sources:

- n.d. (no date of publication)
- para. (no page given, so paragraph number is used)

ADDITIONAL APA REFERENCE LIST FORMATS

Book with editor, but no author—editor(s), date, title, place of publication, publisher.

Babic, G.V. (Ed). (2008). *Words to inspire writers*. Sidney: F. C. Sach & Sons, Publishers.

Book not in first edition—after title, insert edition.

> Turvey, T. (2008) *Criminal profiling: An introduction to behavioral evidence analysis* (3rd ed.). San Diego: Elsevier-Academic Press.

Work within an anthology—list the author you cited, title of the work you cited, year, "In" followed by editor(s), title of book, page numbers, location, publisher.

> Lahiri, J. (2008). This blessed house. In B. Hitchcock & V. Kouidis (Eds.), *American short stories* (8th ed.) (pp. 742–754). New York: Pearson-Longman.

Newspaper article—author, date, title of article, newspaper title, section and page.

> Thomas, K. (2008, April 1). Issue for athletes: protest on Darfur at Olympics. *New York Times*, p. A1.

Personal communications: interviews, lectures, e-mails—use book or magazine format if you read the interview, but if you conducted the interview yourself or personally heard the lecture, a citation in the reference list isn't needed because the information is not recoverable. You should, however, cite them in your essay, like this: (R. Stevens, personal communication, Sept. 20, 2008).

Corporate or group author—corporation name, date, title, document number (if any), location, printing company.

> Spring Nextel. (2007, April). *Subscriber agreement: General terms & conditions of service.* Reston, VA: Sprint Nextel Products.

Brochure or pamphlet—author or group, year, title, format [in brackets], place of publication, publisher.

> U.S. Environmental Protection Agency (2008). *Renovate right: Important lead hazard information for families, child care providers, and schools* [Pamphlet]. Washington, DC: U.S. EPA.

Television program—producer, director, or writer (if any) followed by his or her job title in parentheses, date of broadcast, title of episode (if any), title of program, [Television broadcast], location of broadcast, network name.

> Rudolf, T. (Producer). (2008, April 14). Level one. In *Rise of the video game* [Television broadcast]. New York: Discovery Channel.

Film, videocassette, or DVD—name of producer, director, or writer (if any) followed by his or her job title in parentheses, year, title of episode (if any), title of film, [Motion picture], location, production company.

> Clooney, G. (Narrator). (2008). *Sand and sorrow*. [Motion picture].
> United States: Home Box Office.

Music recording—writer, date, song title, recording artist if different than writer, "On" followed by album title, medium, location, production company (recording date if different than copyright date). "n.d." here means no copyright date could be found.

> Elington, D., & Webster, P (n.d.). I've got it bad and that ain't
> good. [Recorded by B. Holiday]. On *Blues collection: disk 1* [CD].
> St. Laurent, Quebec, Canada: Madacy Entertainment. (1997).

Audio recording—speaker (Speaker), year, title of work, medium, location, distributor.

> Tertzakian, P. (Speaker). (2008). *A thousand barrels a second: The coming oil break point and the challenges facing an energy dependent world.*
> (CD). Burlington, NC: American Media International.

ELECTRONIC SOURCES
Previously Unpublished Electronic Sources
"Previously unpublished" means that the electronic source has NOT been printed. Although some information below may not be provided, give whatever is mentioned. At a minimum, include:

- document title
- date placed online or on CD-ROM
- date of retrieval
- URL (if the site provides a search page, use that Web address).

Article only available on the Web—author, date published to Web, title of article, title of Web site, date retrieved [from] URL.

> Leamy, E. (2008, April 14). Creative consumer: In debt? Consider
> counseling. *ABC News*. Retrieved April 15, 2008, from http://
> abcnewsgo.com

Professional or personal Web site article—author, date published to Web, title of Web page, title of Web site, retrieval date, URL.

> Ashliman, D. L. (2008, April 6). Folklore and mythology electronic texts.
> *Folktexts: A library of folktales, folklore, fairy tales, and mythology.* Retrieved
> April 6, 2008, from http://www.pitt.edu/~dash/folktexts.html

Permanently stored newsgroup or bulletin board posting—author, date sent to Web, title taken from subject line, message identifier (if any), "Message posted to" followed by the URL.

Brown, D. (2008, April 11). Female morals. Message posted to
http://news.interbulletin.com/cgi-bin/ibwrn/artl=37820/alt
.sci.sociology

PREVIOUSLY PUBLISHED ELECTRONIC SOURCES

"Previously published" means the source was originally printed on paper, then converted to electronic form. Because it's assumed that the electronic version is the same as the printed version, follow the traditional APA formats, but insert [Electronic version] right after the title of article or book. **Only if you think that the format has changed,** also tack on the following electronic information:

- Date retrieved
- If applicable, name of computerized database italicized, (*General One-File*, *ERIC, NY Times Online,* etc.)
- If applicable, the document number
- Website address

Article from a database—APA citation for the article (in this case, a journal article with volumes), date of retrieval, database, document number. Note: No document number was available.

Hedgecoe, A. (2001, December). Schizophrenia and the narrative of enlightened geneticization. *Social Studies of Science,* 31(6), 875–911. Retrieved July 1, 2008, from *JSTOR.*

Articles from online magazine or journal—APA citation for the article (in this case, a monthly journal) [Electronic version] after article title, date of retrieval, "from" complete URL.

Learmonth, A. E., Lamberth, R., & Rovee-Collier, C. (2005). The social context of imitation in infancy [Electronic version]. *Journal of Experimental Child Psychology,* 91, 397–314. Retrieved July 25, 2008, from http://www.sciencedirect .com/science/journal/00220965

Book on the Internet that was previously published—APA citation for book plus [Electronic version], retrieval date, "from" complete URL.

Mandela, N. (1995). *Long walk to freedom: The autobiography of Nelson Mandela* [Electronic version]. New York: Little, Brown. Retrieved July 2, 2008, from http://www.obsus.com/obs/english/books/ Mandela/Mandela.html

■ **PRACTICE 15-24** Arrange the following bibliographic information using the appropriate APA Reference format:

- Newspaper title: Milwaukee Journal Sentinel
- Author: Susanne Rust
- Original publication date: 7 April 2008
- Page: No page given; paragraph 1
- Computerized index used: *General OneFile* by Gale Cengage Learning
- URL: http://find.galegroup.com/itx/start.do?prodId=ITOF
- Article title: "Bird Flu Fears Wane"
- Date of access: 13 April 2008

■ **PRACTICE 15-25** Bring to class a book, a magazine or newspaper, and an Internet article. Be prepared to use them to create an APA-style Reference list.

■ **PRACTICE 15-26** Create a Reference list using all the sources you found in researching your topic from Practice 15-3.

Revising Research Writing

- Reread only the introduction and the topic sentences to make sure they support your thesis statement.
- Does each paragraph fit in its section of the essay?
- Did you support your ideas with vivid details and striking facts?
- Edit long-winded quotations or paraphrases to the most vivid or relevant sections; eliminate the rest.
- Make sure each source has a smooth tagline, citation, and your own commentary tying it to the thesis.
- Research papers usually restate the thesis in the conclusion.
- Do all sources used in your essay appear in your Works Cited or Reference list?
- Works Cited or Reference list entries should follow citation formats exactly, including capitalization and punctuation.
- Review sentences for word choice, spelling, and mechanics.

Writing Suggestions and Class Discussions

1. Ten years from now—in your chosen career—what two research projects might likely come your way?
2. What research does your employer need done now?

3. List three topics you'd like to research in college for personal use—consumer, health, or hobby topics, for instance. See pages 338–339 for more ideas.

4. Take one topic from #3 and do a Brain teaser list of key research questions. What do you want to know? See page 339 for tips.

5. Narrow two of these topics until they interest you:
   - Changing family patterns
   - Natural disasters
   - Terrorism
   - Religious principles

6. Make a list of key research questions, and do a Brain teaser list on one narrowed topic from #5.

7. Research Scavenger Hunt: Pick any one topic created in #1 through #6 and find information on it from each of these sources:
   - A computer index like those listed on pages 347–48
   - Your library's electronic book catalog
   - A governmental Web site
   - A news Web site, like *ABC.com* or *CNN.com*

   List the source in proper format and then paraphrase what you learned as an annotated bibliography.

8. Pick any famous historical event: the Stock Market Crash of 1929, the bombing of Pearl Harbor, the first moon landing, for examples. Use your library's electronic indexes to find two articles written on it. Read the articles, summarizing both and quoting one strong sentence from each. Turn in your notes with complete works cited information attached.

9. Do the same as #8, but use the Internet to find two sources.

10. Look up the *New York Times* for the day you were born. What were the main headlines for the day? Was there any significance in them to your birth?

11. Using the *Statistical Abstract of the United States* (www.census.gov/compendia/statab) or another almanac, find an interesting fact about two of these topics. List complete bibliographic information and comment on the significance of each statistic:
    - Crime
    - Marriage
    - Sports
    - Ecology
    - Your own topic

12. Peer groups will develop research questions for one of the following topics and establish a list of sources to contact or read:
    • Space exploration
    • Same-sex marriage
    • Illegal immigrants
    • Single fathers
    • Self-defense murders of abusive spouses/parents
    • Pregnant drug addicts

13. Works Cited Exercise: Find 10 sources on a topic on which you might write a research paper. Try for a mix of books, reference works, magazines, newspapers and Internet sources. Assemble it in proper bibliographic form.

14. Annotated Bibliography Exercise: Pick four sources from #13, read them, and write a brief paragraph for each that summarizes its main points. See page 357 for annotated bibliography formats.

15. **Write a career research paper** to investigate thoroughly a career you're considering. Combine library and non-library resources, including one formal interview with a person who holds the kind of job you want. Your list of key research questions should include all the hard information you want to know about the career—the gutsy truth about its ecstasies and agonies. Examine job outlook, pay, hazards, work environment, personal growth potential, and benefits. Finally, evaluate your research and decide if this career fits your interests and abilities.

A student who interviewed a lawyer found there was "no gavel-pounding or cries of 'order! order!' but simple, solemn procedure." The lawyer admitted liking pinstripe suits and shiny black briefcases from "the horn of plenty." A student interviewing a special education teacher for emotionally disturbed children was taken to a developmental center for half a day where "it is a major accomplishment to have a kid say 'hi' to you."

For more ideas about this topic, see page 247 and the sample essay on page 420.

STUDENT ESSAY USING MLA DOCUMENTATION

Quakers: America's First Feminists
Carol Nobles

Quakers, or the Society of Friends, are quiet rebels whose tireless humanitarian efforts have led to reforms protecting the rights of

→

slaves, Native Americans, the poor, the insane, and prisoners. But they were most outstanding as the first American feminists.

European Quakers brought to the New World their fundamental belief in the spiritual equality of men and women. Three hundred years ago when women were traditionally denied so many rights accepted today, Quaker women were allowed—even encouraged—to preach, prophesize and share responsibility (Specht n. pag.). Because of this reputation, in 1655 Boston Puritans lay in wait for Mary Fisher and Ann Austin—the first Quaker women to arrive from England—believing they were dangerous non-believers and women who would not submit to men. These women were stripped, searched for signs of witchcraft, imprisoned for five weeks, then shipped back to England (MacLean n. pag.).

Puritan belief in male domination contrasted with Quaker ways and set the stage for 40 years of persecution. Quaker leader William Penn was far more accepting of feminism. In the only witch trial held in Pennsylvania, Penn is said to have asked the accused woman, "Art thou a witch? Hast thou ridden through the air on a broomstick?" When she replied she had, Penn simply said that he knew no law against that. She was found guilty of "the common fame of a witch, but not of being one" and was released, not burned at the stake (Bacon, *Mothers of Feminism* 29). This more liberal attitude contrasts vividly with the burning of women accused of witchcraft in Massachusetts by Puritans.

When not polishing their public speaking skills by preaching, Quaker women held business meetings which further developed early feminist ideas. One researcher notes that Quaker women were leaders in the women's rights movement in the 19th century and credits "the women's training in business meetings with providing the necessary experience" for that leadership (Bacon, *Mothers of Feminism* 42).

In addition, couples wishing to marry had to appear twice before the women's, as well as the men's, meetings. Parental permission was needed, but Quakers, unlike many other religions at the time, did not force a daughter to marry without her consent. During the ceremony, no legalistic vows were repeated, but declarations of love and faithfulness were made by both bride and groom. The following guideline for marriage appeared in the *Pennsylvania Chronicle* on January 8, 1770:

They were so one, that none could say,

→

Which of them rul'd or whether did obey.
He ruled, because she would obey; and she
In so obeying, rul'd as well as he. (Frost 172)

This clearly modified the bride's "love, honor, and obey" vow of the traditional wedding.

Quaker feminism grew from their belief that God exists inside every person. Because of this, a Quaker cannot manipulate or exploit *any* person without offending God. One male Quaker said of women, "Nor can you give their opinion, beliefs or feelings less regard than your own" (Hubbard 86). This was nearly 300 years before women could vote, an equal rights amendment was defeated, and women demanded equal pay for equal work. A paper from *Women's Studies* discusses the dilemma feminism has with Christianity, which traditionally oppressed women: "Feminist theologians debate whether or not Christianity can possibly empower women. Some say that since Christianity is rooted in a patriarchal past, it can never shed patriarchal values; others argue that Christ's teachings are anti-authoritarian and, in some cases, feminist. For the Quakers, therefore, feminism was a necessary consequence of religious belief" (Michaelson n. pag.). This contrasts sharply with traditional religions and prepared the way for more liberal attitudes in most Christian religions—many years later.

Modern feminism, of course, defends the rights of many oppressed people, not just women. Here too, the Quakers were feminists ahead of their time. While other European settlers regarded the Indians as "heathen savages, the Quakers saw them as children of God and treated them with consequent respect" (Bacon, *The Quiet Rebels* 46). They also deplored the plight of slaves. In 1770, the sect encouraged its members to release their slaves, making it a disciplinary matter (Jordan n. pag.). Quaker minister and mother of ten, Sarah Harrison of Philadelphia, travelled throughout the southern states preaching emancipation and is credited with the freeing of some 200 slaves (Bacon, *Mothers of Feminism* 32). Quakers seemed to realize something feminism did not discover for many decades: that when one group is oppressed, all people are oppressed.

These early feminists used tactics still successful today. Members boycotted cotton and sugar—slave labor products. Women conducted schools for black children and published anti-slavery articles in newspapers. In 1865, Baltimore Quakers opened a normal school, four industrial schools, and over 70 elementary schools for Negroes.

→

During and after the Civil War, women Friends nursed and clothed blacks in newly freed slave settlements (Bacon, *The Quiet Rebels* 46).

In yet another area, Quaker feminists fought for equal rights. Quaker Elizabeth Fry was an influential leader in prison reform. She succeeded in separating men and women prisoners and hardened criminals from first offenders (West 321). One observer's journal entry from June 11, 1842 stated:

"Elizabeth Fry took us to Coldbath Fields Prison. It is, on the whole, the best of our houses of correction, thou[gh] a severe one, as whipping and the treadmill are still allowed. It was sad to see the poor exhausted women ever toiling upward without a chance of progress." (West 321)

Did this early feminist realize the significance of her last sentence? Could she imagine the "glass ceiling" many women today bump against?

Although one can see the origins of American feminism in the Quakers, Puritan anti-women values continued dominating the culture; yet these early Quaker women were the prelude. One historian estimates that Quaker women "comprised 30% of the pioneers in prison reform, 40% of the women abolitionists and 15% of suffragists born before 1830" (Bacon, *Mothers of Feminism* 1).

Social change is a slow process, and today's Quakers continue their humanitarian efforts, active in such issues as human rights abuses in Africa and Central America and nuclear weapons. And women's rights remain a central concern. The title of a newsletter at their last meeting locally sums them up best: "The Friendly Nuisance."

Works Cited

Bacon, Margaret H. *Mothers of Feminism*. Philadelphia: Quaker Press, 1995.

---. *The Quiet Rebels*. Wallingford, PA: Pendle Hill, 1999.

Frost, J. William. *The Quaker Family in Colonial America*. New York: St. Martin's Press, 1975.

Hubbard, Geoffrey. *Quaker by Convincement*. Philadelphia: Quaker Press, 1985.

→

Jordan, Ryan. "The Dilemma of Quaker Pacifism in a Slaveholding Republic." *Civil War History* (Mar. 2007). *Infotrac.* 17 Aug. 2008 <http://www.infotrac-college.com>.

MacLean, Maggie. "Quaker Women." *History of American Women.* 7 July 2007. 13 Aug. 2008 <http://www.womenhistory. blogspot.com/2008/01/mary-fisher.quakers.html>.

Michaelson, Patricia. "Religious Bases of 18th Century Feminism." *Women's Studies*, 22.5 (June 1993): 281+. *InfoTrac.* 15 Aug. 2008 <http://www.infotrac-college.com>.

Specht, Neva Jean. "Women of One or Many Bonnets?" *NWSA Journal* 15.2 (Summer 2003): 27-44. *Infotrac.* 15 Aug. 2008 <http://www.infotrac-college.com>.

West, Jessamyn. *The Quaker Reader.* Wallingford, PA: Pendle Hill, 1992.

ANALYSIS

Introduction: Quakers as "quiet rebels" makes for an interesting start, since rebellion typically is associated with chaos. The lesser known humanitarian efforts of the Quakers spark readers' interest.

Thesis: The thesis is clear and concise, and it assertively establishes a central point expected to be proven. The words "most outstanding" may be pushing it.

Ideas: The essay effectively identifies little known social activism of female Quakers in contrast with historical Puritan values. I learned many interesting aspects of Quaker beliefs, especially that because God resides in all people, to hurt others is to hurt God. This insight added complexity to the essay. I wonder, though, if generalizations of Puritans or other Christian sects were too broad. Also, were there nonreligious people also heartily advocating for equality?

Details: There are plenty of them, including percentages in the second to last paragraph. Great! The author, however, could have included more facts about Quakers' treatment of Native Americans, as many as she had for the enslaved and imprisoned. Also, the journal entry about Elizabeth Fry needs a clearer connection to the "glass ceiling" experienced by many of today's women. Finally, "Negro" seems dated, but it's hard to tell if it's used in the context of Quaker history, or a replacement for "black" found elsewhere.

Citations: In-text citations flow smoothly with taglines, and they are properly formatted, including block quotes and the multiple works by Margaret Bacon. I can easily distinguish the author's ideas from her sources. The essay's length and number of sources used are finely balanced.

Works Cited: Entries abide by MLA formulas exactly, even typing "---" to tell readers two of Margaret Bacon's books were used. The electronic source entries are flawless. This attention to detail increases the credibility of the essay. I am concerned, though, that some works are dated. Because of the essay's quality and the fact it examines 300 years of unchanged history, I can forgive the author.

☑ Peer Review Checklist for Research

Author: _____

One aspect of this draft I'd like the reviewer to comment on is:

_____

Reviewer: _____

Reviewer

	Strong	Average	Weak
Thesis is clear			
Ideas: Freshness, insight			
Details: Plenty of them			
Vividness			
Organization: Logical/easy to follow			
In-text Citations: Proper format			
Research smoothly worked in			
Works Cited: Format			
Strength of sources			

My response to the author's question:

The strongest part of this paper is:

Two suggestions I have are:

A Collection of Student Writings

16

Journals and Blogs

JOURNALS PRESERVE OUR THOUGHTS, GIVE US A PLACE to be brutally honest without committing ourselves publicly, and help us see our own lives more clearly. **You write journals freestyle, not to create a finished product, but to stir up your mind.** Journals help us realize how much there really is to our lives. They should closely record sights, sounds, facts, and conversation—the hard details of life. They preserve the history of your life but should also search for meaning behind those details. A diary records what you did and when and superficially tells how you felt. **A journal explains the significance of what happened. It seeks intense moments, insights, conflicting feelings.** You can reflect on events in your life or the news, describe a person, place, or thing, remember your past, react to books or films, or record ideas for papers.

> Go into yourself.
> —RAINER MARIA RILKE

> Look the world straight in the eye.
> —HELEN KELLER

    A blog is usually more polished than a private journal since you are writing for other people, but most blogs share the journal's personal feel, even if the blog is directed toward a social issue like gay rights, abortion or military conflict. Some people feel more reluctant to share their inner selves online, while others find it liberating and exciting. Many soldiers fighting in Iraq (on all sides) publish blogs, some to inform others, some to persuade others, some just to figure out how they feel about what they experienced and to have a record of it.

Selections from Journal
Richard L. Shields

Nov. 2

I'm sitting on a wooden bench in a holding cell. It's 7 A.M. I'm writing this on toilet paper. It's Monday. If I were home the TV would be on. My orange backpack would be lying on the carpet beside the couch. My homework would be strewn across the coffee table. If I didn't crawl out & clean up pretty soon I'd be late for KW's math class. I'd feel good about being fifty and going to college—if I was home.

A deputy turns the lock and gestures with his finger. "Time for prints Mister Shields," he says as he holds the cell door open. I follow him to the printing area. There are cells on either side of the main corridor. Arms and hands hang out. Black, white, old & withered, restless & youthful. Faceless with one bond in common. We've all been accused.

My life is spinning backward, like reverse English on a cue ball. Slowly at first—then gaining momentum. Faster and faster. Left hand corner pocket. Scratch! You lose.

Feb. 20

The minute I saw the words "Highland Park" in the newspaper headline, I found myself standing in a bygone era. I was 10 and blazing a trail through Highland Park. My knapsack was filled—rib-sticking peanut butter and jelly sandwich, Oreos, Milk Duds, and Black Crows. Also 2 creme donuts, licorice twists, and Mary Janes I'd been stashing in a shoebox under my bed. I even had Daddy's thermos brimmed with life-saving lemonade. Oh, I remember.

My ears were finely tuned to autumn leaves as they crunched and knuckled under each trail-blazing step. I was on a mission. No longer was I Dickie Shields. I was Crispus Atticus. I was Nat Turner. I was Harriet Tubman. Leading a band of rag-tag runaway slaves through the dense underbrush along the park perimeter.

"Look out boy!" I'd shout. "Dontcha get too close to de edge! Goodman Road out yonder. Ol' massa's men be comin' long dat road afore long. Y'll keep up now."

I crawled along the hill, stopping only to put my ear to the ground to listen for horse hooves. Steam fogged my coke-bottle

→

glasses. My hands sweat. Weak from exposure, I began to hear the howl of bloodhounds. "You got to go on!" I whispered through clenched teeth. I groped feverishly in my empty knapsack, curling around one last melting Milk Dud. It was mangled, fuzzy from knapsack innards. My face squinched as I thought of typhus, gangrene, and TB.

What would ol' Frederick Douglass do? What would Harriet Tubman do? Die on the underground trail and leave her runaways to fend for themselves, their dream of Canada shattered? Or would she risk disease by eating a fuzzy, melted Milk Dud? I broke into whispered song: "Go down Moses, way down in Egypt Land, Tell ol' Pharaoh, let my people go!" I knew what I must do. I blew hard on the Milk Dud, kissed it to God, and plunged it into my mouth. And my strength returned. "C'mon, y'all," I shouted. "Canada!"

DISCUSSION

1. If you were advising Richard to develop one of these journal entries into an essay, which would you push hardest? Why?
2. Write your own journal entries on a low point in your life, a family member, or a childhood fantasy.

Selections from Journal
Tina Thompson

1.

I can't forget the things my mother did to me and move on with life. I want to forgive and forget but don't know how. Maybe if I write it all down, I can get it out of my system, stop feeling sorry for myself and begin to have a normal relationship with my mother.

2.

My sister and I had torn a pair of stockings. "Do you think I am made out of money?" my mother said. "Do you think I can go stand

→

on my head and spit money to replace everything you ruin?" In her hand was the belt! It dangled, quivering like a snake having an epileptic seizure. My stomach lurched. I scurried on hands and knees to reach my sister. We had to hide! She put her hands over her head, pleaded with Mom not to. But nothing could stop her in a rage. The strap swooshed and the heavy buckle jingled. Then WHACK! WHACK! Leather and metal against my back. The air rushed from my lungs and it hurt breathing again. My sister's eyes bulged. We scratched and clawed our way onto the bed as the belt stung us. My back throbbed like a thumb hit with a hammer. When we were driven against the wall, we scaled it like rock climbers for the window ledge above us. Somehow we scrambled on the two and a half-inch sill.

Mom laughed at our climbing, her round body shaking like Santa Claus. Then she turned and stalked out. My sister and I fell from our perch onto the mattress. Our backs were bruised and bleeding. Our hearts pounded like scared rabbits. We grabbed our blankets and dove under the bed. Maybe we would be safe in the dark for a while.

3.

When I turned 18, my boyfriend gave me a puppy. He was gray with white specks but had a face swollen like a blowfish. He was so bloated that his ears stuck out like Yoda's in *Star Wars*, so I named him Yoda. He was big, wild, and slightly retarded, but he was all mine! He slept with me every night. I even got him his own pillow and blanket. When I came home from school, Yoda would be waiting by the door, his whole body wagging.

One day my mother thrust my brother's glasses into my hand. The lenses were gone and the frame was mangled. It looked like someone had them for lunch. "Do you know how much these glasses cost me? 170 bucks! Your brother found Yoda eating them."

"Where is he?" I knew something was wrong, horrible.

"Hah! I took him to the pound." She gloated.

"You fat, ugly witch!" I knew I was in trouble as soon as I said the words, and ran into the dining room. She bounded after me like a crazed elephant on the warpath. She didn't bother going around the table, but scrambled right across it and dug her nails into my shoulder. But I was so furious it didn't hurt. She'd beaten so much

→

hatred into me, I had plenty to spill out. I dug my nails back into her. She screamed at me and threw me into the wall and yanked my hair, throwing me on my back onto the dining room table. She punched me, each blow like a sledgehammer to my ribs. My legs kicked to keep her off, so she pinned me under her 300 pounds. The old table cracked. My brother screamed. When the table collapsed, I was pinned between the splintered wood and her body. My sister tugged at Mom, yelling, "Are you crazy? You'll kill Tina!" Then Mom took after my sister. Then all of us jumped our mother, writhing and thrashing around the room, stumbling over broken table legs, crashing chairs and pictures to the floor. "This'll be the last time you ever lay a hand on us," we vowed. And she never did again. After the police broke it up, I left home for good. I could no longer take her rage and I realized I could no longer contain my own.

To this day I don't know how to act around her. She owes us an explanation and an apology we've never gotten. Maybe someday, if she can't find the courage to talk about it, I will.

DISCUSSION

1. What would you say to Tina if you could write her a letter in response to this journal?
2. Write your own series of journal entries focused on exploring your memories of a close relative. Don't worry about making it all stick together.
3. Describe a pet and what it meant to you.

NARRATIVE ESSAYS

Pa's Secret
Carol Nobles

My great-grandfather died on a Monday—which upset my grandma's schedule. On Mondays, Grandma changed the bedding, hung up the week's wash, and sliced Sunday's leftover roast beef. But this Monday there were arrangements to make.

→

Actually, she'd already begun preparations the day after Pa (my great-grandfather) was taken to the nursing home. Grandma had wedged open his bedroom door and hammered at the sealed windows. Pa was forever cold, even in summer, so they hadn't been opened in years. Panting from the exertion, Grandma said to me, "We've got to air this room out. God knows it needs it."

I only half listened, for I'd never been in Pa's bedroom even though he lived with us two years. I was eight when his second wife died and he moved in. His bedroom door was always shut, but occasionally I'd pass through the hall as he emerged, and a warm, spicy odor sneaked out behind him. The scent reminded me of an old crumpled tobacco pouch I once found hidden in the barn. Maybe Pa had something like that hidden in his room. Why else would he lock his door? If something was in there, now Grandma would find it. She never missed anything.

Grandma watched Pa closely during his last year because he began losing his mind. Today we call it Alzheimer's disease, but back then Grandma only saw it as another chore thrust on her. Pa spent mornings reading the newspaper while huddled next to the kitchen stove, occasionally puffing a cigar suspended from his mouth. Some days he'd forget to flick the ashes, and when they'd drop to the floor Grandma dove on him like a hovering hawk. She'd shriek, "Pa, put that thing out. One of these days you'll start the house afire. You shouldn't smoke those filthy things anyway." Pa never answered, never. He'd just puff and read and reread.

One Sunday, I sat at the table sticking Silly Putty against the comics, imprinting and then stretching Dagwood into all sorts of disproportions, when some live ashes must have embedded in Pa's sweater. Grandma yelled, "Pa! You're on fire!" He just sat there, little smoke streams lifting off his sleeve, while Grandma poured water on him. Only when he felt the wetness did he finally look up with a confused expression. I laughed so hard.

Once, a neighbor called to announce that Pa was "going pee" under the maple tree. Grandma was so mad she must have forgot I was only 10. "That old man's lucky I took him in," she sputtered. "He never cared for me when he was supposed to. My mother died when I was 13, and he took to drink and stayed away nights. Left me all alone for days. But when he asked to live here, I never said

→

a word, just took him in. Not a word! And what gratitude do I get? That dirty old man!"

What angered Grandma most was when he got a girlfriend who lived in the old people's home. Grandma would whisper, "Just watch now. That old fool's in the bathroom sprucin' himself up for that old biddy up at the home. At his age!"

One afternoon, Grandma and I stood in a crowd at the bus stop when she spied Pa strolling down the street with his lady friend. As the bus arrived, she pushed our way to the front and dragged me to a seat so she could watch them pass. "Look at that now, will you? She's got a corsage pinned to her dress. So that's what he's doing with his money. The old fool."

The courtship was short-lived because within months Pa began to shuffle to breakfast unshaven and soon lost his appetite completely. So Grandma called the doctor. A few weeks later I awoke to strange voices on the stairs. Peeking out the door, I spotted two men in white jackets maneuvering a cot around a corner of the hall—headed for Pa's room. Muffled voices were drowned by Pa's "No, no. Don't take me. No." Pleading cracked his voice. Grandma tried calming him, but he wasn't listening, and he moaned steadily.

Later I heard Grandma on the phone saying they'd taken him to St. Mary's Nursing Home: "He's all swollen up down there. The doctor said he only had a few days, but it was going to get messy and this was the best way. I hated to do it, Rose, but I just couldn't handle him anymore."

The next afternoon, Grandma took me to see Pa because it might be for the last time. I asked her, didn't she think I was too young, but she said it was the right thing. At the front desk, a nun glided to us. Tucked into her waist, her rosary beads clicked together as we wordlessly followed her to the room.

It had three other beds. You couldn't see the sick people in them, but you knew they were there by the bulges. They lay flat, motionless, sunken under sheets. I didn't look. I didn't want to see their faces.

"He's in the corner," whispered the nun. She tugged a wooden dowel, opening curtains that hid his bed. It didn't look like Pa, but more like a bunch of bones jutting at funny angles. His pale, wrinkled nightshirt was pulled above his waist, his knees tucked into a fetal

→

position. His legs seemed forced apart by a bulging, angry purplish-red swelling that he fingered.

"Pa! Stop that! Don't do that," Grandma hissed. She tugged at his nightshirt, trying to cover him, but it only made him moan. She grabbed at his hands to stop him from touching himself, but it only made him try harder. The nun whipped up the sheet wadded at the bottom of the bed and covered him, but then he wailed. That's when I left.

On the way home, curled in the back seat of the bus, I tried to remember Pa rocking in his chair, Pa playing cards with me, Pa any way but how I'd just seen him. If he had any more secrets in his bedroom, I hoped Grandma wouldn't tell me.

DISCUSSION

1. What aspect of this essay seems strongest to you? If you could suggest changes to the author in a workshop, what would you say?
2. Study how the author creates conflict. Does the essay start *in medias res?* Point out all conflicts. Describe how the conflict grows more complicated.
3. Study character. There are three vivid people here; how are they made distinct through dialogue and descriptive details? Discuss Grandma's motivation and complexity.
4. The young girl takes little direct part in the action. What does she contribute to the story?
5. Outline the time sequence in the essay. Can you explain why the author might have arranged some parts as she did? Is it too complicated?
6. Study some of the little telling details: Pa's locked room getting aired out and its "spicy" odor; the Dagwood and Silly Putty; and one other you found significant. What do they add to the story?
7. Comment on the last line of the essay.
8. What is the essay's message or theme?
9. Freewrite a page about a family secret or an eccentric relative in your family.

REVISED ESSAY (ORIGINAL IN CHAPTER 7)

Bastard
Miguel Martinez

A child born out of wedlock is called bastard, illegitimate, or lust child. I know. I am a bastard. When I was five, I asked my mother where Daddy was. I only had a vague idea of what a daddy was. I had heard the word used in kindergarten, but didn't understand the principle behind it. Among the many misconceptions about one-parent children is that we feel as though something is missing. We don't. There is no instinct telling us there should be another. We just accept the one parent we have.

My mother told me the best lie she could. She explained that my father had died shortly after I was born. He was supposed to have been a college professor. I accepted this. But her uneasiness about him kept me from asking more.

I have always been gentle with my mother. When she was young, her mother abandoned her, her three sisters, and a brother. They were all placed in a Catholic orphanage. Two of her sisters found good foster homes, and had decent chances at life. Not my mother.

Earlier this year I was required to get a copy of my birth certificate. I learned there were two kinds. The common one states that you were indeed born. The actual file copy, however, is loaded with information. I examined this one carefully. No father was listed. I had given up on learning anything new about my life when I caught a glimpse of the previous children section. It tells how many times the mother has carried to term, how many were born alive or stillborn prior to the birth certificate. I found out my mother had a child before me.

When I first saw that, things clicked into place. My mother had always vowed she was going to keep me. She struggled raising me, working as a waitress, and keeping odd hours. She was paranoid about someone finding me left by myself. I can look back now and see why.

As I won't ask her what really happened in her youth, I can only guess. I think she used sex as a love substitute, looking to men to give her the love she was not getting at the orphanage. I assume she got pregnant while living there and was forced to give the child

→

up for adoption. This would explain why she would always tell me, "No one is going to take you away from me." By 18, she was probably defiant, and went out and lived. I can see a wild streak in her now, when she refers cryptically to New York City bars and roller skates or firecrackers in birthday cakes. I guess she met my father there, and on a fateful November evening, I came into being.

She tells me that shortly after I was born, she moved to North Rose, where she took a job as a live-in caretaker for an elderly couple. I am told that she wasn't allowed in her mother's house with me, and my grandmother once refused to loan my mother money for a needed hospital visit. It makes you wonder about family.

As for me, I grew up basically alone, as my mother would either be working or sleeping when I was at home. I don't resent that, if the alternative was an orphanage. My mother protected me with her lie about my father being dead; imagine what school would have been like for me if it was known I was a bastard. As it was, my friends sympathized.

Looking back, I think I should have realized something was amiss earlier than I did. A certain conversation always haunted me. It took place with a school administrator, who asked, "What was your mother's maiden name?"

I replied, "Martinez."

"No," he'd say, "I want your mother's maiden name."

"Martinez."

"That's her married name. I need her name before she was married."

Again, I would respond "Martinez" and get flustered. I suppose I didn't want to know.

I never really thought of my father. It seemed silly to wonder about someone who had no influence on my life. Nor can he ever. If I do wonder, maybe it's just a selfish desire to know if I have any inherited health problems.

I finally found out that I was a bastard when I joined the Navy. I had quit school and travelled around the country for a year, with no direction in my life. My mother despaired—pleaded with me to enlist. This was the only time she admitted I needed a male influence in my life. While I didn't agree, I felt that I had failed her by quitting high school and I agreed to join.

→

As I glanced through the mound of government forms before me, I saw a paper that my mother had signed stating that I had been born out of wedlock, and that my father did not support me. I think she had to submit this to allow me to join the service as a minor. When I saw the paper, I was surprised, but didn't care. What influence did this man have on my life? Didn't he just supply the raw material? To acknowledge that he had any claim on me would be just as absurd as saying a marble stonecutter can lay claim to an artist's sculpture.

The night before I left for boot camp, before I went out for my last fling with the guys, my mother sat me down and told me that my father was still alive. She told me his name and the city he lived in. She said she was telling me in case I wanted to contact him. I remember my mother was nervous, and I sensed it was a sort of loyalty test, for if I did seek him out, it would have been a slap in her face. I responded that I didn't want to contact him; there was no need. She smiled. I had kept her fragile world intact.

In time, I did get curious enough to look up his phone number, but not to call him. I think I just wanted to affirm that he was. The only thing about fathers I really wonder about is what kind I will make.

DISCUSSION

1. You may want to read the early draft of this essay in Chapter 7. How has the writer responded to peer comments and suggestions? What has the essay gained in revision?

2. Has it lost anything you liked about the early draft? What suggestions would you make if the writer were to revise this draft?

3. The author says his grandmother abandoned his mother and then refers to the grandmother refusing to lend money to his mother. Should he explain how they met again later in life or would it pull the essay off track?

4. Freewrite a page starting a story about a label people have put on you and the conflict it created. How do you deal with it?

5. Write a letter to the author of this essay, explaining what the concept of "bastard" means to you.

Midnight Diner
Michael Y. Rodgers

Diners always seem to be warm, busy, friendly, happy places. That's why on a recent Friday night, returning from a long day's work and needing something to help me through the last ten miles, I stopped at a diner for a cup of soup. A diner at midnight, however, is not a diner at noon. I stopped in front of the dreary gray aluminum building that resembled an old railroad car. A half-lit neon sign blinked, "Fresh Barbecue Ribs," and the colors reflected on the puddled parking lot. An empty wine bottle scraped as it rolled back and forth on the cement entrance step. I pulled the door and walked through, but it slammed shut so fast behind me, it almost snapped on my fingers.

The diner was clean and too quiet. Customers slouched over their plates, but there was no waitress on duty. I smelt stale grease and heard only the slight hum of the empty refrigerated pastry case. Most of the booths were empty, sitting back to back in their black, crushed velvet upholstery. On each black and white checkered table were glass salt and pepper shakers, a ketchup bottle and sugar packets waiting for the sunrise crowd. I peeked through the round window of the swinging door that led to the kitchen. All I saw were a shiny stainless steel range, blackened pans, long steel knives and forks hanging on hooks.

I slid onto a wooden seat at the counter. Three men in wrinkled work shirts and with stubbled faces sat near me, smoking cigars and staring into their coffees as if lost in space. I guessed they were shift workers who didn't want to go home yet. Then I noticed a thin young man with a mop of curly black braids. He wore stiff, new jeans with a black, Ralph Lauren polo shirt unbuttoned at the neck, exposing his black, hairless chest. He wore a blank expression as he picked at a plate of limp French fries. For a second I wondered if he was watching me like I was watching him. He looked like he might have just ended a disappointing date.

At the other occupied booth sat a middle-aged black couple. They hadn't gotten any food yet. The guy was staring off into space, tapping his spoon against his palm while the woman drew lines on her napkin with a fork. I felt the loneliness rising around me like water. Why would this couple stop here? There were no candlelight

→

dinners on the menu. This was a diner for the lonely. Not me, of course. I just wanted a cup of soup. Hot soup, that's all.

The young man with the braids left without finishing his fries. I glanced down at his table. A phone number was written on a napkin and the words, "Call me!!" Whew. There's a lot of it around. I wondered if I looked as lonely as everyone else.

Finally a tired waitress with deep black, round eyes and a grease-stained pink uniform approached me with her pad. Under her fake red hair, I noticed black roots. She said, "Can I take your order?"

"A cup of soup," I said, wanting to eat fast and get out. After gulping it down, I rushed to pay and exit into the night. As I reached the wet parking lot, I realized that the young man with the braids and who left the number behind was standing beside my car. Strange that he'd still be here. "Hey, you need a ride or something?" I said. He just stared at me, and I noticed the way the pale moonlight sculpted the curves of his face. Outside, he looked healthy and young. Hmm, I thought. What should I do with this one?

When I was at my door, he said, "Can you drop me off uptown?"

I stared him dead in the eyes. "I'll take you, but no hanky panky."

"I can't promise you that," he said. "I'm lonely."

We slid into my car, and I knew the long miles ahead would still be lonely and not easy. But that night, I'd rather have temporary company than be stuck in a midnight diner.

DISCUSSION

1. Look for how Michael uses sense details in this essay. How many senses are used and where?
2. How do contrasts between dark and light contribute to the effect?
3. What seems to be the theme he's working with?
4. List a dozen details about diners he could have used but didn't. See if you can insert a couple into the essay that will add something to it.
5. Write a list of details about an eerie place you once visited, and then write a short essay that tries to capture the mood.

Daddy Dearest
Christina Kennison

In the doorway with an ear-to-ear grin, my father's face shows creases and pain lines as he gathers his strength to raise a hand in hello. Although he's forty-three, his jet black hair is as wispy as a new-born baby's. Black framed glasses slide down his nose, and he stares blankly, lips parted, droplets of drool forming in the corners of his lips. The drops pool, then run down and off his chin, landing on a towel he wears as a bib. As we go inside, my father's jerky limp from childhood polio resembles a rubber band that snaps at each step. His Old Spice aftershave stings my nose as I trail after.

The apartment could be Blockbuster with its shelves filled with videos. Hundreds. "Dad, did you get more movies?"

He breathes heavily, gurgling rising from his throat as he gathers enough air to reply. He chokes on his saliva, then gives up and just nods. As I sit, I hear "Hi, Chrissy!" from my father's wife, my step-mother, who is calling from the kitchen where she hides out. Sharon is a few fries short of a Happy Meal. "I hope you don't mind spa-ghetti," she says.

I tell my father the spaghetti better be as good as he claims. At this he laughs, but it looks as though he's choking. Then there's nothing but silence, dead air that makes my ears ring. I do not know what to say to break it, but luckily, the sizzle of water hitting a burner in the kitchen does the job, followed by Sharon's little girl giggle and an "oops!" That and Dad trying to slur directions to Sharon for how to boil water ease my nerves.

Dad turns to me and gathers himself. "UUGHT OOMY U AAN AACH?" This takes him two minutes to say, and as he talks, the im-age of a falling down drunk comes to mind. I have to ask him to repeat this three times before I understand.

"What movie do I want to watch?" I guess finally.

"Yah." He puffs in relief that I got it.

I walk to the video shelves. He stands and almost falls. After he snaps himself to balance, he joins me, stumbling and dragging his elastic leg. I remind myself that my father had a brain tumor and has been on medication for seizures since he had surgery. In November he suffered his second stroke and has not fully recovered. "How about this one?" I hold up *Sleepy Hollow*. My father nods and shoves it into

→

the VCR. The volume is so high, my ears scream. A nervous tick makes me tap my foot so my shoelace beats against my shoe. Just as the previews end and the film is about to start, my stepmother announces that dinner is ready. More like a nurse than a daughter, I help my father to the table. I sit across from him, forgetting that I will have to watch him eat. Sharon gives him plenty of napkins and tightens his bib. As I eat, I soon stare past my father at the television. Almost all the food he manages to get on his fork is shaken onto his bib and face, and when he opens his mouth to get the little that's left, drool flies out. It's been nearly four years since I last saw him, and even though I knew he was sick, I did not understand how hard it would be to see him this way. I pity his suffering and humiliation, and it also hurts just because he is my Dad and I have to see him deteriorate.

"UUGT OO U INK?" he slobbers between bites of food.

I shake my head. "Spell it," I say, not wanting him to waste so much energy when he could use the American Sign Language he knows. Only after he spells it twice with shaky hands do I understand. "The spaghetti is very good," I smile. *Sleepy Hollow*—the horror movie—has become background noise.

After dinner, I start toward the kitchen to help with the dishes. "No!" my father says, motioning me to the couch. He plops down, and I sit. The movie is nothing, just a bright blue screen. The horror is here. I stay only another 15 minutes, although it feels like an eternity. When I say my good-byes, I promise to call later in the week. As I hug my father, he falls into me, and a tear rolls down his cheek.

Driving home, I know I helped cheer him up. It was a tear of joy, I tell myself. But my satisfaction in cheering him fades. I feel bad he is this way, but also that I am related to him. Before his sickness, he didn't visit me, saying he did not have time. I wonder if I would bother to visit him if he were not the way he is, if I didn't pity him. I don't know. As I drive, I plan my week. He will wait for my call. And now that I have the upper hand, I wonder if I will.

DISCUSSION

1. What is the main conflict in this story? How does Christina keep us guessing about what's going on?

2. What roles do the video, the stepmother, and the spaghetti play? How are they symbolic?

3. What are the best descriptive details?
4. How do you feel about the father at the end? Then try to state the theme of this story (think especially about the last line).
5. Write about a relationship of yours that is *not* what is usually expected. Start with a key *moment*, not a summary or background.

---

49 Hours in Afghanistan
Christopher Butler

The weather was cool in Afghanistan, compared to the 125-degree heat in Kuwait. I remember thinking that I should have brought an extra poncho liner because the nights would be cold. I had no idea that being cold would soon be the least of my worries. Two hours later my team made a link-up with the local who would take us to the Taliban and Al-Qaeda cells below the Uzbekistan border. The guide bothered me from the get-go. He seemed angry or maybe frustrated and kept shifting from foot to foot.

After several hours we came to a ridge with a narrow, rocky lane that led down into a valley. In the distance I saw a small village and a few farms—the first green since we crossed the border. Until then we had been walking in a landscape painted solely in shades of brown and tan.

About 250 meters from the village, we attracted a crowd. They smelled like stale cigarettes mixed with something else I didn't recognize, and they shadowed us on both sides and from behind. Their murmuring sounded harsh and angry. The tension rasped across my nerves like a file. I distinctly remember thinking we were cattle being herded to the slaughter. Some of the other team members seemed apprehensive as well, and I wondered what the hell I had gotten myself into by "volunteering" to tag along. "Volunteering" is an Army joke. More often than not, you don't willingly agree to do any specific task but rather get "volunteered" by a superior.

We worked through a village of crumbling stone and mud shacks that might have been thrown together 200 years ago. With the mob behind us, we approached another large crowd outside a building and were soon immersed in a sea of alien faces. My attention was drawn to their eyes. Anger and deep sorrow, the kind that comes from generations of oppression, were in their eyes. At that moment

→

I understood that they were not angry with us. I felt incredible relief. We took up security positions, which seemed ludicrous in the midst of a crowd, and watched while the chief entered with our guide.

When he emerged, his face was stunned. Whatever he had seen disturbed the hardened demeanor of this seasoned soldier. He spoke briefly with a couple of team members and within moments I was inside with two other men. I was hit by a terrible, sweet, acrid, metallic stench that could only be blood. My nerves jumped inside my skin, my vision sharpened and my heart pounded as I gulped air like a fish out of water.

We were channeled to the middle of the house where a blood-soaked sheet lay on the floor. I did not want to see what was beneath that slip of fabric. But someone yanked it off, and any innocence I had went with it. Underneath lay an unidentifiable mass of blood and flesh. A man explained it was a mother and two girls from the village. They had been murdered and mutilated, their tongues ripped out, jaws broken, nipples cut off and sexually disfigured. Someone screamed, "This is how they treat us! We are nothing to them!" Waves of emotion broke inside me; tears rolled down my face.

A villager grabbed my wrist and pulled me through another door. I struggled to free myself and glanced in panic for the other troops who were right behind. Pushed into a small room, we were cramped. Again, the stench assaulted my nostrils, and bile rose in my throat. On a bed lay another bloody sheet. I remember thinking it strange that this one wasn't nearly as red as the first. When removed, there was another body that appeared to be a man's. He was bound, but his body was unharmed except for the head. I could not register what I saw. His eyes sat in their sockets, but there were no eyelids, no lips to cover his teeth, no nostrils. In horror I realized that the skin had been peeled off his skull. This time I threw up.

Through his brother's ravings, we learned that the Taliban had found this man's family guilty of not being true to the word of Allah as written in the Quran. They forced his brother to watch the brutal and cowardly destruction of his wife and daughters. When he defied them, they tied him to his bed and brought the other villagers to watch while they "stole his identity so that Allah would not know him and not accept him into heaven." He was alive when they started.

→

The main thought that penetrated my emotional fog was, "I'm glad I'm an American." Until that day I thought of freedom, like most Americans, in terms of the Bill of Rights, complete with waving flags and mom's apple pie, ignorant of the rest of the world's woes and too arrogant to care. I believed that as Americans, we were entitled to a life of indulgence. I recall thinking that it was selfish and irresponsible for me to think this way after witnessing what these people had to endure, but I did just the same. I thought, this would never happen in America, and we may not be perfect, but our government doesn't go around torturing and killing people in the name of God. I was thankful and proud to come from such a great place where we don't live in caves and mud huts, where our government protects us from radical groups. I could go home and forget this.

Early the next morning we set off into the hills to search for more evidence of Al-Qaeda and their link to the Taliban. We climbed uphill for hours, but my thoughts were still trapped in that village house. They do this in the name of their God? What kind of God requires blood? Isn't Allah supposed to be a loving God?

I was so preoccupied that I didn't hear the first shots. I dropped to the ground and looked for cover before consciously understanding we were under attack. Once again, I found myself in disbelief. What the hell is this! Who's shooting? They can't be shooting at us—we're Americans! I am still amazed at my ignorance of how other cultures view Americans.

But we really were being shot at, and we needed to return fire. Normally soldiers are bound by rules that tell them what is a legal target and what is not. But there were no rules of engagement now. We fired at anything that moved or didn't move. We were engaged with an unknown number of an unknown enemy; man against man; one lives; one dies.

Under such extreme stress, a cocktail of chemicals and emotions takes over, and your conscious mind disengages while your body does what it needs to do. For me it was a double shot of adrenaline mixed with fear and anger. I thought, these were the same bastards that tortured those people, and we should kill them all—slowly. I laughed and fired my weapon like a lunatic. The sudden lack of constraint had me laughing. I felt the kind of freedom people cannot have and still be civilized. No emotional or moral barriers existed in those moments. Unbound from my own humanity, I stood

→

on the shore of my inner abyss where primal instincts raged, and felt compelled to dive in. I was terrified at what I could become. I hope I never feel that free again.

Then came the familiar humming whoosh of incoming mortar rounds. You only have to hear it once to know. Voices yelled, "Incoming!" and we dove down. After the impact, the chief called a direction, and we took off to get beyond the mortars' range. I heard them coming again and dove to ground. One round landed so close I was dazed by the concussion. I couldn't hear anything but when everyone else moved, I ran too. One man yelled in my face and I could just make out, "Are you all right?"

"Yeah, I'm good!" I yelled back, but he stared at my hand.

My glove was torn open and blood dripped. I tried to grasp my rifle, but my fingers wouldn't work and it fell. What the hell? I was too dazed to realize I'd been wounded. Then the pain blasted through my hand. I screamed. As I tried to see what had happened to my hand, time slowed, like a movie moving frame by frame. Drop by drop blood fell from my glove, splashing on my tan leather boots and the brown dirt. Someone led me by the arm. We had to keep moving, so I ran too. Finally, the shells, bullets and noise stopped.

I sat on the medi-vac helicopter, staring at my mauled hand and thinking how my long-held beliefs in freedom had been shattered. I was no longer the young, idealistic soldier who would save the world by spreading democracy and the American way. I had to rethink what I wanted to do with the freedom I did have. I had been in Afghanistan 49 hours and felt as though I had aged 20 years. It was September 1, 2001. In ten days, the whole world would know what Al-Qaeda was.

DISCUSSION

1. What is the significance of these lines: "I felt the kind of freedom people cannot have and still be civilized" and "I was terrified at what I could become"? What is his message about freedom?
2. How do the two major scenes connect to each other?
3. Has your own feeling about freedom changed since the "wounding" of western democracies in the terrorist attacks?
4. What is the significance of the date at the end?
5. **Visual Rhetoric:** Compare the ideas expressed in the essay to the war pictures on pages 37–38 and 285.

Autumn Escape
Brandon Littleton

The heat of long summer days passes, and the leaves on the hard-woods begin to change from greens to an orchestra of reds, yellows and golds. The sweet scent of grapes left on the vine fills the air. The wind carries a chill that makes you wish for a sweater, and the sky is littered with birds following a migratory path that reaches far beyond my wildest dreams. If only I could take up flight and join them on their journey.

When I was about eleven, I often dreamt of fall. It signaled a time of year my brothers and I exhausted ourselves on hunts, draining every last drop of light from the autumn sun. We all loved the freedom that Mother Nature gave us. Growing up in a poor family makes creative dreamers out of young boys. While neighborhood kids were playing catch with their dads, we were fashioning a bat and ball from a branch and rocks. There is no louder crack heard by a boy of five than that of a pine limb crushing a piece of granite. Well, that is except for one.

I was born in Port Angeles, a semi-small city on the northwestern coast of Washington state. For five years of my childhood, my family lived in a shack in the Elwa valley just north of the place of my birth. It was the kind of home that passers by would mistake as abandoned. Run-down barns and farm equipment from a century before sank into a field of uncut grass and thistles kept in only by an old tattered barbed wire fence. It had the look that a painter dreams of capturing on canvas and a land owner dreams of selling.

My father was a logger who looked like he hadn't slept in years. His face and hands were gritty and worn from sun and saw. His clothes were tattered and his jaw line covered with an untrimmed, wispy beard. My mother was aged far beyond her years by poverty and a pack of six wild kids. She rarely smiled, but she did all she could to be a hen shielding her chicks from dangers by concealing them under her wings.

I don't think I will ever know what kept them together for seventeen years other than us kids. One day as they argued, my eldest brother tried to intervene for peace. My father crushed his jaw with a single punch. My mother screamed for the rest of us to run out the front door and not look back. As we fled down the front steps, my mother at our heels and my father clumping after us, she paused. To one side of the staircase was one of our pine limb baseball bats.

→

She grabbed it and drew back. As my father raged through the front door, she drove through with a full swing and met him with four pounds of pine. My father's granite knees rang out with a crack louder than any child's home run. We spent the remainder of the day with Mother Nature in the autumn woods near our home. There are some things that a child should never see, and this is one of them. I can still hear the crack of the bat.

In my life, the only certainty is nature. She is my escape from the pressures I have endured and still endure. Her face changes with the seasons, and at times she can be unforgiving, but she is there when I need her. Even when it is intolerable outside, she still covers my soul like warm wings. I live for her glow in autumn when her beauties and strengths burn one last time before lying to rest for winter.

Discussion/Writing

1. Reread the first paragraph and explain what it contributes to the essay that someone might not realize during the first reading.
2. This essay uses the iceberg technique (page 189). Pick two details that suggest more than they seem to say. Which spots would you have liked the author to explain more? Or argue why they are best left unexplained.
3. Write a paragraph that connects setting (weather, the seasons, time of day, and/or location) to a story that happened to you. Try not to explain too explicitly.

Informative Essays

INFORMATIVE CONTRAST ESSAY

Food for Thought
Yeou-jih Yang

Mr. Chen took a short break from the steamy kitchen. Even though he was sweaty, he had a sense of accomplishment and satisfaction. He ducked out of the kitchen and scanned the dining room. Most tables were full. He watched a man shaking something vigorously into his food.

→

"What's that, Daddy?" asked a little girl who sat beside him.

"Soy sauce; you're supposed to put it on Chinese food."

Chen's heart sank. He retreated into the kitchen. "You should see what they do to my dishes!" he exclaimed. "After I spend so much time blending just the right seasoning, plup! It's all gone!"

Welcome to the West, or conversely, to the East. Dining experience is often a gate through which we can peek into a different culture. By examining it, you can not only enjoy food better, but also understand another culture and people, maybe even getting along better and promoting peace.

In Chef Chen's case, he had cut the meat and vegetables into bite-size pieces. He had chosen bright orange or red carrots, thick round scallops, curly pink shrimps, tender beef, green tree-shaped broccoli, yellow bamboo shoots, mixed them and gave a quick stir in the wok over intense flames. Then he blended in the sauce that he created. His masterpiece!

Its smell provoked the gastric glands. Its appearance had a master painter's color and composition. Its taste made the tongue sing. It was a culture communicator inviting the eater to examine it and appreciate it. Just like tasting fine wines or desserts, we shouldn't just flush or gulp it down the throat. The stomach may be filled, but the head will stay empty and the senses idle.

Chinese dining is filled with loud greetings, bright lights, and crowded seating. In contrast, American dining appears quite harmonious—candlelight, soft, soothing music, and well-matched tableware. Peeling off this superficial appearance, we will find a different philosophy underneath.

To understand, first you must know that the Chinese believe the universe consists of two opposite forces: yin, a negative force, and yang, a positive force. Only if these two are balanced can there be harmony and peace. This applies to food too. Meat is usually yang and vegetables are yin. A balance produces a peaceful dish. The Chinese avoid extremities.

For example, they don't drink icy cold water while eating a hot dish. They avoid conflict. For the same reason there are no knives at the table. Everything needing cutting is already done in the kitchen. The Chinese can't understand the western style of cutting meat at the dinner table, nor the swing from ice water to hot soup back to cold

→

salad followed by a hot entrée and ending with a cold dessert. To Chinese, this causes conflict and unbalance.

"Would you pass the mashed potatoes, please?" someone may politely request at the end of an American rectangular table. With these interruptions, cutting food with two hands and switching the fork from one hand to the other, it can get pretty busy. The Chinese prefer a round table so everyone has equal access to the food. The use of chopsticks with precut food doesn't require switching, so everything is more direct and peaceful.

One day last summer while visiting from Taiwan, my in-laws, armed with a dictionary, local map, some basic sentences, and a lot of curiosity, ventured into town by themselves. When they returned, my father-in-law said, "When I order a steak, the waiter bombed me with a chain of questions: 'How would you like your steak, sir: well done, medium, or rare? What kind of dressing would you prefer? We have French, Italian, Thousand Island, and house. Potato? Baked, mashed, or fried?' There! I thought steak was a simple American food."

My mother-in-law nodded. "All I wanted was an American hamburger, but they asked me how do I want my burger done, do I want lettuce or tomato on it or both? Leave out onion? Keep pickle in? Do I want ketchup, mayonnaise, or mustard in it?" She continued, "Like a tailor, they will make exactly what you want. The problem is, I don't know what an American burger should be. A Chinese chef doesn't make you make all these choices to enjoy it."

When we go to different restaurants, we have the chance to fill our stomachs, but also to fill our thoughts.

DISCUSSION

1. Rate this essay for surprise value in ideas and detail. What do you know now that you didn't before?
2. How does the author make comparing Chinese and American eating habits interesting?
3. How is the essay structured? Outline its main sections.
4. Think of two types of food or eating styles from different cultures. Draw up a list of comparisons or contrasts, looking for some "food for thought" behind the surface differences.
5. If you read this essay in a class workshop, what suggestions would you offer the author?

INFORMATIVE PROCESS ESSAY

The Autopsy
Gregory F. Matula

The county hospital. People come here to mend broken bodies, but it's also where those whose time has been cut short are sent to find out why. In the back, almost like an embarrassing family member kept out of sight, is the medical examiner's office. This is where the fine art of forensic medicine is practiced.

Above the door a sign reads, "What you see, what you hear, when you leave, leave it here!" A reminder of the sensitive investigations conducted here. There is complete silence except for a constantly ringing telephone. Three walls in the holding room are covered with tile and the fourth with what appears to be metal refrigeration doors.

This is the world of Dr. Nicholas Forbes, the medical examiner who will be performing today's autopsy. When he enters, his assistant briefs him about the corpse's death. She was a 59-year-old woman whose automobile struck a tree during good driving conditions with clear visibility.

I follow Dr. Forbes into the examining room, and I'm given a gown and mask to protect myself and my clothes from flying debris and blood. In the center are two metal beds that work like draining boards. Holes in the top layer allow water running beneath to wash away the blood that spills. There are instruments, wash basins, and hoses placed around the room for easy access.

On one metal bed lies the naked body of the dead woman. Stitches stretch from the navel to rib cage and continue under each breast almost to the armpit. This is from a brief preautopsy exam performed just after the accident. Abrasions cover her body. Dr. Forbes's job is to determine what might have caused the car accident.

As he disappears to scrub up, his two assistants diligently reopen the cuts made the night before, and the room fills with an aroma best described as that of menstrual blood. One inserts a long needle into the woman's eyes to draw fluid. From this fluid they can determine if there was alcohol in her system. After exposing the rib cage by moving the breasts up and to the side, the gentlemen use a pliers-like tool to cut the ribs and remove them. Now the lungs are visible.

With the precision and delicacy of a butcher, one assistant lifts and cuts out organs. The lungs and heart are plopped on the table.

→

A hose suctions out a pool of dark blood from the cavity. From a brief inspection, the man notices that her liver is badly mangled and adds it to the vital body parts. When the pile of organs grows too large for the table, he pulls out a metal bin and dumps them in.

Is this what life is to become? A bunch of scraps thrown in a pile, like giblets for the gravy? It's been said we are "food for worms." I wonder if worms like giblets. Humans tend to think "It won't happen to me," "I can handle it," or "Only old people die." However, the Bible says in James 4:14, "Whereas ye know not what shall be on the morrow. For what is life? It is even a vapor, that appeareth for a little time, and vanisheth away." How fragile we really are.

My thoughts are interrupted by a high-pitched whizzing sound. The man has completely gutted the corpse. All that remains is the empty cavity of the woman's torso with her head and appendages. The sound comes from a saw that looks like a drill with a disk. In the empty cavity the man saws the woman's backbone. After a moment he pulls out what looks like a flat oval-shaped dog biscuit. He explains it's a vertebra—to be used for a bone marrow specimen. He points out the spinal cord. It's thin and flimsy, like thick thread.

Next, the man walks to the head of the table, and without a word about what's next, grabs her scalp at the center of her head and folds it over her face. There, directly before me emerges a human skull. Not a picture, not a movie, not a computer replica, but a real skull fresh from its fleshy cage. He wipes it so it almost shines, as if gloating about its ability to protect its cargo. The saw resumes, and its pitch drops under the strain. Then the man uses a small prying instrument to pop the cap he'd just cut.

I'm privileged to see firsthand the most perplexing organ of the human body. The brain is creamy with black-etched grooves. It's so powerful yet so delicate that it indents like a sponge when the man takes hold and removes it. This magnificent piece of flesh isn't just thrown into the bin like the rest. It's treated royally, set apart on the examining tray. It will be saved for last.

After scrubbing up, the doctor reappears, steps to the table, and makes a visual inspection. He presses a foot pedal and talks into a microphone. In his foreign accent, he announces the time, then picks through the organs in the bin for the heart. He weighs it and announces the result into the microphone. He cuts the heart open for an internal examination and records a few observations. Then,

→

like a butcher discarding excess fat, he drops the organ into a pail lined with a plastic bag.

One by one, the doctor examines each organ externally and internally in the same manner. He has obviously conducted this procedure more often than he might care to calculate.

Dr. Forbes pauses for a moment. In deep thought, he taps a tune on the examining tray with an instrument. For the first time I realize there's an actual person behind that surgical mask. He calls me over to see something unusual in the lung. He explains how he determined she had sclerosis. I'm lost in the medical terms, but it doesn't stop him. He jokes about the red lungs with black tobacco spots having beautiful color just before he throws them into the pail.

Next is the trachea. He explains how it changes as a woman ages and causes her voice to deepen. He cuts intricate samples of each piece of flesh. He begins to quiz me on my knowledge of bodily organs and, like a game show host, he gongs me when I'm wrong.

Dr. Forbes appears to be surprised, when examining the stomach and liver, to see there is no gallbladder. He checks the bin and motions an assistant to look for a scar on the woman to see if it had been removed by surgery. No scar. The doctor notes this into the microphone. He then makes an incision into the stomach to empty its contents into a sample cup. "Well, look what we have here!" he says, as about thirty little yellow pills appear.

At this point, Dr. Forbes realizes this is a suicide. So far, he's determined she did not die on impact, because pieces of her liver were found in her lungs, proving aspiration after the accident. The pills in the stomach weren't even slightly digested, suggesting that she took them just before getting into her car. Due to her frenzied state, she must have driven her car into the tree because she couldn't wait for the pills to take effect. The doctor briefs me on the mental state of suicides.

While Dr. Forbes turns over the pills to the toxicologist for further examination, his assistant returns the skull cap and sews the scalp back together. After inspecting all the organs, Dr. Forbes cuts into the brain as easily as slicing pâté. I cringe at the thought of all the memories it once held. It's almost as if with each cut, 59 years of history are erased bit by bit. To me, the inside of the brain is the most beautiful part of the body. The white portions are distinct,

→

highlighted with a creamy layer and graceful lines. If one glance at it doesn't cause you to believe in Creation and the miracle of human-kind, then nothing ever will.

Done, Dr. Forbes presses the microphone pedal and announces, "Cause of death, pending toxicology report. Autopsy complete at 11:32."

DISCUSSION

1. What are the steps in the process described? Which steps does the author dwell on and which skim over? Say why you agree or disagree with his emphasis.

2. This is mostly an objective informative essay. Do the passages in which the author muses on the meaning of what he witnesses fit? Explain.

3. Think of how you could use firsthand witness to write a great informative essay. List three processes readers and you might be interested in, and a few notes about how you would go about it. Greg received permission to observe the autopsy simply so he could write a college paper.

INFORMATIVE CLASSIFICATION ESSAY

Marijuana Smokers
Jacqueline M. Mathis

Joe struggled to lift his lead eyeballs as the sun glared into his bedroom. "Crap," he groaned, "It's 1:30 already." He rolled over and searched the room for his bong, drifting his gaze until he located the tall red statue. Groggily, he stood, picked up a lighter and his bag of weed. He packed the bowl head lazily, spilling some potent buds onto the carpet. He lit up and breathed a sigh of relief. This is the life, he thought.

Joe had to hustle to get ready for his 2:30 appointment. It felt like only twenty minutes when someone busted through the front door—a man with a shaggy mop of curls, a marijuana leaf blatantly displayed on a T-shirt, and frayed corduroys. "Adam, what the hell are you doing?" Joe asked.

→

"Aw, sorry man. I know I'm late. I tried to be on time. You know, smoker's delay," Adam said.

"No, dumb ass. I was talking about busting through my front door. Show some respect and knock next time." As they sat on the couch, Adam asked Joe if he was selling in dimes. He only had twenty dollars, but he needed to get high, something to carry him over for a couple days. Annoyed, Joe broke up an eighth he had set aside for Adam, re-bagged it and sent him on his way.

Joe flipped on the T.V. and lit the joint he had rolled to smoke with Adam. What a cheap bastard, he thought to himself. Not even five minutes into *Change of Heart,* the phone rang. He glanced at the caller I.D., but the number was blocked. He picked up and was greeted with a soft hello. It was his next appointment, calling to say he'd be there in ten minutes.

Five minutes later, he heard a soft rapping at the door. One, two, three hesitant knocks. There stood a lanky man in a suit and tie–the real estate agent. He followed Joe to the couch and shared a joint. He inhaled deeply and held the sweet smoke a long time. "How's work going?" Joe asked.

"Oh, you know, it's going. I have this really good offer on a house I showed earlier this week, but it's been a little slow." Richard counted out three hundred in fifties and handed Joe the money. Joe carefully weighed the weed on a digital scale, showing Richard for his approval. "Thanks Joe, I really appreciate it. You always hook me up. I'll call you in a couple weeks." With that, Richard was out the door.

Not long after, Cindy bounced in with her friend Stacey. They giggled more than they talked. They choked on the joint when Joe passed it and commented on how ripped they were. They each put in twenty toward an eighth, and their eyes lit when they held the green in their hands. "Thank you so much, Joey. I really wanted to smoke this weekend at Stacey's party," Cindy said. They declined on hitting the joint again; they had a very low tolerance. Hell, they didn't even notice that Joe didn't weigh the weed. They each gave him a hug and bounced.

Well that was interesting, Joe thought. He reached into the bagged ounce he had set aside for himself, and rolled a quick joint up. Two seconds later, the phone rang.

Although the behaviors of marijuana smokers tend to overlap, there are distinct classifications of usage and lifestyles. Four common

→

types are "Slacker-Stoners," "High-Achieving-Stress-Relieving-Paranoids," "Wannabe-Smokers," and "Capitalists."

Adam is a typical "Slacker-Stoner." They dress casually, hang in groups with the same slacking habits and indulge frequently. They smoke anything from swag to rare kind buds and use all types of smoking tools. They always have a bowl and a few buds on them. They openly advocate smoking and legalizing marijuana. Typically with low grades and attendance, this group skips school or work to smoke. These are the guys we see frequently stereotyped in movies like *Jay and Silent Bob*—low motivation, no goals and low paid, or nonexistent, jobs. You wouldn't be surprised to find the pizza delivery boy is in this group.

Richard is an example of a High-Achieving-Stress-Relieving-Paranoid. People tend to forget successful business people and students who pull straight A's smoke weed too. This group doesn't let its use of marijuana affect its goals or work habits. They are often closet smokers or just keep a low profile. This group takes extra precautions not to get caught; they block numbers and keep Visine on them at all times. They buy kind bud, the truly potent stuff, in large quantities, maybe twice a month. They keep a rational hold on their habit; they realize the addiction but excuse it as "self-medication." Smoking is an escape for this group, marijuana a pleasant, relaxing, easy escape from stress.

Cindy is a Boastful-Wannabe-Social-Smoker. She wants everyone to know she does it, because it makes her naughty. She doesn't do it often, and never alone. Since her use is so rare, marijuana does not affect her thinking, attendance, grades, or income as it does the other groups, but it does affect things like her driving. You will never hear another group say, "I can't drive when I'm high." Heavier users adapt to marijuana. This group's rare usage does not allow for adaptation. For her, weed is just social fun.

Joe is the Capitalist. Dealers usually smoke and appreciate the demand for buds by others in need. He can charge whatever he wants, smoke whenever he wants, and live how he pleases. This group tends to extremes: Very Uptight or Extremely Laid Back. These people are at a high risk for brushes with the law. They succeed by word of mouth and are caught by word of mouth. This group lives on the edge and thrives on danger. Behind the scene, Joe is the man who continues the cycle and keeps us all high. We like Joe, don't we?

Discussion/Writing

1. Suggest additional details for two of the four types that Jacqueline classified.
2. This essay has two styles of writing separated by a break. Does this work well? What about the last sentence? Explain.
3. Rate this essay for surprise value. What parts are freshest? Least fresh?
4. Set up a classification system like this for some other *user group* – drinkers, car drivers or computer users. Create headings and under each add notes for details.

INFORMATIVE ESSENTIALS ESSAY—CAREER RESEARCH

Mental Health Counselling
Judy Robbins

At the tender age of 47, I may have finally decided what I want to be when I grow up: a mental health counselor. I have always worked in the healthcare field and want to help others. I did have some concerns about the degree required, the "market" for mental health counselors, the income I could expect and the difficulty of keeping my own sanity while helping others cope with heavy burdens.

A mental health counselor must have at least a bachelor's degree. This allows you to do social work, but only under supervision. To have a private practice, you must have a master's degree ("Social Workers," *CollegeGrad.com* n. pag.). Even after obtaining a master's degree, you still must be supervised before being credentialed by insurance companies. This allows the new graduate to learn more on the job and protects fragile clients from mistakes.

To discover more about the career, I interviewed Bill McGough, LMSW, who has a private practice in Honeoye Falls, NY. Although McGough possesses certification as a substance abuse counselor, his primary focus is with people who have difficulty coping with personal problems. He said, "Mental health counselors . . . assist people who are having a hard time coping. They could be facing a psycho-physical problem or having a hard time coping with stress from major life changes such as the death of a loved one, a failed marriage, returning to college after many years, or the loss of a job." He prefers not to counsel only people with addiction problems,

→

but those with a wide variety of issues, as this makes his profession more interesting.

People looking to work in the area of social work can expect the employment market to grow faster than average until the year 2012. This is directly related to the rapid growth of the elderly and aging baby boomers who create demand for health and social services ("Social Workers," *Occupational . . .* n. pag.). Another reason for growth is that mental health counseling is more acceptable than it used to be. People who openly sought help for emotional problems used to be viewed as damaged goods and treated as outcasts.

Most social workers have a 40-hour week. However, many work late hours and weekends to catch the edge of the market. Despite changing attitudes, most people still do not want to tell employers they are getting counseling and seek counselors who will make appointments that do not interfere with their jobs.

The key to a successful practice is to find an area not being "served" by another mental health counselor, notes McGough, especially in rural areas. Rural people typically resist travelling into the "city" for treatment and suffer more isolation in their communities. McGough says, "When I started out, I was not above going to people's homes to see them for the first couple of appointments. I would see people from Honeoye Falls southward, some of them very leery of us city folks! To gain their trust, I met with them in their homes, and after I established rapport with them, they would agree to meet at my office (n. pag.).

For 2007, a graduate of a master's program in social work earned a median income of $40,093. Of course this income depends on your area of social work. Someone in medical and public health will earn more than someone in substance abuse ("Salary Survey Report" n. pag.). McGough said that the rate for a local mental health counselor is $85 per hour. Insurance companies dictate the amount that counselors can charge.

When I asked McGough how he maintains his sanity listening to patient after patient's grief and horrors, he admitted it can be tough. For example, he currently has a client who sought help because her great aunt died and left diamond earrings to her sister and not her. Although this may sound trivial to listen to, this is a major issue to her. McGough hopes to shift her focus to what she can do to overcome

→

her feelings of hurt and resentment. Sometimes a counselor must deal with more painful issues like childhood abuse, so it is important to have a support resource oneself. McGough says his faith and belief in God makes it easier to handle those situations.

I am excited about the prospects for my future as a mental health counselor. I envision this profession as one in which I can grow old, one in which I can work no matter where I live. I understand there will be years of challenge as I learn my trade, but I hope to help people struggling with issues that interfere with their health and well being. You see, I too needed help once, and there was someone who, in spite of my reluctance, helped me. I look forward to doing the same for others.

Works Cited

McGough, William, LMSW. Personal interview. 2 December 2006.

Pistoe, Carol. "Mental Health Counselling: Identity and Distinctiveness." *ERICDigest*. n.d. 4 Dec. 2006 <http://www.ericdigests.org>.

"Salary Survey Report for Degree: Master of Social Work." *PayScale. Com*. 18 Jan. 2008. 26 Jan. 2008 <http://www.Payscale.com>.

"Social Workers." *CollegeGrad.com*. n.d. 3 Dec. 2006 <http://www.collegegrad.com/careers>.

"Social Workers." *Occupational Outlook Handbook, 2004-05 Edition*. 2005. 18 Dec. 2006 <http://www.bls.gov/oco/print/ocos060.htm>.

DISCUSSION

1. List the issues Judy promised to cover in the introductory paragraph. Does she do so in the order given? Which of her four areas has the most specific information? Did any need more details? Explain.

2. What is your personal evaluation of this career after reading this essay? Why would you be interested in a career as a mental health counselor?

3. What does Judy not discuss that you think are key issues?
4. Make a list of the top five things you want from a job. How does your present job or the one you are pursuing through college match up?
5. List 10 questions you'd ask someone in the kind of career you want.

The Persuasive Essay

You will write many business or professional letters in your life: cover letters for job applications, letters of recommendation, letters to co-workers, bosses, employees, government agencies, and clients. You will write letters to lawyers, banks, medical organizations, and credit card companies disputing charges or asking for information or help. Your writing must look professional to be taken seriously. The professional letter follows a strict format:

- Single space with double spaces between paragraphs.
- Do not indent paragraphs.
- Your address in the upper-left corner.
- Skip a line and write the date.
- Skip a line and write your audience's name, title, and address on the left.
- Skip another line and write the salutation ("Dear Ms. Lesser:" for example).
- The letter should state its purpose in the opening paragraph and say exactly what you want your reader to do.
- The closing ("Sincerely," for example) goes on the left side of the page. Skip several lines where you will sign your name with pen, then type your name.

PROFESSIONAL E-MAIL

Your style can relax when you e-mail friends or family. But professional e-mail substitutes for a business letter or memorandum and should be as formal as one.

- Check spelling and punctuation.
- Spell out contractions.
- Avoid emoticons such as the happy face ☺ or frown ☹.
- Spell out e-mail acronyms ("BTW" should be "By the way," and "TIA" should be "Thanks in advance").

- Change cutesy or weird addresses like "Goofygirl@AOL.com" to something that will make an employer more confident about hiring you.
- Use the "subject" box at the top to let your reader know this is not a virus or spam.
- Do not use a heading, salutation, or closing because e-mail is in memorandum format. If you want a heading so the reader will have your home address, write in professional letter format and send it as an attachment to a brief e-mail that announces what is in the attachment.
- Choose a common font like New Times Roman or Courier because some fancy fonts do not travel well by e-mail and arrive in "Martian."
- Your message should be concise, direct and professional.
- Do not dash off quick replies to upsetting or professionally important e-mails. Draft a reply, but do not send it until you have had time to rethink and revise carefully.

E-MAIL OR SNAIL MAIL?

Should you send your professional letter by standard postal delivery or by e-mail? E-mail arrives instantaneously and includes any original correspondence the person sent you so you don't have to summarize it as you do in snail mail. But for first correspondence, most people hesitate to open e-mails from strangers to avoid viruses. I have accidentally deleted messages from people I knew because I did not recognize their e-mail name. Help your reader overcome this resistance with a clear subject line.

It's nice to make quick replies without dragging out envelopes and stamps, but e-mail can be too fast for your own good. Important replies need rethinking and incubation, not just proofreading. Save a draft for a day before letting it go. Stamped mail still has advantages, however. It will sit on a person's desk until he does something about it. It's easier to tap "delete" to e-mail than throw away a personal letter. A paper letter is also more private. E-mail is basically a public letter that can be accessed by your boss or fellow employees if sent to your work computer, by family members who know how to retrieve old communications on your home computer, by people who buy your old computer, and by snoopy hackers.

Can you think of other advantages or disadvantages for either type of mail? Or which situations might be better suited for e-mail or snail mail?

PERSUASIVE LETTERS

Hanson Street ICF
Newton Area NYDA

June 13, 2009
Brad A. Walker

Director of Employee Relations
New York Developmental Association
Newton, NY 14620

Dear Mr. Walker:

At 6:03 as I enter the group home I am bombarded by screaming and banging. Don, a co-worker, is slumped against the door of the time-out room, hand diligently on the door lock. Dark circles hang under his eyes. He is utterly exhausted. "Long night?" I ask. He can't hear me. Inside the room, G. L. pounds her fists against the metal door.

As a residential treatment specialist at the Developmental Association, I experience stress on many levels. I have begun to pop Rolaids like candy, and my body is bruised and scratched. I deeply enjoy most aspects of my job: helping residents use a toothbrush, participate in sensory stimulation, or practice sign language. I am part physical therapist, part social worker. Working with the retarded is both important and inspiring.

But every two years we have a 75% turnover rate of employees. The house is in a constant state of retraining, which detracts from the quality and amount of goal work with residents. Someone hired a month ago cannot relate well to residents or implement programs. We need to make changes to prevent the burnout caused by unnecessary stress.

One cause of stress is the time-out room used by three of the ten residents at my house. According to G. L.'s plan, for instance, when she becomes disruptive or assaultive, she will be "escorted" to the time-out room. The escort requires two staff members trained in SCIP (strategies in crisis intervention and prevention) to physically relocate G. L. Her arms are held, SCIP staff secure her between them with their hips, and she is forcibly moved. In her agitated state, she lashes and thrashes feet, arms, and head to cause damage.

→

This occurs daily, up to five times in a single afternoon. She is kept in the time-out room for up to an hour where she will yell and bang the electromagnetically locked door. Staff must hold the button at all times or she can exit.

H. T. also exhibits violent behavior. He becomes impatient and disruptive if forced to wait—for dinner, for instance. If ignored, he hurls anything within reach at staff, engages in SIB (self-injurious behavior), breaks windows or furniture, and assaults staff members. He is strong enough to dislocate arms and snap wrists.

Here are some strategies to reduce these stresses.

We could introduce a more dynamic program to vent staff frustration. Our present biweekly meetings deal with modification-to-behavior plans. We could devote more time to good old-fashioned gripe sessions. These would be confidential, nothing would be taken personally, and nothing would be exempt from discussion. Empathy from administration during these meetings is crucial. I have observed that older NYDA administrative members tend to dismiss our grievances—when we do voice them—by saying, "Boy, you should have been here ten years ago. *That* was stress." Maybe so, but it is exhausting now, and they should be more receptive to our suggestions.

We should have access to stress management courses designed for our specific work problems, as well as to teach us how to catch up on sleep after an overnight and manage time better. A group membership at the local YMCA could vent pent-up anxiety and frustration. Ideally, we should have access to deprogramming sessions with a psychologist after particularly bad episodes. We are expected to fulfill our responsibilities regardless of how angry we are at getting spit on, slapped, scratched, bitten, and pulled by the hair. We're frustrated having a behavior plan work successfully one day and blowing up the next. We know each resident has potential; when this potential is not realized, we blame ourselves. We need to know our supervisors support our efforts and understand; we often feel they do not. Making available *any* of these suggestions will show we are taken seriously, respected and appreciated.

My duties at NYDA are not without rewards, but it is increasingly difficult to feel the enthusiasm I once did. Walking into the Hanson Street ICF is like entering a pro wrestling match that does not let up until my ten-hour shift is over. My ears often ring on the drive home.

→

These stresses detract from my goal: to do something positive and learn about myself and the human condition, not just turn a profit with my head in the sand. I do not regret working with the mentally retarded, but at the current stress level, I do not think I will continue after finishing my education. I don't want to be a coffee-gulping, chain-smoking burnout by the time I'm twenty-five. Please consider these proposals for the good of all of us.

Sincerely,

Craig Lammes

Craig Lammes
Residential Treatment Specialist

DISCUSSION

1. What are the main ideas of this letter? What are the best supporting details?
2. The author is writing for an audience who knows something of the subject. If you are not familiar with the operation of group homes, you may feel a bit left out as an audience. Find some word choices that indicate this.
3. What does the author say to avoid sounding like a mere complainer?
4. Write a formal letter to your employer or a public official to suggest a policy change (one page maximum, single spaced).

Note: The following letter a student wrote to her boss, the owner/director of a dance studio where the author worked as a dance instructor.

Dear Shirl Bonaldi:

There are a few things I would like to discuss with you. I feel your business needs extreme improvements.

First, your attendance record lacks by a lot. You are the director of a dance studio, and you have put in only two full weeks this

→

whole year. At least one day a week you have cancelled class or gotten another teacher to cover for you. As a result of these constant absences, students have lost confidence in you. For example, one of your most advanced students, Kelly Fisher, refused to do competition because she felt she wouldn't get enough practice. A student can only practice so much on her own. She needs a teacher's advice and corrections to really improve and be successful in competition. Your students are beginning to doubt your ability because they don't see it very much.

Secondly, you have lost your enthusiasm. You used to come to class with your tights, leotards, and proper shoes. Now you wear jeans and sneakers. It is a bad influence on the little kids. Now they come unprepared. When asked where their stuff is, they say, "Miss Shirl doesn't have her things, so why do I need them?" You never dance anymore. You just sit in your chair and dictate what you want done. You make it easy on yourself. You take all the advanced classes and leave the other teachers with the beginner and baby classes. Where is your desire to teach and dance? You have already lost two students, and you will continue to lose more if you don't think about what I'm saying.

There is one last point: the treatment of your employees. I have been working for you for three years, and I've gotten the same pay all that time. I'm teaching as many classes as you are. I also pay $104 a month to take lessons from you. When I finally had the nerve to ask for a raise, you laughed at me. I understand you may not have been able to afford it, but you were inconsiderate.

The students miss how you once were: energetic, enthusiastic, and caring for all of us. You could use these again. Please think about it. Thank you for your time.

Sincerely,

Tina Maenza

Tina Maenza

DISCUSSION

1. Comment on the letter's tone. How do you think the author's audience would react? Suggest where and how you might revise for tone.

2. Outline the letter. What are the key arguments? Discuss their validity. Are they supported with sufficient detail?

3. If you have complaints about your boss or place of employment, write a brainteaser list. In peer groups or in class, discuss how to achieve the proper tone in presenting them.

4. How does this letter's format fall short?

---

10 Hometown Boulevard
Rochester, NY 14611

January 23, 2009
Mr. Eric Goodman
Chief Engineer
Time Warner Communications
Rochester, NY 14620

Dear Mr. Goodman:

I'm writing this letter to remind you why I should be promoted to the Master Control Supervisor position.

First, my professionalism and communication skills not only have helped employees perform effectively but also helped the company succeed. Edwin Cowls, the Production Manager, said this at our 2008 award ceremony when he awarded me the plaque for best communication skills. You patted me on that back then too, remember? Your last two quarterly reviews credited my professionalism; both said I was your number one man.

In March, 2004, I was hired for the Master Control Operator position which I still hold. Since then I have obtained the knowledge and hands-on experience needed to supervise the other operators in the department. I am experienced in all the systems in the master control area, including Newsplay. This system was brought on line during 1998. As you may recall, this was the first digital system in the city to run local and worldwide news clips 24 hours a day. Most of the system's bugs are now resolved due to my discrepancy reports to the engineers—such as the system freezing so that on air a newscaster looked like someone has pressed "pause" on a DVD. Louth, the digital system that runs Channel 26 (WB), is also fairly new. But because of my daily troubleshooting and repairs, it's now 98% effective.

→

I was the one sent to learn Seachange, another new system, and you had me train the other operators with it. These are the responsibilities of a supervisor.

You may be reluctant to promote me to Supervisor because I have not been employed as long as two other operators. But I have spoken to them, and they do not want the promotion themselves because they would need to make a shift change. They said I'm already their supervisor and that you should make it legitimate. Both feel I'm the best qualified because I do all the instruction and implementation already. They assured me if I were promoted that there would be no problem.

You may prefer to promote someone from outside who has supervisory experience. But who would train and instruct this new hire on the department's systems? Me. Why go through that and incur needless expense when you have someone in your department to fill the position? You may have forgotten that I do have training in supervision—during my six-year military career, I attended classes in supervision and held a supervisory position my last three years. I am currently attending college, which adds depth to my career file.

I believe I have completely refreshed your memory on my accomplishments and work performance. I now rely on your keen judgment to see that I am the applicant most qualified and suitable for the position of Supervising Master Control Operator.

Sincerely,

Willie F. Nelson, Jr.

Willie F. Nelson, Jr.

DISCUSSION

1. If you were Willie's boss, would you be convinced by this letter? Why or why not?
2. Rewrite any phrases you'd consider changing. Explain why.
3. What possible refutations does the author raise and answer? Are there any other possible objections Willie does not raise?
4. Write a letter to your boss, outlining why you deserve a promotion or raise.

PERSONAL PERSUASIVE LETTER

May 30, 2009

Dear Greg,

Hi, how are you? Probably scared, shocked and confused. I am too. But I need to talk to you about our future and our baby's too. As I'm sure you realize, our future is now going to be unimaginably more difficult than we thought. I know I can do it, though, and you can too. I have a lot of faith in the two of us. But although we could do it apart, if that's what you truly wish, we both know that it will be a thousand times easier together.

As far as our relationship goes, I don't see any reason why we should break up. Things were really going well between us before. Now you avoid me at all costs and refuse to speak to me over the phone. I am willing to forgive all that. I want us to move forward *together* into this new part of our lives. We should do this for ourselves, but—more importantly—we need to do it for our baby. We need to preserve our relationship for the sake of the emotional support you as a father can provide the baby and me. I need to be strong for the baby, and I need your help. Please try to see this from my perspective. I *can't* run away; I *can't* hide, I really need you now, Greg—more than ever.

The biggest point I want to make is this: *our baby will need a dad.* If it's a boy, who's going to teach him to play football, fix cars or handle girls? If it's a girl, who's going to be there to threaten her boyfriends, tell her she's not old enough to wear make-up and that her skirts are too short? Don't deny her the chance to be "daddy's little girl." Now, I know you are probably thinking, "Teach my kid how to handle girls or not to wear short skirts? How can I possibly do that considering the mess I'm in now? How can I teach my kid about the world when I haven't figured it out yet?" But the truth is that no dad ever has. Parents just teach their kids what they *do* know. They try to help them in all the ways they can. You can do that, Greg—I know you can. Remember that fatherhood is as much a learning experience as childhood.

If you don't decide to be part of our baby's life now, think about that someday down the road when you will inevitably run into him. Then you will have to look into your child's hurt, innocent eyes and tell

→

him you didn't love him enough to be his dad—the pain and loneliness you knew you would cause in his life wasn't enough to make you want to stay. And I know you, Greg; I know you haven't the heart to do that. Even if you don't want to be a dad, our baby will want to have you as one. You owe it to him. After all, you're half the reason he's here. For your own sake, though, think of all you'll miss. You won't get to see your baby's first steps, his first Christmas; you won't know his first words or the look on his face when he tells you he loves you. Imagine your life without your father and all the things he did for you that our baby won't have.

I realize you feel stuck between a rock and a hard place right now. But you aren't, and everything can be fine. Nothing will be fine, though, unless you are willing to put in the effort to make it so. I need you desperately right now, and in eight months our baby will too. I hope you will see past your fears and choose willingly to do what you know is right. Greg, please come back and be a father to our baby.

All My Love, Always,
Britni

Britni (Bellwood)

DISCUSSION

1. Discuss the tone of this letter. How does the author reach past the rage one might expect? Are there any sections where you think the tone could be better for her audience?

2. Write a brief reply to this letter as if you were Greg. He might agree to come back, but if he does not, what reasons might he give? Try not to invent things, but pick up cues from Britni's letter.

THE PERSUASIVE ESSAY

The Beginning of the End of Freedom
Kevin Giunta

In the weeks following September 11, 2001, 19-year-old Murat Kurnaz, a German citizen, traveled to Pakistan for religious study; while there, he was arrested at a Pakistani checkpoint, handed over

→

to U.S. officials and sent to the U.S. base in Kandahar, Afghanistan and eventually Guantanamo Bay. Murat was detained by U.S. officials as an unlawful enemy combatant lacking the rights of a P.O.W. and far from the protection of any court. U.S. military intelligence wrote, "Criminal investigation task force has no definite link [or] evidence of detainee having an association with al Qaeda or making any specific threat toward to the U.S.," but Kurnaz was not released for 5 years ("Ex-terror Detainee" n. pag.). Murat's story may seem like an Orwellian horror, but these are legal activities for the government to engage in with an unprecedented opacity from public scrutiny. Under the Presidency of George W. Bush, Americans' civil rights were infringed upon as a cost of the war against terrorism; but this violates the fourth amendment set in place to protect the people from their own government. The federal government does not have the right to undermine civil liberties in the way it has with the passing of anti-terrorism legislation.

The Fourth Amendment of the Bill of Rights says, "The right of the people to be secure in their persons, houses, papers and effects, against unreasonable searches and seizures, shall not be violated, and no Warrants shall issue, but upon probable cause, supported by Oath of affirmation, and particularly described the place to be searched, and the person or things to be seized" ("Constitution of the United States" n. pag.). The restrictions were added to the constitution for the safety of citizens against abusive government. Today law enforcement agencies such as Immigration and Customs Enforcement undermine civil rights to increase their own power, claiming the authority is necessary to help fight threats to the American people including terrorists and illegal immigrants. It is wrong and naïve for the federal government to believe that any threat to the American people is more important than protecting the freedoms that the country is based on.

Unconstitutional legislation is not limited to anti-terrorism and the USA PATRIOT act; there are many situations in which members of the federal government are not required to abide by civil law when protecting the people of the United States from national threats. For example, the government is allowed to

→

undercut civil liberties in the realm of immigration. It is legal for Immigration and Customs Enforcement also known as ICE agents to enter the home of a believed illegal immigrant without a warrant and place the suspected illegal immigrant under arrest; because Miranda rights do not apply to immigrants, basic rights are denied to both legal *and* illegal immigrants. Simply put, ICE agents do not need a warrant to enter an immigrant's home, place them under arrest, take them out of state, deny them the rights to a public attorney and hold them indefinitely. As ICE special agent Peter J. Smith put it, "We don't need warrants to make arrests" (Preston n. pag.). Not only does the government not need a warrant to harass immigrants in this country, but once the arrest is made, the government is within its rights to detain the person in question indefinitely ("Immigration Policy" n. pag.). This is extremely alarming. It is true that non-citizens do not hold the same rights as US citizens; but no matter what a person's citizenship, all people should be treated fairly and as human be-ings. It is almost incomprehensible that the government would deny anyone basic human rights, no matter what the situation. To undermine the basic civil rights of any man defies what our coun-try is based upon.

Immigrants legal or not are not the only ones in danger of hav-ing their rights undermined by our government, for U.S. citizens are now subject to the same dangers due to the passing of the USA PATRIOT act by Congress. The USA PATRIOT act allows for "sneak-and-peek" warrants which allow investigations to be made without a warrant and in secret, and it also allows the federal government to search citizens' records without their knowledge. The new power granted to law enforcement is dangerous for two reasons; first the permission to search one's records without a warrant is a direct violation of the Fourth Amendment, and more importantly the secrecy in which investigations may be conducted makes public scrutiny of government practices nearly impossible. If the public is unable to see how the government conducts its searches, then it is impossible to know if the searches are unrea-sonable and therefore in conflict with the constitution and citizens' rights. The government claims that the reason for newly passed legislation is to protect citizens from the threats of terrorism—but

→

is this true? The answer is no; of the 155 known "sneak-and peek" search warrants served by the Justice Department in 2005, almost all were used on common crimes such as drug charges and violent crimes, not terrorism ("Patriot Act Evasions" n. pag.). This shows that we have faltered under the fears of our times and allowed our freedoms to be sacrificed for protection. We have forgotten the great men and women of our country's history who fought and died fearlessly for the freedoms we readily gave up to the power hungry.

Although the situation seems dreadful and unjust, the American people still have the power to undo this infringement on our rights and freedoms. The people of the United States must realize our government's blunder in putting security before freedom, for the most important role of the government of the United States of America is to protect the freedoms of its people—no matter the cost. We must remember that the freedom and equality of all men is what our great nation was founded upon and that ". . . all men are created equal, that they are endowed by their Creator with certain unalienable Rights, that among these are Life, Liberty and the pursuit of happiness." ("Declaration of Independence" n. pag.). Although we live in frightening times with terrorism a looming threat, it is important that we not lose sight of our values in the face of fear.

Works Cited

"Constitution of the United States." *Funk & Wagnalls New World Encyclopedia*. EBSCO. Monroe Community College Library. 30 Mar. 2008 <http://search.ebscohost.com>.

"Declaration of Independence." *Funk & Wagnalls New World Encyclopedia*. EBSCO. Monroe Community College Library. 30 Mar. 2008 <http://web.ebscohost.com>.

"Ex-Terror Detainee Says U.S. Tortured Him." *CBS News*. 28 Mar. 2008. 30 Mar. 2008 <http://www.cbsnews.com>.

"Immigration Policy in U.S. is Criticized by U.N. Aide." *New York Times*. 8 Mar. 2008: A11.

→

"Patriot Act Evasions." *Nation.* 2 May 2005. Academic Search
    Premier. EBSCO. Monroe Community College Library.
    21 Mar. 2008 <http://searchebscohost.com>.
Preston, Julia. "No Need for a Warrant, You're an Immigrant."
    New York Times. 14 Oct. 2007. *InfoTrac.* 28 Mar. 2008
    <www.infotrac-college.com>.

DISCUSSION

1. What are the author's thesis and main supporting arguments?
2. What would someone opposed say? Write a few sentences as if you were an opponent, then try to answer the objection.
3. Write a position statement on some public issue on which you have strong opinions. List two or three reasons to support your position and one strong objection someone might raise.
4. Evaluate this essay using the Peer Review Checklist in Chapter 13.

ESSAY PRESENTING BOTH SIDES OF A CONTROVERSY

Sterilization for Sale
Lauren Weaver

Lashanda Jackson looked worn out and as thin as a rail as she entered into a clinic the size of a shack on the south side of Los Angeles. She was there for a pregnancy test—again. Lashanda is twenty-six years old and has been pregnant thirty-seven times. Why so many? She prostitutes to support her crack habit. When an "accident" happens on her job site, a child is conceived. "Damn, not again," she says as she hears the results of number thirty-eight. She is only one of thousands of women in California and the rest of the United States with the same problem. A controversial solution to this problem is called the C.R.A.C.K. program (California's Reduction of Addicted Children Kinship). The program pays addicts like Lashanda two hundred dollars to go through a sterilization operation. I have done an internship for my father, one of the founders

→

of the organization, for the past two summers and have heard arguments for both sides of the program, which will likely have both positive and negative long-term effects.

One obvious result of this program will be to reduce the number of babies born addicted to crack and heroin. The forty-three women who have followed through with the program so far had conceived a total of three hundred and twelve times prior to sterilization. Of the one hundred and sixteen children who lived to be born, all were addicted. Some argue that reducing the number of addicted babies would greatly reduce the amount of money taxpayers spend on medical costs and foster care for these children.

One of the highest rates of abuse and neglect come from addicted mothers towards their addicted children. Addicted children tend to be difficult to begin with, showing more symptoms of ADD, learning disabilities, health problems, and overall irritability. Handing a child like this to a parent under the influence can be a dangerous combination. The C.R.A.C.K. program, its supporters say, will reduce the number of addicted mothers caring for addicted children and therefore the amount of abuse and neglect.

Some who oppose the program protest that an addict will have two hundred dollars to spend on her habit, money that likely will end up in the pockets of drug dealers. Many of those against the program state that they would not be as opposed to it if the money was offered on a food card or in clothing or furniture vouchers.

Others against the program feel that women who participate in the program for the money as a quick fix are not capable of thinking about the long-term effects on their lives. The process is irreversible, and although it has not yet been an issue, some fear it may be in the future if the sterilized women sober up and want children.

If women who participate in the program can't get pregnant, will they bother to use contraceptives? Will that increase STD and AIDS rates? Some say yes, some say no. If a woman who is addicted and prostituting to support her habit is not using protection because she knows she is not capable of conceiving, she could be a likely target for disease. However, program supporters feel that the women were obviously not using protection to begin with, and many already had HIV or AIDS from sexual contact or intravenous drug use. Not being sterilized will only add the risk of passing a disease on to a child she may carry in the future.

→

The women could also have harmful health effects from the actual procedure. There is always a risk in an operation that requires sedation. Women may also have to undergo hormone therapy to prevent their voices from deepening and growing facial hair due to the drop in the amount of estrogen their bodies will produce post-operation. However, most are fairly young, the average age being twenty-seven, and there have been no documented cases of complications to date. The women also go through a very selective orientation process during which the risks and outcomes are explained. All women sign papers of consent and understanding ahead of time.

Lashanda Jackson did follow through with the sterilization and was given the two hundred dollars cash. She will never have to go to the clinic for a pregnancy test again and so far says she has no regrets. However, if she wishes to clean up her life and have children in the future, she will not have that option. She has given birth to five children previously, but has custody of none. Two are in a home for children with retardation and disabilities, and the other three have been diagnosed with ADHD and live in three separate foster homes. Working for the program has been challenging and eye opening. It has also put me on the front lines to hear testimony both for and against C.R.A.C.K. The program is in its infancy at only two years old. Perhaps the best judgment of its success or failure will be time.

Discussion/Writing

1. This essay avoids taking a direct stand. Does the author seem to have a preference? Is her presentation fair? Support your views.

2. What other effects might such a program have that the author does *not* raise?

3. If you were to take a stand for or against the California sterilization program, what would it be? How would you refute the other side's main arguments?

4. Present arguments for *both* sides on a controversy without giving away your viewpoint. Give equal space, detail and accuracy to both sides.

Researched Persuasive Essay using MLA-Style Documentation

· ·

Genetically Modified Food
Caroline Ward

Somewhere in Southeast Asia, a little girl in a poor village has a problem. She cannot see well anymore, especially at night, and will eventually go blind. She is sick because her immune system cannot fight infections. In fact, there is a fifty percent chance she will die—all because her diet consists mainly of rice, and rice does not have enough beta-carotene for her body to convert into vitamin A ("Vitamin Deficiency" 34). But there is hope for her and the other 800 million people in the world suffering from malnutrition (James 21). Scientists are developing genetically modified foods with nutritional enhancements, such as rice with higher levels of beta-carotene, increased resistance to disease and drought, higher yield, and the ability to grow in salty or nutritionally deficit soil.

"Genetically modified" (GM) essentially means that scientists have taken DNA from one plant or organism that has a desirable trait, like disease resistance, and spliced it into DNA from a plant that does not have that trait. GM foods particularly benefit developing countries, which are the least equipped to feed their people. Much of the soil available for farming in countries like Brazil, Colombia, Venezuela, and Indonesia cannot sustain crops because it is either too acidic or lacks nutrients, and it has been that way since "before humankind appeared on the planet" (Borlaug 135). GM crops that can grow in bad soil and higher-yielding GM crops can provide possible solutions to this problem.

Unlike farmers in the United States and other developed countries, plant disease and drought can completely devastate some farmers in Asia, South America, and Africa. These farmers depend on harvests to feed their families for an entire year. If they lose their crops to disease or drought, they go hungry. If genetic engineering provides crops that are more resistant to disease or drought, those farmers and their families have a much better chance of surviving.

GM foods can also be beneficial to developed countries like the USA. One benefit of herbicide tolerant crops (ones engineered to

→

survive weed killing treatments) is that farmers should be able to use gentler chemical sprays on the crops. The same goes for insect resistant crops like *Bt* corn, which is modified to produce a natural bacterium that is toxic to some common insect pests. Robert Horsch of the Monsanto Company, a leading manufacturer of GM seeds, also claims that *Bt* corn has a five to fifteen percent higher yield than non-GM corn, because the farmers use gentler chemical sprays (63). Increased nutritional value can also be beneficial. Won't kids (and adults) across the country rejoice if they have to eat fewer vegetables to get the same amount of vitamins and minerals?

Despite these promises, many people are skeptical of genetically modified foods because of the risks. First, they are concerned about possible adverse effects of GM foods on our health. Some claim that a genetically engineered substance designed to make dairy cows produce more milk, called recombinant bovine somatotropin (rbST) or recombinant bovine growth hormone (rBGH), can be dangerous to humans.

Ronnie Cummins, director of the Organic Consumers Association, argues that milk from those cows contains high levels of IGF-1, a protein hormone similar to insulin that has been shown to promote cancer in humans (39). However, protein hormones have no effect when ingested orally, which is why diabetics need to *inject* insulin. Additionally, IGF-I is normally present in milk, and the difference in levels is very small. Therefore, the Food and Drug Administration (FDA) has determined that IGF-I in milk from rbST–supplemented cows poses no significant health risk (United States, FDA, CVM n. pag.).

Some people have also voiced concerns about antibiotic residues in milk from rbST-supplemented cows, because they do have a slightly greater chance of developing udder infections that need to be treated with antibiotics (United States, FDA, CVM n. pag.). The overuse of antibiotics can lead to germs and bacteria evolving and developing resistances to antibiotics. If that happens, doctors could not fight viruses, making it possible for a common stomach flu to become an epidemic. However, milk from cows treated with antibiotics is discarded for several days, and new milk is tested for antibiotics before it goes to a milk processing plant. If the milk tests positive for residues, it is rejected for human consumption immediately (United States, FDA, CFSAN n. pag.).

→

Cummins and other opponents of GM foods also worry about the risk of allergic reactions. In 1996, Pioneer Hi-Bred spliced DNA from Brazil nuts into soybeans because the nuts contain an amino acid that natural soybeans have little of, and they were searching for a more nutritious animal feed. But researchers at the University of Nebraska found that the modified soybeans could cause allergic reactions in people sensitive to Brazil nuts. The company ceased plans for production, and the soybeans never made it onto the market (36). Milk, nuts, fish, and wheat cause most people's allergies (DeGregori 127). However, if the use of DNA from these foods is limited and properly labeled, then the risk of potentially dangerous allergic reactions should be greatly reduced.

Safety testing is essential, as the soybean case proves, but the tests themselves must be conducted carefully. In 1995, the Rowett Research Institute in Scotland hired British biochemist Arpad Pusztai to conduct a government-funded independent study on genetically engineered potatoes. All was well until 1998, when Pusztai announced preliminary findings that the GM potatoes were damaging the lab rats' immune systems and digestive tracts. Support for GM crops and food was already shaky in Europe, and Pusztai's announcement added fuel to the fire. The director of the Institute himself looked into Pusztai's work and discovered the experiments were flawed. The researchers had "included too few animals per diet group, and lacked controls such as a standard rodent diet" (Kuiper et al. n. pag.). Pusztai and his team were suspended and the experiments were never completed.

Another issue is the effect of GM crops on the environment and wildlife. In 1998, a study claimed that pollen from *Bt* corn was toxic to Monarch butterflies, who feed on milkweed that grows in and around cornfields. However, this study was done in the laboratory by feeding the butterflies milkweed dusted with *Bt* corn pollen in much higher concentrations than would ever be found in a normal field. After a field study, a group of independent researchers concluded that the actual risk to Monarch butterflies was negligible (Sears et al. 6).

However, there is the possibility, especially with *Bt* crops, of insects and weeds becoming resistant to herbicides and pesticides. Organic farmers have been spraying *Bt* on their crops for years, but

→

they have been careful to use it sparingly, because they knew the insects would eventually evolve and develop immunity to *Bt*. The *Bt* crops, however, chum out their pesticide all the time, regardless of whether or not they have an insect problem. The insects are then much more likely to become resistant, like the antibiotic-resistant viruses previously mentioned (Halweil 142).

Though evolution can't be stopped and eventually the insects and weeds will develop resistance, the Environmental Protection Agency has instituted safeguards to slow the process. Farmers who use *Bt* crops are required to set aside part of their fields for regular crops, therefore allowing "insects that have acquired some *Bt* resistance to breed with those that have not, diluting the resistance trait" (Brown 57). Furthermore, a new genetic engineering technique being developed could help avoid these risks almost entirely, because most insects and weeds are exposed to genetic modification through plant pollen. With this new technique, all of the modified genes would be carried through the plants' female reproductive systems; therefore, the pollen (which is male) would not contain any modified genes (Jung 31).

Some people are also concerned about intellectual property rights (IPRs). Under current IPR laws, private corporations can patent their genetically engineered seeds, making it illegal for farmers to save seeds from their harvest for next year's crop, unlike with traditionally bred plants. Some companies have employed "terminator" technology that renders the seeds sterile (Cummins 80). Even if the farmers tried to save seeds for next year's crop, they simply wouldn't grow. This means they need to buy seed every year, and while some commercial growers can handle this expense, most small-scale farmers cannot.

Without patents, though, private corporations would have no way to commercialize their product and make a profit on it, and therefore no reason to invest in this research. Without investments from corporations, biotechnology research would depend on the government for funding. Since it cannot usually give science top priority, it is unlikely research would progress much.

Unfortunately, there is no easy solution to the intellectual property rights problem. GM seeds are more expensive than regular seeds and will be for a while. But farmers may be able to eventually

→

reduce their production costs by using fewer chemical pesticides and raise profits by getting a higher yield per crop.

For developing countries, some private companies are working on agreements with foreign governments and researchers to help them reap some benefits of GM crops and foods. For instance, Robert Horsch says that Monsanto is sharing its "intellectual property and technical knowledge" on disease resistant sweet potatoes with Kenyan scientists (63). The U.S. government is also working on bills to aid developing countries in conducting their own GM research. Congress recently held a hearing about funding the National Science Foundation's (NSF) research into agricultural biotechnology, including genetic modification. One of the bills proposed authorized the NSF to establish research partnerships with scientists in developing countries (United States, Committee on Science 2). At the hearing, Dr. Mary Clutter, an assistant director of the NSF, said, "Perhaps the single most effective way to help the developing world . . . is to provide the solid scientific knowledge base and efficient research tools, including trained scientists, that can be applied to local problems" (Clutter n. pag.).

In light of my research, I believe genetically modified foods have great promise, especially to developing countries that desperately need to feed their people. The possible benefits seem to outweigh the risks, especially when I consider the 800 million people in the world like that little girl in Southeast Asia.

With regard to the GM foods already on the market, I believe they are safe for consumers. The companies producing these crops and foods have done extensive analyses that have been reviewed and approved by the FDA. As I have shown, many of the arguments frequently raised against GM foods can be easily refuted. However, I hope more independent studies will be conducted to show skeptics that GM foods are safe and can be beneficial to people through increased nutritional value; higher yield; and resistance to insects, herbicides, drought, bad soil conditions, and disease.

Works Cited

Borlaug, Norman. *Genetically Engineered Food Could End World Hunger.* Genetic Engineering: Opposing Viewpoints. Opposing Viewpoints Series. James Torr, ed. Greenhaven Press, Inc., CA: 2001. 129–136.

Brown, Kathryn. "Seeds of Concern." *Scientific American* April 2001: 50–57.

Clutter, Mary. *Agricultural Biotechnology Research.* Testimony at the Hearing on Strengthening NSF Sponsored Agricultural Biotechnology Research. U.S. House of Representatives, Committee on Science, Subcommittee on Research. Washington: 25 Sept. 2001. EBSCOhost. EBSCO Publishing. Central Maine Technical College Lib. 28 Sept. 2001, <http://www.ebscohost.com>.

Cummins, Ronnie, and Ben Lilliston. *Genetically Engineered Food: A Self-Defense Guide for Consumers.* Marlowe and Company: New York, 2000.

DeGregori, Thomas R. *Genetically Engineered Food Is Not Dangerous.* Genetic Engineering: Opposing Viewpoints. Opposing Viewpoints Series. James Torr, ed. Greenhaven Press, Inc., CA: 2001. 119–128.

Halweil, Brian. *Genetically Engineered Food Will Not Help End World Hunger.* Genetic Engineering: Opposing Viewpoints. Opposing Viewpoints Series. James Torr, ed. Greenhaven Press, Inc., CA: 2001.137–146.

Horsch, Robert B. Interview with Sasha Nemecek. "Does the World Need GM Foods?" *Scientific American* Apr. 2001: 62–65.

James, Clive. *Transgenic Crops Worldwide: Current Situation and Future Outlook.* Agricultural Biotechnology in Developing Countries: Towards Optimizing Benefits for the Poor. Matin Qaim, Anatole F. Krattiger and Joachim von Braun, eds. Kluwer Academic Publishers, Netherlands: 2000. 11–23.

Jung, Christian. *Molecular Tools for Plant Breeding.* Agricultural Biotechnology in Developing Countries: Towards Optimizing Benefits for the Poor. Matin Qaim, Anatole F. Krattiger and Joachim von Braun, eds. Kluwer Academic Publishers. Netherlands: 2000. 25–37.

→

Kuiper, Harry A., Hub P.J.M. Noteborn, and Ad A.C.M. Peijnenburg. "Adequacy of Methods for Testing the Safety of Genetically Modified Foods." *Lancet* 16 Oct., 1999. Vol. 354, Issue 9187, p. 13151. *EBSCOhost*. EBSCO Publishing. Central Maine Technical College Lib. 8 Oct. 2001 <http://www.ebscohost.com>.

Sears, Mark K, et al. *Impact of Bt Corn Pollen on Monarch Butterfly Populations: A Risk Assessment.* Proceedings of the National Academy of Sciences of USA. 14 Sept. 2000. 3 Oct. 2001 <http://www.pnas.org/cgi/doi/pnas.21132999>.

U.S. House of Representatives, Committee on Science, Subcommittee on Research. *Hearing Charter: Strengthening NSF Sponsored Agricultural Biotechnology Research.* Washington: 25 Sept. 2001. 3 Oct. 2001 <http://www.house.gov/science/research/sep25/res_charter_09250 l.htm>.

---.Food and Drug Administration, Center for Food Safety and Applied Nutrition. 2000. *National Milk Drug Residue Data Base: Fiscal Year 2000 Annual Report.* 11 Dec. 2001 <http://www.cfsan.fda.gov/-ear/milkrp00.html>.

---.Food and Drug Administration, Center for Veterinary Medicine. 1998. *Report on the Food and Drug Administration's Review of the Safety of Bovine Somatotropin.* 2 Dec. 2001 <http://www.fda.gov/cvm/index/bst/RBRPTFNL.htm>.

"Vitamin Deficiency, Dependency, and Toxicity." *Merck Manual of Diagnosis and Therapy.* 17th ed. Merck Research Laboratories, NJ: 1999. 33–51.

DISCUSSION

1. Would more anecdotes like the one in the introduction have improved or detracted from the essay? Explain.

2. What does the author do to show she is an ethical arguer?

3. Outline the essay's main headings. How much is devoted to proposing an idea and how much to refutation? Do you agree with the proportion? Explain.

4. Think of one other worry or concern about GM food that was not raised. Are you more or less willing to accept GM food after reading this research paper?

Literary Research Paper Using Comparison and MLA Documentation

....

Responsibility and the Odyssey
John Barzelay

In the first pages of Homer's *Odyssey*, the Greek God Zeus introduces the theme of responsibility: "Ah, how shameless—the way these mortals blame the gods. From us alone, they say, come all their miseries. Yes, but they themselves, with their own reckless ways, compound their pains beyond their proper share" (Homer 78). The tale will demonstrate how irresponsible men are held accountable for their excesses. It will take twenty years to transform Odysseus from a fearless, irreverent, reckless boy into a responsible, self-controlled man.

Now consider the controversy surrounding attention deficit disorder—and how the *Odyssey* addresses this problem. ADD is used to describe an inattentive, overactive, noncompliant child with poor impulse control (Breggin n. pag.). Four million ADD-diagnosed children each year are prescribed Ritalin, a stimulant medication (Diller, "Nearly" n. pag.).

In a letter to the *New York Times,* one physician asks whether vague and subjective symptoms including "often fights with hands or feet or squirms in seat . . . leaves seat in classroom" and "has difficulty awaiting turn" could be explained by something other than a neurological problem. He suggests that many factors may lead children to behave this way: "a spirited, creative nature that defies conformity . . . inconsistent discipline or lack of unconditional love . . . boring and oversized classrooms . . . ." In short, the ADD label is "attached to children who are in reality deprived of appropriate adult attention" (Breggin n. pag.). The National Institute of Health admits that there is no valid diagnostic test for ADD (Huffington n. pag.). Neurologist Fred Baughman cites estimates of the frequency of ADD that vary from 1 in 3 to 1 in 1,000 and asks, "Is ADD, after all, in the eye of the beholder?" (Breggin and Breggin n. pag.).

Early in the book, Homer describes the misery that Odysseus's wife and son endure at the hands of brazen suitors who hope to wed the supposed widow, Penelope. Odysseus's son, Telemachus,

→

blames the god Zeus for his misfortune: "Zeus is to blame. He deals to each and every laborer on this earth whatever doom he pleases" (Homer 89). These are the words of a boy who sees himself as a helpless victim. This self-image perpetuates his victimization.

But growing up means becoming responsible for oneself. And Telemachus's transformation from child to adult begins when the goddess Athena arouses his dormant manhood by instructing him: "Think how to drive these suitors from your hall at daybreak. Summon the island's lords to full assembly, give your orders to all and call the gods to witness. Tell the suitors to scatter sail in quest for news of your father. Then . . . think hard for a way to kill these suitors. You must not cling to your boyhood any longer. It is time you were a man" (86–89). She shows Telemachus he is not helpless, that passivity makes him guilty of complicity.

This same phenomenon occurs with children diagnosed with ADD. Studies show that labeled children tend to hold themselves less accountable for their behavior. The ADD label encourages victim-like passivity or a sense of persecution. One author says, "Self-image for children is highly dependent on peer opinion. . . . Once labeled, it may take them well into adulthood to learn that they have a choice" (Diller, "Culture" n. pag.).

The suitors indignantly deny any responsibility for devouring Odysseus's family's worldly goods by blaming Penelope for being so attractive (Homer 96–99). By fixing blame on her, they rationalize their outrageous behavior.

Just so, we find that diagnosing children as ADD merely relieves us of responsibility. Diller says, "Parents of children who receive the diagnosis often describe the event as tremendously liberating and empowering. The idea that their problems are not of their own making but controlled by skewed brain chemistry and genetics represents salvation from a sense of failure" ("Culture" n. pag.). Shockingly, while prescriptions of Ritalin to children diagnosed with ADD jumped 20% since 1989, the percentage of those receiving psychotherapy dropped from 40 to 25% (Huffington n. pag.). Such statistics show that health-care providers prefer relatively cheap drugs to costly therapy. It also demonstrates our lazy culture's inclination to medicate social problems rather than act on them. Diane McGuinness describes the crossroad in the debate concerning

→

ADD: "Research . . . indicates that ADD and hyperactivity as 'syndromes' simply do not exist. We have invented a disease, given it medical sanction, and now must disown it. The major question is how we go about destroying the monster we have created . . . and still save face" (Breggin n. pag.).

The brazen suitors show that to enjoy one's folly, a man will embrace with dogmatic fervor any explanation that relieves him of responsibility, even if the consequences of doing nothing are horrible. Odysseus revenges himself on the suitors, cracking open their skulls and washing the floor in their blood (Homer 448–51).

The failure to correct the ADD fallacy will also have serious consequences. One developmental psychologist at UC Berkeley reports that children on Ritalin are three times more likely to develop a taste for cocaine. The Drug Enforcement Agency reports increasing Ritalin abuse among adolescents. Huffington concludes, "When the government spends $16 billion a year on the drug war, and when more than half those in jail are nonviolent drug offenders, isn't it time we connect the dots between prescription drugs and street drugs? How many more prisons do we have to build to jail offenders who, earlier in life, we have drugged with abandon?" (n. pag.). Not only are we turning out Ritalin zombies; we have made the concepts of self-discipline and freedom of choice obsolete. This indicts our society, but the real tragedy is the child whose life is needlessly and irreparably harmed.

In Odysseus's encounter with Polyphemus the Cyclops, both Polyphemus and Odysseus first reject responsibility. Polyphemus, the son of Poseidon, harbors no fear of Zeus. For when Odysseus entreats him for hospitality in the name of Zeus who guards all guests, the Cyclops contemptuously eats two of Odysseus's men. Likewise, Odysseus, whose lineage springs from Zeus, blinds the one-eyed son of Poseidon to escape.

As the crew escapes, Odysseus taunts the Cyclops and proudly announces who has humiliated Poseidon's son. Polyphemus groans back: "Oh no, no—that prophesy [was made] years ago. It all comes back to me with a vengeance now! Telemachus warned me all this would come to pass someday, that I'd be blinded here at the hands of one Odysseus. Come here, Odysseus, let me give you a guest gift and urge Poseidon . . . to speed you home. I am his son . . . and

→

he will heal me if he pleases" (Homer 227). Polyphemus realizes his own reckless sacrilege caused his pain. Offering a guest gift shows his respect for Zeus.

Odysseus, however, brimming with indignation and pride, shows contempt for Poseidon in responding, "Heal you . . . Would to god I could strip you of life and breath and ship you down to the House of Death as surely as no one will heal your eye, not even your earth-quake god himself!" (Homer 227–28). Odysseus's blind arrogance incurs Poseidon's wrath, and it takes 20 years of pounding, rocking, sea-sickening misery to clear his vision. Home at last, he must face another disaster his blindness allowed to happen—the suitors for his wife's hand.

Like Odysseus, we are no longer blind. Twenty-five years of drifting on a fallacy and sowing the seeds of disaster have passed. As the evidence mounts, we can no longer plead ignorance. ADD simply does not exist as the widespread condition psychiatry once claimed. Society must now decide whether it will acknowledge its culpability and minimize the damage, like Polyphemus, or turn a blind eye to the disastrous long-term effects, like Odysseus. Society should leave behind its fantastic explanations and prescription drugs, stop avoiding responsibility, and liberate itself from victimhood.

Works Cited

Breggin, Peter R. "Whose Attention Deficit Disorder Does Ritalin Test?' *New York Times* 20 May 1996: A14. 2 Mar. 1999 <http://www.breggin.com/newyork times.html>.

Breggin, Peter, and Ginger Ross Breggin. "The Hazards of Testing 'Attention-Deficit/Hyperactivity Disorder' with Methylphenidate (Ritalin)." *Center for the Study of Psychiatry and Psychology.* n.d. 2 Mar. 1999 <http://www.breggin.com/newyorktimes.html>.

Diller, Lawrence H. "The Culture of ADD." *Docdiller.* n.d. 2 Mar. 1999 <http://www.docdiller.com/html/six-1.htm>.

Diller, Lawrence H. "Nearly 5 Million Americans Take Ritalin Daily." *Docdiller.* n.d. 2 Mar. 1999 <http://www.docdiller.com>.

→

Homer. *Odyssey*. New York: Penguin, 1997.

Huffington, Arianna. "U.S. Attention Deficit on Legal Drug Risk." *Center for the Study of Psychiatry and Psychology*. n.d. 2 Mar. 1999 <http://breggin.com/ritalin AH2.html>.

DISCUSSION

1. Evaluate the sources used in this essay.
2. Is the author's focus primarily on the *Odyssey* as literature or on ADD?
3. Are there any flaws in the comparison between the two?

Handbook of English

17

Myths about the English Language

Myth #1: There is a logical reason for our language's rules. **Reality:** Rules of language are a *convenience*. There's no reason why "cat" can't be spelled "rat," "hat," or "lypd." The letters and sounds of words have no logical connection to objects they represent. Language is simply an agreement people make that they will share these arbitrary definitions. **Communication and complex thoughts would be impossible without such an agreement. That agreement is called "standard English" and it is the language used for government, education, business, and publishing—in other words, the language that provides a person with money, prestige, power, and status.**

Myth #2: Standard English is chiseled on stone tablets. **Reality:** Our language constantly changes. English is really a combination of old German, Celtic, Latin, French, Spanish, Norse, and many other languages that it met through history. English also mixed and matched grammar the way no other language ever has. This makes English the most creative, inclusive, and perhaps democratic language in the world, but also the most contradictory and confusing. It is still changing today. Shakespeare would only know about half of the words we use today. Rules only slow down the changes.

Sanity is perhaps the ability to punctuate.

—W. H. AUDEN

You just can't trust the English language.

—NEDRA LAMAR

There's only one "z" in "is."

—GEORGE S. KAUFMAN

451

Myths about English Usage

Myth #3: You cannot begin sentences with "and," "but" or "or" because these conjunctions must join two things. **Reality:** Prestigious writers often start sentences with these words because they're great transitions. Computer grammar checks pounce on this because it is something they *can* do. Ignore them.

Myth #4: Put commas where you hear a pause. **Reality:** Do this and you'll be wrong about half the time because pauses come where semicolons, colons, dashes, periods, and no punctuation are right. Commas indicate where key elements of sentences must be separated for clarity. Learn the rules in the handbook.

Myth #5: Don't use "I" because it makes your writing sound too personal. **Reality:** Which is better: "I think" or "One might think"? The impersonal "one" is a tone-killer in all but the most formal writing, and an "I" hides behind it anyway. Don't shout "Me! Me! Me!" at readers, but don't worry about squashing every "I."

Myth #6: Computers will fix your errors. **Reality:** Use spell-checkers and grammar-checkers, of course! But learn enough yourself to catch what computers miss—especially commas and usage errors—and to know when your computer gets spooked by our illogical language and finds errors where there are none.

Myth #7: Your job as a writer is to avoid mistakes, and your professor's job as a teacher is to correct mistakes. **Reality:** Your job is to say something worth saying with the most vivid details and most accurate words and to keep mistakes to a minimum so they don't interfere. Your professor's job is to help you do all three. Grammar mistakes irritate readers and teachers, but what they care about most are great ideas, details, and language.

Myth #8: Passing this course proves you have mastered English. **Reality:** Passing is one step forward in your lifetime of writing. Enjoy the journey.

Punctuation

Punctuation is a quiet signal. You absorb it without thinking, as you do with small words like "if" or "and."

When you mispunctuate, a reader can usually figure out what you intended to say. But you make her read twice what should only have to be read once, and you may give her an entirely wrong idea. For instance, reread the first sentence in this paragraph without the comma. Doesn't it sound for a second that you're punctuating a reader? Sometimes punctuation errors can be more serious. Look at these two sentences:

- All foreign fruit plants are free from duty.
- All foreign fruit, plants are free from duty.

The first means that young trees and bushes that will bear fruit may enter the country without paying an import fee. The second means all fruit as well as plants are duty free. The comma in the second sentence means two items are duty free. Number 1 was what The United States Congress intended in a law it passed. But a congressional clerk punctuated incorrectly as it is in 2 and the error cost the United States $2 million in lost import taxes before the law could be re-approved without the comma.

, COMMA

1. Use a Comma to Separate an Introductory Clause or Phrase from the Main Subject and Verb of the Sentence. The comma signals the end of introductory words and the beginning of the sentence's main subject **(S)** and verb **(V)**. For example:

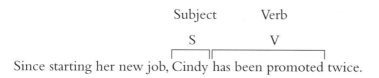

The typical English sentence starts with its subject (a noun), tells you what the subject does (the verb), and usually ends with a modifier **(M)** that further explains what these two are up to.

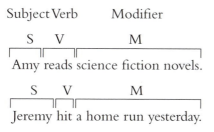

Even when sentences are longer, the "normal" pattern still holds.

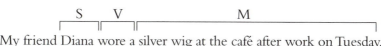

However, when the modifier comes first as it does in the sentence you're reading now and you're desperately looking for the main subject and verb,

the writer must help by marking the end of the introductory words with a comma (after the word "verb" here. "Writer" is the subject, and "must help" is the verb). **Hint:** If the following words begin a sentence, you will usually need a comma at the end of the introductory words:

If	Since	When	Because
As	Although	Before	After
In	On	At	With

Verbs ending in "ing"

If I get an A in Chemistry, I will explode with joy.

Because he was running late for his midterm exam, John dashed out of the locker room wearing only his sneakers and a smile.

Wearing only his sneakers and a smile, John dashed out of the locker room.

If it's a very short introductory phrase, there's no need for the comma because a good reader can see the entire sentence as a unit.

In a moment we will join you.

Before the film Jackie told us the whole plot.

At noon we'll go home.

Even if it's short, however, introductory words that would confuse a reader if unpunctuated need to be separated:

Next to Janis, Bob is ugly. (Bob looks ugly when compared to Janis. If the comma followed "next," it would mean that Janis thought Bob was ugly.)

■ **PRACTICE 17-1** Write five sentences about any subject. Start them with these five words: if, when, since, although, as.

2. A Comma Separates Items Listed in a Series.

Mario walked into the faculty locker room by accident and found a pile of moldy papers, a textbook, and a retired Latin professor on the floor. He dropped his sneakers, socks, and towel.

The serial comma before the conjunction is preferred, but not necessary.

This rule also applies to a series of adjectives modifying the same noun—but *only* if you can substitute an "and" for the comma.

> The Latin professor gave a musical, sputtering snore. His nose was a pinkish red and matched his pink, red, and tan socks. (The commas after "musical" and "pink" could each be replaced by "and." An "and" cannot be put between "pinkish" and "red," so that gets no comma.)

> **Wrong:** The professor gave a most, musical snore. (An "and" cannot be substituted for the comma.)

■ **PRACTICE 17-2** How would you punctuate these sentences:
A television "survivor" needs a lack of fear a lack of inhibition and a lack of brains.
The dean recited an amazing itemized list of Jill's violations of college policy.

, 3. A Comma Separates Two Groups of Words that Could Be Punctuated as Separate Sentences When These Sentences Are Joined by a Conjunction. These are the conjunctions:

and	**nor**
but	**for**
or	**so**

This comma tells readers a complete thought has just ended, and they must regroup to look for a new subject and verb.

```
       S      V            M              C      S
Mario nudged the Latin Professor with one foot, and the professor

       V            M
muttered a few phrases from Cicero.
```

He could scream for help, or he could leave quietly and say nothing.

If the reader sees an "and" or other conjunction and *no comma,* the signal is different. It tells the reader that whatever is on the right side of the conjunction still refers back to the subject or verb on the left side:

$$\text{S} \quad \text{V} \quad\quad \text{M} \quad\quad\quad \text{C} \quad\quad\quad \text{M}$$

Mario asked if the professor was hurt or if he could get him a Latin text. ("Mario asked" applies to both "if" clauses.)

The professor grunted and asked if he was in Rome. ("Professor" before the "and" applies to both verbs "grunted" and "asked.")

Hint: When you come to any conjunction, separately read what is written before the conjunction and what is written after the conjunction. If *both* are complete sentences, you need a comma. If either part is less than a complete sentence, don't use a comma.

■ **PRACTICE 17-3** Punctuate the following:

Cruella kicked the Dalmatian in the side and then laughed wickedly.

Paul Bunyan had a giant blue ox named Babe and they traveled together decimating forests and calling it progress.

■ **PRACTICE 17-4** Write two sentences that contain an "and." One should require a comma before the "and," and one should not.

, 4. Commas Separate Nonessentials from the Main Sentence. This is one of the uses of commas that frequently occurs when you hear pauses in a sentence, but you will do two stars better if you understand the logic behind it. When you have a *parenthetical comment,* a comment like this one that sounds as though it belongs between parentheses, you must separate it. The commas signal the reader that we are making a side trip. To test whether you need commas, see if the sentence makes sense if you leave out the words in question.

$$\text{S} \quad\quad\quad \text{M} \quad\quad\quad\quad \text{V} \quad\quad\quad \text{M}$$

Mario, his pulse starting to race, began backing toward the locker room door. (First modifier can be left out without damaging the main idea of sentence—needed.)

The Latin professor, who wore only gray tweed undershorts, shouted, *"Illiterati non carborundum."*

Mario, however, was racing for the health office.

Remember, if the words in question are essential to understanding the sentence, *don't* use commas; commas set off nonessential information. The following are both correct as they are:

George Smith, who plagiarized a term paper, was expelled from college.

All students who plagiarize term papers should be expelled from college. (In the second, "who plagiarize term papers" cannot be dropped from the sentence—it is essential to the meaning, so there are no commas.)

The following sentences are both correct as they stand. But how does the meaning change when we add the commas?

The president of the college says the professor is misinformed.

The president of the college, says the professor, is misinformed.

How would this sentence from the *Wall Street Journal* change if we removed the comma?

In the past decade small stocks returned 13%, above their 12% annual gain since 1926.

A group of words at the end of a sentence can also be considered extra information. If the words are necessary to the main idea in the sentence, *do not use a comma*.

Write all test answers in the blue book, remembering to skip lines. ("Remembering". . ." is extra information.)

The war is over because we starved the enemy into submission. (The *reason* the war is over is the key idea, so "because". . ." is necessary.)

Don't leave the party if you've been drinking. ("If". . ." is necessary.)

Place marker words or phrases are considered nonessentials and set off with commas. Place markers are expressions like "thirdly," "in conclusion," "therefore," "next," "however," and "on the other hand."

■ **PRACTICE 17-5** Punctuate the following:
Senator Windbag on the other hand voted for the law.
Meeting Martin O'Malley the mayor of Baltimore was the big moment of the trip.
Directly witnessing child abuse however can change a person's mind about its seriousness.

, 5. Use a Comma to Separate Quotations from Taglines.

(See the section on quotations on page 462.)

Gloria told the class, "Julius Caesar was a Roman geezer."

9 **6. Use a Comma after the Greeting in a Personal Letter. Business Letters Use a Colon.**

Dear Wendy,
Dear Senator Cumulous:

9 **7. Use a Comma to Separate Direct Address of Someone.**

Sarah, would you come here?
I wish you'd look at this, Doctor.

9 **8. Use a Comma to Separate the Day from the Year in a Date:**

September 19, 2009.

9 **9. Use a Comma to Separate What Would Be Separate Lines in an Address:**

I visited my former lawyer at Cell Block 33, 12 Dawson Street, Sing Sing Prison, San Francisco, California 92758.

■ **PRACTICE 17-6** Illustrate the first five comma rules by creating a sentence for each that uses commas correctly.

■ **PRACTICE 17-7** **Comma Exercise.** Correct any comma errors in the following:

TO: ALL STUDENTS   May 3 2009

FROM: DR. R. J. FACTOTUM

       Dean of Academic Studies

RE: Graduation Competency Exam

The college is instituting a competency examination which must   5
be passed to graduate so all students should study the following
questions carefully.

BIOLOGY PRACTICUM, Part 1. Create life with your Bunsen burner
a test tube and two spoonfuls of the cafeteria's Jell-o.

Part 2. After your professor approves your life-form you should   10
make it evolve to the level of an earthworm or a TV talk show host
whichever comes first.

BIOLOGY WRITTEN TEST. The platypus lays eggs like a bird, swims
like a fish, and has hair like a mammal but it has no wings, gills, or

eyelashes. If a female platypus were to mate with a polar bear what   15
would be the genetic makeup of the offspring?

PHILOSOPHY. Using Socratic and Aristotelian methods of inquiry
you must explain life. What will humans assuming they still exist
then believe life means in the year 2050? Be concise, and specific.

ENGLISH. From memory, rewrite *Moby Dick,* also called *The Whale*   20
or *Hamlet.*

MATH, Part 1. Applying the principles of probability studied in
Math 151 you must defeat your math professor at blackjack poker
or gin rummy. A deck of unmarked unopened cards must be sup-
plied by the student.   25

Part 2. Students must divide any number by zero, and record the
result if they live.

Answer Key to Comma Practice 17-7
Line

1. Separate day from year in date. "... 3, 2009 ..."
6. Separate two complete sentences joined by a conjunction. "... gradu-
    ate, so ..."
8. Separate items in a series. "... burner, a test tube ..." Comma after
    "tube" is optional, but be consistent.
10. Separate introductory words. "... form, you ..."
11. Separate nonessential information. "... host, whichever ..."
14. Separate two complete sentences joined by conjunction. "... mam-
    mal, but ..."
15. Separate introductory words. "... bear, what ..."
17. Separate introductory words. "... inquiry, you ..."
18. Separate parenthetical, nonessential information. "... humans, assum-
    ing they still exist then, believe ..."
19. No comma before conjunction unless there are two sentences.
    "... concise and ..."
20. Separate end of parenthetical material. "... *Whale,* or ..."
23. Separate introductory material. "... 151, you ..."
23. Separate items in a series. "... blackjack, poker ..." Comma after
    "poker" is optional.
24. Separate items in a series. "... unmarked, unopened ..."
26. No comma before conjunction unless there are two sentences.
    "... zero and ..."

SEMICOLON

Semicolons Connect Two Complete Sentences That Are Closely Related. The words on both sides of a semicolon must be independent sentences; you could have a period there instead.

> Hawaii has the Liberty Bowl; Florida has the Gator Bowl.

> We can satisfy almost all our energy needs with solar power; the main energy needed is the effort to pass the laws.

> **Wrong:** Our soccer team lost by a 7–4 score; even though they had twice as many shots on goal as our opponents. (What follows the semicolon is not a complete sentence.)

> **Wrong:** There are two billion hungry people on earth, that's more than all the people who lived in the entire nineteenth century! (The comma should be a semicolon because there are two complete sentences.)

Do _not_ use a semicolon when two sentences are joined by a conjunction; a comma is used there.

> **Wrong:** The boss wants sales; and he wants them now.

_Do_ use a semicolon if two sentences are separated by "however," "therefore," "yet," or "nevertheless" (the conjunctive adverbs).

> Colorado River University may have carp in its river, but Colorado Creek College has trout in its pond. (comma comes before the conjunction.)

> Colorado River University may have carp in its river; however, Colorado Creek College has trout in its pond. (semicolon before a "however" joining two complete sentences.)

COLON

A Colon's Main Use Is to Emphasize a Sharp Break Between a Statement and Something That Follows: a List, a Comment, a Quotation, a Question, or an Explanation. Hint: think of a colon as meaning "that is" or "namely." If one of these sounds right, a colon is your best choice.

> Three things would make the Student Union perfect: a popcorn vendor, sawdust spread on the floor, and a ringmaster.

> Everyone should remember Henry David Thoreau's last words: "Moose, Indian."

Because the colon is used only when you want to make a dramatic break, do not use it when your list or explanation follows *smoothly* from what comes before:

Wrong: This handbook consists of: rules, rules, and more rules.

■ **PRACTICE 17-8** Create a sentence using a semicolon correctly and another correctly using a colon.

OTHER PUNCTUATION

! **EXCLAMATION POINT:** They're overused! They shout too much!! Save them for big moments!!! Don't use more than one!!!

— **DASH:** You are never required to use a dash—commas, colons, or parentheses can always substitute for the dash, for it **separates a nonessential part of the sentence from the main idea** (see comma rule 4). A dash has more flair than commas, so poets—Emily Dickinson, for instance—like to use them.

> Professor Snerdman—a burly bull of a man with flaming red hair—charges into his lectures just looking for a student foolish enough to wave his hand.

— **HYPHEN:** A hyphen indicates **a word split** at the end of a typed line. *Only* divide words at syllable breaks—which are indicated in dictionaries. Hyphens also **connect groups of words that function as a single unit:** a happy-go-lucky boss is not a happy boss, go boss, or lucky boss. If you can substitute an "and" at the problem location, use a comma.

> sister-in-law
>
> my thirty-first birthday
>
> two-thirds vote
>
> the hairy, old horse

( ) **PARENTHESES: Parentheses separate nonessential information** (definitions, citations for sources, or by-the-way comments like this) from the main text. No punctuation marks should precede a parenthesis, and all punctuation that normally would come at that point should follow the end parenthesis mark. (The exception is a parenthetical statement that is a complete sentence, like this one.)

> When General Motors fired the Flint auto workers (7,000 in August and another 6,000 in October), the city's tax base collapsed.

General Motors fired 13,000 Flint auto workers in August and October. **(**The city's tax base collapsed.**)**

66 99 QUOTATION MARKS

66 99 **1. Put quotation marks around the titles of short works** (poems, articles, chapters of books), **but use italics or underlining to indicate works long enough to be published on their own** (books, long plays, magazines, newspapers).

> In his research paper, Michael documented the following sources: *The Missoula Times-Union,* O. Henry's "The Gift of the Magi," *Jaws,* a *Newsweek* article called "Bloodshot in Boise," and the entry "Worms" in *Encarta.*

Sacred works (Bible, Quran) and **public documents** (United States Constitution) are *not* italicized or underlined.

66 99 **2. Use quotation marks to indicate speech reported word for word.** If you're doing research, you must record exactly what the writer wrote. If you want to leave out some of what was said, use **ellipsis marks.** Three dots mean you've left out part of a sentence; four dots mean you've left out a sentence or more, or you've left off the end of the sentence you're quoting.

> The press secretary reported, "Senator Jones flew to Hawaii 81 times . . . and to Aruba 79 times while in office."

> Joseph Campbell's best advice was, "Follow your bliss."

If you're writing **dialogue in a narrative,** you also must use quotation marks around what the speakers say. If you don't feel you can report accurately, summarize and *do not* use quotation marks.

> "What a blast!" Billy yelled as he lit the fuse.

> **OR** As he lit the fuse, Billy said he was having a blast.

Here are other guidelines for dialogue:

- Never quote two or more people in dialogue in the same paragraph. If a second person speaks, start a new paragraph, even if only for one word.
- Use **taglines** to identify speakers. A simple "he said" is usually better than "he threateningly implied." In dialogue between only two people, you may leave the taglines out once in a while if it's clear who is speaking.
- Punctuate taglines with commas.
- People's thoughts are *not* put in quotation marks.

SAMPLE DIALOGUE, TAGLINES, AND THOUGHTS

Ricardo approached the registration counter waving a letter. "This says I can't graduate," he said.

"That's right," the secretary said. "See, you haven't completed your program's new course in witchcraft."

"Witchcraft! I'm going into telecommunications."

"Well," she said, "maybe the college curriculum committee thinks you need a broader perspective." Great, Ricardo thought.

■ **PRACTICE 17-9** Write three lines of dialogue in which two speakers exchange ideas. Have fun with it, but punctuate correctly.

3. **Use quotation marks around a word or phrase being referred to as a word.**

The word "computer" comes from "compute."

I want to examine the term "software."

4. **Use single quotation marks for quotations within a quotation.**

Doctor Seaver says, "We must understand poverty, not simply 'pity the suffering of the poor,' as my colleague stated."

Single quotation marks are made with the apostrophe key.

5. **Punctuating quotations.** At the end of quotations, periods and commas go before the quotation mark; semicolons and colons follow it. Question marks and exclamation marks go before the end quotation if they are part of the quotation, after it if they apply to the sentence as a whole.

Merle said, "trick or treat"; then he snapped open his suitcase.

How can we elect a man who says, "Kiss my grits"?

Darren's last question was, "What's for supper?"

Do *not* combine a comma with other punctuation marks in quotations.

Wrong: Ingrid asked, "Where's my scented soap?", and Brian confessed he thought it was Halloween candy. (The comma after the question mark must be deleted, even though it is required by comma rule number 3.)

❯ APOSTROPHE

❯ 1. Use an apostrophe to form a contraction; the apostrophe is located where the missing letters normally would be.

>don't (do not)
>
>who's (who is)
>
>it's (it is)

❯ 2. Use an apostrophe to form possessives. To form the possessive of *all singular nouns* (including those already ending in "s") and *plural* nouns *not* ending in "s," add " 's."

>Pete's ball
>
>James's hat
>
>men's cars
>
>people's park

For plural nouns already ending in "s," only add an apostrophe.

>schools' rules
>
>enemies' weapons
>
>cats' tails

What does the following sentence mean? "I saw cats' eyes staring at me from the woods." It means more than one cat was staring. If it had been "cat's," only one cat was staring.

The apostrophe's two uses conflict where they overlap: at the possessive pronouns. Grammarians awarded the apostrophe to the contractions—who's (who is) and it's (it is)—and allowed the possessive pronouns to be possessive even though they don't have apostrophes: whose, its, his, ours, hers, and so on.

>It's raining outside. (it is)
>
>The sky let loose its heavy rains. (possessive it)
>
>Who's coming to the party? (who is)
>
>Whose party is it? (possessive who)

■ **PRACTICE 17-10** Write a series of sentences that correctly use a dash, a hyphen in a compound word, titles of a chapter and a book, a quotation, a contraction, and a possessive plural. Circle each use.

Capitalization

· ·

1. **Capitalize the first word in every sentence or intentional sentence fragment.**
2. **Capitalize the first letter of all words in a proper noun.**

A proper noun is the name of a specific person, place, thing, organization, or event.

Frederick Douglass	October
Maine	the Northwest
Orange County	Kodak Corporation
San Juan Hill	*Webster's New World Dictionary*
Lake Michigan	Tuesday
the planet Earth	Grandma (but "my grandmother")

Do *not* capitalize the seasons (winter) or general directions (Go northeast a mile).

3. **Capitalize the first word and all important words in a title.**

The Moon and Sixpence

A Dance of Thieves

"Rommel the Desert Fox"

■ **PRACTICE 17-11 Punctuation Exercise.** Correct any errors in punctuation and capitalization in the following:

May 2, 2009

12 Pit Road
Citrus, FL 32881

Marla G. Snooker
President   5
Snooker sales corp.
17 Lemon Lane
Citrus, FL 32881

Dear President Snooker,

I regret that my wife Loretta and I will not be able to attend the   10
companys annual dinner dance at the Elegant Memories diner. Since

Loretta returned to college full time I'm living with a human volcano and its tough keeping up with her. She tears through four classes, and three hours in the library. When Loretta and I arrive home she's still full of energy, however, I'm ready for a nap.   15

All of a sudden she knows about Psychology and even talks to me in spanish. She wants to discuss "Hamlet" and Ode to Joy with me. It's wonderful she's learning so much but I'm worn out listening. At 2 A.M. she'll be reading that yellow marker attached to her hand.

"Do you feel like discussing picassos paintings?" she'll say. "It's   20
2 A.M.!" I'll groan. "Put some zip in your life," she'll say.

A four-hour party will kill me and Loretta has to finish her research paper about illegal whale hunting. There's one thing I need most rest. I hope that you our president will understand.

Sincerely,   25
Boris Backwater

Boris Backwater

KEY TO PRACTICE 17-11

Line

6. Capitalize proper nouns. "... Sales Corp."
9. Colon used in greeting of formal letter. "... Snooker:"
10. Separate interrupter with commas. Dashes acceptable instead of commas. "... wife, Loretta, and ..."
11. Possessive requires apostrophe. "company's"
11. Capitalize proper noun. "Diner"
12. Comma separates introductory material. "... time, I'm ..."
12. Comma separates two complete sentences joined by conjunction. "... volcano, and ..."
13. Contraction, not possessive. "it's"
13. Comma before conjunction *only* if it joins two complete sentences. There's just one here. "... classes and ..."
14. Comma separates introductory words. "... home, she's ..."
15. Semicolon joins two complete sentences when "however" or "therefore" is used. A comma would be used if "but" had been used. "... energy; however ..."
16. It's generic, not a proper noun. "psychology"

17. Capitalize words derived from proper nouns (Spain). "Spanish"

17. Hamlet should be underlined or italicized as a book-length work.

17. "Ode to Joy" must have quotation marks around it—title of a short work.

18. Comma separates two complete sentences joined by conjunction. ". . . much, but . . ."

19. Comma separates nonessential information (unless she's really reading the marker). ". . . reading, that . . ."

20. Capitalize people's names and use apostrophe for the possessive. "Picasso's"

20. New paragraph before "It's." A new paragraph starts when there's a second speaker quoted.

21. New paragraph before "Put."

22. Comma separates two complete sentences joined with a conjunction. " . . . me, and . . ."

23. Colon (or dash) should mark the sharp break. ". . . most: rest."

24. Commas (or dashes) separate nonessential interrupters. ". . . you, our president, will . . ."

Sentence Structure

SENTENCE FRAGMENT

The "normal" English sentence has a subject, verb, and possibly a modifier. Anything less is a sentence fragment or incomplete sentence. Why do English teachers make a big deal about it? Because it shows whether or not you recognize the basic unit of the language.

Most sentence fragments are not like the following: "John the house early" or "Left the house early." Most fragments occur when a writer is nervous about writing a long sentence or when a writer confuses a verb *form* with a main verb. Look at these examples:

> **Fragment:** Rosario put away her teddy bear, kissed her goldfish goodbye, and tore up the photos of her high school boyfriend when she headed off to college. Which turned out to have more fish than good-looking guys.

> **Fragment:** The first college guy she dated reminded her of her guppy. Because he puckered every time she looked at him.

Both examples are typical fragments that should be attached to the previous sentence. The first example lacks a subject in the second part—it needs to refer back to "college" to make sense. The second fragment does have a subject and verb, but it also begins with a "because," which turns what follows into a *dependent clause*. It depends on the first part to have complete meaning. There's no theoretical limit to the length of an English sentence (James Joyce may hold the record with a 50-page sentence in *Ulysses*).

Beware of these key words:

- because
- since
- if
- although
- as
- who
- which
- verbs ending in "ing"

If any of these words begin a sentence, it should be in an introductory phrase or clause with a comma separating it from the main subject and verb. If there is no such place, you've probably written a sentence fragment.

How to fix a sentence fragment:

- Attach the fragment to the previous sentence if it completes the thought.
- Add a subject and/or verb if needed.

Legitimate uses of sentence fragments: to answer your own rhetorical question or to create a fragmented impression in dramatic scenes.

Legitimate Fragment: Why do politicians lie to the public? Because the public wants to be lied to.

Legitimate Fragments: Whack! The stick caught the side of his head. Whack. Dizzy. Spinning images of the windows. Whack! Sal went down.

RUN-ON SENTENCE (COMMA SPLICE)

A run-on sentence is two sentences joined together without proper punctuation. What difference does it make? Here is an actual invitation some professors at my college received for an end-of-the-semester party: "Come to the party and forget your exams, spouses and other attached persons are welcome." We all thought it was going to be a wild party until realizing, at the end of the sentence, that we were only to forget exams. In this case the writer should have either substituted a semicolon for the comma or put a period there and capitalized the "s" in spouses.

Run-on: From the parking lot, Emily listened to the roar of the jets landing at the airport she wished she were going somewhere. (Second sentence begins after "airport.")

Run-on: Tom's biology experiment had an unexpected result, his frog grabbed a scalpel and hopped for freedom. (Second sentence begins after "result.")

Run-on: The security guards pursued the frog toward the student cafeteria, however, the amphibian made good its escape. (Second sentence begins before "however." If a "but" had been there, a comma would be proper.)

How to fix run-on sentences: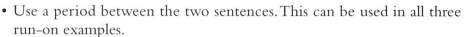
- Use a period between the two sentences. This can be used in all three run-on examples.
- Use a semicolon between the two sentences. This can be used in all three run-on examples.
- Add a comma and conjunction (and, or, but, so, for, nor) between the two sentences if it sounds logical. An "and" could be used in the first run-on example and a "but" in the third, instead of "however." None of the conjunctions seem to fit the second example.
- Make the second sentence a dependent clause attached to the first sentence by adding one of these words between the two sentences: because, since, if, when, although, as. You should NOT use a comma if you use this option. "When" or "because" could be used in the second example.

It may help you to understand sentence structure better if we examine the three types of sentences: simple, compound, and complex. The following abbreviations are used:

S—subject of sentence

V—verb of sentence

M—modifier

C—conjunction

DCl—dependent clause

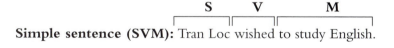

Simple sentence (SVM): Tran Loc wished to study English.

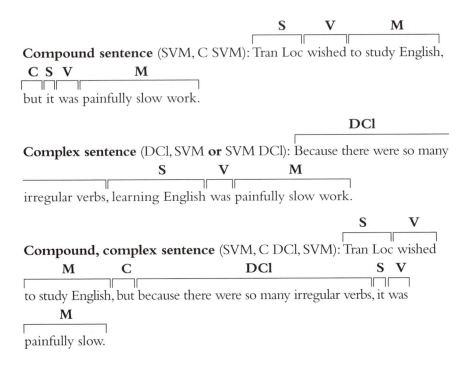

Compound sentence (SVM, C SVM): Tran Loc wished to study English, but it was painfully slow work.

Complex sentence (DCl, SVM **or** SVM DCl): Because there were so many irregular verbs, learning English was painfully slow work.

Compound, complex sentence (SVM, C DCl, SVM): Tran Loc wished to study English, but because there were so many irregular verbs, it was painfully slow.

■ **PRACTICE 17-12** Write one sample sentence of your own to illustrate each of the four types of sentences. Label the parts as illustrated here.

MISPLACED MODIFIERS

A modifier is a word or group of words that describes or adds details to another word or group of words. The italicized sections in the examples are modifiers:

> Chantel played the *Baldwin grand* piano.

> *With tenderness,* Randolph rocked the *beautiful, bald* baby.

The modifier must be placed next to the thing it modifies, or it may accidentally describe something else with comic results:

> **Misplaced:** For Sale: One maple table by elderly lady *with chipped legs.* (an actual newspaper ad)

> **Misplaced:** I was on my way to the doctor's *with rear end trouble* when my car's rear axle gave way, causing the accident.

> **Misplaced:** The accident was caused by a little guy in a small car *with a big mouth.*

The placement of one modifying word can change the meaning of a sentence. How do the following sentences differ?

In the poker game Hector almost won $500.

In the poker game Hector won almost $500.

Consider this gruesome, unintended meaning I once found in a paper:

Misplaced: The police arrested a man in the Mt. Hope Cemetery who said he was digging up corpses trying to make some extra money.

Corrected: The police arrested a man digging up corpses in the Mt. Hope Cemetery; he said he was doing it to make some extra money.

■ **PRACTICE 17-13** Correct any sentence fragments, run-ons, or misplaced modifiers your professor marked on your last paper.

Agreement

"Agreement" means the parts of a sentence are in harmony so readers are not confused. Here are three kinds of agreement to strive for.

TENSE
All verbs must agree in tense unless you clearly prepare a reader for a time shift. **Generally speaking, if your essay starts in the past tense, it should use the past tense throughout. Stay in the present if you start there.**

José *came* to my house and *asked* to use my computer.

José *comes* to my house and *asks* to use my computer.

José *came* to my house often, but now that he *has* his own computer, he *stays* away. ("Now" prepares us for time shift.)

Wrong: José *came* to my house and *asks* to use my computer.

SUBJECT–VERB AGREEMENT
Subjects and their verbs must agree, meaning singular subjects require singular verbs and plural subjects require plural verbs.

For college students, the most common source of mistakes is a **collective noun**—which is a subject that includes more than one individual but is thought of as a unit, so it requires a singular verb.

The wolf pack devours deer. (collective singular)

Wolves devour deer. (plural)

The community is going bankrupt. (collective singular)

Many area businesses are going bankrupt. (plural)

The government decides who is drafted. (collective singular)

Bureaucrats decide who is drafted. (plural)

Everyone is writing a paper this week. (collective singular)

All students are writing papers this week. (plural)

Dual subjects require a plural verb:

Sheri and Rolfe study two hours each night. (But Sheri studies two hours each night.)

NOUN–PRONOUN AGREEMENT

Pronouns represent nouns and must therefore be of the same gender and number (singular or plural) as the nouns they represent.

Paulo wants *his* paper typed.

The dog doesn't care if *its* paper is typed.

Everyone wants *her* hair short these days.

Wrong: A paper should show their writer's style. (its)

Spelling

I am a bad speller. I *need* a dictionary so I don't look stupid. For 35 years I have had to say to myself i before e except after c every time I've spelled *believe* or *receive*. (And it took me another 10 years to learn that this does not apply to *foreign* or *neighbor*.) Spelling just doesn't "come" to some people, and I'll always rely on a dictionary more than most people do.

For the same reason people judge others based on looks or clothes, readers judge writing skills partly by the surface appearance of the paper. Fair or not, it's done. So the final task before typing any paper is to check the spelling of all words you're not 100% certain about. It'll be worth the two minutes it takes. If you simply can't find a word, look up a synonym in a dictionary or thesaurus and your word may appear in the definition.

Your word processor's spell-checker will catch no more than 75% of your misspellings. "My hat was a white pail" looks just fine to most computers, even though you meant, "My cat has a white tail."

NUMBERS

Spell out numbers nine and under and spell out all numbers (even those 10 and *over*) that start sentences. Numbers 10 and over are written as numerals. *But* if you compare numbers (for example, "9 or 10"), both numbers must be in the same format. If you spell out the number, you must also spell out "percent," "degrees" and "cents" instead of using the symbols %, °, ¢.

- At the conference, five women arrived late.
- Twenty-five customers complained yesterday.
- Another 15 people left after lunch.
- By Christmas, only 20% of our merchandise remained.

Weird Words

WEIRD SINGULARS AND PLURALS

Singular Form	Plural Form	Singular Form	Plural Form
Analysis	analyses	medium	media
Crisis	crises	mouse	mice
Datum	data	sheep	sheep
Deer	deer	species	species
Fish	fish	thesis	theses

IRREGULAR VERBS

Normally you add "ed" or "d" to verbs to form the past and past participle (action that began in the past and continues):

Base Form	Past Tense	Past Participle
I walk	I walked	I have walked
We implore	We implored	We have implored

But some English verbs are rebellious. **Here are the most common irregular verbs:**

Base Form	Past Tense	Past Participle
awake	awoke, awakened	awakened, awoken
become	became	became
begin	began	begun
bite	bit	bitten
blow	blew	blown
break	broke	broken

Base Form	Past Tense	Past Participle
bring	brought	brought
build	built	built
buy	bought	bought
catch	caught	caught
choose	chose	chosen
come	came	come
creep	crept	crept
deal	dealt	dealt
dig	dug	dug
do	did	done
draw	drew	drawn
dream	dreamed, dreamt	dreamed, dreamt
drink	drank	drunk
drive	drove	driven
eat	ate	eaten
fall	fell	fallen
feel	felt	felt
fight	fought	fought
find	found	found
fly	flew	flown
forget	forgot	forgotten, forgot
forgive	forgave	forgiven
freeze	froze	frozen
get	got	gotten, got
give	gave	given
go	went	gone
grow	grew	grown
have	had	had
hear	heard	heard
hide	hid	hidden
hurt	hurt	hurt
keep	kept	kept
know	knew	known
lay (place)	laid	laid
lead	led	led
leave	left	left
lie (recline)	lay	lain
lose	lost	lost
make	made	made
mean	meant	meant

Base Form	Past Tense	Past Participle
pay	paid	paid
read	read	read
ride	rode	ridden
ring	rang	rung
say	said	said
see	saw	seen
set	set	set
shake	shook	shaken
show	showed	showed, shown
sing	sang	sung
sink	sank	sunk
sit	sat	sat
speak	spoke	spoken
steal	stole	stolen
strike	struck	struck
swear	swore	sworn
swim	swam	swum
take	took	taken
teach	taught	taught
tear	tore	torn
think	thought	thought
throw	threw	thrown
wear	wore	worn
write	wrote	written

Odd Pairs

Adapt means to modify to fit: Professor Cruz adapted his lecture for a class of elementary pupils.

Adopt means to accept as one's own: Professor Cruz adopted a less-formal attitude toward the children.

Bring is used only for movement closer: Bring the cat here.

Take is used for all other movement: Take the cat with you when you leave.

Can is used when the *ability* to perform a task is the issue: Can Mervin swim across the bay to the island?

May is used when *permission* to do something is the issue: His mother says he may not try the swim.

Conscience refers to one's sense of morals: My conscience won't allow me to eat lamb.

Conscious refers to being aware or awake: I'm just too conscious of how farmers mistreat lambs.

Lose means to be defeated or misplace something. It is a verb: Gina will lose her tennis match.

Loose is an adjective meaning detached: Gina stepped on a loose ball and twisted her ankle.

Sensuous refers to situations that have rich appeal to our five senses: It was a sensuous night with balmy breezes, fireflies, and the aroma of fresh cut hay.

Sensual also refers to arousing the senses, but in a distinctly sexual way: The sensual night in the garden stirred Romeo and Juliet's passions.

Set is used when you place an object down: Franz set the plate on the counter. **Wrong:** Grandma said Franz should set awhile with her.

Sit is used only if the subject seats itself: Franz would sit by his sick guppy for hours.

Who is used when referring to subjects in sentences that *perform* actions. "Who" stands for "he" or "she": Who entered my room last night? (He entered.)

Whom is used when referring to objects that *receive* actions and stands for "him" or "her": You left with whom? (You left with her.)
   To whom are you speaking? (Receives action)
   The man who drove the car was drunk (Performs the action)

Mechanics

Foreign words: Use italics for words from foreign languages: *bon voyage, cerveza, prosit.* **Note:** if a word has been officially absorbed into English (lasagna, aloha, gung ho, kangaroo), do **not** italicize. A good dictionary will indicate if a word is still considered foreign or has been adopted.

Common abbreviations and symbols:

Apt. (apartment)

rpm (revolutions per minute)

¢ (cents)

° (degrees)

P.M. *or* p.m. (noon-to-midnight: three p.m.)

A.D. (*anno domini.* Precedes year: A.D. 975)

Two-letter postal code (for U.S. states)

Rev. (reverend. Place before name: Rev. Smith)

M.D. (place after full name: Mary Smith, M.D.)

e.g. (for example. Followed by a comma and example)

c. *or* ca. (about. When referring to dates)

mph (miles per hour)

$ (dollars)

% (percent)

A.M. *or* a.m. (midnight-to-noon time reference: Six a.m.)

B.C. (Before Christ. Follows year: 58 B.C.)

No. *or* no. (number)

mg, km (milligrams, kilometers)

Dr. (doctor. Place before name: Dr. Smith)

Ph.D. (doctor of philosophy. Place after full name: Mary Smith, Ph.D.)

i.e. (that is. Followed by a comma and an explanation)

vs. *or* v. (versus)

FORMAT FOR COLLEGE PAPERS

Paper: white, 8½ by 11, one side only

Font: 12 point Courier or New Times.

Ink: Black

Margins: Left justify with one inch on all sides

Heading: Your name, course title, and date in upper-left corner

Title: One-fourth from top of page, centered, all in capitals. Separate title page common only in papers of 10 pages or more.

Double space.

Number pages in upper right

Staple: upper-left corner

Dictionary of Usage

· ·

The 25 Most Commonly Misused Words in English

advice, advise

Advice is a noun, meaning "guidance."

His father's advice was to study liberal arts.

Advise is a verb, meaning "counsel" or "give advice to."

His father advised him to study liberal arts.

affect, effect

Affect is a verb that means "influence."

The president's budget cuts affected public television.

Effect may be either a noun or verb, although it is used as a noun 99% of the time. As a verb, it means "accomplish."

> The president's public television cuts effected a $2 million savings nationwide.

As a noun, *effect* means "impact" or "result."

> The cuts have had two effects locally: longer auctions and longer membership drives.

all right
"Alright" is not standard English. Would you write "alwrong?"

a lot
This is the only way it appears; don't use "alot" in such sentences as this: "Don't make a lot of spelling mistakes."
The word "allot" is a verb, meaning to "distribute shares."

among, between
Between is used with two items or persons.

> After graduating, he had to choose between a career in business and working for his father.

Among is used with three or more items.

> After graduating, he had to choose among a career in business, working for his father, or continuing for a master's degree.

amount, number
Amount is used with uncountable things.

> An amazing amount of work goes into completing a college course.

Number is used with countable things.

> What number of hours do you study for an average college course?

Amount applies to sand, weight, and volumes. But if you count the grains of sand in your navel someday, it will be a number, not an amount. *Number* applies to people, years, and dollars.

Being that, being as
Use "since" or "because" instead.

> Since it rained so hard, we stayed home from college.

> **Wrong:** Being as it rained so hard, we stayed home from college.

etc.
Try to avoid *etc.* It sounds lazy. If you do use it, don't write "and etc." *Etc.* means "and others."

farther, further

Farther means "a greater distance" and should be used only to refer to space and time.

> If I have to travel any farther between classes, I'm going to wear roller skates to school.

Further means "more" or "besides." It's used with ideas or abstractions.

> Our professor is always saying, "Let's go into that further." And after we exhaust the topic, he always seems to say, "Further, we should consider . . ."

few, little

Few is used with countable items.

> Few students know this college was once a prison farm.

Little is used with uncountable items.

> Some would say how little the place has changed.

good, well

Good is an adjective and should always modify a noun, never a verb.

> Her essay made several good proposals.

> **Wrong:** She runs good. She feels good. She talks good.

Well is an adverb and should modify a verb.

> She runs well, feels well, and talks well.

its, it's

Its is the possessive of "it"; *it's* means "it is."

> It's a shame a deer can't shoot back at its hunters.

lie, lay

To lie means "to recline" and should be used if the reclining object or person can be thought of as doing it under its own power.

> He lies down. The dog lies in the shade.

To lay means "to put in place" and should be used if another person or force puts the object in that position.

> Dad lays the baby in the crib. I lay the book on the table.

Lie and *lay* are complicated because they're irregular verbs and the past tense of *lie* is the same as the present tense of *lay*.

Lie	**Lay**
I lie down. (today)	I lay it down. (today)
I lay down. (yesterday)	I laid it down. (yesterday)
I have lain down.	I have laid it down.
I am lying down.	I am laying it down.
I was lying down.	I was laying it down.

mad, angry

Mad means "insane." A person can be mad, but not "mad at" you. Use "angry."

might of, could of, would of, should of, must of

These verbs do not exist. "Of" should be the helping verb "have."

> Inez should have used "have" when she wrote the note to her teacher that said: "I must of got a hundred on the test—I studied all afternoon."

We may confuse this because the contraction "might've" (might have) sounds like the incorrect form.

myself

A pretentious word to avoid.

> **Wrong:** Ethel came with myself to the airport. (Use "me" instead)

> **Wrong:** I myself did not believe him. ("I" alone says it.)

prejudice

This requires a "d" ending when used with a helper verb—"is," "was," "are," or "were."

> Dorothy is prejudiced.

raise, rise

You *raise* an object or person, but you *rise* yourself.

> Rocky raised his fist when he won the 100-yard dash.

> Peter had to rise from where he'd fallen on the track to see his opponent celebrate.

than, then

Than is comparative.

> Alaska has fewer people than Rhode Island.

Then refers to time.

> Then we drove home.

that, which, and who

Who should be used to refer to people. *That* and *which* are used to refer to things or ideas.

> Amy, *who* led the team to the state finals, broke her ankle in the final minutes of the regular-season game, an accident *that* cost the team its playoff game.

> **Wrong:** The man that lives next door is bald.

there, they're, their

There refers to a place, *they're* is a contraction for "they are," and *their* is the possessive of "they."

> They're going to take their tennis game over there on court three.

to, too

If you mean "very" or "also," use "too." **Hint:** The extra "o" suggests excess.

> It's too hot to go anywhere; it's humid, too.

try to

People often say "try and" when they mean *try to.*

> We'll try to start the engine.

> **Wrong:** Let's try and go to the party. (You're not doing two things, only one.)

unique

Unique means one of a kind, not just unusual.

> Moe is unique if he has antennae and speaks Martian.

your, you're

Misusing these is a professional embarrassment. *Your* is possessive; *you're* is the contraction for "you are."

> You're going to get in trouble if you misuse your words, but you're going to be a star if your writing is correct as well as lively.

■ **PRACTICE 17-14 Summary Exercise.** For each of the following, write a sentence that:

1. Starts with "because," "since," or "if."
2. Has a "however" in the middle.
3. Contains two sentences joined with an "and."

4. Contains an "and" but does not contain two complete sentences.
5. Uses a colon.
6. Includes a quotation.
7. Uses a singular possessive.
8. Uses a plural possessive.
9. Contains an interrupter phrase.
10. Has a dash.
11. Is followed by a legitimate sentence fragment.
12. Includes two words in the usage section that you have had trouble with.
13. Includes a semicolon.
14. Includes two words you frequently misspell.
15. Uses "in conclusion" or "lastly."

■ **PRACTICE 17-15 Summary Exercise.** Correct any errors in punctuation, sentence structure, spelling, or usage in the following:

December 3, 2008

Wade Biggs
Personnel Director
Fudge Motors, Inc.
Detroit, Michigan 11391

Dear Mr. Biggs,

Attached to this letter you will find my résumé. Which lists my employment and academic background. I hope your still considering me for the job in the swedish division of the company.

I used to make alot of errors in English but I received some good advise from one of my prof's at college, and now I write good. My prof told me the kind of affect bad grammar has on a potential employer who has hundreds of people to choose between. I know I'll go farther if I know how to use a semicolon; as in this sentence. Its important, to, knowing the difference among words like "amount" and "number." When you study wrighting since Third Grade as I have you soon learn to punctuate and use correct sentence structure. Although its hard sometimes if you hav'nt lain the rules down in front of yourself.

Commas for instance should mark two sentences connected with a conjunction. They also set off interrupters, these words block the flow of a sentence. Sitting like a frog flattened in the road, my prof told us to watch out for the sentence fragment. "Beware the galloping run-on he lectured us and shun the frivolous, comma." After I memorized these rules I knew I'd be an employee any company would of been proud to hire.

Sincerely,

Gustov Osterly

Gustov Osterly

■ **PRACTICE 17-16** Write a letter to the students who will take your writing course next term. Give them advice that will help them do well, and close by explaining two grammar or usage rules they must know. Give an illustration for each.

■ **PRACTICE 17-17** Exchange papers with a fellow student for peer review. Read each others' work once only for punctuation, a second time only for word use, and a third time only for sentence fragments and run-on sentences.

Appendix
The Real Rules for Writing Classes (And Maybe Life)

- Show up.
- Play hard—it's the only way to have fun and improve.
- Figure out what you're good at and exploit it; figure out what you're weak at and work on it.
- An honest effort does not guarantee an A, but it almost always prevents failure.
- Thou shalt not steal.
- Each day is a chance to start fresh. If you tell yourself, "I'm no good in English," you chain the weight of the past to your ankles.
- Bad things happen to everyone; those who succeed find a way to keep going when the sharks attack.
- Writers live more in 24 hours than most people because they look intensely at things.
- Smart people ask for help before it's too late.
- Do more than the minimum required.
- Defensive living and defensive writing ensure only mediocrity. To accomplish anything outstanding requires some risk.
- Love far more things than you hate.
- Parties last one night; your grades last a lifetime.
- Inspiration is rarely luck; it knocks on the doors of people who try hard and care about what they're doing.
- A hard assignment is an invitation to be better than you are now.
- Write a rule of your own here: _____
_____ .

> In writing you start where you are and you do it poorly. You do it afraid. And something happens.
> —ANNE LAMONT

- Write one of your professor's rules here: _____ .
- Ask a person you admire for a rule and write it here: _____ .
- Life is often unfair and will break these rules when it chooses; you can persevere anyway.

Index

A TROUBLESHOOTING GUIDE TO WRITING

Note: Many of these "problems" are normal procedure for most writers.

Problem	Possible Causes	Possible Cures	Chapter Reference
I don't know what to write about.	Unclear about assignment or purpose in writing.	Reread text. Reread assignment. Ask professor.	
	Unclear about audience.	Visualize an audience and write to it.	1, 12 13, 15
I can't start.	No ideas or vague ideas. Insufficient detail or visualization.	Brainteasers.	2–3
	Introduction jitters.	Start with main idea. Use intro brain teaser.	6
	Insecure about thinking. Fear of risk.	Overcome blocks and strive for honesty.	1, 3
I start but then stall.	Ideas fuzzy or incomplete.	More brain teasers.	3
	Poor writing environment. Fear of messiness/risk.	Overcome these blocks.	6
I can't put my ideas or notes together.	You need a main point or headings.	Work on thesis/outline.	5
I keep writing the same idea–going nowhere.	Insufficient ideas/details.	More brain teasers.	2–3
	Redundancy.	Cut to essential idea.	7–8
I know what I want to say but not how to say it.	Word paralysis.	Freewrite, loop, or try oral composition. Talk to peers.	5–6